SPYING ON THE REICH

ON
THE REICH

THE COLD WAR
AGAINST HITLER

R. T. HOWARD

OXFORD
UNIVERSITY PRESS

OXFORD
UNIVERSITY PRESS

Great Clarendon Street, Oxford, OX2 6DP,
United Kingdom

Oxford University Press is a department of the University of Oxford.
It furthers the University's objective of excellence in research, scholarship,
and education by publishing worldwide. Oxford is a registered trade mark of
Oxford University Press in the UK and in certain other countries

First Edition published in 2023

Impression: 1

Published in the United States of America by Oxford University Press
198 Madison Avenue, New York, NY 10016, United States of America

British Library Cataloguing in Publication Data

Data available

Library of Congress Control Number: 2022940113

ISBN 978–0–19–286299–0

Printed and bound in the UK by
Clays Ltd, Elcograf S.p.A.

Contents

Abbreviations

AN	Archives Nationales, Paris
A/S	Au sujet de ('About')
CCCA	Churchill College Cambridge Archive
DBFP	Documents on British Foreign Policy
DDF	Documents diplomatiques français
DRC	Defence Requirements Committee
EHR	*English Historical Review*
HJ	*Historical Journal*
IMCC	Inter-Allied Military Commission of Control
INS	*Intelligence and National Security*
IWM	Imperial War Museum, London
ODNB	*Oxford Dictionary of National Biography*
PCO	Passport Control Office(r)
PRO	Public Record Office
SHD	Le Service Historique de la Défense, Paris
SIS	Secret Intelligence Service
SR	Service de Renseignements
TNA	The National Archives, Kew

A Note on Sources

Documentary sources for the pre-war period are highly fragmentary. Many secret French and German archives were lost or destroyed—sometimes deliberately—during the Second World War. Nor did the French governments of the Third Republic keep official records of their discussions. Although since 1916 British governments have kept records that are usually released to the public after thirty years, SIS reports remain closed to the public. This book has attempted to piece together some of the surviving fragments, and the clues to and glimpses of this secret world that emerge from public records and published memoirs.

List of plates

'I have an instinctive mistrust of diplomats who want to convey the impression of being well informed, of rumours that are manipulated by private agendas, and of fake news spun out by Goebbels' press service...a piece of information, from a trustworthy source and with value, can be distorted by the time foreign embassies get hold of it and put it onto a secret telegram.'

Paul Stehlin, French Air Attaché Berlin (1936–9)

'Many intelligence reports in war are contradictory; even more are false, and most are uncertain...In short, most intelligence is false.'

Carl von Clausewitz, *On War*

Map 1. Europe in 1920, after the territorial changes imposed by the Treaty of Versailles

Introduction

Early in the afternoon of 1 February 1939, a middle-aged man called Walther Friedrich Marath arrived at the Hebron Hotel in central Copenhagen. He showed the receptionist his passport to prove who he was and then made his way, suitcase in hand, to his comfortable, although simple and sparse, single room on the top floor. To the hotel staff, there was nothing about this guest that seemed unusual, other than the fact that he had a noticeably strong German accent. Such visitors were always coming and going.[1]

His real name was Felix Waldemar Pötzsch and he was in fact a highly valued British Intelligence agent who was tasked with obtaining vital information about what was happening inside Hitler's Reich. His spy handler—an Englishman he knew only as 'Karl'—had provided him with a forged passport that had allowed him to reach Danish shores and get through customs unchallenged. And it was Karl's substantial cash payment that would pay his expenses over the months ahead.

In return, Karl wanted information about Hitler's Reich. And alone in his room, Pötzsch looked out to the harbour, a few hundred yards before him, and across to the sea beyond, and began to draw up plans to obtain it.

This was not the first time that the mysterious Englishman had helped him. Over the preceding year, Karl had enabled him to evade the clutches of the Belgian and Dutch governments: both of these neutral countries had come under strong German pressure to crack down

---

1. This account is based on the proceedings of the Copenhagen City Court. See Københavns Byret. 10. A Afd. Særlige Straffesager. A-1 1939–1967. Retsbog 1939 1 2–1949 12 30.

on the British and French spy rings that operated from this foreign soil against Germany. And in Holland, where the Nazi secret services had infiltrated British Intelligence operations with stunning success, the Gestapo had also been hot on his heels until Karl had once again helped him keep one step ahead and slip unnoticed into Denmark.

There was one simple reason why the British Secret Intelligence Service (SIS) was prepared to go to such lengths, and to some expense, to help Pötzsch. The British government was desperately short of accurate, up-to-date information about the state of the German armed forces, and it was on this vital matter that this well-networked individual had something to offer.

Born in Bad Schmiedeberg near Wittenberg in Saxony, Pötzsch had joined the German navy in 1911, when he was just 18, and served on the cruiser *Emden* as a seaman. It was not long before he saw action, for within just months his ship had been ordered to suppress an uprising of native people in the Pacific Islands against German rule, a brief and bloody episode that was by all accounts marred by brutality on the part of the overlords. Later, in the First World War, he took part in pitched sea battles and skirmishes against the Royal Navy in the North Sea.

But Pötzsch had always had another interest besides seamanship. He had joined the left-wing Social Democratic Party when he was a teenager and subsequently became closely involved in its activities, and those of some international Marxist groups, in and around the port of Bremen. Before long, he had been appointed as one of the party's local representatives, and by the early 1920s was helping to organize strikes, protests, and demonstrations, as well as fighting street battles, against a variety of political opponents, including Adolf Hitler's fast-growing National Socialist Party.

Hitler's accession to power, in early 1933, put the fear of God into Pötzsch, who soon fled his homeland, narrowly escaping arrest by crossing firstly into Holland and then, shortly afterwards, to Belgium. But he had no intention of giving up the fight against his political opponents. He immediately made contact with his fellow exiles, who were equally determined to rally domestic opposition to Hitler and to help other political exiles find places to live and work. And he kept in regular touch with his contacts in the German underground back home, sending them anti-Nazi leaflets and pamphlets that they could quietly distribute. But in early 1937 he fell out with his fellow exiles and was expelled from their governing committee.

It was at this point that Pötzsch had become acquainted with a British official called Edward Kayser, who was based at the British Passport Control Office (PCO) in Brussels. In Belgium, as elsewhere, the PCO provided a cover for British Intelligence operations, and in this role Kayser was responsible for recruiting and running agents. Foreign intelligence services generally considered exiles to be a suspect source of information but Kayser was willing to take a chance. He introduced himself as 'Karl'—Pötzsch never discovered his real name—and the two men soon struck up a good rapport.[2]

The German exile now became a full-time paid British agent, lured by a tempting amount of money and wanting to do something to undermine Hitler's regime. He had numerous contacts amongst his friends, family, and comrades back in Germany who were in a position to tell him what he, and Karl, wanted to find out. He would write to them, using a series of post office boxes to make contact and employing a similarly discreet method to pick up the anonymous and carefully worded letters they sent back. Soon he had cast light on some of the Reich's military secrets, including a number of technical developments the Germans had implemented, notably to the armour plate used by their new battleships.

But Karl's most pressing priority was to obtain accurate and up-to-date information on the state of the German navy, which the SIS had been instructed to 'make every endeavour' to find out more about. Nearly two years before, in the summer of 1937, he had instructed Pötzsch to visit Denmark to investigate reports that the Germans were building ports and harbours on the island of Sylt in the North Sea, a capability that would have serious repercussions for the Royal Navy and for British security. Rumours had also long been flying about top-secret aviation experiments that the Nazis were supposedly carrying out in the area [see below Chapter 2]. But if Hitler's ships were dangerously below the radar, Denmark was a good place to find out more because, as the head of the SIS argued, it was 'by its geographical

---

2. Exiles—'alarmist statements...seem to be always prevalent among refugees and/or prominent anti-Nazis': see 'Most Secret Memorandum', 9 Mar 1939, FO 1093/86 TNA. 'Too much attention should not be paid to the views of emigrés whose connections (in the Reich) are solely with the opposition'—Memo from British consul in Vienna to Kirkpatrick, 19 May 1939, FO 371/23008 TNA.

position...very favourably situated' for intelligence-gathering on Germany.[3]

Now Karl had asked him to find out more about the specifications and capabilities of the German navy, and to do so, on this second trip, Pötzsch planned to ingratiate himself with some of the German sailors who frequented the Danish ports. He would pose as a salesman, peddling hair tonic, to introduce himself and then buy them drinks and get them talking. Soon he had acquired detailed information about the movements of German vessels and knew exactly when they were due to arrive and depart so that he could appear at just the right moment. At the same time, he wrote cryptic, coded messages to his Bremen contacts and asked them for the information he needed.[4]

Felix Pötzsch was just one of many foot soldiers of a Cold War against the Third Reich in the years that preceded the Second World War, as their respective governments sought *détente* with Hitler—'a settlement in Europe and a sense of stability'—brokered by a policy of appeasement. This Cold War then continued from March 1939, when policymakers surrendered appeasement and instead made threats of war, until the German invasion of Poland on 1 September, when those threats were realized.[5]

This Cold War was not a campaign of covert destabilization, comparable to the efforts that the American government, for example, waged against the Cuban regime of Fidel Castro in the years that followed the revolution in Havana in 1959. It was instead an effort of intelligence-gathering, as a number of foreign governments scrambled to gauge the threat posed by a regime in Berlin that became increasingly belligerent and hostile but remained highly opaque and unpredictable.

This effort involved gathering accurate information about not just the Nazi regime's resources and capabilities but also about the mindset

---

3. 'Make every endeavour'—Keith Jeffery *MI6: The History of the Secret Intelligence Service 1909–1949* Bloomsbury (2011) 279. Sylt—British concern about Sylt becomes clear in WO 190/460 and 474 TNA, and from a parliamentary question in April 1938; https://api.parliament.uk/historic-hansard/commons/1938/apr/13/island-of-sylt-naval-air-base>. Denmark—Jeffery 279.

4. Karl's instructions—Sagsnummer 68.418, Danish National Archives, Copenhagen. Pötzsch was arrested in Apr 1939 and in June sentenced to six months in prison for spying. The German government suspected him of complicity in a series of bombings on German vessels and made numerous attempts to extradite him.

5. Settlement in Europe—Neville Chamberlain, 31 Oct 1938, CAB 23/96 TNA.

and ambitions of its leaders and the attitudes of ordinary people, upon whom even the most tyrannical regime is to some degree ultimately dependent. And although there were moments of relative cooperation between Berlin and some of its neighbouring governments, notably during the 'honeymoon period' of the mid-1930s, when the Nazi authorities granted foreign access to some previously restricted installations and factories, this effort of espionage was always undertaken in an atmosphere of mutual suspicion and mistrust, and always at great personal risk to those who stood at its frontline.

The challenge of monitoring and assessing Nazi Germany was one that confronted the whole of Europe, which watched and listened to Hitler and his henchmen with growing alarm and which worked hard to find out more about what was really happening within the borders of the Reich. Even neutral states, such as Switzerland, Sweden, Holland, and Belgium, could not afford to look away from a country that had committed sacrilege against Belgium's neutrality in 1914, when the German army had used its territory as a convenient gateway into France. European leaders were also well aware that the outbreak of another catastrophic conflict would create waves of refugees who would flood across their borders.

Nor could more distant countries afford to look away. Despite its strictly isolationist approach in the 1930s, the United States government was deeply conscious of the seismic economic damage that another world war would inflict, particularly at a time of global depression, as well as of the strategic realignment that would then eventuate, especially at an hour when Washington might need comrades-in-arms against a communist, 'Bolshevik', order that had seized power in Russia in 1917. As the secretary of state, Henry L Stimson, argued in 1935, 'a great war anywhere in the world today will seriously affect all the nations, whether they go into that war or not'.[6]

But while spying on the Reich was always an international effort, there were of course some countries that stood closer to the frontline of the Cold War than others.

At the very forefront were Czechoslovakia, Austria, and Romania. Hitler had openly described his ambitions to seize control over stretches of foreign territory where ethnic Germans lived, and he also

6. Stimson—radio broadcast, Oct 1935: transcript in the files of the British Embassy, Washington, FO 115/3408 TNA.

had every reason to cast a rapacious eye upon the raw materials and infrastructure that these other countries could boast but which the German economy, particularly its war machine, painfully lacked. Germany should start its 'racial fight', as the dictator once said, against those states which hosted 'oilfields, rubber, treasures of the earth'. Romania's massive oil reserves represented a glittering prize, while Czechoslovakia's giant Skoda munitions plant at Pilsen was also firmly in Hitler's sights. He had outlined his plans in his 1925 autobiographical manifesto, *Mein Kampf,* as well as in his unpublished but revealing *Second Book,* written in 1928.[7]

But the two countries that mattered most in the Cold War against Hitler were Britain and France. This was not because they had more reason than any other to feel a sense of threat. On the contrary, the *Führer* consistently reiterated his peaceful intentions towards both countries, prompting some politicians of the time and historians of the present day to even question whether their involvement in the Second World War was ever necessary. Instead, Britain and France matter most in the story of foreign espionage against Germany because of their military and economic might.[8]

Stricken though both were by economic hardship, and still traumatized by the experience of the First World War, only these two countries had the resources to take effective action against Germany. This was not necessarily military action, although the French possessed a mighty landed army and the British a formidable navy: both could instead also have mounted an economic embargo, sanctioned by the League of Nations (the forerunner of the United Nations), that could conceivably have starved both the people and the economy of Germany. The Soviet Union was the only other European (or semi-European) country that could have posed a similar such threat to the Reich in the 1930s, but it was at this time too embroiled in its own internecine struggles, waged by a leader too focused on finding and executing his domestic enemies, real and imaginary, to mount an effective challenge. Josef Stalin was bleeding his own country red. His critics in any case argued that the Soviet military was like a bear

---

7. 'Racial fight'—Piers Brendon *The Dark Valley* Jonathan Cape (2000) 467. Hitler's *Second Book* was written in 1928 but was unpublished until 1961. The text was discovered in May 1945.
8. British involvement in WW2, or at least the timing of it, has been questioned by, for example, Peter Hitchens in *The Phoney Victory: The World War II Illusion* IB Tauris (2018).

defending its home territory, capable of fending off an invader but not of launching an offensive beyond its borders.[9]

It was the relative might of the two cross-Channel neighbours that makes the relationship between their governments, and their spy services in particular, so integral to the story of the international effort to monitor and understand Hitler's Germany in the 1930s.

Throughout this decade, this 'relationship' was little more than a flirtatious liaison between two partners. The two partners began to embrace only suddenly, in early 1939. And intimate though it latterly became, this relationship was at every stage riven by a state of mistrust and rivalry, characteristic of two countries that had been rivals and adversaries for centuries. Even in the spring of 1938, when Germany posed a strong threat, the French secret services were still closely monitoring the activities of 'notoriously anti-French' and 'very dangerous' British intelligence agents, notably in North Africa, where they were judged guilty of secret 'collusion' with Spanish nationalists against French interests. At the same time, numerous figures in the British cabinet, including the prime minister, Neville Chamberlain, wanted to avoid making a commitment to Paris: there was still time, they argued, for their policy of appeasement to satisfy Hitler's demands and avoid war.[10]

While the political relationship between Britain and France was central to the loose 'network' of foreign spy agencies that watched the Reich, several other countries also played their part. In particular, there was also close contact between the French and the Czechs, who had signed a vaguely worded treaty of 'alliance and friendship' in January 1924, and the Poles, who had also struck up a similarly worded alliance with Paris in 1921. Other countries also stood at the outer fringes of this loose network, including Holland, which despite its supposed neutrality gave underhand, low-level assistance to the British, as well as to the German, intelligence services.

Each of these countries had their respective spy services whose relations both mirrored but also helped to shape those of their political masters. Sometimes these services pulled closer together because their

9. Royal Navy—see Joseph Maiolo *The Royal Navy and Nazi Germany 1933–9: A Study in Appeasement* Palgrave Macmillan (1998). Soviet critics—see 'Military Value of Russia', 24 Apr 1939, CAB 27/624 TNA.

10. On French suspicions of and rivalry with the British, see 'Services Spéciaux Britanniques', 12 Mar 1937 and 'Anglais en France', 7NN 2229 SHD.

governments were doing so, while at other times, like the 'tail wagging the dog', those governments were pushed closer together by the advent of some particularly startling piece of intelligence. Secret information about a resurgent Germany gradually brought the governments of Great Britain and France closer together in the course of the 1930s. In the words of Robert and Isabelle Tombs, the Anglo-French relationship was forged by 'a German matchmaker all could agree to hate', while Peter Jackson writes that 'the volume of documentation concerning the importance of the Franco-British entente in French diplomatic archives increases in direct proportion to the growth of German military power'. As Hitler's demands became more assertive from 1936 and intelligence information more alarming, both governments orchestrated the same policy of appeasement that was designed at least to buy more time. And in the spring of 1939, a series of erroneous intelligence reports, emanating from highly questionable sources, prompted firstly Britain and then France to make a commitment to the defence of Poland that led both countries along a path to a conflagration that erupted six months later. Equally, the French government sometimes regarded closer links between its own spy service and the British as a precursor to a military alliance, which would in turn create a political treaty: this made the British particularly wary of and resistant to any intelligence cooperation, which did not become intimate, constant, and systematic until the eve of the Second World War.[11]

There are other reasons why this international spy network presents a complex picture. One is that the relationships between all foreign governments were constantly evolving. When, for example, Paris signed a treaty of mutual assistance with Moscow in May 1935, relations cooled between France and Poland, which had highly acrimonious relations with the Soviets. And after the Munich agreement, which was seen in Prague as a sell-out by a French ally that had sworn, fourteen years before, to provide 'aid and assistance', so too did the Czech intelligence services move away from their French counterparts and become closer with the British. Sometimes, too, the relations between the British and French spy services proved to be as choppy and unpredictable as the waters of the English Channel: for example, there was a

---

11. Robert and Isabelle Tombs *That Sweet Enemy: The French and the British from the Sun King to the Present* Penguin (2006) 514. Peter Jackson *France and the Nazi Menace* OUP (2000) 246.

flurry of intelligence-sharing between them in the late summer of 1938 that broke off in October and November before resuming again in December.[12]

Equally, this network was often entirely asymmetric because information did not flow equally, in a reciprocal manner, between any of these actors. Despite their shared fears of Germany, there was little or no contact but much ill-feeling between Warsaw and Prague: the Poles made no secret of their loathing for the Czech government and wanted to seize pieces of Czech territory, notably the border town of Teschen, while the Czechs were also wary of links between Warsaw and the government of Hungary, with which they also had their own territorial disputes.

Above all, other intelligence services nearly always shared far more information with their British counterparts than they received back. This was partly because in London the sharing of classified information with any foreign government was strictly regulated by a ministerial committee. But its members knew that other countries needed the support of Great Britain more than the British, whose politicians and general public wanted to remain aloof from continental alliances after the calamities of the First World War, felt they needed them. France, by contrast, could not so easily afford the luxury of such choices, most obviously because it was confronted by a long border with Germany rather than being protected by the relative sanctity of the 'silver sea', above all by the twenty miles of the English Channel. The SIS—which was often referred to throughout Europe as 'The Intelligence Service' or 'British Intelligence'—was also highly mistrustful of its Czech counterparts because of Prague's links with the Soviet Union, fearing that Moscow could exploit them to infiltrate its own ranks or compromise its own sources, even though it was of course more than willing to accept any information that the Czechs passed on. Such fears became more prevalent from June 1935, when President Beneš visited Moscow 'on a personally conducted tour' during which his 'enthusiasm' for the Soviets 'rose to lyrical heights'.[13]

12. Jackson in Martin Alexander and William Philpott (eds) *Anglo-French Defence Relations between the Wars* Palgrave Macmillan (2002) 142.
13. Ministerial committee—Hinsley *British Intelligence* CUP (1979),Vol 1, 39, 488. 'This precious stone set in a silver sea'—Shakespeare's *Richard II*, 2. 1. Czech mistrust—FW Winterbotham *The Nazi Connection* Dell (1978) 213; see also Peter Neville, 'Nevile Henderson and Basil Newton: Two British Envoys in the Czech Crisis 1938', in Erik

But however complex, shifting, and asymmetric the relationships between them, these intelligence agencies all shared the same ends that brought them, in such a varied way, closer together. The central, basic function of every foreign intelligence agency is of course to predict and gauge external threats to the country it is entrusted to guard: as the historian of this subject, FH Hinsley, has written, 'intelligence is an activity that has to perform three functions. Information has to be acquired; it has to be analysed and interpreted; and it has to be put into the hands of those who use it.' And from 1933, and to some extent before, the analysis and interpretation of information showed that the threat posed by Germany was growing fast.[14]

This involved making accurate assessments of the existing quality and quantity of Germany's armed forces, and predicting their future strength. Throughout the 1930s, this meant seeing through a Nazi cloak of deception. To begin with, Hitler used this cloak to hide the manic pace of his covert rearmament plans. But then, from the spring of 1935, he deployed it to cast a shadow, conjuring a terrifying but inflated misleading image of German power in a bid to intimidate his critics and opponents.

Of particular interest to all these foreign onlookers was the strength of Hitler's air force. By the 1930s, warplanes had acquired a far greater range and striking power, leading some contemporaries to credit them with the potential to deal a 'knock-out blow' against civilian targets.

This image of an overwhelmingly powerful 'strategic' air force, rather than one that 'tactically' supported an army's advance on the ground, was the stuff of the nightmare visions that had originally been conjured by HG Wells in his 1908 work *The War in the Air* and subsequently gripped the imagination of senior figures such as the former prime minister AJ Balfour, who declared that 300 French bombers could render London uninhabitable by delivering 'a continuous torrent of high explosives at the rate of 75 tons a day for an indefinite period'.[15]

Far from being a flight of fancy, such fears had seemed to become a deadly reality during the First World War, when German warplanes thundered over British skies, and then during the Spanish Civil War

Goldstein and Igor Lukes (eds) *The Munich Crisis, 1938: Prelude to World War II* Frank Cass (1999). Enthusiasm—Addison to Hoare, 24 June 1935 FO 371/19461 TNA.

14. Hinsley 8.

15. AJ Balfour, 29 May 1922, CID 106-A, TNA.

(1936–9), when the town of Guernica was devastated in the space of just hours, killing around 1,700 civilians. And when Mussolini's warplanes dropped gas bombs to quell local insurgents in Abyssinia in 1935, many people's fears were propelled sky-high. Fearful that 'the bomber would always get through' against air defences that had an unproven value, leading governmental figures such as the British diplomat Robert Vansittart argued that an enemy air force was 'the arm in which we are likely to be faced in the future with the most bitter armament race . . . a far more formidable danger than anything in the way of naval or military armaments'. His peers in the Committee of Imperial Defence even anticipated half a million casualties in Britain in the first weeks of a conflict with Germany, taking a series of drastic precautionary steps that laid the foundations of the National Health Service.[16]

But accurately judging the true strength of Hitler's air force, like his other military resources, was a hugely demanding task. It posed questions not just about how many planes the Germans possessed but about a wide variety of other issues. Foreign spy chiefs needed to know about the training and aptitude of the German pilots, and how reliable and well serviced their planes were. When those planes were in the air, how manoeuvrable were they, and how many planes and pilots did the Luftwaffe have in reserve? Assessing the rate at which the Germans would continue to build up their strength of their air force, and of all their other armaments, was equally daunting since this depended on such factors as the availability of raw materials, notably oil and rubber, and of skilled labour. And in the offices of the Air Ministry in London, experts also furiously debated issues such as Germanic 'efficiency', which some claimed would exert a powerful brake on Germany's industrial output. Of course, 'predictions' and 'forecasts' of production were in any case never likely to be more than 'guestimates', given such variable factors as periods of consolidation, shortages of raw materials, human exhaustion, and the strain on the wider economy.[17]

---

16. 'The bomber will always get through'—Stanley Baldwin to the House of Commons, 10 Nov 1932. Vansittart to Hankey, 18 Jan 1933. Norman Rose *Vansittart* Heinemann (1978) 127–8. NHS—Tombs and Tombs 529. The dangers of a 'knock-out blow' were described in, for example, the governmental paper DP(P), 22–5 Mar 1938, CAB 16/83 TNA, see Hinsley 81.

17. Such factors moderate Air Ministry assessments of Luftwaffe strength in 1938, as German aircraft production slumped after Munich. See CAB 4/26–7 TNA.

Spying on the Reich also involved making informed judgements about the attitudes, mindset, and opinions prevalent within Nazi Germany, such as the state of morale of its armed forces, and the ambitions and temperament of the governing elite that made or influenced key decisions of policy. Above all, was Hitler determined to fight aggressive wars against foreign targets, or was he just an opportunist? Were his outpourings in *Mein Kampf* and his posthumously published *Second Book* those of a dreamer or a blueprint for conquest that he was determined to realize? Were Hitler and his cohorts, like Hermann Göring, really just rearming Germany at such a furious rate because such a programme offered a quick fix to the scourge of mass unemployment, which had helped to bring them to power in 1933 and which had virtually disappeared by 1937? And did they, or did ordinary Germans, want *Wehrfreiheit* ('military freedom') not as a means of waging aggressive wars of foreign conquest but more as a sign of national pride, as many commentators, well versed in German and Prussian history, argued?

The views of the wider general public also mattered because 'public opinion does not percolate Herr Hitler's ears...but will still count, if not before, in the extremity of the trenches'. But were ordinary Germans strongly influenced by Nazi propaganda, and how susceptible would they be to British radio broadcasts? These were questions of political intelligence that the British Foreign Office and its French counterpart, the Foreign Ministry in Paris (the 'Quai d'Orsay'), tried to answer, although they also fell within the remit of their respective intelligence services because Germany was a strategic threat to both countries.[18]

The difficulties of making any such judgement were self-evident: 'the principal trouble', as the foreign secretary, the 1st Earl of Halifax, wrote during the Sudeten Crisis in September 1938, 'remains that we cannot possibly tell, however much we may guess, what is going on inside the brains of the one man who matters'.[19]

Even as relatively late as 1937, it was far from clear if Hitler wanted economic supremacy in continental Europe, to acquire colonies in the developing world, or to unleash outright war. Some wondered if he would see Britain and France as the true threat to Germany or else cut

18. Percolate—British Consul, Frankfurt, to Whitehall 22 Mar 1939, FO 371/23006 TNA.
    Political intelligence—Hinsley 17.
19. Halifax to Runciman, 6 Sept 1938, FO 800/309 TNA.

a deal with the West that would allow him to undertake *Drang nach Osten* ('March to the East'). But trying to make any assessment was immensely difficult when Hitler discussed his key decisions with only the smallest and most intimate of circles. Some observers wondered if even this was a false assumption: 'Hitler lives more and more in a practically hermetically sealed case and no one seems even to know who his chief advisers are,' wrote Sir Nevile Henderson, the British ambassador in Berlin from 1937 until 1939. 'Possibly no one.' As a result, observers were 'constantly groping in the dark'.[20]

Sometimes, too, Hitler would reach a decision at either the last minute or at unpredictable, even random moments as his instincts dictated, while he would also frequently and very rapidly change his mind. 'Not even Herr Hitler's intimates, according to one of them, knew for certain if he would really risk a world war,' as one SIS assessment judged at the end of 1938. His decision to march into the Rhineland in 1936, for example, was taken only two weeks before he gave the order. 'It is impossible to know anything for certain in a regime where all depends on the will of a single individual whom one does not see,' lamented Henderson. When dealing with such 'incalculability', as a senior diplomat, Gladwyn Jebb, called it, intelligence reports were likely to be speculative and of limited value. Or, as the British military attaché in Prague wrote, 'the factors involved are so multiple and complex that it is impossible...to arrive at any reasonable conclusion'.[21]

Foreign spy agencies were also confronted by a police state that quickly built a security apparatus of terrifying ruthlessness and efficiency. The German police not only had powers to make arbitrary arrests and indefinitely detain suspects but did not flinch from carrying out brutal punishments that were unthinkable elsewhere in Western Europe. Political opponents were sometimes hacked to pieces with pickaxes—a fate that descended upon the conservative politician Gustav von Kahr during the 'Night of the Long Knives' in 1934—while traitors were typically beheaded. And anyone deemed an 'enemy' of the Reich could easily be despatched to concentration camps, such as Dachau near Munich, that were described by one inmate as 'a veritable chamber

---

20. Henderson to Cadogan, 20 July 1938, DBFP III series, Vol 1, 1938, No 524.
21. SIS 1938—Jeffery 309. Henderson—DBFP III series, Vol 2, 643, No 3. Jebb— 'Hitler...is to a large extent incalculable', Jeffery 304. Prague—Stronge to Newton, 6 Sept 1938, CAB 21/949 TNA.

of horrors run by sadistic maniacs' and where life was 'more brutal, more savage, more sadistically bloody than anything we had ever imagined'. Soon, Germany's borders, and its increasingly numerous military sites, were also sealed and closely monitored. Not surprisingly, the task of finding well-placed and genuine informers, and running those agents without being detected, was difficult in the extreme. 'We needed the secrets of a country', as the head of the Czech spy service later wrote, 'where people spoke in whispers.'[22]

The challenges of casting light on such an opaque enemy also had an unfortunate consequence, which provides an underlying sub-theme of this book. Desperate to obtain reliable information and unable to verify the material that they did acquire, some intelligence services and their governments were vulnerable to falling under the spell of charlatans who made unproven assertions about what was happening within Germany. As Jebb wrote in a SIS memorandum in March 1939, 'politicians are only too apt to let themselves be swayed by backstairs gossip and precipitated into decisions which they afterwards regret'. In theory, of course, this did not happen: 'no agent's report is ever put forward unless he has been tested over a long period and the reliability or otherwise of his reports proved beyond doubt'. But in practice it was often far from clear who really fell into this category. British officials were of course well aware of this danger—in July 1938 Chamberlain himself referred to 'unchecked reports from unofficial sources'—but could not evade it.[23]

It is likely, for example, that the Polish spy Jerzy Sosnowski, and perhaps the British informer and 'fixer' William de Ropp, fell into this category for some and perhaps all of the duration of their careers, since both were paid considerable sums of money by their respective spymasters in return for providing material whose value continues to remain, at best, unclear. Equally, it was tempting to unwittingly exaggerate the importance of the personal opinions and impressions of individuals who perhaps never claimed to know more than they actually did. When the celebrated American aviator Charles Lindbergh and the French air chief General Joseph Vuillemin visited German aircraft factories and aerodromes in the mid- to late 1930s and described what

22. Dachau—Brendon *Dark Valley* 256. Whispers—*Master of Spies: The Memoirs of General Frantisek Moravec* Bodley Head (1975) 53.
23. Jebb memo—31 Mar 1939, FO 1093/86 TNA. Chamberlain—CAB 23/94 PRO. Hinsley 81.

they saw, their eyewitness accounts were in fact pie in the sky. But they were taken at face value by experts who viewed their superficial accounts without the scepticism that they merited.

It is into this same category that private intelligence networks also fall. Throughout the 1930s, the dearth of accurate intelligence meant that the British and French governments, and their respective spy services, were more inclined to turn to such parallel agencies, which influential figures, such as the diplomats Robert Vansittart and Lord Lloyd, set up as they made their own, sometimes frantic, efforts to monitor the Reich and to warn the outside world about what they found, or thought they found. This was partly because 'official' agencies were so short of cash, and partly too because of the desperate need for information about a rapidly growing threat.

On the upside, these networks could sometimes offer hugely valuable information that might otherwise have been missed: Malcolm Christie, who put the Air Ministry in touch with a high-level informant in the Luftwaffe, provides one such example. But equally there were occasions when these private spy services used unverified sources to make unverifiable claims that would not, in all likelihood, have progressed far if ventured within the offices of the British or any other professional espionage agency. This was true, for example, of the claims put forward in March 1939 by the journalist Ian Colvin, who was granted immediate access to key decision-makers in Whitehall at a crucial moment.

Perhaps this shortcoming is what Sir Alexander Cadogan later referred to when, towards the end of his life, he reread his diary of the events of the late 1930s and described 'the impression of a number of amateurs fumbling about with insoluble problems': he doubtlessly had in mind 'amateurs' at every level, not just those in the very highest office. But he made a more specific reference to the dangers of private networks in a memorandum written in early 1939, as rumours of German plans abounded:

Our agents are, of course, bound to report rumours or items of information which come into their possession: they exercise a certain amount of discrimination themselves, but naturally do not take the responsibility of too much selection, and it is our job here to weigh up the information which we receive and try to draw more or less reasonable conclusions from it.[24]

---

24. Amateurs—quoted in *The Diaries of Sir Alexander Cadogan 1938–45*, 30 Mar 1939, Cassell (1971), 166. Cadogan to Henderson, 28 Feb 1938 FO 800/270 TNA.

This danger, of dubious sources making unverifiable claims that are then given too much credit too soon, has at least two unfortunate outcomes.

One is a loss of credibility. Any source that produces bad and unreliable material quickly forfeits its reputation, or finds it impossible to win one. But this is most undesirable if the source is capable of producing, perhaps even sporadically and occasionally, valuable material in the future. In the spring of 1939, for example, senior British diplomats became increasingly sceptical about the value of well-connected German informants such as Dr Carl Goerdeler, who 'tries to curdle our blood by overstating his case', even though his contacts were impressive and their reports sometimes accurate. Even more unfortunate is a situation in which one unreliable source also tarnishes the reputation of others, even though they may be quite different and have no connection. As Sir Alexander Cadogan wrote, 'our sources of information have lately become so prolific (and blood-curdling) that I am beginning to regard them all with a degree of suspicion'.[25]

The other, obvious, danger is that bad intelligence can easily bounce decision-makers into making poor decisions. Again, in the spring of 1939, the British and French governments made a rushed and very questionable commitment to defend Poland on the grounds of very dubious 'intelligence reports' about an imminent German attack. It is hard not to be reminded of parallels from the contemporary age, in which charlatans had credence and dossiers of 'intelligence' were deliberately 'sexed up' in a bid to seduce public opinion.[26]

These are important themes of a story that starts not in 1933, when Hitler became chancellor of Germany, but much earlier, when a shattered and defeated nation gradually and secretly began to rearm.

---

25. Goerdeler—minute by Sir Orme Sargent, 12 Feb 1939, FO 371/22963 TNA. Cadogan—2 Feb 1939, FO 371/22963 TNA.
26. The case for the US invasion of Iraq in 2003 was based on the false 'intelligence' provided by such figures as 'Agent Curveball'. In 2002, the British SIS was also instructed to 'sex up' its published dossier on Iraqi arms.

I

Germany Reawakens

Early in the morning of 6 October 1920, a walker in Forstenrieder Park, outside Munich, was suddenly confronted by a shocking scene that made him stop and stare in disbelief, filling him with an overwhelming sense of revulsion.

Hanging from a rope barely a dozen yards before him, and swinging silently in the breeze, was the lifeless body of a young woman. Stunned and sickened by what he saw, he nonetheless recovered his senses and walked closer. As he did so, he saw a note, writ large and strung around her neck. Its message was simple, crude and shocking: '*You Bitch! You have Betrayed Your Country. The Black Hand Have Delivered Justice!*'

Later that day, the local police found out that the victim, who was barely out of her teens, was a young Munich woman by the name of Marie Sandmayr.

The facts of her case were unfortunate. Some months before she had been working as a domestic servant in the luxurious home of a Bavarian aristocrat. She had left suddenly, probably sacked for some minor indiscretion, and had then seen a poster in the street that offered a reward for information about hidden arms caches in Germany. Whether out of financial hardship or vindictiveness, she had then approached the police with details of what she knew, or claimed to know. What happened after that was unclear but someone, perhaps in the ranks of the police, hadn't liked what she was doing and had taken the law into their own hands.

At around the same time, a number of other ordinary German civilians, all of whom had led seemingly innocent and innocuous lives, also died mysterious and violent deaths, often in or around Munich. Amongst them was a local waiter who had also threatened to tip off the authorities about another illegal cache of arms and who may have demanded payment to buy his silence. Again, word got round and he paid the heaviest possible price: he was shot several times in the head by an unknown assassin before his body was weighed down with heavy stones and dropped into the murky depths of the River Isar.

Then, in March 1921, the body of Hans Hartung, a young German man, was found in a stream, while two other corpses were also found hanging in Forstenrieder Park. Their torsos also bore macabre messages that were similar in style and tone as the note that had proclaimed the fate of Miss Sandmayr: '*I am a rat who betrayed the Fatherland*', went one, in an unconvincing attempt to make the death look like suicide, '*so I die by my own hand*'.[1]

This series of brutal murders later became known as the *Femegerichte* killings. This was a reference to 'vigilante courts', prevalent in parts of medieval Germany, that were not run by the state but instead organized by self-appointed judges: not only had these courts passed sentence on their unfortunate victims but their henchmen had also pinned notes, with excoriating messages, on the chests of those they executed. And now, all these centuries later, the same unpleasant practices had been revived in the near-anarchic conditions of the Weimar Republic by a self-proclaimed 'Black Reichswehr'. This was a mysterious network of violent German nationalists, expert in the dark arts, that had sympathizers, and perhaps even an active leadership, at the very heart of the German government.[2]

Very little was known to outsiders about this 'Black Reichswehr', a term that explains the reference to the 'Black Hand' that wrote and carried out its macabre writ of execution on Miss Sandmayr. In the Reichstag, the defence minister, Otto Gessler, once proclaimed that it was an act of treason to even mention it in public, let alone to ask searching questions. But there was no real doubt about its ultimate purpose. This secretive organization, comprising serving or former members of the German armed forces, was sworn to help Germany defy international agreements and to rearm itself after its shattering

1. Arthur D Brenner, 'Feme Murder: Paramilitary "Self-Justice" in Weimar Germany', in Bruce D Campbell and Arthur D Brenner (eds) *Death Squads in Global Perspective: Murder with Deniability* Palgrave Macmillan (2002) 57–84; Robert Waite *Vanguard of Nazism* W. W. Norton (2007) 221.
2. These murders came to light in 1929, when Carl von Ossietzky and Walter Kreiser published an article about the secret rearmament of Germany. At a later trial (1930–1) Ossietzky alleged that these killings were instigated by the top, on the orders of figures such as Generals von Bock, Schleicher, and Seeckt.

defeat in the First World War. Most of its victims, including those who had met their grisly end in Forstenrieder Park, had seemed to pose a threat to such plans.

In fact, Gessler, Sandmayr, and the two dozen or so other victims of the 'Black Reichswehr' were amongst the first victims of Germany's post-1918 rearmament. This was a process that began to unfold in the ruins, smoke, chaos, and bloodshed of a shattered nation, resolutely defeated in the First World War, and culminated, two decades later, in the outbreak of the Second. Their bloodied, lifeless corpses were an unmistakable sign that in Germany there were fanatics prepared to kill anyone who obstructed their bid to reassert what they regarded as their country's rightful place in the world. And they were a stark reminder to various foreign intelligence agencies across Europe and beyond of how this defeated nation, although vanquished, could still cast aside its shackles and pose a clear threat to others.

A deadly game of German deception and of foreign investigation and espionage, one that was to last throughout those two subsequent decades, had already begun.

In this Cold War, whose stakes could hardly have been higher, one participant was represented by a succession of German politicians, senior officers, and industrialists who, for a number of different reasons, wanted to rearm their homeland.

Some of these individuals were motivated by professional pride or by a desire to defend their homeland from foreign attack. The Germans had crushed foreign invasions before, notably in the summer of 1914, when the Russian army had moved into East Prussia in the first few weeks of the Great War. But they could not be sure about doing so again, particularly if they were confronted by the nightmare scenario that had so haunted their predecessors—the prospect of simultaneous attack on two fronts. At the Second Battle of the Marne in 1914, German strategists warned, the Russian offensive in the east had diverted their soldiers from a French assault in the west. Others, however, wanted to restore what they regarded as Germany's rightful place in the world, with the influence and territories it deserved. Only later, after Adolf Hitler's accession to power in Berlin in 1933, were such limited ambitions dwarfed by an orchestrated, murderous, and diabolical programme of territorial conquest.

On the opposing side were the foreign intelligence services of several surrounding countries which, after the turmoil of the First World

War, harboured deep fears of a resurgent Germany. Amongst them were Romania, Yugoslavia, and the Soviet Union. But the most important, given their military and economic power, were the British and French, whose spy chiefs worked hard to monitor and to thwart the covert German efforts to rearm, and sometimes to warn their political masters about what was happening.

Both countries feared Germany for good reason. Nearly one and a half million French soldiers had died in the Great War, and in just one prolonged, agonizing encounter, fought at Verdun in the course of 1916 against an enemy that had sworn to 'bleed France white', the French army had sacrificed around 160,000 men. In Paris, such fears went back to at least the mid-1860s, when Bismarck's Prussia started to win a series of stunning military victories that culminated in a humiliating defeat of France during the brief but decisive war of 1870–1 and the creation of the state of Germany. The French had subsequently felt overshadowed by their neighbour and haunted by fears of their own relative decline: since the 1890s, Germany had boasted a more powerful economy and a substantially larger population, which was still growing at a time when France's own was diminishing. And French fears of another war against Germany, or indeed any adversary, were heightened by their traumatic experience of the political instability that frequently ensues after a major defeat in the field: in 1870, humiliation and surrender on the battlefield had been followed by revolution and carnage in the streets of Paris.

The British had also lost heavily in the Great War, sacrificing around three-quarters of a million in a war that very arguably bestowed no obvious benefits and whose justification had always been open to question. From the moment of victory in November 1918, the British were as determined as the French, and other powers, to introduce a peace settlement that would prevent such a catastrophe from ever happening again. A young British diplomat, Harold Nicolson, revealed these understandable but absurdly high hopes when he later described how 'we were preparing not Peace only but Eternal Peace. There was about us the halo of some divine mission.' But the British pushed for a more lenient line than France against Germany, gripped as they were by fears of another nightmare becoming a terrifying reality. Winston Churchill, a junior minister in Lloyd George's cabinet, called this nightmare 'the plague bacillus of Bolshevism' that had already infected Russia and brought down the czar in the revolution in 1917. Now, like a deadly virus, it seemed ready to sweep west, into Germany and beyond, and such a threat needed to be locked down only with compromise and conciliation, not by threats.[3]

On 28 June 1919, seven months after the ceasefire, large crowds gathered outside the vast Palace of Versailles near Paris to watch the arrival of the great names of the day, including President Woodrow Wilson, the British leader David Lloyd George, and the French prime minister Georges Clemenceau, who then signed a treaty that would, its advocates hoped, consign the last conflict as 'the war to end wars'.

But in the words of one diplomat who witnessed the grandiose proceedings, it was 'the utmost insult to Germany', one that was always likely to stir up a resentment, bitterness, and feelings of vengeance within the defeated nation. In the Great Hall of Mirrors, where the delegates signed their treaty, they had seen reflections of their own emotions rather than the true state of Germany. This was partly, perhaps largely, because the French took a harshly vindictive line, pushing for draconian measures against a defeated adversary. These feelings also merged with economic jealousy and insecurity, and perhaps with fears that the French nation had lost its old fighting spirit and would in the future be unable to defend itself: powerful waves of pacifist sentiment were at this time sweeping through the country, prompting Churchill to claim that France was 'armed to the teeth but pacifist to the core' and forcing cadets at the military academy at St Cyr to wear only civilian dress when they went outside, for fear of provoking abuse or even assaults by members of the public. And on the streets outside Versailles, French pacifists attacked the German delegation on their arrival, pelting them with rotten fruit and other missiles.[4]

But while London urged moderation, fearing a nationalist reaction that would play into the hands of German communists, Clemenceau showed little clemency and insisted that the Treaty of Versailles should impose massive financial reparations and tear whole strips of territory away from the vanquished state. Chief amongst these was the creation of an unnatural 'corridor' of Polish territory in what had previously been East Prussia. This gave the newly formed state of Poland access to

3. Nicholson—Harold Nicolson *Peacemaking 1919* Grosset & Dunlap (1971) 106–7. Churchill—William Manchester *The Last Lion* Little, Brown and Company (1983) 680.
4. Insult—Brendon *Dark Valley* 18. St Cyr—in 1934 the pacifist Rassemblement Universel pour la Paix had 16 million followers. Churchill—*The Gathering Storm* Cassell (1964) 40.

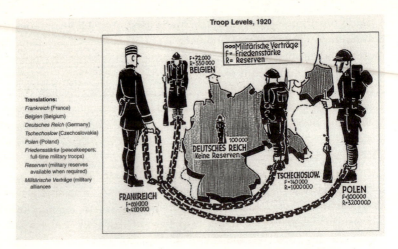

Figure 1. A contemporary depiction of troops levels in Western Europe in 1920

the sea but nonetheless drove a wedge between East Prussia and the rest of Germany. It was always an issue that looked likely to start a future conflict.

In addition, the French reclaimed Alsace and Lorraine while the treaty also gave them two German territories for the next fifteen years—the coal-producing region of the Saarland and the Rhineland, which became a neutral, demilitarized zone.

But because the armed forces unmistakably represented their country's greatness, as well as being the most obvious guarantee of their self-defence, the 'Disarmament Clauses' of the Versailles Treaty were amongst those that caused the most indignation for many Germans. These imposed severe restrictions upon the number of soldiers, just 100,000, that Germany was now allowed to have (see Figure 1). To prevent any reserves being built, officers were also required to serve for twenty-five years and ordinary soldiers for twelve. The Germans were also prohibited from producing any new arms and forced to destroy any stockpiles of arms or else surrender them to the Allied forces. Similarly harsh conditions were imposed on Germany's navy, while its air force was outlawed altogether.

The French also wanted other guarantees of their national security, notably a defensive alliance with Great Britain. The government's great fear, as the prime minister Édouard Herriot later told his generals, was that 'one day France would find herself alone facing Germany'.[5]

Such an alliance represented a great prize. Britain's immense financial power had enabled it to raise American loans that subsidized the entire Allied war effort, and bucked up morale, during the First World War. And because the immense might of the Royal Navy had kept this war effort afloat, British support was vital in the event of any future conflict. In the Great War, the British fleet had contained the German navy, guarded merchant shipping, and blockaded the Axis powers. In any future conflict, it would allow France to concentrate on controlling the Mediterranean, which provided a 'vital artery' to its colonial territories in North Africa and beyond. 'With its navy, its military potential, its immense economic resources and especially its fidelity to engagements', observed the French ambassador in London in early 1922, 'Britain is as precious an ally in wartime as its political influence, moral authority and loyalty make it in peacetime.'[6]

The French had craved an alliance with Great Britain long before the First World War. In 1904 the two countries had promised to resolve some of their differences but French diplomats wanted to convert this 'Entente Cordiale' into a formal alliance: their own mistrust of the British, of 'Perfidious Albion', was outweighed by their fear and suspicion of Germany. Nor did such fears of their eastern neighbour abate after 1918.

For Georges Clemenceau, this meant that an understanding with Great Britain was the 'essential basis' of his foreign policy. He would not and could not help the Poles in the event of a German attack, he told them, unless the British first helped him. Clemenceau even offered to build and pay for the construction of a Channel tunnel that would allow a British expeditionary force to come to the defence of France within just hours. 'Only with the help of John Bull—his powerful navy, his burgeoning modern air force and his immense imperial resources', as Piers Brendon puts it, 'could Marianne survive a prolonged Teutonic assault.'[7]

5. Anthony Adamthwaite *The Making of the Second World War* Routledge (1977) 194.
6. Quoted in Peter Jackson, 'French Security and a British "Continental Commitment" after the First World War: A Reassessment', *EHR* (Apr 2011), 350.
7. Tunnel—the British had vetoed an earlier proposal, in 1883, on the grounds that the French might invade Britain; Brendon *Dark Valley* 503.

But now, as before, John Bull rebuffed Marianne's advances. After the horrors of the Great War, isolationist sentiment was strong in London. There seemed to be no compelling reason to tie a knot that would drag Britain to the altar of another, perhaps quite unnecessary, war on the continent. In London, maintaining a balance of power across the Channel would not help Britain to defend her empire but could instead easily distract and divert its resources from those more vital interests: this was set to become all the more important a consideration after 1931, when Imperial Japan presented a rapidly growing threat to the security of British India and Australia. And any such further entanglements would also be likely to prove very expensive, imposing more costs on war-weary British taxpayers at a time when their vast empire was already burdensome. As the prime minister Neville Chamberlain was to lament a few years later, 'if only it wasn't for Germany, we would be having such a wonderful time just now... what a frightful bill do we owe to Master Hitler, damn him'.[8]

France needed Britain, in other words, more than the British needed the French. As an island power, the British did not share the same sense of vulnerability that had long afflicted their neighbours.

If the British were deeply wary of any continental alliances, they were even more mistrustful of striking one with France. This reflected long centuries of rivalry and war that had woven stories of Joan of Arc and Agincourt, Napoleon and Trafalgar, the Norman Conquest, and of British success and French humiliation at Fashoda in East Africa, deep into the national tapestries of both countries. Despite moments of cooperation, such as those of the Crimean War, and some close personal friendships amongst rulers and political elites, relations were typically 'deeply ambivalent' between two countries that became allies only after the onset of the Great War in August 1914. These sentiments of rivalry and suspicion were mutual: 'people in this country forget all too easily... that there are just as many Anglophobes in France as there are Francophobes in England. Indeed perhaps there are more', as Robert Vansittart wrote.[9]

8. RJ Overy and A Wheatcroft *The Road to War: The Origins of World War 2* Vintage (2009) 78.
9. Fashoda—there had been a stand-off between British and French contingents at Fashoda in East Africa in July 1898 before the French backed down. 'Deep ambivalence'—Tombs and Tombs 442. Personal friendships—see Theo Aronson *Queen Victoria and the Bonapartes* Cassell (1972). The 1904 Entente Cordiale was essentially just an agreement to resolve colonial differences. Vansittart—quoted in Talbot Imlay 'The

Such mistrust between London and Paris persisted throughout the First World War and beyond. Despite their united front against a common enemy, the Great War had aggravated rather than healed the animosity that many British people felt for their continental neighbour. 'Anti-French feeling among ex-soldiers amounted almost to an obsession', wrote the celebrated war poet Robert Graves, while one British aristocrat echoed the views of many of his fellow soldiers when he exclaimed that if 'another war comes...I hope the partners will be changed'. Clemenceau's uncompromising line at Versailles stirred up even more anti-French feeling, even amongst Francophiles like Sir Austen Chamberlain and Winston Churchill, who were shocked by the harsh French approach.[10]

Other post-war incidents reinforced such views. During the 'Chanak Crisis' of September 1922, for example, the French had infuriated London by pulling their troops out of disputed territories in the Ottoman Empire, leaving British soldiers exposed and isolated. There could scarcely have been any better way of entrenching the anti-French prejudices of figures such as Sir Maurice Hankey, who regarded the French as duplicitous and unreliable, and of the foreign secretary, Lord Curzon, who lamented that 'the Great Power from whom we most have to fear in the future is France'. At almost the same time, the British air staff felt that the prospect of war with France was 'the greatest menace to this country'.[11]

Britain and France, in other words, were 'most dear enemies' that had been superficially allied in war but now continued to be profoundly divided in peace. Nor did such British suspicions of France abate throughout the 1920s: the Locarno Treaty, signed in 1925 by leaders of Western European countries who agreed amongst themselves to respect their existing borders, was seen as a means of protecting Germany against France at least as much as anything else: in the eyes of David Lloyd George, for example, the French were striving to

Making of the Anglo-French Alliance', in Alexander & Philpott (eds) *Anglo-French Defence Relations* 104.

10. Graves and Clemenceau quoted in Brendon *Dark Valley* 150; on post-WWI rivalry see in general James Barr *The Line in the Sand* W. W. Norton (2011).

11. Curzon—quoted in M Dockrill, *British Establishment Perspectives on France 1936–40* Palgrave Macmillan (1999) 2. Menace—Anthony Adamthwaite *Grandeur and Misery* Bloomsbury (1994) 74.

acquire hegemony in Western Europe and trying to rope in Britain behind.[12]

The French, however, were wise to be so concerned about their security. For while the remnants of the German army sometimes provoked ridicule from foreign observers—on occasion by using fake tanks, made of wood, canvas, and cardboard, on parades and on exercises— Berlin was in fact making a determined effort to rearm almost as soon as the Treaty of Versailles had been signed, and perhaps even before.

Some of this covert gun-running was driven purely by profit. Some destitute employees in the arms industry, and elsewhere, were prepared to sell secrets to anyone who offered generous bribes. In 1921, for example, the French foreign spy service, the Deuxième Bureau, offered significant sums to several employees of a German company that was developing blueprints of a new aircraft that the French agents were particularly keen to see: the designs were smuggled out of the factory and taken, hidden inside a suitcase, to a hotel rendezvous with undercover French operatives.[13]

Another such renegade was not a German national but a Dutchman. The fortunes of Anthony Fokker, aged just 28 at the end of the Great War, had risen sky-high when he developed and then manufactured several highly successful types of aircraft. Just months after the Versailles Treaty came into force, and as the inspectors started to home in on his factories, he smuggled the bulk of his personal savings onto foreign soil, hiding these vast cash sums in suitcases that were then moved out of Germany, firstly on a boat and then, subsequently, by train. Within just a few weeks, Fokker had spirited his planes, 400 engines, and a great deal of other material into neutral Holland.[14]

---

12. The only 'commitment' to France that the British made was the Anglo-French Treaty (Defence of France) Act of 1919 but this was conditional upon an alliance with America that Lloyd George knew was very unlikely to ever materialize: the Republican majority in the US Senate rejected the Versailles peace agreements to prevent further overseas commitments. Lloyd George—French Memo of 13–14 Dec 1928, 7NN 2797 SHD.

13. 'A/S de Wizinger, Yohanna', 7 Sept 1929, 7NN 2182, SHD. In this text, the 'Deuxième Bureau' is used, out of convenience, as a blanket term to cover six different intelligence agencies in France. Of these six, the spy service of the army general staff was the most important. This was divided into the Service de Renseignements (SR), which gathered information and forwarded it to the Deuxième Bureau, whose officers evaluated it and forwarded it to the general staff.

14. Anthony Fokker *The Flying Dutchman* Penguin Books (1938); Barton Whaley *Covert German Rearmament, 1919–1939: Deception and Misperception*, Foreign Intelligence Book Series (1984) 4–5.

But if Fokker's actions were motivated more by profit and careerism, many others were concerned with the grandeur of their homeland: as some foreign observers noticed, in Germany the status of the army was indistinguishable from feelings of national pride. The other chief consideration was of course the national security of a country that was threatened on both its eastern and western fronts. Such fears were felt most deeply by the acting head of the German army, General Hans Friedrich von Seeckt, who was dismayed by Germany's defeat and surrender in 1918 and regarded the Versailles Treaty as a 'poison' that was capable of killing Germany 'spiritually' as well as militarily. He and his fellow generals were now determined to hide Germany's covert rearmament from the watching eye of the victorious Allies, who had set up an international body for that very purpose.[15]

Britain and France liaised closely as they watched and monitored a defeated Germany but this was not an interaction between their respective intelligence services, whose eyes were focused more on events in Russia and the apparent threat posed by communism. It was instead undertaken by the Inter-Allied Military Commission of Control (IMCC) that the Treaty of Versailles had set up to ensure the 'complete execution' of its disarmament clauses.[16]

Headquartered at the impressive Hotel Adlon in central Berlin, the Commission was run by nine senior Allied officers, four of whom were French and two British. They organized and supervised inspections by their officials, who were scattered all over the defeated nation and who had immense freedom to travel 'to any point whatever in German territory' and inspect whatever, and whenever, they thought fit. These inspectors pooled their information but also shared their findings with their respective governments and intelligence services, who were entrusted with assessing the information that they received and bringing their conclusions to the attention of their political masters.[17]

The inspectors initially notched up an impressive balance sheet of information, and it looked as though their surveillance of post-war Germany was reaping handsome dividends. By the early 1920s, they

15. Indistinguishable—'The Military Situation in Germany', 10 Apr 1929, CAB-24/203/21 TNA. Von Seeckt—FL Carsten *The Reichswehr and Politics 1918–33* Clarendon Press (1966) Ch III.
16. Threat of communism—Jeffery Ch 6.
17. Freedom—Articles 159–213, the Military, Naval and Air Clauses of the Versailles Treaty, 28 June 1919. Charles Nollet *Une Expérience de Désarmement* Gallimard (1932).

had visited thousands of sites, supervised the dynamiting of entire infrastructure, and disabled many more specialized industrial tools and machinery, which had sustained the German war effort for four long years. During one particularly energetic six-week period alone, between September and October 1924, they carried out more than 200 inspections at factories that had manufactured vast quantities of arms throughout the war. And at Essen in the Ruhr, the site of the vast industrial conglomerate that the Krupp family had built up over decades, several inspectors set up a permanent residence at a guesthouse, using it as a base from which to make snap inspections and to interview visiting businessmen and factory officials.[18]

But although they were unaware of it, they were often chasing shadows. They spent considerable amounts of time inspecting facilities whose bosses had been illicitly tipped off and at other times were deliberately fed with false leads: on one occasion they made a long and fruitless journey to investigate a fallacious story about a factory whose 'prams' could somehow be reassembled into machine guns. In truth, some arms were built surreptitiously in workshops away from main factories and then hidden on heathland or in sand dunes. Behind a façade of cooperation with the Allies, German factory owners and operatives often tried to circumvent the rules: 'padlocks, milk cans, cash registers, rail-mending machines, refuse carts and similar rubbish appeared really innocent, and locomotives and motor cars appeared perfectly "peaceful"', as the arms magnate Gustav Krupp wrote afterwards. Industrialists became particularly expert in the arts of deception, for example by 'spreading out equipment in an exaggerated manner', as the inspectors themselves noted, to make their workshops look sparser than they really were.[19]

By the mid-1920s, an increasing number of German industrialists and commanders were also following the example of Anthony Fokker by offshoring their enterprises. This was true of Gustav Krupp, who deeply resented a treaty designed to keep 'the German people...enslaved forever'. Looking abroad to find places to store, research, and develop arms, he made good use of an old machinery plant, once run by AB Landswerk,

18. Six weeks—IMCC Memo, 20 Nov 1924, WO 32/5797 TNA. At Essen, inspectors supervised the destruction of property amounting to more than 104 million gold marks belonging to the Krupp family; 9,300 machines, weighing around 60k tons; 801,420 industrial tools, and 379 installations.
19. Padlocks—chapter written in Apr 1941 for the Todt Org, International Military Tribunal, Nuremberg 1946–7, Doc D-64. Spreading out—25 Nov 1924, WO 32/5797 TNA.

at Landskrona in southern Sweden, and also bought shipbuilding yards in Rotterdam, where he set up a special centre for ordnance manufacture that was staffed by German experts from the major naval base at Kiel. He also established a number of other such companies in Barcelona, Bilbao, and Cadiz where U-boats were now built and tested.[20]

The German authorities also proved duplicitous. It was no coincidence that, just as the Germans began to act against both the spirit and the letter of the Versailles Treaty on such a scale, they also started to show some superficial cooperation with the Allied inspectors. There has been a 'marked improvement in general attitude' by 'the Germans [who] have changed their attitude very considerably in the last month', wrote a delighted Colonel McGrath of the IMCC's Berlin office in March 1925. This was partly because there was strong international pressure on Germany to comply with its obligations, for in February 1925 the IMCC had issued a General Report that called on Berlin to make a greater effort and concluded that a strenuous effort was needed to enforce the Versailles Treaty. But the Germans also wanted to drive wedges between the Allies. Such divisions existed within the ranks of the IMCC, in which hardliners like Morgan and its French director, Charles Nollet, took issue with the more moderate and trusting approach of colleagues such as General Sir Francis Bingham. But the rift they really wanted to exploit lay between the French and the more moderate British.[21]

In the early 1920s, Paris continued to take the most hawkish line, even pushing for more direct Allied control over Germany rather than supervising the efforts of the German government to enforce the terms of the treaty. Such demands had prompted Viscount D'Abernon, the British ambassador in Berlin, to write that 'I consider the French demand for the total disarmament of all *Einwohnerwehr* [citizens' defence] and similar organizations almost insane…the French do not appear to understand that the real danger is communist disorder.' A respectable German army, ran the British argument, would not only be in a position to crush any communist revolt but would also give a degree of national pride that would stop the country falling into the hands of extremists.[22]

20. Krupp—chapter written in Apr 1941 for the Todt Org, International Military Tribunal, Nuremberg 1946–7, Doc D-64. U-boats—Bernhard Menne *Krupp: Lords of Essen* William Hodge & Co (1957) 365–7.
21. McGrath—'IAMCC in Germany', 24 Mar 1924 WO 32/5797 TNA.
22. Hawkish line—Martin Alexander, 'Did the Deuxième Bureau Work?' *INS* 318; D'Abernon, *Diary I, Versailles to Rapallo 1920–22* Hodder & Stoughton (1929), 92–3.

But these Anglo-French differences became more pronounced from March 1926, when the Germans had applied for admission to the League of Nations while also demanding that all international inspections and controls should be swept away: Germany had respected the demands of the Versailles Treaty, argued Berlin fallaciously, and the inspectors had served their purpose and should now leave.

The French immediately resisted these calls and compiled a long and detailed dossier of German violations of the treaty: Berlin was massaging its figures, Paris claimed, akin to squeezing a heavyweight into a corset. It was really maintaining an enormous number of NCOs and generals while also organizing illegal paramilitaries, hiding forbidden weapons and concealing its growing links with Russia. 'Germany', the French argued, 'has not shown good faith in carrying out her obligations, and there are still a number of important points covered by the "time-limit" clauses which remain to be fulfilled.'[23]

At the same time, Paris insisted on maintaining Allied troops in the Rhineland, and still worked hard, without success, to lure Britain into a formal defensive alliance. The importance of British support had become particularly clear in 1923, when the French government had retaliated against Berlin's failure to pay some of the reparations, imposed by the 1919 treaty, by sending troops into the Ruhr district in a bid to seize control over its valuable resources. But the subsequent international furore forced the French to beat a retreat and reminded them that they needed British diplomatic as well as military support. But there was no sea-change of opinion across the Channel, and still London refused an alliance with its old enemy: critics argued that it would be viewed in Berlin as a potential threat and risked inflaming nationalist sentiment, playing into communist hands. Instead, the British government wanted to bring an immediate end to the inspections, arguing that they stifled a spirit of reconciliation that would heal divisions and prevent another tragedy, comparable to the First World War.

But in December 1926, deeply alarmed at the possibility that Germany might soon be freed from Allied military control, the French War Ministry produced another alarming report warning that Germany was far more dangerous than recognized: citing evidence of hidden stockpiles of arms, it estimated that Germany could call up more than six million men and half a million officers and NCOs, while also raising

23. 'Report on Situation Concerning Inspections', 2 Feb 1925, WO 32/5797 TNA.

120–50 divisions of frontline troops. In fact, such claims were a desperate attempt to keep the inspectors in Germany, and the French Foreign Ministry disputed them.[24]

To the alarm and horror of Paris, it was the British line that won the day when, on 31 January 1927, the IMCC formally pulled out of its Berlin headquarters and ended its eight-year presence in Germany. Military control over the country now passed to the League of Nations, and no foreign government or agency had any automatic legal right to investigate German military affairs beyond the Rhineland, where both countries continued to station troops. 'By this date', the War Office in London stated proudly, 'the numbers, organization and equipment of the German Army had, broadly speaking, been brought into conformity with the provisions of the Treaty of Versailles.' But privately many of those who were familiar with events in Germany were furious, claiming that the British government had been far too quick to overlook overwhelming evidence of German rearmament.[25]

There was by this time another, more specific, reason why some foreign observers were feeling a sense of alarm about German affairs. This was the sudden, spectacular rise of a young Austrian fanatic called Adolf Hitler, whose National Socialist movement was attracting an increasing number of followers, particularly in and around the politically turbulent city of Munich. It was to find out more about this nationalist firebrand that the young Truman Smith, acting as an assistant US army attaché, had been tasked in 1922. Travelling through Bavaria, Smith had noted how 'the National Socialists are increasing their strength rapidly'. Hitler was, in his view, 'a pure and simple adventurer [but] a real character [who] is exploiting all latent discontent to increase his party's strength'. The threat he posed was greater because he 'thoroughly understands the Bavarian psychology'. Smith, like others, could see, and sense, that trouble was brewing.[26]

24. Richard J Shuster *German Rearmament After World War I* Routledge (2006) 161.
25. War Office—FO Memo from Berlin, 25 Nov 1924, WO 32/5797 TNA. Furious—see in general JH Morgan *Assize of Arms* OUP (1945), 124; John P Fox, 'Britain and the Inter-Allied Military Commission of Control 1925–26', *Journal of Contemporary History* (Apr 1969) 149.
26. Truman Smith, Letter of 15 Nov 1922—*Berlin Alert: The Memoirs and Reports of Truman Smith*, ed. Robert Hessen, Hoover Institution Press (1984) 48.

2

Foreign Spies Keep Watch

As the last of the international inspectors left Germany, they passed the mantle of intelligence-gathering to their respective spying agencies, who were now entrusted with the task of monitoring developments within Germany's borders and gauging the potential threat that they posed.

It was upon the British and French that the burden now fell. The United States did not maintain any full-time intelligence presence on German soil and instead only posted serving diplomats and attachés at its embassy in Berlin, all of whom lacked specialist training in espionage. The Czech spy services were at this stage run by just a handful of military officers, whose attention was focused largely on the much more immediate threat of a Polish attack on disputed territories whilst also suffering from 'an outdated preoccupation with Austria and its Habsburg restoration'. And Moscow's gaze was too distracted by the bloody political turmoil at home to focus on potential threats that might, in a worst-case scenario and at some distant future point, perhaps eventually materialize.[1]

During the Great War, the SIS and the Bureau had worked closely together, even setting up a joint command, based in Folkestone in Kent, that was focused on tracking and neutralizing German agents who were operating on Allied soil. But even at these moments of greatest danger, such shared challenges could not create more than a superficial unity between two countries whose relations had for centuries been characterized by outright enmity, rivalry, suspicion, and jealousy.[2]

1. Moravec 43.
2. Folkestone—Olivier Forcade *La République secrète* Nouveau monde (2008) 32–3.

Such mistrust lingered after the Armistice. Both services, it is true, continued to work together on matters of mutual concern, such as monitoring Bolshevik agents on Western soil and Japanese espionage on the British fleet in the English Channel, which in 1925 was the subject of correspondence between two heads of department, Colonels Stewart and Henri Lainey. And from the mid-1920s, the SIS also ran a number of stations in France that tracked Soviet agents and sympathizers, making use of Paris-based emigrés to obtain information about what was happening within Russia. This was done with the full knowledge, and at times the full cooperation, of the French authorities. But the wider picture revealed an image of rivalry or even open competition for influence in several other parts of the world.[3]

This became particularly clear soon after the signing of the Versailles Treaty, when the head of the Deuxième Bureau, Colonel Charles Fournier, had written a telling memorandum that bore a revealing testimony: now that the war had ended, he argued, 'the exchange of confidential information (with Great Britain) was no longer necessary, and would even have a serious downside'. Henceforth, he continued, information should only be shared if it concerned 'an historic issue rather than one that gives an assessment of our present or future capabilities'. Any such exchange of information would also have to go through 'the proper channels, and through the military attachés' who were stationed at the respective embassies in foreign capitals.[4]

And although they were working together to supervise post-war Germany, the two countries also kept a close and wary eye on each other's activities: in July 1927, for example, a suspicious military attaché at the French embassy in Berlin picked up signs that the British were establishing *relations cordiales* with the German army. Such games of rivalry were played out, above all, in the Netherlands, where the French reported that the SIS was using banking and commercial operations to hide its activities, and suspected that it was also seeking to penetrate the Deuxième Bureau's local intelligence networks and buy off its agents. So strong were French suspicions of British intelligence activities in the Low Countries, particularly of the SIS heads of station in Rotterdam, Captain Richard Tinsley and Major Hugh Dalton, that Colonel Lainey set up an enquiry into the matter. And in North Africa

---

3. Japanese fleet—Forcade 206. Soviet agents—Jeffery 289.
4. Forcade 204.

the Bureau shadowed suspected SIS operatives such as HR Owen and the 'enigmatic' Guy Loftus, whose meetings with Major Fox, the British consul at Bizerte and an 'undoubted' British agent, aroused great suspicion of an 'Anglo-Saxon' plot against French interests.[5]

Given the wide channel between them, it was not surprising that the two spying agencies missed crucial information about the state of a 'German army [that] seems to have disappeared from public view . . . in a way that arouses suspicion'. In April 1926, the army general staff in Berlin had issued a directive for planning what became known as 'the first armaments programme', one that would start the following year and finish in 1932. Its estimates were based on a threefold, or even ninefold, increase above their supposed level. Yet neither the SIS nor the Bureau appear to have been aware of this order.[6]

But their independent efforts had some success at detecting Germany's covert rearmament outside its borders. Holland was a particular concern, not least because its economy was so closely integrated into Germany's industrial heartland, and French agents kept a very close eye on two businesses that were based in Amsterdam. One was Rhodius Königs, an import–export business that was suspected of having undercover links with both Krupp and Siemens, and the other was IPU, a German-owned press agency run by Peter Kirner that was seen as a cover for German intelligence. In 1925, the Bureau had three agents in its Dutch network who were 'focused on the comings and goings at Fokker's factories', as well as another two operatives who concentrated on researching military intelligence about Germany. These agents were tasked with 'obtaining solid information about the German military', in addition to other duties that included monitoring arms trafficking to North Africa, and tracking both communist and German influence in, and infiltration of, Holland and elsewhere. The British also began to watch Kirner, whose activities became the subject of Anglo-French correspondence in the mid-1920s, and the two agencies discovered that his press agency was running German agents

5. French attaché—7 July 1927, 7NN 2583 SHD. Tinsley and Dalton—20 Aug 1920, 7NN 395/101 SHD. Owen and Loftus—'A/S d'un Anglais Suspect: Loftus', 13 Jan 1928, 7NN 3198 SHD; 'A/S du nomme HR Owen', 12 Dec 1933, 7NN 3203 SHD.
6. German army—'Germany seems determined to hide its army, doubtlessly to convince outsiders it has disarmed', 7 July 1927, 7NN 2583 SHD. Estimates—for example, an increase in the number of machine guns from 12,000 to 20,000 between 1927 and 1931, nearly six times the figure authorized by the Allies.

tasked with obtaining economic intelligence, notably about petrol and foodstuffs.[7]

The French also now focused more attention on Denmark. In 1927 the Deuxième Bureau had noted how well positioned it was as a base for spying on the Reich as well as commenting upon the 'pro-French sympathies' of its intelligence officers, who allowed the Bureau's officers 'a lot more freedom' to undertake espionage activities than in Holland, even if it was 'much harder in Denmark to recruit informers'. Based in Copenhagen, the Bureau's agents regularly travelled to Hamburg, Kiel, and Stettin, where they liaised with French consuls to determine ways of obtaining information about illicit German rearmament.[8]

Working independently, both agencies were also successful at detecting the new and highly covert liaison between Russia and Germany. The Deuxième Bureau had first become aware of growing commercial links between the two countries as early as the spring of 1922, when an informer at the German embassy in Paris passed on important information about the secret terms of the Rapallo Treaty: German businesses, the source claimed, had been given special concessions to exploit Russia's mines and to manufacture heavy artillery for its army. The French also detected indications of a sudden increase in German exports to the east and stepped up their surveillance of a businessman, Hugo Stinnes, who seemed to be at the heart of many of these suspect trade deals. And in 1924 the Estonian government also tipped off the Deuxième Bureau about the growing links between Germany and Russia.[9]

It was not long before the emergent Berlin–Moscow axis became an open secret, one that the mainstream press picked up. On 3 December 1926, *The Manchester Guardian* published 'startling disclosures' about Germany's 'secret plan' with Russia. Over the preceding five years, shouted the dramatic headline, there had been 'cargoes of munitions from Russia to Germany'. German personnel—there was no indication of their numbers—had also been covertly visiting several training centres that had been quietly set up a few years before, in blatant

7. Solid information—'Voyage du Lt-Col Lainey à La Haye', 19–21 Nov 1925, 7NN 2151 SHD. Kirner—Forcade 235–6.
8. 'Service de l'attaché militaire', 1 Apr 1927, 7NN 2151 SHD.
9. Concessions—Forcade 495. Stinnes—Forcade 496. Estonia—Georges Castellan *Le Réarmement du Reich 1930–35* Plon (1954) 179.

defiance of the Versailles Treaty. These illicit activities, it continued, had been orchestrated by 'secret military societies' in Berlin 'with the connivance of officers of the Reichswehr and some high officials, at least, of the Ministry of War', although the report claimed that the involvement of the German minister of war, Dr Otto Gessler, was 'still uncertain'.[10]

The report seems to have been quietly overlooked by the British officials who were now organizing the withdrawal of the Allied arms inspectors from Germany. Others paid more attention to the more reassuring public gestures that Berlin was making towards the outside world: at Locarno, the previous year, the German foreign minister Gustav Stresemann had accepted Western Europe's existing borders and championed a spirit of international goodwill, just as in 1928 he went on to sign the Kellogg–Briand Pact that renounced war as an instrument of foreign policy. But word continued to leak out about what was really going on between Berlin and Moscow. Just six weeks later, on 19 January 1927, the *Münchener Post* also published details of a high-level German delegation that had gone to Russia to conclude a deal for the production of a new fighter plane.

The existence of such links between Russia and Germany, however, told the foreign spy agencies very little. They needed much more information, over a very wide spectrum of issues, to gauge any possible German threat. In particular, they had to know not just about the quality and quantity of Germany's existing resources but also about what its leaders were trying to do. Did they just want to maintain this very modest effort and build up only a relatively negligible military force? And if they were going to be more ambitious, did they simply want to defend their homeland against foreign incursion—hardly an unreasonable aim, when between them Poland and France had 134 army divisions to boast of—rather than launch an aggressive war to seize back lost territories? Berlin also had other potential motives for rearming. If the Germans wanted to produce arms to sell them to foreign buyers, the world over, then that also made perfect sense at a time of recession and such high unemployment. Nor, for that matter, did there seem to be anything necessarily unreasonable about the German

10. 'Cargoes of Munitions from Russia to Germany', *The Manchester Guardian*, 3 Dec 1926.

claim for *Gleichberechtigung* ('equality') with other countries, however exactly that was defined.

One source of such information was Poland, another close ally of the French and a natural partner against an aggressive Germany. The Bolsheviks had swept away the rule of the czars and, by doing so, deprived France of its traditional ally, Imperial Russia. In Paris, politicians and generals saw Poland as a more reliable and trustworthy ally than the revolutionary Bolshevik regime in Moscow.

France and Poland had enjoyed close political, military, and intelligence cooperation since 1919, when the Poles had gone to war with the Bolsheviks over disputed borders in present-day Ukraine. Soon after the clashes began, the French sent a military mission that strongly supported the Polish war effort, particularly during a Red Army counter-offensive in the spring of 1920. By the time a ceasefire was struck and the war was over, in May the following year, France and Poland had already signed a series of pacts, each promising to give the other 'mutual aid' in the event of German 'aggression' whilst also calling for 'cooperation' on military matters.

France's willingness to strike up an alliance with the Poles was neither whole-hearted nor shared by other governments in Europe. The Poles appeared to have ambitions that were out of all proportion to their true status: 'The Poles regarded themselves as an independent power,' as AJP Taylor has written, 'blindly confident in their own strength.' But this raised suspicions amongst outsiders who wondered if the Poles were really untrustworthy and willing to do deals with anyone if it suited them. Nonetheless, by the mid-1920s the French wanted a pact with Warsaw because it was in their interest to do so, offering them some semblance of security in the absence of British, American, and Soviet support. By the time this agreement was signed, in February 1921, the Deuxième Bureau already had a permanent representative stationed in Warsaw who formed part of the military mission. Information was exchanged about a variety of matters of mutual concern, including the activities of Russian and communist agents in Poland and elsewhere, as well as developments inside Germany. In April 1926 this led to the signing of another secret deal between the two countries: under its terms, the Poles agreed to focus their intelligence activities on the eastern half of Germany while the French concentrated on the west, following a line of demarcation that ran between Stettin, Berlin, and Leipzig. Both would share the information they obtained, as well as any details about the activities of German agents on their own soil.[11]

In particular, Warsaw needed to know if the Germans were actively planning to make some aggressive territorial claims, perhaps by seizing and prising the 'Corridor' from Polish hands, or taking back control over the disputed city of Köningsberg. Neither they nor their French and British counterparts knew that the German top brass had already drawn up a list of very assertive foreign policy aims that included winning back the Rhineland and acquiring control over Austria and 'areas essential to her economy'—a reference to the Polish Corridor, Polish Upper Silesia, and the Saar.[12]

Given their fears of attack from both east and west, Polish ministers were prepared to spend significant sums of money on their foreign intelligence service, the Second Department of the general staff, which was run by around 200 officers, more than three times the number of its French equivalent. And besides allocating such resources, the Poles also had some very good informers amongst the millions of ethnic Poles who had, for decades, lived under a German flag. Nearly all spoke the German language like natives and were also highly familiar with the places, customs, and mindset of their former compatriots.

Just such an individual came to the attention of the head of the Second Department in or around 1926.

Speaking perfect German and having served in the First World War as a cavalry officer in the Austro-Hungarian army, Jerzy ('Jerry') Sosnowski cut the kind of dashing figure that the spy chiefs felt sure would win admiration in Berlin: just 30 years old, his youthful good looks and energy, perfect manners, and charm were a heady mix. And he had an impressive track record of melting female hearts, having had passionate affairs with a number of glamorous high-society women, amongst them the wife, nearly two decades his senior, of his commanding officer.

It was his remarkable success with women that probably helped bring him to the Department's attention, since one of his numerous

---

11. Pact with Warsaw - AJP Taylor *The Origins of the Second World War* Penguin (1963) 242–3. Secret Deal - Forcade 270–1.
12. Edward W Bennett *German Rearmament and the West, 1932–1933* Princeton University Press (reprint 2015) 20.

lovers, Maria Wlotny, was an active Polish spy, codenamed 'Agent Z30' or 'Antoinette'. Sosnowski had been shocked and sickened by Wlotny's sudden grisly end in an 'accident' after the Department's chiefs discovered that she was a double agent and then staged her death to avoid the humiliation of a public trial. But by the mid-1920s Sosnowski was too engulfed by personal debt, nearly all of it incurred by a lavish lifestyle intended to satisfy his lovers, to turn down a job offer working for the Polish foreign spy service.[13]

But his handlers must have had their doubts about their new recruit. He was not, as he liked to claim, really of aristocratic lineage at all. Though he loved to refer to himself as 'von' Sosnowski, he was in fact the son of a plumber and had grown up in very simple surroundings in the city of Lvov in south-eastern Poland. He had joined the army to stop his life going down the drain but there was no evidence that he took part in any fighting action in the Great War, as he often liked to say. He was really experienced only in other affairs. And if he declared his unremitting love for every woman who fell into his arms, this did not stop him from immediately looking elsewhere. A man who was so unfaithful in love would have been most unlikely to have had any other loyalties.

But the Polish spies were prepared to overlook such doubts and inconsistencies. With overstretched resources that were focused on the threat from Moscow and on potential disputes with Czechoslovakia as well as Germany, they could hardly afford to turn down an opportunity to recruit and run such an agent. Soon they had devised a plan. Since Sosnowski was a former cavalryman who had also shown a passionate post-war interest in racing, he could easily establish himself in Berlin as a horse breeder. In such a role, he would have a perfect excuse to attend horse races, where well-connected people, particularly high-society women, tended to go. He could then use his formidable and proven charm to watch thoroughbreds, establish contacts, and get the information that his handlers wanted. They were willing to subsidize all his expenses, including those incurred by buying and breeding studs, dining in the best restaurants, living the high life, and paying hefty bribes, provided that their protégé got the information he

13. Accident—André Brissaud *The Nazi Secret Service* Corgi (1972) 104. See in general Bernard Newman *The Sosnowski Affair* Werner Laurie (1954).

needed. In the spring of 1928, Sosnowski moved to Berlin and began his new life as an undercover agent.

Meanwhile, both the British and French intelligence services were working independently to find out more about what was happening in Germany. Much of their information came from open sources of information, notably newspapers, Reichstag debates, on-the-spot observations, and photographs which, when pieced together, could sometimes yield some interesting and significant facts. In the late 1920s, for example, the British noticed that German generals were starting to retire at much younger ages than before. Maybe this was just coincidence but there was a worrying possibility that Berlin was deliberately, and quite cunningly, building up a reserve of top people who could be suddenly brought back into service in the event of a national emergency.[14]

Even just a few words could sometimes reveal so much: in 1927, for example, the widow of a German airman placed a memorial notice in the press for her husband had who had died 'in distant Russia for his fatherland, while working as an airman'. There were reports, too, of an increase in the number of civilians who had been tried, convicted, and executed for the crime of *Landesverrat*: this was officially an act of treason against the state's security, although the real offence was thought, probably correctly, to have been the unauthorized disclosure of illegal rearmament activities.[15]

So too could a meticulous reading of government accounts sometimes indicate that sizeable chunks of money were being quietly siphoned off for unexplained reasons. These accounts did not quite add up. The Allied spy agencies soon noticed that the cost, or supposed cost, of German materials was much higher than their foreign equivalents: why did the Germans need to spend so much more to produce metal or wood for their armaments than their British and French counterparts? The British military attaché in Berlin reckoned that German military expenditure was often about twice or even three times greater than its equivalent British spending 'on similar items'. He also felt that the Germans possessed a considerable amount of unauthorized equipment and were illegally subsidizing companies that were in a position to manufacture arms.[16]

14. Bennett *German Rearmament* 81.
15. Lionel Kochan, 'General von Seeckt', *Contemporary Review*, Vol 178 (July 1950) 37.
16. Accounts, Landesverrat—Bennett *German Rearmament* 18. 'German Military Expenditure'—Memo of 10 July 1931, FO 371/15225 TNA.

Both the SIS and the Bureau flagged these inconsistencies to their respective chiefs, and in February 1930 Field Marshal Sir George Milne, the chief of the imperial staff, signed a report noting that, if the Germans really were sticking to their supposed limits, as they claimed, then a single German mortar cost nearly twice as much as a British field gun, and 120 times the cost of its British equivalent. The following summer, the sharp-eyed British military attaché in Berlin, Colonel James Marshall-Cornwall, also noticed how German military spending was not falling in step with the wider fall in commodity prices brought about by the global economic slump.[17]

The same concerns were voiced at the highest levels of the French capital. In February 1932, the Bureau informed Prime Minister André Tardieu that Germany was spending more on arms than it had even in 1913, when it had maintained a much bigger army. The French also discovered that some military expenses were being disguised in other ways, for example by being paid from the budgets not of the War Ministry but of other government departments. However, these concerns were overlooked and no protests were voiced to Berlin, partly because of the difficulties of proving where and how money was spent.[18]

How many of these intelligence reports were seen by political chiefs in Paris and London is often impossible to judge. Key decision-makers might have viewed them but rarely made any note of doing so, and only the foreign and war secretaries are known to have seen Rumbold's and Marshall-Cornwall's reports about German violations of Versailles. Very few SIS reports have either survived—most were destroyed after being read—or been revealed, and some cabinet papers make only very generalized references to 'secret intelligence'. French records are even more meagre, partly because many secret French papers were lost or destroyed but also because the governments of the Third Republic (1870–1940) did not keep official minutes of their discussions in the same way as their British counterparts: no minutes or records were taken during ministerial meetings.[19]

But some material was deliberately suppressed, overlooked, or downplayed because it was in one way or another inconvenient. In

17. Bennett *German Rearmament* 81–2.
18. WO Memo, 5 Aug 1931, FO 371/15225 TNA.
19. Jeffery 302.

Paris, there was an atmosphere of 'intellectual suffocation' that allowed
the intelligence service and its reports to be regarded with 'disdain',
particularly if they were seen to question 'adherence to rules and les-
sons acquired at enormous expense in the trenches of 1914–18'. Even
if they did reach the highest level, they had little or no impact if they
told political chiefs what they did not want to know. At this time, the
British government was less interested in discovering evidence of a
covert German rearmament programme than in winning Berlin's support for a disarmament convention that would guarantee long-term
peace. And when, in March 1932, British ministers did undertake a
defence review, they were preoccupied with the growing dangers that
Japan seemed to pose in the Far East.[20]

Some specific intelligence reports certainly deserved to be noticed.
By the late 1920s, for example, there were signs of growing German
interest in gas warfare. In 1928 a Spanish military commission had
visited Germany to study this subject and, the following July, British
spies obtained photographs of a secret German manual, which dealt
with every aspect of the use and manufacture of these gases. The SIS
also received a copy of the syllabus of the several secret gas training
schools in or near to Berlin, notably the Kaiser Wilhelm Institute, as
well as those located at some university research departments. At the
same time, reports emerged of soldiers being secretly trained at an
artillery range at Jüterbog in north-eastern Germany, at an experimental centre at Kummersdorf, south of the capital, and at a camp at
Dallgow-Döberitz in the north-east, where there had been 'trials of
combined high explosive and gas shells, trench mortar gas shells,
experimenting with gas mines and with special rustless metal gas containers'. Furthermore, the Hamburg firm of Stolzenburg was thought
to be illicitly producing gas near Samara in Russia, while by this time
the SIS and the Deuxième Bureau were well aware that several Russia
factories employed German experts who helped research and develop
and produce poison gas that was manufactured in Russia before being
smuggled back into Germany.[21]

---

20. 1914–18—Douglas Porch, 'French Intelligence and the Fall of France 1930-40', *INS*
    (1989) 30–1; Bennett *German Rearmament* 90–1.
21. 'Summary of Breaches of the Treaty of Versailles', 1933 document AIR 2/1353 TNA;
    these factories were listed by M. René Marchand in a series of articles in *La Liberté* in
    June 1931.

There were other indications of covert German activities. In January 1931, for example, the SIS received some alarming reports from a British arms dealer called David Ball. True to his line of work, Ball was naturally a shady character but in the past he had willingly cooperated with the British government and kept Whitehall closely informed of his commercial activities, particularly when, in the late 1920s, he had exported arms to China and other volatile parts of the Far East. But in the late 1920s he had been quietly approached by several German nationals who had been interested in purchasing surplus war stock, particularly naval mines. Whether these attempts at procurement were for Germany's own rearmament or for illegal export elsewhere in the world, notably to China or Turkey, was unclear but Ball reported these advances to Vice-Admiral Cecil Usborne, the director of naval intelligence.[22]

Spurred on by such reports, British and French spies worked hard to find out more about what was going on behind closed German doors. In 1930, two French officers were arrested for openly photographing anti-aircraft batteries at an artillery barracks in Königsberg, while the following year French officials pressed the Dutch government to allow them access to several sites where they suspected that German manufacturers had offshored their work. Under great pressure, the Dutch government relented and granted the French military attaché permission to access the two depots, one at Krimpen and the other at Martenshök, that had been the source of his concern. The attaché was alarmed at the size and potential output of the factory, and argued that the arms and material could all be moved to Germany in a matter of a few days, which the Dutch government would be powerless to stop. This presented a 'great danger' to France, he concluded.[23]

One site that aroused particular suspicion was located at Rechlin in Mecklenburg, on the south-east coast of Germany's second largest inland waters, Lake Müritz. Its very location was enough to raise eyebrows, and British intelligence reports commented on its 'isolated' position where 'it is possible to carry out tests on all types of aircraft in absolute privacy . . . and avoid unwelcome foreign interests'. From the late 1920s, reports had also emerged that the Germans had set up a

22. 'Alleged German Attempts to purchase naval mines', 26, 28 Jan 1931, FO 371/15221 TNA.
23. These fears were realized in Nov 1933. Castellan 415.

secret air base there which they were using to carry out firing tests and night training, as well as to fly to and from Lipetsk. Reports, perhaps groundless, also emerged of 'pilotless aeroplane experiments' being undertaken at this site. Other reports referred to 'secret trials in bomb-dropping and machine gun work' being undertaken there.[24]

Given its location, Rechlin posed a real challenge for foreign intelligence officers. British spies made serious efforts to find out more but did not succeed until April 1932, when the British air attaché, Group Captain JH Herring, was granted permission to visit a civilian flying school at Warnemünde, on the Baltic Sea. Taking his chance and becoming conveniently lost, close to Rechlin, on his way back to Berlin, he saw from a distance of just a few miles a single seater plane which had crash-landed in a nearby cornfield. A British SIS officer, Group Captain Frederick Winterbotham, also considered using local agents to hire a boat and sail as close as possible to the site, although it remains unclear if these plans were ever put into effect.[25]

'Freddy' Winterbotham was set to become an important player in the efforts of British Intelligence to monitor Germany. After the Great War, he had initially set up his own business—in the field of pig farming—that suffered badly during the economic depression, forcing him to search for other lines of work. But his wartime career saved his bacon. As a former pilot in the Great War, he had a good knowledge of, and interest in, matters of aviation, and after spending eighteen months in a prisoner-of-war camp, having been shot down behind enemy lines, he spoke reasonable German. Admiral Hugh Sinclair, the head of the SIS, recognized his potential and in 1929 offered him a role as his chief of air intelligence and as a liaison officer with the air staff's own intelligence department.[26]

Other reports of Germany's illicit rearmament came from chance encounters or from travellers who were public-spirited enough to inform their respective governments about what they witnessed. On 22 August 1930, for example, the civilian ship *Krakus* was sailing along the German coast, close to Kiel, when passengers saw German

24. Experiments—'Infringements of the Air Clauses of the Treaty of Versailles', 4 July 1933, AIR 2/1353 TNA. Secret trials—'German Military and Naval Aviation', 18 Mar 1933, ADM 116/2945 TNA.
25. Cornfield—'Infringements of the Air Clauses of the Treaty of Versailles', 4 July 1933, AIR 2/1353 TNA. Winterbotham *Nazi Connection* 168.
26. Winterbotham *Nazi Connection* 28–30.

warships undertaking a practice firing exercise, targeting a towed, pilotless plane. This was consistent with other information, drawn from Polish press reports, about German planes flying 'in pairs, the lead one towing the target, which is fired at by the following machine', near the island of Sylt, off Schleswig-Holstein. Casual conversations with other foreign representatives in Berlin also sometimes yielded unexpected results: the French first became aware of German plans for a militia because they were told of them by the American military attaché, who was in turn informed directly by the Germans.[27]

But still the big, unanswered question was 'why'. Were the Germans covertly rearming just to defend themselves and use only diplomatic means to win back the places they had lost? Or would they be likely to pursue a more aggressive agenda, attacking their neighbours to return them to German sovereignty?

On this vital point, foreign observers were divided. In January 1930, a French intelligence report concluded that 'in its present state, Germany does not seem to be steering an aggressive course. It does nonetheless seek to restore its power and be ready to take advantage of any favourable opportunities that may arise.' This did not prevent, however, the Deuxième Bureau from drawing up contingency plans in the event of a sudden German attack into the Rhineland and beyond.[28]

But other reports struck a sombre tone as they gauged the mood and feelings of the general German public. One British diplomatic briefing, written in 1929, was based on the conversations that spies and government representatives had held with ordinary Germans over such matters. 'It is small wonder', ran the report, 'that the whole nation reacts violently' against the present state of affairs, in which Germany was treated so harshly and unfairly. 'The desire to redress the balance is universal throughout the country, and the resulting manifestations of a militarist nature become obvious to the most superficial observer.' As a result, everywhere there was 'resentment' and 'after ten years . . . a strong desire . . . to increase the military strength of Germany'. And just as dangerous to the outside world, the report continued, was the fragile state of the country's politics and institutions: 'the weakness of the German Republic lies not only in the fact that as yet it commands no affection,

27. *Krakus*—Castellan 153. Sylt—'Illegal Activities in Aviation', Appendix C, June 1933 AIR 2/1353 TNA.
28. 'La Situation de l'Allemagne', 1 Jan 1930; Plan de Renseignements, 11 Jan 1930, 7NN 2530 SHD.

but still more in the political immaturity of the German people and in their failure so far to make a reasonable use of the democratic forms of government'. Altogether, these developments were 'menacing'. Such views were soon echoed by the British ambassador, Sir Horace Rumbold, who reported that 'most Germans have no affection for disarmament in the abstract', adding that a war with Poland would be highly popular amongst Germans.[29]

Put together, such fragments of information were drawing a picture that alarmed many observers. And one individual who was by now watching developments in Germany with particular alarm was the newly appointed permanent undersecretary at the Foreign Office, Robert Vansittart, who had taken up his post in November 1929.

A man of wide interests and great natural talent—he wrote novels, plays, and poetry, and was a champion tennis player as well as excelling at numerous other sports—Vansittart had a wide variety of contacts across the world, which he made great use of to track the apparent resurgence of Germany. His 'fertile mind and unequalled knowledge of European politics and personalities were invaluable to me', as Sir Samuel Hoare, the foreign secretary, later wrote.[30]

But within a year of taking office, 'Van' was deeply disillusioned by the quality and quantity of SIS reports on Germany. British Intelligence, he felt, was not only desperate for funds but still focused largely on the Soviet Union and communism at the expense of the real, and much closer threat, to British interests. He instead proposed setting up his independent intelligence service that could focus entirely on what was happening inside Germany, and whose findings he could then forward to anyone he chose, including his close friend, Winston Churchill, who shared his deep mistrust and fear of Germany.

The person to whom Van now turned was a 54-year-old former army officer by the name of Colonel (later Sir) Claude Dansey.

With a hawk nose, dark-rimmed glasses, a small moustache, and piercing eyes, Dansey looked the part of the imperial adventurer that he had once played, having previously fought against a succession of enemies, ranging from the Boers of South Africa to the mullahs of the North-West Frontier, on various fronts of the Empire. He was also an

29. 'The Military Situation in Germany', 10 Apr 1929, CAB-24/203/21 TNA; Rumbold—Bennett German Rearmament 89.
30. DBFP, II series, Vol 15 No 258, n 4.

experienced intelligence officer who had a love for the romance and adventure of spying: his staff noticed his fondness for aliases and his tendency to carry numerous bogus visiting cards, bearing such exotic names as 'Captain Charles Pomfret-Seymour CBE, DSO, RN', although he sometimes forgot which of these different names he was supposed to be using.[31]

Although it is unclear exactly when and how the two men had met, Vansittart soon approached Dansey, who was at this time heading the SIS station in Rome under the usual cover of a passport control officer, and asked him to help to set up this network.

Between them, Dansey and Vansittart planned on utilizing the constant flow of information that came from a succession of foreign visitors to Germany, ranging from bankers, businessmen, industrialists, journalists, and politicians. Both men were personally acquainted with a great many of these visitors, some of whom made fleeting trips to the Reich, while others were expatriates who were based there permanently. All, however, were willing to provide information in a patriotic spirit and would not expect or demand any payment for their services. The Dansey–Vansittart intelligence service, in other words, would not be constrained by the financial pressures that were so badly afflicting the SIS.

British archives provide some examples of such informants, whose unusual stories illustrate how this private intelligence network operated. In the summer of 1939, for example, a former British journalist by the name of Geoffrey Pike ran a team of ten agents inside the Reich, mostly in and around Frankfurt, who were based at and who reported to 'four posts'. As war approached, all were tasked with posing as golfers who could challenge a Frankfurt club to a competition. This gave them a chance to gauge 'the state of public opinion in Germany' by posing a series of carefully crafted questions and recording the answers. Several of the 'golfers' quickly discerned that 'there was a surprisingly large body of opinion in Germany hostile to the present regime', but as war approached, Pike ordered all of them to leave the country for their own safety, asking one of them to travel to Berlin to leave their reports at the British embassy.[32]

---

31. Christopher Andrew *Secret Service: The Making of the British Intelligence Community* Hodder & Stoughton (1986), 381.
32. 'Mr Pyke', 23 Aug 1939, FO 371/23009 TNA.

But appealing though Vansittart's idea sounded, it had one obvious flaw: if ministers and government officials were going to run their own private spying networks, then there was a clear risk that intelligence-gathering was going to become not only fragmented but highly suspect. Dansey and Vansittart would be relying upon sources whose credentials and claims were unverified and unverifiable. And instead of being carefully assessed by trained intelligence officers, who were tasked with challenging them, such sources and their claims could easily be fast-tracked and brought to the immediate attention of decision-makers who took them on trust. This hardly boded well for the future.

3

The Rise of Hitler

In the summer of 1931, a hefty dossier on German violations of the Versailles Treaty landed on the desks of Whitehall officials. It came courtesy of the French government, and detailed many highly technical infringements of the disarmament clauses, most of which were based on unspecified 'sources' that readers were asked to take on trust. In London, the documents naturally provoked a sharp debate about how the issue of covert German rearmament, which was now starting to surpass Soviet Russia as a matter of national security, should be dealt with.

In the offices and conference rooms of Whitehall, a consensus quickly emerged that the document certainly contained 'a considerable element of truth'. 'Both the French and British military authorities are pretty certain that the Germans have spent unjustifiably large sums on certain items in their Reichswehr budget,' ran one British report, 'that they do possess equipment unauthorized under the Treaty of Versailles and that subsidies are being granted to actual and potential German manufacturers...a good case could be made out for joint representation on the subject.' Unfortunately, however, it was also marred by 'serious errors and exaggerations' as well as being 'hastily compiled' with 'numerous arithmetical inaccuracies'.[1]

The French, in other words, had politicized some of the intelligence that was coming their way and risked losing credibility by doing so. The challenge of gathering accurate intelligence on post-war Germany had become manipulated, or 'skewed', by individuals who had their own vested interests in 'sexing up' the dossier.[2]

---

1. AJ Creedy memo, 20 July 1931, FO 371/15225 TNA.
2. See above page 16, footnote 26.

The British felt that 'one of its objects may be to disseminate propaganda with a view to the Disarmament Conference'. As an international summit on the subject loomed in Geneva, the British were more inclined than Paris to take a compromising position towards increasingly vocal German demands for 'equality', which Berlin formally demanded the following summer. The French government was under strong domestic pressure to resist these demands, and just a few months before, French nationalists had even disrupted the proceedings of an earlier disarmament conference in Paris in a rampage that was broadcast on live radio to an astonished and outraged audience.[3]

More generally, it remains very possible, although it cannot be proven, that French officials were manipulating 'intelligence' on Germany in a bid to lure Britain into the longer-term defensive alliance that Clemenceau had fought for but failed to win. Exaggerating the German threat was one way of enticing Britain out of her post-1918 state of isolation and committing her to act in unison against not only a resurgent Reich but other adversaries, real or imaginary, such as the Soviet Union. And at home, the French government felt under strong popular pressure to be seen to act. As communism and fears of communism surged and peaked in France, even a socialist politician, Ferdinand Buisson, excoriated 'Bolshevik' activity as a 'perpetual menace to civilisation...in any country where communism should win the day it would be the end of everything'.[4]

The exaggerated French reports may also have reflected the influence of military chiefs who were fighting their corner for a bigger military budget, or at least avoid swingeing cuts at a time of economic crisis. This may have been why, in 1932, a further series of official papers warned that Germany's fleet of passenger, cargo, and mail-carrying aircraft could be immediately converted into a fleet of bombers capable of dropping 170 tonnes of explosives on Paris every day. Their authors were right that the Germans had plans to convert civilian planes into bombers, but they considerably exaggerated the speed and ease with which this could be done.[5]

Another motive was economic jealousy. The French wanted to maintain their tight grip over Germany, repressing its industry and

3. Objects—Memo, 20 July 1931, FO 371/15225 TNA.
4. Quoted in Adamthwaite *France and the Coming of the Second World War* Frank Cass (1977) 26.
5. Jackson *France and the Nazi Menace* 49.

exacting painful reparations, in order to constrain a country whose massive economic power had outpaced and overshadowed their own since the 1890s. At a time when such rivalry was heightened by global recession and by the drastic fall in the value of the mark, which gave German exporters a big competitive advantage, the French intelligence services became increasingly preoccupied with economic espionage, while German counter-intelligence stepped up its own efforts to thwart them, keeping close watch on a number of French companies that it deemed to be in a secret joint venture with the Deuxième Bureau.

Much of this game of economic espionage and counter-espionage was played out along the banks and on the waters of the Rhine, where the French continued to maintain a military presence. In a bid to find out if the Germans were importing war materials, French patrol boats closely monitored maritime traffic and sometimes also obstructed it, knowing that such heavy tactics would give them a commercial advantage and aware that they could officially justify this approach because the Versailles Treaty banned or restricted the import of certain goods.[6]

There were other possible motives. The poor quality of the Bureau's reports may have reflected its low status in French society, which had 'serious consequences on the quality of intelligence passed on to the high command'. This meant that, because they were 'annoyed that their message was not striking home, intelligence officers raised the tone of their reports (and) exaggerated the numbers of German soldiers, tanks and aircraft'.[7]

But equally some, if not all, of the reports may not have been deliberately skewed at all. A good number were based on accurate information but unintentionally faulty analysis. In 1921, for example, French intelligence had estimated that, in addition to the Reichswehr's regular forces, Germany could also field an army of 2.4 million 'volunteers' who would 'without any doubt respond immediately to a decree of mobilization'. In fact, these 'volunteers' had almost no formal training, and the Germans could only field seven divisions. Yet these absurdly inflated figures prompted French strategists to aim to build a force of

6. Forcade 498. On German accusations of French economic espionage see *Koelnische Volksseitung*, 6 Feb 1930.
7. Porch 'French Intelligence' 37–8.

eighty divisions to save a Polish army of fifty divisions from a German invasion.[8]

Other reports may also have accurately but uncritically portrayed flawed information from agents on the ground. This is because a good deal of the information that Paris passed on to London emanated from Polish sources. In October 1930, for example, the Polish Second Department had given General Henri Castellan of the Deuxième Bureau a major report on German rearmament. Further flows of information from Warsaw followed, notably in October 1932, when the Poles provided Paris with two further major studies, one of which charted a dramatic uplift in the number of pilots and gave details about their organization, while the other detailed how and where these pilots were trained. Castellan was alarmed to see that, over the preceding year, the Germans had sharply increased their output of pilots, who were ostensibly trained as 'acrobats' for 'sporting events'.[9]

But the earlier Polish reports were also based largely on information from a single source: Jerry Sosnowski. This 'secret agent' was not, however, all he claimed, and his story instead illustrates the dangers and difficulties of intelligence-gathering in any foreign environment. This enigmatic figure was, in every likelihood, really little more than a charlatan.

Just as Polish spy chiefs had hoped, the dashing young cavalryman had proven to be a winner at making friends and influencing people in high places. The Berlin horse races had, after all, proved to be a fruitful hunting ground, not least for well-placed sources of information. Although Sosnowski had taken several months to find his feet, he soon proved adept at striking up conversations with military officials, their wives, girlfriends, and secretaries, dropping in casual and offhand questions about their present role and future plans, and memorizing whatever he could. But his best source of information was his association with a young, glamorous, and well-placed German lady.

Benita von Zollikofer-Altenklingen, or Benita von Falkenhayn as she became after her second marriage, was born into an aristocratic family that could trace its lineage back to the time of Charlemagne. The daughter of a senior officer in Kaiser Wilhelm II's army, she had a privileged upbringing, spending time in Switzerland and England and

8. Jackson *France and the Nazi Menace* 48.
9. Polish report—Castellan 186–95. Two studies—Castellan 150–4.

becoming a highly adept swimmer and horse rider. But harder times followed Germany's defeat, as the Weimar Republic spiralled into economic chaos, while a few years later her father's death wreaked financial hardship on her family. Such stresses did not help her marriage, which met an inharmonious end when she was still just in her late twenties, and it was at this difficult stage in her life that she took up a secretarial post, on meagre pay, at the Reichswehr ministry in Berlin. Not long afterwards, she also met Jerry Sosnowksi.

An attractive young woman, who dressed with a strong fashion sense and presented herself well, in the true manner of the product of a finishing school, Benita had little trouble attracting men. She made a tempting target for Sosnowski, who would have seen her mixing in high circles at the races, and perhaps recognized her vulnerability at this difficult time of her life. As he spoke with her, at a bar at the Berlin races sometime around 1929, he not only charmed but also impressed her with the sums of money he had at his disposal. Within weeks, he was offering to render her well-heeled, and a very intense, passionate affair now followed.

Benita had access to a good many of the General Staff's top-secret documents, which she was entrusted with typing and copying as well as keeping safe, and now became the source of much of the highly confidential intelligence that made its way firstly to Warsaw and then to both Paris and London. She had easy access to details about the new organization and structure of the Reichswehr as well as information about German agents inside Poland. She was, in every sense, a prize catch.

This, at least, was the story that Sosnowski told, or rather sold, to his handlers in Warsaw. But by the time that he was sending such material back home, Sosnowski's story was starting to cause alarm.

Not only was he demanding even more money to fund his 'expenses' but doubts were growing about the quality of his information. Impressive though some of it had at first seemed, there was little that a reasonably well-informed observer of Germany could not guess at, and no evidence to back any of it up. True, Sosnowski exposed some German agents in Poland but, on their arrest and after their interrogation, it became clear that they were not of any particular value. Salacious details were now also emerging about how he was obtaining some of this 'intelligence'. The Polish 'agent' had told lurid stories of scandalous parties in Berlin, at which well-bred girls were blackmailed

after being secretly photographed in positions as sensitive as those they
worked in. But these stories never seemed plausible, even by the louche
standards of the Weimar Republic.

The spy chiefs in Warsaw became even more suspicious when
Sosnowski started to take extreme liberties with his personal safety,
ignoring orders to return home and openly compromising the Polish
embassy in Berlin which, like every diplomatic post, was not officially
supposed to be implicated in espionage. Soon the 'count' was demanding
ludicrously high payments for documents whose value was unclear.
And when a Polish intelligence officer visited Berlin and met 'Martha',
one of Sosnowski's supposed sources of information, he found that she
was someone of no importance, bearing no special knowledge, and
offering no unique access to anyone or anything that did. It also
seemed much more likely that Benita von Falkenhayn was also really
just a double agent who had been instructed to become romantically
involved with Sosnowski and provide him with false information that
he could pass on to his handlers in Warsaw. To make his story more
plausible and justify his high price, Sosnowski then invented the existence of other 'agents' he claimed to have recruited, and fabricated the
stories of the parties in Berlin. When he eventually returned to Poland,
exchanged with a German prisoner in the spring of 1936, Sosnowski
was imprisoned for fraud and high treason.[10]

The story of Sosnowski's charade is a reminder of how easily any
intelligence service can fall victim to charlatans, particularly those who
tell them what they want to hear and particularly when they are desperate for information about an elusive target or opaque foe. And the
officers of the Second Department, like their counterparts in Paris and
London, were increasingly keen to find out what was happening inside
a neighbouring country that was not only covertly rearming but also
politically highly unstable.

German politics had become much more volatile after the withdrawal of British and French troops from the Rhineland. In 1929, a
cash-strapped British government, under the Labour Party's Ramsay
MacDonald, had been the first to pull out, followed some months later
by the French, who now closed their bases at Koblenz and Mainz.

---

10. Invention—Newman; André Brissaud *The Nazi Secret Service* Corgi Books (1975)
    Ch 7. Benita von Falkenhayn was beheaded for treason in 1935. She was most likely
    the victim of Nazi politics because of her aristocratic family background.

Their withdrawal induced a powerful wave of nationalist fervour that surged into German politics, and upon which Hitler's National Socialist Party was now riding high.

The officers of the Deuxième Bureau had already noted the burgeoning support for Hitler's party but even they were taken aback by the Reichstag elections of September 1930. Hitler now seized nearly twenty per cent of the total vote, stealing 6.4 million votes, and overnight had increased his representation in the Reichstag from just twelve seats to 107 out of the total of 577. This had happened against a backdrop of three million unemployed and mass poverty that had deeply concerned the French Foreign Ministry, which noted how Hitler's party exploited such 'misery' by distributing food and water at very cheap prices. Suddenly the prospect of Nazi government, or a stake in a coalition, was far from unthinkable. 'Fantastic', wrote the Nazi propagandist Joseph Goebbels, scarcely believing his luck, 'an unbelievable advance…I hadn't expected that.' At the polls no less than in the streets, Hitler was smashing his opponents.[11]

For the French, Germany once again constituted a very real strategic threat that the Deuxième Bureau was now carefully assessing. Initially, French observers in Berlin had been dismissive and even contemptuous of the Nazi movement. In the corridors of French power, Hitler was typically referred to as the 'house painter from Vienna' and rated as a 'third-rate street demagogue' whose rhetoric embodied 'the most violent and distasteful extremes in German culture and politics—rabid nationalism and visceral racism'. But now he was taken much more seriously and became the subject of a detailed study by analysts who read *Mein Kampf*, Hitler's personal testimony that he wrote during a period of imprisonment in the mid-1920s, and who looked carefully at his party manifesto. General Maurice-Henri Gauché, for example, put much emphasis on a word-by-word scrutiny of the book arguing that it was 'a crucial document, fundamental and perfectly valuable' as an intelligence source, and one that 'governed Hitler's future behaviour'. Prophetically, another report warned that 'a young generation of Germans imbued with the Nazi ideology will certainly constitute the gravest threat to peace in Europe in the years to come'.

11. Bureau report on 1930 election—'Augmentation du nombre des partisans d'Hitler', 24 June 1929, 7NN 2584 SHD. Misery—'La Situation à Lorrach', 6 Nov 1931, F/7/13428 AN. Goebbels—quoted in Richard Evans *The Third Reich in Power* Penguin (1975) 261.

The military attaché in Berlin, General Gaston Renondeau, also felt compelled to argue that 'if Hitler becomes Chancellor, then Germany will be transformed into one huge military barracks'.[12]

Other foreign representatives in Berlin, who were now well aware of the growing spectre of a Nazi government, echoed such warnings. In December 1931, the British ambassador Sir Horace Rumbold wrote to the newly appointed foreign secretary, Sir John Simon, to report on violations of the Versailles Treaty. These, he felt, 'may well be the thin edge of the wedge', particularly when there was a 'revival of militarist sentiment'. But making matters much worse was 'the speed with which the National Socialist movement is now spreading, and the possibility [arises] of them being either in the Government or in power next Spring'. Such was the momentum of Hitler's rise, he argued, 'that higher officers in the army who six months ago spoke disparagingly of the Nazi movement have now, under pressure from the ground swell in the junior ranks, turned round and are swimming with the tide'. Rumbold cited the example of General Kurt von Schleicher, a 'political general . . . who last year was an ardent opponent of the Nazis' but who was now 'trimming his sails to a possible change of the political wind'.[13]

But to his frustration, the British secret service had until this time been run by a foreign secretary, Arthur Henderson, who was not only highly suspicious of the SIS, wanting only minimal dealings with it, but who regarded the Soviet Union and international communism as a much greater threat than Germany. The service was also still very short of funds, at least as much as any other government department. Vansittart noted that he 'had to work Henderson into his best mood' before discreetly producing his estimates for the SIS budget, which would invariably prompt the foreign secretary to 'pause, sign and sigh'. On the ground, station chiefs found their 'biggest headache . . . the necessity of accounting for every single penny and trying to justify the

---

12. Threat—'Le Mouvement national-socialiste en Allemagne', 11 Feb 1930, 7NN 2585 SHD; Jackson, *France and the Nazi Menace* 55. *Mein Kampf*—'Programme du Parti National-Socialiste', 4 May 1932, 7NN 2623 SHD; Le Deuxième Bureau Au Travail, General Maurice-Henri Gauché 32. *Mein Kampf* was not published in France until 1938. Younger generation—'L'Attitude de l'Allemagne à l'égard de la France', 2 Apr 1931, 7NN 2638 SHD. Renondeau—'Service du travail obligatoire', 24 Feb 1932, 7NN 2588 SHD; Jackson *France and the Nazi Menace* 55.
13. Rumbold to Simon, 11 Dec 1931 FO 371/10A TNA. Col Marshall-Cornwall to Rumbold, 9 Dec 1931, FO 371/15225 TNA.

expenses we had to render monthly'. Expenses were sent to a figure in Whitehall 'who treated public money as if it were his own and seemed almost to begrudge every penny we spent'.[14]

Such constraints exasperated not just Rumbold but also others who detected seismic political shifts within Germany. Marshall-Cornwall had always taken a very moderate tone, arguing in 1931 that German actions 'may be justifiably regarded as designed purely for self-defence' adding that the country was not 'at present a danger to any neighbouring power'. But he now felt that 'a change of system is . . . being actively prepared'. He argued that 'the danger is not imminent but it is throwing its shadow ahead. Infractions of the treaty restrictions have lately become more frequent and less concealed.'[15]

Visiting Berlin, the French prime minister, Édouard Herriot, shared this sense of alarm when he witnessed a demonstration of *Wehrsport* by 'German youth [who] gave an exhibition of such things as the methods of getting through barbed wire entanglements', as well as showing expertise in pursuits such as map-reading and target-shooting. After the show, Herriot felt sure that 'Germany is deliberately building up again her former military power', adding that 'I am now for the first time convinced that the Germans mean war as soon as they are strong enough to do so'. On his return to Paris, French officials made renewed threats against Germany, including threats of reoccupying the Rhineland. But these were never followed up, mainly because France was too engulfed in political chaos to take decisive action: Herriot's administration, his third in eight years, only lasted another three months.[16]

But obtaining accurate information about Germany's covert rearmament was still proving to be very difficult and became harder still after the French retreat from the Rhineland in 1930. The Anglo-French presence there had always closely monitored much of the covert rearmament that was, or would have been, concentrated in its big industrial centres: 'the way was clear', as a secret British report later stated, 'for the beginning of the illicit rearmament of Germany'. German progress was slow, especially so long as the Allied forces were in occupation of the Rhineland. But its evacuation was completed in

14. Hinsley 49–51; Andrew 348.
15. Col Marshall-Cornwall to Rumbold, 21 Dec 1931, FO 371/15225 TNA.
16. Hampton to Simon, Paris, 7 Sept, 19 Oct 1932 FO 800/291 TNA.

the summer of 1930. In particular, the French bases at Koblenz and Mainz had served as highly successful recruiting grounds for under-cover agents, many of them 'drop-ins' who had arrived uninvited, unexpected but never unwelcome, to offer their services in return for payment. Based on German soil, the French were also able to keep close tabs on the German economy, more specifically its demand for the raw materials used to manufacture arms.[17]

Filling this void after 1930 was no easy task for the Bureau's German department, led by Colonel Edmond Laurent, even if it already had more analysts than all of the agency's other departments combined. Its staff searched hard for possible informers amongst German expatriate workers who had left their recession-stricken homeland, with temporary permits, and gone to France to search for work or take up job offers. Typically impoverished and often in debt, they were potentially easy prey for French agents, who offered them lucrative sums in exchange for any valuable information they could obtain on their return. Other sources included the ranks of the French Foreign Legion, which had long been a magnet for professional German soldiers frustrated by the shackled state of the Reichswehr. The French spy service instructed recruiting officers at the Legion's offices and barracks to debrief all German applicants and pass on any information about the true state of Germany's armed forces.[18]

In December 1931, a French intelligence report focused on the growing importance of obtaining new sources of information inside Germany. 'The recruitment of agents inside Germany has been stepped up', its authors noted, 'and the results have been reasonably satisfactory' since 'a certain number of agents' had been found, particularly in the south-east, where they were handled by the post at Metz. The French spying chiefs were cautiously optimistic about their ability to find more informants, noting that 'there are numerous officials who are in debt, or who don't want to sacrifice their high outgoings, and who may be willing to reach out to us if they can find a way of doing so'. They also sought to make the most of political turmoil inside Germany, where 'the growing prospect of civil war' would help recruitment,

17. British reports—'Germany's Illegal Rearmament', Mar 1934, CAB 24/248/18 TNA. French bases—Michel Gardner *La Guerre secrète des Services Spéciaux français 1933–45* Plon (1967) 28. Economy—Forcade 145.

18. Easy prey—Forcade 166. Legion—Réunion de Colonel Laurent, 13 Dec 1931, 7NN 2693 SHD; Henri Navarre, *Le Service de Renseignements 1871–1944* Plon (1978) 51.

notably amongst communists 'who can be a very useful source of information about the state of German industry'. They needed to address a shortage, however, of 'high level agents' inside the military.[19]

But the highly fragmented, and often unconfirmed, reports that fell into their hands did not give intelligence agencies enough to go on. Much more detailed and higher-level information was urgently needed, not least about the motives and ambitions of any German rearmament. But the authorities in Berlin were now tightening their internal security, cracking down on economic espionage, which was at times indistinguishable from military matters and which aroused strong feelings amongst many Germans: they suspected the French, in particular, of using the issue of disarmament as an excuse to steal industrial secrets. They had always taken a hard line on anyone caught illicitly selling industrial secrets, such as two chemists who were found guilty in November 1930 of providing an unnamed foreign power with details of industrial processes, and who were both given prison sentences and fines. And a former soldier who was deemed guilty of selling secrets 'to three foreign powers' was given fifteen years' hard labour. But in March 1932, the government overhauled existing laws on the matter and introduced draconian new penalties, sharply increasing prison sentences from one to five years for anyone who revealed any confidential details about such matters as industrial processes.[20]

The German authorities also toughened up security around their military sites and tightened up the flow of confidential information. In April, they banned foreigners from visiting some of their military and industrial factories, notably those owned by Heinkel and Arado, and when, in the same month, Group Captain Herring again visited a civilian flying school at Warnemünde aerodrome and saw two Arado planes on the runway, he was taken aback by 'much unpleasantness for those responsible for the indiscretion'. A further sign of a more assertive German attitude emerged when the Defence Ministry in Berlin started to censor the amount of published information about its military officers. This was no coincidence. If the Allies had been able to review these lists, then they would immediately have seen that the total number of officers in the army and navy exceeded the number per-

19. Réunion de Colonel Laurent, 13 Dec 1931, 7NN 2693 SHD.
20. Two chemists—'Condamnations prononcées par Le Tribunal de Dusseldorf pour espionnage économique', 18 Nov 1930, F/7/13427 AN. Soldier—'Contre-Espionnage', 7NN 3096 SHD. New laws—Forcade 508.

mitted under the Versailles restrictions. Equally, someone who careful
sifted this information might have noticed that some officers were
retiring earlier than they were allowed, allowing the Germans to train
more of them.[21]

Foreign spy chiefs did their best to counteract the tightening grip of
German domestic security. In late 1931, for example, two Deuxième
Bureau undercover agents in Germany—codenamed MA 279 and B
609—disappeared, prompting the agency's chiefs to draw up a new set
of guidelines to help their undercover agents evade detection and capture. In future, they were required to keep their cross-border movements to an absolute minimum, on the grounds that they had a much
greater chance of being detected as they crossed any frontier; case
officers were instructed to closely research Germany's entire borders to
find weak points—in addition to several already located along the
Belgian and Czech frontiers—where agents could slip across unnoticed
or unchallenged; written communications had to be made in German,
rather than French; there should be greater use of anonymous post office
boxes, which could easily be abandoned if there was a chance they had
been discovered; and more efficient and surreptitious ways of posting
covert photos from Germany back to France were introduced.[22]

But still the foreign spy chiefs had only snippets of information that
came to them in dribs and drabs. In April, an informer saw heavy artillery being moved to the Döberitz training ground in Berlin while
further stories also emerged of the Germans quietly building defensive
lines on the Polish and Czech borders, ostensibly to reclaim land for
agricultural use. Reports were also filtering through that the Germans
had set up a training centre in Russia, codenamed Kama Camp, for
tanks and armoured cars, although frustratingly only very few hard
facts were known about it. 'The greatest secrecy has, however, been
maintained about this camp', as a British report stated, 'and information as to its exact location has never been obtained. Full details of the
nature of the work which is carried out are also lacking.'[23]

Over the summer, the British military attaché in Berlin also obtained
photos of a new close-support gun that the Reichswehr had started to
use, while another 'secret source' obtained a descriptive booklet about

21. Herring—'Interview with Bolle', 10 June 1933, AIR 2/1353 TNA.
22. 'Mesures Nouvelles', 13 Dec 1931, 7NN 2693 SHD.
23. 'Memorandum on German Rearmament', AIR 2/1353 TNA.

a 7.5 cm gun made by the state-owned firm Rheinmetall. And towards
the end of the year, 'documents from a reliable source' showed that the
German police were using unauthorized weapons, including heavy
machine guns, all surface cars, and communications and signals equipment: in one district alone, 184 out of 850 officers had been given
training in the use of heavy arms. In such a murky environment, it was
perhaps inevitable that stories of extraordinary German technical
developments would also start to emerge. These included a series of
intriguing reports, quite unfounded, of a 'Death Ray' that forced any
aircraft that crossed its path to land, as well as stories of 'pilotless aeroplanes... controlled by wireless'. Other stories also reached the desks of
the Deuxième Bureau of German scientists developing a gas that neu-
tralized petrol, rendering vehicles immobile, and disabled machine
guns and other weapons in a matter of minutes.[24]

For foreign spy chiefs, and for others who were watching Germany
with growing concern, 1932 brought more bad news. In May, President
Paul von Hindenburg dismissed the chancellor, Heinrich Brüning,
who was not only highly critical of the Nazi Party but who was equally
hostile towards Germany's rearmament. As a later British document
observed, 'the replacement of Dr Brüning in May 1932 by the reac-
tionary government of Papen put an end to the restraining influence
hitherto exerted in Germany by the parties of the Left. From that
moment on, the process of rearmament began to be systematized and
accelerated.' Until his dismissal, it had seemed 'legitimate to hope that
the forces of the Left in Germany would be able to keep in check any
attempt at serious rearmament. But democracy in the Weimar
Republic had by this time run amok: from 1930 there was no longer
an effective parliamentary majority that was taking responsibility for
government.[25]

Filling this void was all the more urgent because by the summer of
1932 Hitler was getting closer to seizing the reins of power, his party's
fortunes hugely bolstered by the advent of economic calamity, trig-

24. Reliable source—'Germany's Illegal Rearmament', Mar 1934 CAB 24/248/18 TNA.
    Death Ray—Report, 30 Sept 1933; 'Memo on German Rearmament', June 1933, AIR
    3/1353 TNA. Petrol—'Nouveau Gaz Capable d'Arrêter Les Moteurs', 4 Aug 1936,
    7NN 3114 SHD; A/S Des Armements, 18 Sept 1935, 7NN 3141 SHD.
25. British document—Germany's Illegal Rearmament, 18 Mar 1934, CAB 24/248/18
    TNA. The largest political party, the Social Democrats, practised 'constructive absten-
    tion' (voting neither for nor against motions) and soon the Reichstag kept dissolving
    its own sessions.

gered by the Wall Street Crash in October 1929, and of mass unemployment. In the Reichstag elections held in July, the Nazis more than doubled their representation, winning 230 seats out of a total of 608.

The French government scrambled to obtain information about Germany's rearmament. 'I have no illusions. I am convinced that Germany wishes to rearm,' as Édouard Herriot stated in October 1932. 'Tomorrow it will be a policy of territorial demands.' In Paris, Colonel Laurent of French intelligence ordered an urgent effort to monitor Germany, warning of dire consequences if 'Hitler takes power and monopolises it... and seals the borders'. He needed to unearth as much information as possible to win international support, above all from the British, for concerted diplomatic, and conceivably military, action against a resurgent Reich. Fortunately more information flowed from Warsaw: in 1932, the Poles sent Paris nearly 200 documents, with revealing information about the numbers and activities of German border guards and paramilitaries. The Deuxième Bureau also intercepted the post of some key individuals who were based on French soil: the European representative of the American engineering firm Curtiss Writh, for example, was closely watched, and in September 1932 French spies discovered that an undercover operative in Berlin, working for the German government, was secretly in touch with him in a bid to place an illicit order for twelve planes.[26]

The French wanted to acquire more information quickly because London was still showing no signs of striking up any alliance. It was far from clear that some key decision-makers in London were even reading the reports that Paris had sent them, and of those who did, some were also guilty of wishful thinking: in 1932 General Sir George Milne, the chief of imperial general staff, even predicted that, by the end of the decade, Germany would still be at the mercy of France or Poland. Other British officials took a much more moderate approach than Paris wanted, maintaining their faith in a new disarmament convention that would also oblige the French to reduce the own arsenal. In such a scenario, the Germans could plausibly claim they had achieved 'equality' even if they then chose not to rearm.[27]

26. Herriot—quoted in Henry Kissinger *Diplomacy* Pocket Books (1994) 285. Poles—7NN 2636 SHD. Planes—'Commande d'avions pour le compte de la Reichswehr', 5 Sept 1932, F/7/13429 AN.
27. Milne—'Disarmament', 28 Oct 1932, CAB 24/234 TNA; Bennett *German Rearmament* 43. Equality—Hampton to Simon, 7 Sept 1932, FO 800/29 TNA.

French officials now sent more 'intelligence reports' to London, hoping to cause alarm. In June 1932, Herriot handed the British prime minister, Stanley Baldwin, a number of secret documents, which included information about illegal caches of German arms in Holland. But the British viewed the report as a recycling of existing material, and felt that much was based on dubious sources. 'Their main interest . . . is the insight gained into the rather meagre sources of information about German activities which the French have at their disposal.'[28]

But they would not be meagre for much longer. By the summer of 1932, the heads of the Deuxième Bureau were feeling more than a mere tinge of self-satisfaction about a new agent that their spies had, for some weeks, been grooming and who would soon be proving his worth to both the French and their British allies.

28. 'Very Secret MI3 Memo', 27 June 1932, WO 190/150 TNA.

4

The New Mood in Berlin 1933

In late July 1933, exactly six months after Hitler had become German chancellor, the French ambassador in London handed another weighty file on German rearmament over to the Foreign Office. The French government was now pushing for a formal investigation into the matter by the League of Nations, and its long and lengthy document, entitled *Germany's Main Breaches of the Versailles Treaty*, represented a call for British support.[1]

The French certainly painted an alarming picture. Based on 'a mass of secret information [that] indicates the manufacture and use of prohibited aircraft and war material' as well as 'the export [of war material] on a large scale', they claimed that Berlin had exploited loopholes in the 1919 Treaty to create an army around three times the size of its supposed total, as well as a police force more than twice its permitted strength. The document added that the 'manufacture of war material has been resumed and developed in a large number of factories not authorized by the IMCC'. And it also detailed a good number of other violations of the Versailles Treaty, including the development of 'sporting' aviation, the training of excessive numbers of commercial pilots, a failure to record and publish registrations of new pilots and their planes, and the granting of illegal subsidies. All of this explained, as a senior French official argued, the 'rapid growth' of German factories and the big jump in demand for raw materials, even if it was impossible at this stage to judge the exact speed and scale of German rearmament.[2]

1. 'Principaux Manquements allemands aux clauses du Traité de Versailles', 4 Aug 1933, AIR 2/1354 TNA.
2. Castellan 268.

The French government, it was clear, was rattled. It has 'long been gravely preoccupied with the evidence which they possess of German rearmament', as one senior Whitehall official noted. 'Nor is this information confined to official circles: it is constantly brought before the public by the press. Opinion has, therefore, long been aware that Germany is rearming.' But they also detected an element of deliberate exaggeration on the part of the French as they tried to win London's backing. 'French policy is now peculiarly susceptible to leadership by Great Britain,' as Sir Ronald Campbell argued in a Whitehall memorandum.[3]

This was partly because any international arms limitation agreement would have meant that France, no less than Germany, would have to renounce some of its weapons. But Paris would only agree to this, Campbell continued, 'if convinced that Great Britain, whose influence if exercised she knows will be decisive, is with her'. At a time of the 'subsidence of democracy' in Europe and elsewhere, 'France looks to England to stand by her in upholding the principles upon which both are founded'. The prime minister, Édouard Daladier, also needed full British support to secure parliamentary approval for his compromises. But Campbell, like everyone else in London, was unaware of just how bleak matters looked in Paris: at this time, French intelligence analysts judged Great Britain, like America, to be at serious risk of adopting a 'benevolent neutrality' in the event of a clash between France and Germany, even if the British were felt to be 'less inclined' than the Italians to lend Berlin their support.[4]

But whatever the motives of those who wrote, or distributed, the file, the British accepted a good many of the charges, notably French allegations of illegal military flying. However, the French dossier failed to make a big impact in London because most of its details merely confirmed what Whitehall already knew. This lack of impact angered the French, who were now 'at a loss to understand our refusal to check the evidence' and dismayed by 'the unfortunate impression' the British made.[5]

There was one highly intriguing reference, however, that could not have failed to become a source of concern. The information from

3. Campbell to Simon, Memo from Paris 16 Sept 1933, AIR 2/1355 TNA.
4. 'La neutralité bienveillante des pays anglo-saxons' 'Plan de Renseignements', 15 Sept 1933, 7NN 2530 SHD.
5. Telegram from Paris, 2 Dec 1933, AIR 2/1355 TNA.

across the Channel emanated from 'a reliable source'—a reference to a high-value intelligence asset, known as 'un grand'—somewhere in Hitler's Reich. If this was true, then his or her price tag was incalculable: as Napoleon Bonaparte had once said, 'one spy in the right place is worth 20,000 men in the field'. But who exactly was this mysterious source, and to what exactly did he or she have access?[6]

The phrase 'a reliable source' would have seized interest in London because, despite their misgivings about relying too heavily on France, the British could at this time scarcely afford to look away from developments in Germany.

Although Hitler initially led a coalition and spent several months establishing and consolidating his grip on power, he wasted no time in rearming Germany. 'Almost overnight', as one of Hitler's top generals wrote later, the tank corps 'liberated itself from the constraints of the Versailles Treaty'. And within the space of just a fortnight, the new chancellor had appointed his old comrade, Hermann Göring, to form a new 'Air Transport Ministry' whose true role was not as innocuous as it sounded. Organized and run by an official, Erhard Milch, who argued that air power would be decisive in determining the outcome of future wars, it was really just a cover for the establishment of a military, rather than civilian, air force. 'The process of re-armament of the Reich is today an accomplished fact,' admitted British officials, as they read the French dossier. 'This process is going forward more quickly since the Hitler government came to power...if it were not promptly remedied, [it] would make all attempts at agreement...vain and illusory.'[7]

Foreign observers also quickly noticed a 'hardening of attitude' by the Berlin authorities over military matters. 'The attitude of the German government has recently shown itself so aggressive that it is necessary to take into account the possibility of Germany deciding to rearm on a large scale, either clandestinely or as an open act of defiance,' as a London official noted. And in Berlin, Nazi bigwigs became

6. The French differentiated between agents (*petits agents* and *les grands*) and *informateurs* (*occasionnels* and *honorables correspondants*). Navarre 52–3.
7. Top generals—'The armour plates of our "mock-ups" became visibly stronger...the wooden guns were banished. The reconnaissance detachments were increased to four companies each, anti-tank detachments were organized in three companies. And we began experiments with motorized infantry and tanks.' Heinz Guderian *Achtung-Panzer! The Development of Tank Warfare* Arms and Armour (1999) 162. British officials—2 Aug 1933, AIR 2/1354 TNA.

more belligerent in expressing their 'dissatisfaction... with the status quo' and their ambition to develop 'a spirit which would shrink from no sacrifice in order to reassert [Germany's] position in the world'.[8]

Soon senior German officials were starting to openly admit, even boast, that they were breaking the terms of the 1919 Treaty. 'We are now faced with a more or less official admission that the German government are [sic] rearming and intend to rearm', as Rumbold told Simon at the end of June. There was now 'little or no endeavour to conceal' the construction of military aircraft. The only source of consolation was that, in his view, 'the Germans are not ready to take violent action for years to come'. But the full picture was more alarming still. Unknown to the outside world, Hitler had even hectored to his ministers that 'the next five years must be dedicated to the rearmament of the German people', adding that 'every publicly-supported work-creation scheme must be judged from this standpoint'.[9]

This abrasive German attitude was sometimes unmistakable. On 18 June, for example, the Germans celebrated a National Flying Day, when several Junkers planes performed some very impressive aerobatic displays over Templehof aerodrome, startling visitors from all over the world. But other indications were based on covert observation: as early as April, word reached foreign spy agencies that one of the largest car factories in the country had introduced round-the-clock production shifts. This rapid change of gear had ostensibly been introduced to fulfil a surge in demand for cars but the real reason for the acceleration was that the plant, a former munitions factory, needed to fulfil secret orders for arms. Soon the French government also received insider information, which it forwarded to London, that 'the majority of motor car factories were now engaged in the manufacture of aeroplane machinery'.[10]

Foreign diplomats or spies could not determine much, however, by talking about such matters to ordinary Germans. There was little or no private discussion of the issue of rearmament, argued the British

8. London official—CAB 24/240/16 (C 3579/319/18), 21 Apr 1933 TNA. Bigwigs—Newton to Simon, 2 July 1933, AIR 3/1353 TNA.
9. Rumbold to Simon, 27 June 1933, AIR 3/1353 TNA. Five years—Harold James, *The German Slump* OUP (1986) 381.
10. Change of gear—'Munitions or Motorcars', *Evening Standard*, 8 Apr 1933; *embauche d'ouvriers et vive activité des usines d'automobiles et de fabrication de tubes*, 2 May 1933, 7NN 2591 SHD; Baxter to Boyle, 17 Oct 1933, AIR 2/1355 TNA.

ambassador, because 'Germans are sensitive to a greater degree than people imagine to the moral stigma involved in flouting the Treaty of Versailles.' As he searched for an explanation, he wondered if 'they are perhaps oversensitive on the moral issue' because of the invasion of neutral Belgium in 1914 and because Germany brought America into the war 'by violating international law' on the sinking of the RMS *Lusitania* in 1915.[11]

This mirrored a comparable reluctance in other countries, notably Britain and France, to talk in public about the need for rearmament, partly because it was such an explosive issue so soon after the Armistice: 'public opinion (in Great Britain)...will not tolerate the idea of German rearmament', as Rumbold privately admitted. But in the House of Commons, the 58-year-old MP for Epping, Winston Churchill, denounced 'the tumultuous insurgence of ferocity and war spirit' in Berlin, comparing the new regime in Berlin to the barbarism of pagan times. Nor was the French government always willing to look away from uncomfortable realities, and soon decided to close its main air bases at Thionville and Strasbourg, relocating them at newly created stations at Bordeaux, Toulouse, and in the Rhône Valley, on the grounds that they were too close to the German border and were therefore vulnerable to a pre-emptive strike.[12]

Such fears were shared at the highest level of British Intelligence. As Hitler tightened his grip on power, Admiral Sinclair told Hugh Dalton, his head of station in The Hague, that 'unless a miracle intervened there would be war between France and Germany within a few years'. But obtaining accurate and reliable information about developments there was no easy matter for the simple reason that in 1933 the SIS had very few agents in Germany. 'Almost our only resource in Germany', wrote Commander Reginald 'Rex' Howard of the SIS in February 1934, was William de Ropp, who became 'Agent 821' in the late 1920s. This dearth of intelligence sources was also highlighted by another senior figure in the SIS, Major Malcolm Woollcombe, who lamented the need to 'increase our supply of first-class agents who can provide real authoritative information on German high policy, especially so

11. Memo from Sir Eric Phipps, 24 Nov 1934, CAB 27/572 TNA.
12. Rumbold to Simon, 27 June 1933, AIR 3/1353 TNA. Martin Gilbert *Churchill* Heinemann (1976) Vol 5, 457. Bases—*Evening Standard* 8 Apr 1933.

that we should not be so dependent on de Ropp, who may at any time come under the eye of the Gestapo and drop out of the picture'.[13]

At a time of a growing and pressing need for information but very limited sources, the British were susceptible to the same 'Sosnowski trap' that their Polish counterparts had already fallen into—the lure of charlatans with a convincing and charming exterior that concealed darker motives, amongst which greed was probably prevalent. And it is into just such a category that this other enigmatic figure, as mysterious as the Polish 'count', emerges.

William de Ropp was by birth and upbringing a Lithuanian who had become a naturalized British citizen during the First World War. Resembling 'a perfectly normal Englishman, about 5′10, with fair hair, a slightly reddish moustache and blue eyes, dressed in a good English suit', he fitted well into his new homeland, joining the army and then the Royal Flying Corps in 1917 and going on to marry an Englishwoman. After the war, he had quickly found new work as a journalist, moving to Berlin as a political correspondent for *The Times*. Fluent in English and German as well as other languages, he was well qualified for the job.[14]

De Ropp had first come to the attention of the SIS in the late 1920s, when he fed back to London a series of reports about the links between Russia and Germany. British Intelligence had wanted to know more about the source of this information and in 1931 sent Frederick Winterbotham to meet him in a hotel lounge in Central London.

Winterbotham was quite taken by his guest, whom he found 'highly intelligent [with] a spontaneous, neat sense of humour' and who spoke 'perfect English without any trace of an accent'. The SIS man wanted to do business with a journalist who had access to, and who was very well connected with, the Nazi leadership. On his return to Berlin, de Ropp now began to send London an increasing number of reports about developments in Germany, and also arranged for Winterbotham to meet a senior figure in the Berlin regime, his fellow Lithuanian and the self-styled 'Nazi philosopher', Alfred Rosenberg, who made a two-month-long visit to Britain in the spring of 1932.[15]

13. Howard—Jeffery 295. Woollcombe—Jeffery 301.
14. Winterbotham *Nazi Connection* 34.
15. Winterbotham *Nazi Connection* 32.

But there were some alarming parallels between Sosnowski and de Ropp. Perhaps it was just coincidence that both men claimed to have aristocratic lineage. De Ropp said that he was originally a Lithuanian 'baron' whose ancestral home had been seized by the Bolsheviks in the revolution of 1917, forcing him to flee to Britain. But even if such 'barons' ever existed in Lithuania, there was a nagging possibility that 'Baron de Ropp', like every double agent, was pretending to be something that he wasn't and that his own aristocratic lineage was just as imaginary as that of Hitler's diplomat and future foreign minister, Joachim 'von' Ribbentrop. De Ropp and Sosnowski were also naturalized citizens of their adopted countries, since Sosnowski originated from a city that was at that time part of the Austro-Hungarian Empire before being absorbed into the new state of Poland. And both had a considerable and ingratiating charm that may have blinded their respective spy chiefs to their faults, inconsistencies, and, very possibly, their blatant lies.

Alarmingly, both intelligence services paid these men a considerable amount of money for the 'intelligence' they supplied: just as Sosnowski lived in luxury, courtesy of Polish taxpayers, so too in the early 1930s the SIS paid de Ropp the then very considerable annual sum of £1,000. Yet the value of his reports has never been proven. His early stories of links between Moscow and Berlin do not appear to have added anything new, since the association was already well known to foreign intelligence. He brokered meetings between British and Nazi officials who wanted to improve relations, and to provide the Nazis with propaganda material, rather than expose any secrets. Two years later, when de Ropp introduced Winterbotham to Hitler, the German leader used the opportunity to sell his version of events and persuade his visitor of his good intentions towards Britain: 'all we ask', Hitler told the undercover agent, 'is that Britain should be content to look after her Empire and not interfere with Germany's plans of expansion'. Perhaps de Ropp had a good reason to want to improve relations between London and Berlin: it would leave Hitler free to move east and liberate his homeland from the Bolsheviks.[16]

Despite the sizeable payments he received, it remains unclear how much importance and value the SIS placed on de Ropp as an intelligence source. Although in 1934 Rex Howard noted that he was 'putting

16. Winterbotham *Nazi Connection* 71, Ch 3 *passim*.

out some good stuff at the moment', SIS headquarters also had doubts about his reports and value. In one of his books, written long after the end of the war, Winterbotham implies that the 'baron' may well have been duplicitous, and it is significant that, once war broke out, de Ropp tried to broker an Anglo-German settlement and was judged, by Colonel Dansey, to be just a 'vehicle for Nazi propaganda'.[17]

Any undue importance that the SIS placed upon his reports would have partly reflected the growing difficulties of obtaining information about Germany. 'Since about June 1933 all channels of information [have been] closed', as the British military attaché in Berlin wrote later. 'This policy of secrecy included the closing down…to foreigners of factories manufacturing aeroplanes and aero engines', and aerodromes, where there was 'intense air activity', were being guarded 'with the utmost secrecy'. By this time there was already 'an impenetrable cloak of secrecy in Germany itself—a secrecy which is loyally observed both by the officials of the army, navy and aviation…and by private people', as one British official in Berlin had written. 'All channels of information [are] closed': this policy of secrecy included the closing 'down…to foreigners of factories manufacturing aeroplanes and aero engines'. This also included much more rigorous censorship of German newspapers, which had long been a favourite source of information for foreign observers.[18]

German counter-espionage was also cracking down on foreign spies, real or imaginary. Handling any agents on foreign soil was of course always dangerous at the best of times but in Nazi Germany it was particularly so. Such were the difficulties of building and maintaining an intelligence network in Germany that in October 1933 the head of SIS wrote some very precise instructions to Frank Foley, who ran its station in Berlin from the Passport Control Office, to help him evade detection.

The 48-year-old Foley was hardly a novice at playing the intelligence game. On the contrary, this diminutive, bespectacled, and slightly

17. Howard—Jeffery 295; FW Winterbotham *Secret and Personal* Kimber (1969) 23–4; Jeffery 296.
18. Attaché—'German Rearmament', 23 Nov 1934, AIR 2/1355 TNA. Official—Military Attaché memo to Ambassador Phipps Nov 1934, AIR 2/1355 TNA. Censorship—'Il est difficile d'avoir beaucoup de renseignements, par suite notamment de l'extrême réserve de la presse qui ne laisse plus filtrer le moindre indice intéressant sur l'évolution silencieuse de la Reichswehr,' 3 Oct 1933, 7NN 2592 SHD.

overweight middle-aged man had been in the shadows of this murky world since the Armistice, when the War Office had noticed his courage, initiative, and leadership and headhunted him into the ranks of the Intelligence Service. Soon he was using his fluency in both French and German to recruit and manage a network of agents operating throughout northern Europe. Yet even he may have been taken aback by the very high level of security he was now expected to implement. The briefing that reached him stressed that he could not keep any confidential papers in his office, or even write them there; he would have to put pen to paper at the last available opportunity before they were sent by diplomatic courier, to minimize any chance of losing them, or having them stolen or seized; any meetings with agents should only be held at different meeting places; and on no account should he use the telephone to send any messages.[19]

Pitched against Foley and other foreign operatives inside the Reich were two formidable organizations. One was the German army's intelligence service, the Abwehr ('Security Service') which had been established after the Treaty of Versailles to conduct counter-espionage operations inside Germany: this was the only form of espionage that the treaty allowed the defeated country to undertake. As a department of the Ministry of War, the Abwehr was staffed extensively by personnel from the armed forces, and from January 1935 this small but well-coordinated and efficient organization was headed by Admiral Wilhelm Canaris, a short man with white hair and a reddish face who was 47 years old when he took the role over from his predecessor, Captain Conrad Patzig.

An abstemious individual, who worked unremitting hours and drank water and no more than a single glass of wine every day, Canaris was not without his eccentricities: he was a bachelor who was devoted to his rough-haired dachshunds, which invariably accompanied him on his business trips across Germany, and whose antics, moods, and state of health were frequently mentioned in his official reports. But such idiosyncrasies did not detract from his cleverness and devotion to his country, which were stronger—as his involvement in the July 1944 plot to kill Hitler attests—than his commitment to the Nazi Party. Nor did they stop him from expanding the organization's horizons: under the tutelage of Canaris, the Abwehr began to undertake military espionage in foreign countries as well as within the Reich.

19. Jeffery 296.

Working alongside the Abwehr, and often in competition with it, was the Geheime Staatspolizei—the Secret State Police or 'Gestapo'. Originally set up by Göring, the Gestapo was organized and run by Heinrich Himmler and Reinhard Heydrich and acted as a domestic undercover force whose jurisdiction lay in investigating and preventing political rather than military crimes, even though, in a highly militarized state like Nazi Germany, there was no clear distinction between the two. Boasting unlimited powers of arrest, detention, and execution, it frequently ignored decisions made by Germany's law courts. And amongst both Germans and outsiders, it quickly established its reputation for extreme brutality and ruthlessness.

Between them, these two organizations drastically tightened security along Germany's long borders. Large stretches of the Franco-German border, particularly surrounding the Saar, were highly porous, allowing soldiers or agents from both countries to illicitly cross into each other's territory to undertake reconnaissance missions. In late 1932, the French authorities had been alarmed by reports of such surveillance missions undertaken by German soldiers, who sometimes deliberately strayed across the border. But now French spy chiefs noted that German customs officials and police were exerting much greater control over their western borders, closing down minor roads and sealing off any obscure or unofficial crossing points while keeping much closer watch over railways as well as the main highways, and subjecting travellers to extensive questioning about the purpose of their journey to Germany. The border guards were also reinforced by units of the Nazi paramilitaries, the SA, who brandished automatic weapons, bayonets, and truncheons. This was partly to control the exodus of political refugees from Germany—any German national who wanted to leave his or her homeland now needed a special pass, known as the *Sichtvermerk*—but it was also to stop foreign spies from entering the Reich. On 1 March 1933 French domestic security reported that 'since this morning, German control over their frontiers has been significantly stepped up', not least by border guards 'who were now inspecting passes with particular care'.[20]

This made it much harder for spy handlers to run agents, who had been frequently crossing the border into France to provide information

20. Surveillance—Ministère de l'Intérieur Memo, 16 Feb 1933, F/7/13430 AN. SA—'Événements Politiques en Allemagne', 18 Mar 1933, F/7/13430 AN. The SA (*Sturmabteilung*) were also known as stormtroopers or brownshirts. 1933—Ministère de l'Intérieur Memo, 1 Mar 1933, F/7/13430 AN.

and collect cash payments before heading back home again. From one outstation close to the border, Lieutenant Doudot reported to his superiors in Paris that his most important agent, codenamed Bn 101, was finding it considerably more difficult to move seamlessly between the two countries in the way he was used to. But the Service de Renseignements did have an expert forgery department that could produce fake German passports, of which the Gestapo made determined efforts to obtain copies. There were also vulnerable spots in the border that savvy travellers could exploit: in October 1936, for example, around twenty political dissidents fled a Gestapo crackdown and escaped into France, using a route that ran close to Spicheren in northern France.[21]

In the months that followed Hitler's accession to power, the closely guarded German border presented another challenge to French security. This was the threat of Nazi efforts to incite nationalist sentiment amongst the people of French-controlled territory that the Germans claimed for themselves. In March 1933, for example, Paris officials were alarmed by reports of very provocative Nazi demonstrations at Neulauterbourg by a large group of Hitler supporters who then travelled right up to the border before being stopped. Organized by 'diehard' Nazis who 'harboured hostile sentiments towards France', this demonstration was a 'source of real concern' to French civilians in the area, who were taken aback by the 'audacity' of the demonstrators, as well as to Parisian officials. Just a few weeks later this threat seems to have been realized when a group of Nazi fanatics, posing as tourists, crossed the border by car and arrived in Metz, intent on stirring up pro-German nationalist sentiment. The incident prompted French consulates in Germany to step up their surveillance and vetting of prospective German 'tourists' who wanted to visit France.[22]

The importance of obtaining accurate information about Germany was rapidly becoming more pressing.

21. Doudot—Forcade 310. Forgery—'Concernant l'arrestation du nommé Klempp', 27 July 1938, 7NN 3084 SHD. 1933—'Opération de Police', 5 Oct 1936; 7NN 2352 SHD.
22. 1933—'Agitation Hitleriénne à proximité de la frontière', 11 Mar 1933, F/7/13430 AN. Tourists—see for example 'Entrée en France', 8 Apr 1933; Memo from Police d'État de Metz, 14 Apr 1933, F/7/13430 AN.

5

The Anglo-French Spy
Networks Inside Germany

Confronted by such a closely guarded adversary, but not always willing and able to work together, the British and French foreign intelligence services were forced to make the most of every source at their disposal, as well as to find new ones. But despite the gulf between them, many of the methods they used to do this were the same.

Much of this work was of course undertaken by full-time intelligence officers but 'open intelligence', from sources such as newspapers, observations in the street, and everyday conversations, was gathered by military attachés who were officially assigned to their respective embassies but whose work, in practice, overlapped strongly with those of the spy services.

These attachés were tasked with monitoring every aspect of the country they were based in, including not just its defence policies and armed services but also its politics, economics, and foreign policy. This meant dealing with a huge amount of material. 'I was very much struck with the pressure of work in MA [Military Attaché's] Berlin's office and the great difficulty of competing with the number of reports', wrote one visitor in 1935. 'The strain on the Air Attaché is equally great.' These attachés were therefore carefully chosen for the high levels of commitment and the hard work necessary to discern what was and was not worthy of further attention, and to acquire a formidable grasp of so much information. Unlike their British counterparts, the French attachés would also have to compile annual reports that were invariably highly detailed, beautifully presented, and sometimes hundreds of pages long. They also wrote regular despatches back to Paris, usually at fortnightly intervals although at times of crisis and tension they could be sent every few days or, in a real emergency, communicated over the phone or by telegram.[1]

All military attachés needed a whole host of other skills. They had to not only speak the foreign language of their host country at a very advanced level but also have an affable personality that allowed them to mix and make friends easily. This was important because they were in constant touch with a very wide range of people, from many walks of life, who could provide all sorts of information, ranging from highly technical data to salacious rumour. Sometimes they attended functions and parties where they rubbed shoulders with generals or air chiefs, or even heads of state, who told them, quite openly and without any prompting, vital facts and figures. At other times, they might meet the wife or girlfriend of such a figure and steer the conversation, carefully and with subtlety, towards something they wanted to discuss. It was such casual chats that could be hugely revealing: 'the greatest value is always attached to "unconscious" sources', as a British diplomat wrote, 'that is to say, on what certain persons say when they have no reason to believe that their remarks will be repeated'.[2]

They also needed to meet, and to judge, the steady flow of individuals who walked into their embassy and claimed to have an important story to tell or vital information to reveal: a few of these 'walk-ins' were genuine and worth cultivating although vastly more were merely fantasists, time-wasters, and miscreants who were looking for a quick buck or some undue attention. In 1934, for example, the French judged a German civilian called Richard Klein, who appeared unexpectedly at their Forbach headquarters, to be not a fugitive German spy, as he claimed, but a 'professional crook who turns up everywhere, even in Germany, telling the same sort of story and offering his services in return for payment'. Equally, another German civilian who offered to obtain information disappeared with a detailed list of questions that his French spy handler wanted him to research and answer: he had really just used his undercover mission as a way of deserting the French Foreign Legion and returning back home. An American businessman called Wallace Flynn also approached the French embassy in Washington, offering to use his extensive contacts to track German agents inside France as well as to obtain information about developments

1. 1935—'Report on a Visit to Germany', 14–22 Mar 1935, WO 190/321 TNA.
2. Jebb memo, 31 Mar 1939, FO 1093/86 TNA.

inside Germany, but was judged to be a bit too demanding to be trustworthy: although he was certainly well networked, he raised eyebrows by demanding high fees to cover his 'expenses' at a time of economic depression in the United States. And the veracity of a junior officer in the German army, Lieutenant Walther von Scheve, who offered secrets was also questioned on the grounds that he did not quite look his supposed part, and that he did not speak German at native level.[3]

Other 'sources' may have had the best of intentions but merely peddled rumours. In August 1932, for example, the exiled political activist Grigory Alexinsky sent a handwritten letter to French intelligence officers 'informing' them of covert British financial support for Hitler and his party, alleging that London regarded a possible German annexation of the Ukraine as a means not just of undermining the Soviet government but of diverting Berlin away from the acquisition of overseas colonies. The military attaché needed to have the insight and gut feeling to correctly judge who was what, as well as the ability to strike up a rapport with those who really were what they claimed.[4]

It was also a big asset to be eagle-eyed, and to have a very close knowledge of all military matters. Such skills became very useful assets when the attachés were invited to visit military sites or exercises. After 1933, the German authorities sometimes granted such access as confidence-building measures: for the moment at least, they wanted to 'prove' to the outside world that their intentions were honourable and they were adhering to the Versailles Treaty. However, the attachés' visits were always very closely monitored and carefully restricted, with access to whole sections of those sites usually closed off. This meant that the visitors had to be very astute, with excellent powers of observation, to make the most of their trips: they could even assess the number of workers employed at a given factory, for example, by taking a look at the size of its cafeteria. Given the fact that taking notes in such circumstances was, at best, highly awkward, they also needed to memorize a lot of detail.

3. 'Richard Klein', 9 Apr 1934, 7NN 3196 SHD. Legion—Renseignement, 7 Nov 1932, 7NN 3141 SHD. Flynn—military attaché, French embassy in Washington to Paris, 31 Dec 1932, 7NN 3344 SHD. Von Scheve was later shot for treason—Renseignement, 9 June 1934, 7NN 3201 SHD.
4. Alexinsky—'Londres et Mouvement Hitlerien', 25 Aug 1932, F/7/13429 AN.

These attachés were not officially supposed to undertake intelligence work: if a host country accused foreign diplomats of intelligence activities, then this would have badly obstructed the invaluable tasks that their diplomatic services were supposed to undertake. But in practice the distinction between their official roles and spy work was very unclear, and this meant that the military attaché had a highly ambiguous status: 'just as the soldier's voice was at odds with the diplomat's', as Wesley Wark has argued, 'so too was the requirement for non-partisan reporting at odds with the need to make his views felt. His task was no less than to acquire intelligence without employing the methods of espionage.'[5]

Covert intelligence work, including 'dirty tricks' such as actively procuring and running agents, tapping telephone wires, and placing individuals under observation, was carried out by specialist agencies. French undercover work was the responsibility of the army's Service de Renseignements (the SR, although also known as Services Spéciaux), which obtained information that was then was evaluated by the 'Second Sections' of the general staff of the army, navy, and air force (Deuxième Bureaux).

Most of the SR's operations against Germany were conducted from within France's own borders: the SR station at Lille, for example, was responsible for monitoring northern Germany, Belgium, and Holland, while a post at Metz was assigned responsibility for Luxembourg and the Franco-German border along the Palatinate. The Rhineland and Switzerland were the responsibility of the Belfort post. The head of its Berlin station was Lieutenant Colonel Maurice Dejean, who reported directly to the SR's office in Paris 'without passing through the regular administrative channels', as the French ambassador later admitted. But in 1938, as tension with Germany grew, the SR enhanced its presence in Germany, setting up satellite stations in French consulates at Dresden, Munich, Leipzig, Sarrebruck, and Nuremberg.[6]

French archives sometimes offer tantalizing glimpses of the type of work that these SR operatives undertook. In late September 1938, for example, three undercover agents infiltrated German lines in the Sarre district, wearing German army uniforms to do so. Because this was at

5. Wesley K Wark, 'Three Military Attachés at Berlin in the 1930s', *International History Review*, Vol 9 No 4 (1987) 588.
6. Dejean—Robert J Young, 'French Military Intelligence and Nazi Germany 1938–9', *HJ* (Mar 1985) 276.

the height of the Munich crisis, their likely mission would have been to monitor the scale and degree of German preparations for war with France, Britain, and Czechoslovakia. But daring and resourceful though they were, just one mistake led to their arrest. Having stopped to put some petrol into their jeep, they aroused the suspicions of the petrol attendant by paying in cash rather than using, like every other customer, a requisition ticket. Within minutes the attendant had reported his visitors to the police, who then quickly arrested them. German archives, penned by Abwehr officers who were tasked with surveillance of known French undercover operatives, also describe the skill of their quarry at using hire cars to throw their foe off the trail, moving quickly from vehicle to vehicle before making their way to military sites with hidden cameras.[7]

Some agents, active inside the Reich, were recruited outside Germany. The French domestic security services had considerable expertise at detecting German spies operating on their own soil and recruiting them as double agents. This was a difficult and often highly complex game because each participant had to decide who could be trusted, as the case of Ernest Klempp illustrates.[8]

The Gestapo had arrested the 31-year-old Klempp in 1936, charging him with trying to persuade two of his fellow nationals to leave the Reich and join the fight for the left-wing Republican cause in the Spanish Civil War. Klempp was initially sent to a prison in Karlsruhe before being transferred to a concentration camp near the Dutch border, but in March 1938, the Gestapo offered to release him if, in return, he travelled into France to infiltrate and spy on German exiles there. He was also expected 'to gather as much accurate information as possible' about how they were organized and their sources of funding.

Quietly slipping across the border near Bienwaldmuhle, Klempp rented a house in Strasbourg before the police swooped. The French then tried to recruit him as a double agent, sending him back to Germany with a list of questions—asking, for example, about the strength and location of German armed units in particular places—and giving him a false address, belonging to a 'Madame Mathilde Bores', to write to them with his answers. But Klempp's loyalties were unclear,

---

7. Petrol—Renseignement, 29 Sept 1938, 7NN 3129 SHD. Hire cars—R 58/579, Bundesarchiv Berlin.
8. 'Concernant l'arrestation du nommé Klempp', 27 July 1938, 7NN 3084 SHD.

and he returned to France bearing false information, supplied by his Gestapo contact, and with instructions to watch the military parade in Strasbourg on Bastille Day, which the German spies hoped would reveal clues about the true state of the French army.

Equally, the overseas operations of the British Secret Intelligence Service were not run by diplomats but by its regular staff, who almost invariably worked undercover, like Frank Foley and Edward Kayser, as passport control officers. This gave them, like the military attachés, a very ambiguous position, since they were sometime said to be 'attached' to British missions overseas even though the Foreign Office claimed, at other times, that they had 'no connection'. Such uncertainty could cause problems if foreign governments denied British PCOs their right to diplomatic immunity, something that happened on a number of occasions over a range of incidents, ranging from disorderly conduct after excessive drinking to 'a row over a girlfriend'. Whatever their precise status, they had few of the perks and privileges that mainstream diplomats took for granted while nonetheless being burdened with a great deal of administrative chores. These became intense, almost unbearable, in Germany as growing numbers of Jews clambered to escape Hitler's growing persecution: as early as March 1933, Foley reported that his office was 'overwhelmed' with applications from German Jews 'desperate' to escape the Reich.[9]

Because the PCOs were not officially supposed to undertake intelligence-gathering operations aimed at the same countries they were stationed in, a great deal of SIS operations against Germany were conducted from neighbouring countries, notably Holland and Italy. But in practice British Intelligence surveillance of Germany still depended, as its chiefs acknowledged, upon 'a limited number of Passport Control Officers and representatives anchored to their posts in the capital, and possessing neither the means nor the mobility for covering the many industrial and strategic posts from which essential information can alone be obtained'.[10]

Besides Frank Foley at the Passport Control Office, the SIS was also represented in Berlin by Timothy Breen, who was a press attaché at the embassy and also ran four outstations inside the Reich. These were located at Frankfurt, under Captain MacMichael; Cologne, run by

9. Incidents—Andrew 346–7. Foley—Andrew 379.
10. Memorandum on Secret Service Funds, 9 Oct 1935, CAB 127/371 TNA.

John Lennstrand; Hamburg, under George La Touche; and Munich, headed by AG Tyler. To keep in close touch with their bosses in Berlin and London, all of these undercover intelligence officers made constant use of King's Messengers, hand-picked, highly trained, and trusted couriers who hand-carried diplomatic baggage because of the extreme sensitivity of its contents and the high risk of interception by very efficient domestic intelligence services. The PCOs used this courier network to send material back to their respective capitals, where it could be properly sifted and evaluated by experts at departments such as the Air Ministry, Admiralty, and War Office and, after 1931, the Industrial Intelligence Centre.

Much of the intelligence work was humdrum. From their desks, attachés and operatives would carefully scan local and national newspapers, searching for clues that the German authorities had unwittingly disclosed. This was often a very fruitful source of information because, in the words of Peter Jackson, 'the Nazi desire to cultivate a traditional military ethos took precedence over the intense concern with security'. Others combed through published German documents that could sometimes yield pieces of information. Towards the end of 1933, for example, Frederick Winterbotham closely scrutinized a list of appointments that the German War Office published every year: 'I noticed that each department of the German War Office had an attached officer added to its staff', as he later wrote. Because 'one of the names rang a bell from my First World War flying days .... there was little doubt that this was an Air Staff in training, camouflaged in the War Office'.[11]

Foreign spies had other leads. On the ground, both agencies were apt to place adverts in the local press, offering 'generous pay' in exchange for ill-defined but seemingly easy 'research' work. Intelligence officers would carefully sift through the responses, searching for candidates who were well positioned to provide them with the information they needed but who were also destitute and vulnerable. Representatives of the mysterious 'Research Office', usually located on neutral territory, then made their move.[12]

Spymasters also relied heavily on *informateurs occasionnels* for scraps of information that they then tried to piece together to create a coherent

11. Jackson *France and the Nazi Menace* 26; Winterbotham *Nazi Connection* 102.
12. Navarre 63.

whole. French archives are full of such reports. Typical of such information were eyewitness accounts of German work camps that were set up close to the French border in the summer of 1933, and of the resemblance of a whole section of road, between Heidelberg and Darmstadt, to 'an immense military camp'; or of a German workman who took his children for a walk along a mountain path and saw a considerable amount of electric cable being laid down, before being approached and arrested by hostile security staff who wanted to hide the construction of a Luftwaffe radio station.[13]

But such sources were unverifiable, forcing case officers to pass judgement on their veracity and decide whether more of their precious and overstretched resources needed to be allocated to investigate. Often such reports remained impossible to check and confirm, no matter how many extra resources may have been allocated to following them up. In August 1933, for example, the Bureau acquired information about a German plan to send an undercover trade mission to the United States. Travelling in a flying boat and bearing a very large amount of cash, the German team had been instructed to negotiate a contract with a Detroit car factory for the construction of a number of 'very resilient and very fast-moving' light tanks, made of a special steel, that could then be dissembled and smuggled back into Germany, disguised as tractors. The same informant also flagged some 'large purchases' of tin and cotton from a supplier in Galveston, Houston. Even though his handler emphasized that 'it hasn't yet been possible to verify these intelligence reports', he flagged them to his superiors in Paris.[14]

Some of these unverifiable reports from 'sporadic informers' were much more plausible than others. In the closing months of 1933, for example, the French spy service had contact, probably just on a one-off basis, with a well-heeled expatriate Frenchman who lived in Stuttgart, where he worked for a large shoe manufacturer. His company, he told his contact, had just received an enormous and lucrative order from the German army for five million pairs of boots, all of

13. '*Occasionnels*' were usually army reservists, industrialists, or businessmen travelling in Germany. By contrast, *honorables correspondants* generally stayed in Germany for a longer period of time. 1933—'A/S du movement nationaliste en Allemagne', 27 July 1933, F/7/13431 AN. Mountain path—'A/S Travaux Suspects sur l'Ebersberg', 3 July 1935, 7NN 3114 SHD.

14. 'Tanks légers commandés à Detroit', 21 Aug 1933, F/7/13431 AN.

which were well suited for wartime use, and its staff were having to work day and night to fulfil the order. Such a fragment of information gave the French an indication of the extraordinary speed and scale of German rearmament. More alarming still was a toxic report, received in the spring of 1934 from an expatriate German called Hugo Wertheim, about the establishment of a heavily guarded research centre for bacteriological warfare that was located between Dortmund and Horde: the report was brought to the attention of top people in Paris although it is unclear if it had substance.[15]

German universities also provided a useful source of information, notably about popular attitudes. A German student at Karlsruhe University, whose reports struck the Deuxième Bureau as 'sincere', described the attitudes prevalent amongst his fellow students, claiming that although many had joined the Nazi Party, most had done so only 'out of fear' and because their professional futures would otherwise be compromised. And in 1935 a French student at Freiburg, *un informateur bénévole et occasionnel*, told spy chiefs in Paris about changes to the curriculum that he felt were significant—a course on 'national minorities' had suddenly been introduced, for example—and amendments to term dates that he thought might signal preparations for impending action.[16]

But much harder to verify were the vastly more sweeping and ambitious claims that a French intelligence source, based in Hamburg, made about 'the state of public morale in Germany'. This particular individual was a French national who had lived in the city for sixteen years, working in the automobile trade. Claiming that unemployment, underemployment, harsh conditions, and low living standards were rife in the district as a result of government policies, he informed the Deuxième Bureau that Hitler and his regime were extremely unpopular in the city. There was real 'disillusionment', ran this source, 'that would add to the growing discontent of the masses . . . a certain degree of resistance was starting to make itself felt'. This individual had even stated that 'a sudden uprising was not inconceivable if matters

---

15. Expatriate—'Renseignements Militaires', 13 Oct 1933 AN. Wertheim—Renseignement, 11 May 1934, 7NN 3114 SHD: the veracity of the report remains unclear, since Hitler's bacteriological warfare programme is not known to have started until later.
16. Karlsruhe—'Renseignements sur l'état d'esprit en Allemagne', 29 Sept 1933 AN. Freiburg—'A/S Périodes d'Activité des Universités Allemandes', 2 Feb 1935, 7NN 3114 SHD.

deteriorate over winter', and that it could happen with just the same speed and surprise as the revolution of 1918.[17]

This particular report, from an 'intelligence source' whose value remains unclear, may not have mattered in itself, but it doubtlessly carried extra weight because it seemed to confirm other information that reached the desks of French intelligence officers: shortly before, another report had claimed that there was widespread anger towards Hitler from 'workers and the unemployed' who remained 'unswayed by propaganda and threats. And in November, further information described 'an exceptionally strong fear' of war and a 'particularly great fear of invasion' amongst the people of Hamburg in particular, as well as the northern Rhineland in general, adding that this would provoke 'serious enough trouble in the near future'. Unverified and unverifiable though such reports were, they help to explain why some French politicians remained convinced that Hitler would be toppled by a domestic coup. André Tardieu, the former prime minister, told the French ambassador in Berlin that 'Hitler will not last long. His fate is sealed,' although Sir Eric Phipps cautioned that if the French foreign minister 'anticipated the fall of the Hitler regime', as he had done, then 'he was mistaken'.[18]

However, such minor sources were far from the big prizes that every foreign intelligence officer dreams of recruiting. These were *les grands*, the select individuals who have highly privileged access to the most confidential information.

Such people would very rarely take the initiative and approach foreign spy services independently and unexpectedly but were more typically headhunted and then recruited after months or years of painstaking effort. Undercover agents would find someone who was in some respect vulnerable—perhaps because they were suspected of harbouring covert hostility towards the regime they were supposed to be

17. 'L'État d'esprit de la Population allemande', Interior Ministry, 16 Oct 1934, F/7/13433 AN.
18. Anger—'La "conquête" des opposants en Allemagne', 24 Aug 1934, F/7/13433 AN. November—'L'État d'esprit de la Population Allemande', Interior Ministry, 22 Nov 1934, F/7/13433 AN. 'German Rearmament', Memo from Phipps, 23 Nov 1934, CAB 21/949 TNA. Tardieu—Overy and Wheatcroft 120. By May 1935, French Intelligence concluded that Hitler's regime was strong and that 'all individual interests bow willingly to the general interest of the racial state'. The exception was resistance within the General Staff. See 'Potentiel militaire de l'Allemagne', 7NN 2N 151–3 SHD; Jackson *France and the Nazi Menace* 86.

working for—and then make a careful and timely approach, perhaps after a long period of closet surveillance of their target's daily routines. Even if their prey was open to such an advance, then foreign spies could sometimes need very considerable sums of money to win them over. 'Even when adequate funds are available, it takes at least two-to-three years, under the most favourable circumstances, to establish a satisfactory source in any country,' as one intelligence memorandum stated.[19]

Securing top-quality sources was vital at a time when foreign spy services needed to get a clearer idea not just of German capabilities but also of Hitler's plans. Without such insights, any information about resources had very limited value. A classic case concerned an intelligence report, which reached Paris in the summer of 1933, about some unexpected steps that the German armed forces were suddenly taking to defend some of their key industrial sites in Baden, close to the border with France.

The French had obtained this information by intercepting some documents that the Berlin authorities had sent out to these sites, which were required to 'protect themselves against the immense dangers posed by aerial attacks'. These industrial sites were ordered to undertake a number of other measures, including appointing staff members to take responsibility for protection and to carry out drills in the event of an emergency. But the big, unanswered question was why: were the Germans expecting France to carry out a pre-emptive attack, or were they planning to spark a crisis by undertaking a highly provocative move that might then trigger such a response? Or were the Germans just taking sensible preventive steps against a possible Polish attack on East Prussia, fearful that the French might exploit such an assault? In the summer of 1933, rumours about such a Polish invasion were certainly plentiful. Facts were one thing, but gauging motives and intentions quite another.[20]

Given the sheer difficulty of obtaining high-grade information and of recruiting high-value sources, the SIS was susceptible to French advances in the summer of 1933, even if its political chiefs still balked at the prospect of a formal defensive alliance with Paris. As British

19. 'Memorandum on Secret Service Funds', 9 Oct 1935, CAB 127/371 TNA.
20. Industrial sites—'Concerne la protection aérienne de l'industrie', 14 July 1933, F/7/13431 AN.

defence and security chiefs digested the dossier that the French ambassador had forwarded them at the end of July, Colonel Stewart Menzies, who was at this time the deputy head of the SIS, carefully assessed what the Bureau could offer. In a detailed internal report, he noted the severe budgetary cuts that had forced his French counterparts to cancel some of their overseas and domestic operations but also mentioned some compensatory factors. The French, he pointed out, had close links with the Poles and ran several agents in Germany, although these were 'sleepers' who would be used only in time of war and who were 'definitely forbidden to send in any reports at present': such sleepers were vital, however, to maintain 'a network of resident agents who will be able to remain there under any circumstances, and whose communications are arranged for by cast-iron methods'. He also noted how the French procured many 'high class female agents' to seduce German officers.[21]

But an intriguing and very valuable question remained unanswered. Who exactly was 'the reliable source' that the French had used to obtain some of the information within their dossier?

21. Jeffery 290. Sleepers—'Memorandum on Secret Service Funds', 9 Oct 1935, CAB 127/371 TNA.

6

'The Reliable Source'

In late 1932, a German man in early middle age, smartly dressed and well turned out, walked into a post office in central Berlin and spoke briefly to the clerk behind the counter before showing him some proof of his identity. Without a second thought or a further glance, the clerk disappeared for a moment to fetch an envelope that had been marked for the visitor's attention.

Inside the envelope was a single item—a simple receipt for some luggage that had been left at the city's main railway station, a short distance away. The middle-aged German headed straight there, taking his time, walking slowly and taking care not to hurry or show any other outward signs of stress.

Ten minutes later he had picked up the key to the railway locker, in which he found not a suitcase but a packet. He stuffed it inside his coat and furtively glanced around before he left, just in case someone might be watching, and then headed straight home. He knew that he would be in trouble if, for whatever reason, he was stopped and searched on the way. He would have trouble explaining why he was carrying thousands of reichsmarks, which was the equivalent of several years' salary for the vast majority of Germans. And if the secret police then searched his house, they would find a lot more money hidden away, which surely no amount of excuses could account for.

The 44-year-old Hans-Thilo Schmidt was at this time on the verge of becoming the most important asset on Germany that the French, or indeed any, intelligence service possessed. And on that November day he was picking up his reward for an immensely valuable batch of information that he had passed on to his handlers in Paris.

He was following, by the letter, one of several procedures that the French spy service had so carefully worked out for him to help him stay alive. One golden rule was not to use the postal system unless it was absolutely necessary: it was safer to travel into Switzerland or Belgium and send a letter from there than to use Germany's domestic postal service, which was closely monitored. Only simple postcards, bearing pre-arranged messages that had specific meanings, were acceptable. In 1934, for example, the Gestapo uncovered an informer inside the German army because he posted a newspaper, the Nazi Party daily *Völkischer Beobachter*, to his contact in Poland: perhaps because they had considered this to be an unusual item to send abroad, the Gestapo had intercepted the envelope, looked carefully at the newspaper, and found a number of handwritten notes about confidential military topics hidden within its pages. But Schmidt could at least use the latest types of secret ink in order to arrange meetings with his intelligence contacts at one of several venues. And he was now starting to become accustomed not just to using these procedures but also to living this stressful and precarious existence, just as his French handlers were starting to trust him and to acknowledge the extraordinarily high quality of his information.[1]

Schmidt had first come to the attention of the Deuxième Bureau nearly eighteen months before, when one summer's morning he had walked, uninvited and unexpected, into the French embassy in the German capital and asked to see an intelligence officer. He explained that he had some important information to offer, and took a note of the name of the person he needed to write to.

Several weeks later a letter from Schmidt reached the desk of a senior French intelligence officer in Berlin. He had access to material of the highest order, the German explained, and he would reveal more at a later stage, if a meeting in person could be arranged. The Bureau's bosses were prepared to take the risk and wrote back to the contact address in the letter. A meeting could and would be arranged, at a venue where both parties could feel at relative ease.

On the evening of Sunday 1 November 1931, Schmidt had arrived at a hotel in Verviers in Belgium, close to the German border. As instructed, he reported to a receptionist who handed him a simple note, inviting him to visit a private suite on the first floor. Waiting for him in this highly luxurious set of rooms, and seated in a deep chair,

---

1. The Gestapo and Abwehr noted that foreign spy services would avoid using the post, aware that it was under close watch. See file R 58/579, Bundesarchiv, Berlin.

drawing heavily on an expensive cigar and reading a newspaper, was Rodolphe 'Rex' Lemoine.

Like his visitor, 61-year-old 'Rex' had an unusual professional background, having acquired a conviction for fraud in a French court before being lured into the ranks of the Deuxième Bureau, whose officers clearly recognized some remarkable traits that they felt they could harness and exploit. They doubtlessly judged that his criminal record did not matter, since this enormous, bear-like man had a strong, even mesmeric, personality, as well as a pair of pale blue eyes that exerted a powerful hold on those he met. He was just the right man to recruit prospective agents and then keep a grip on them. And well versed in the arts of the criminal underground, he was also well suited to intelligence work. He was just the person to go to 'if you wanted a passport, real or fake, from any country in the world, to carry out a burglary, or to spirit money or documents across even a closely guarded frontier'.[2]

The visitor was visibly ill at ease but began to relax as they talked, and Lemoine found out more about this new and potentially vital source of information.

Schmidt was a humble clerk in the German army's Cipher Department in Berlin. Married with two children, his life superficially seemed to be no different from any of his office colleagues. But whatever the reason, he was now willing to betray his country and sell details of top-secret military ciphers, which were stored in a safe to which he had highly privileged access. Above all, he continued, he could obtain important information about a new and highly secretive coding machine, called Enigma, that the German armed forces were now using to scramble their messages into what they thought was an indecipherable code. The machine combined a series of wheels, or 'rotors', that were wired to plugboards to create an almost unquantifiable number of coding positions.

The French did not at this stage have the expertise to crack the German codes but knew that, if their visitor was telling the truth, then much of this information, which he said included the codebooks, signalling, and technical data, would be of priceless value, even if months or years of effort might well be needed to make full use of them.

2. See in general Dermot Turing *X,Y and Z* The History Press (2012) 54–5; Hugh Sebag-Montefiore *Enigma: The Battle for the Code* W&N (2004) Ch 2 *passim*; Navarre 72.

As the conversation and drinks began to flow, Rex, like every spy chief, worked hard to decipher his visitor, looking for clues about what was motivating him to betray his country. Part of the answer, he and his counterparts determined, was that their recruit was clearly something of a 'playboy and a rascal', who made no pretence about the fact that he just wanted to make lots of money. With a love of expensive cigars and drinks, and with gambling habits and numerous mistresses to pay for, as well as a wife and several children, he found, like so many other traitors, that he could not make ends meet. And the more he talked, the more it became clear that he suffered from what, in today's world, would be termed sex addiction. He had, and in the past had had, partners, casual girlfriends, and long-term mistresses everywhere, it seemed, and to satisfy them he needed a very large income. These were no empty boasts but later backed up by the disturbing testimony of his children. His interlocutor, a Frenchman and a man of the world, was amazed, and perhaps appalled.[3]

But something else was probably at work in the recesses of Schmidt's mind. It is likely that he felt completely overshadowed by the considerable professional success of his elder brother, who held high rank in the German army. Although, ironically, his brother had helped to secure him his current job in the Cipher department, Hans-Thilo nonetheless still felt a failure by comparison. Betraying the secrets of the German army and his country may have represented a form of revenge.[4]

A week after this initial meeting, the two men met again at the same hotel in Verviers. This time they were more at ease and Rex was accompanied by a cipher expert, 34-year-old Gustave Bertrand, whose jaw dropped when Schmidt produced several top-secret operating manuals for the Enigma machines. Bertrand flicked through the documents in a state of disbelief and then photographed them while Rex handed his visitor a thick wad of cash. It was both a reward for the documents and an expression of personal trust. From this moment on, the middle-aged German had become an undercover French agent, codenamed 'HE' or, as he was usually referred to amongst his handlers, 'Agent Asche'.

Over the weeks that followed, Bertrand and his team combed through every word, drawing, and page of the immensely convoluted documents before them. They knew for sure that this material was genuine. But much of the information was simply beyond their expertise. Bertrand suggested to the heads of the Bureau that they should share Schmidt's documents with their British counterparts. It was better just to swallow their pride and admit that they needed foreign assistance to exploit this astonishing break.

Bertrand's key contact here was the head of SIS's Paris station, an outgoing, flamboyant young Englishman by the name of Wilfred 'Biffy' Dunderdale.

Although just 28 years old, Dunderdale had already led an extraordinary life by the time he arrived in Paris in 1927 as the SIS liaison officer. The son of a shipbroker, he had grown up in Constantinople and as a teenager had used his father's business as a cover to obtain information about the Russian fleet that passed through its waters and docked. At the age of just 16, his father had sent him to Russia to act as a minder and interpreter for some American businessmen who were selling some submarines to the czar. And as soon as he joined British Intelligence in 1921, he was embroiled in the complex and sometimes violent power struggles that broke out in Constantinople at the end of the First World War, thwarting a Turkish coup to seize control of the capital, and then paying off and repatriating those of the sultan's harem who had made their way from other parts of the world.[5]

Speaking French like a native, as well as Russian and Turkish, he enjoyed very close and amicable relations with his counterparts in Paris, who described him as *un camarade séduisant, d'une élégance raffinée*. British visitors commented on this close and sparkling rapport: when David Footman, a senior British diplomat, visited the French capital, he was taken aback by the 'excellent personal relations which [Dunderdale] has already established with his French friends'.[6]

But behind the affability was the seriousness of a dedicated intelligence professional whose office hosted an impressive collection of maps, reports, plans, and photos. Dunderdale immediately recognized the supreme importance of the material that Bertrand had shown him and passed it straight to a team of cryptanalysts in London. Within days,

5. 'Commander Wilfred Dunderdale', *The Times*, 16 Nov 1990.
6. Jeffery 290–1.

British experts at the Government Code and Cypher School (GC&CS) in London were examining the documents with the same rapacity as their French counterparts. They were as impressed by the quality of the information but were equally flummoxed: they needed much more to work on, preferably a perfect replica of an Enigma machine, to get any further forward.

Bertrand now turned to the Poles. Unknown to Bertrand, Polish codebreakers already knew far more about Enigma than they were saying. Two years before, in January 1929, a vigilant customs officer in Warsaw had alerted his bosses to an unusually bulky and weighty box that had been mistakenly sent to Poland from Berlin. The German embassy urgently requested its return but this aroused the suspicions of the Polish authorities, who decided to investigate further. Inside they found an Enigma machine and, before returning it, they were able to take exact measurements and photographs that would enable them to build a replica. When the box was resealed, the Germans had no way of knowing that it had ever been tampered with. The Poles had now taken a big step towards cracking the German codes but still had a long way to go to reach the finishing line.

The head of the Cipher department in Warsaw, 37-year-old Major Gwido Langer, was under strict instructions to keep this intelligence coup quiet, even from Poland's closest allies: the Poles could not risk any unnecessary leaks of information that would alert the Germans to what they had managed to do. Langer informed Bertrand, quite truthfully, that much more information was needed if the codes were to be broken but said nothing about his replica machine. Because the Germans had considerably modified the commercial model of two years before, Langer needed to know more about their latest version if Schmidt's material was to be of any benefit.[7]

By this time, the French intelligence services were pressing their top agent to obtain more information not just about Enigma but about other military matters that he was privy to. Above all, they needed to know more about the existing strength of the Reich's armed forces and Berlin's future plans. The task of gathering intelligence about this covert rearmament programme was entrusted to Lieutenant-Colonel André Perruche.

7. Paul Paillole *Notre espion chez Hitler* Robert Laffont (1985) 40–1; Montefiore 23–4.

Perruche and Rex Lemoine were now in direct competition to get their different material from a single source, who had limited opportunities to obtain such information without arousing suspicion. Perruche sighed with relief when, in the course of 1933, Schmidt began to acquire high-level information about German plans and capabilities from his brother, whom he was on close terms with. His brother, as one French spy later wrote, was inclined to talk to him about top-level secrets 'with such astonishing candour that we wondered if we were living in a dream world'.[8]

To convey whatever information he obtained, Schmidt was ordered to contact his handlers in secret code, although at times he also found other means of doing so: in September 1933 he hiked over the border into Switzerland to post a letter, and on another occasion, he was said to have placed highly confidential information in a carrier bag along with various Bavarian delicatessen foods. Such stories were of course easily exaggerated by the second-hand sources who related them, but there is no doubt that in August 1933 Schmidt provided documents detailing the composition and deployment of the Reichswehr down to company level. It was this information that comprised the dossier that the French handed over to Whitehall in the same month.[9]

Of course, the French never revealed the identity of their new master spy to the British, and did not even publicly acknowledge his existence until years after the war. Schmidt's name and details remained a very closely guarded secret to which only a handful of French officials were privy. The French authorities were willing to indicate only that they did possess a high-value asset—a 'reliable source'—that would naturally give their document more weight.

The British would also have known that, in the summer of 1933, the Deuxième Bureau had a number of other intelligence assets that they themselves lacked. These included a network of listening posts along or close to the border with Germany.

These posts served a number of functions. On the one hand, French spy handlers could keep in regular touch with their network of inform-

8. Navarre 54.
9. Switzerland—Paillole *Notre espion* 158–9. Only fragments of the documents from Schmidt remain in the French archives. See 'Tableaux d'effectifs de la Reichswehr', 7NN 2675 SHD and an undated and untitled dossier of photographs of documents and diagrams from the 'Chef der Heeresleitung'. His story comes mainly from second-hand accounts.

ers inside the Reich and other countries, who often used simple transmitters to receive instructions or send information. The Bureau could
also eavesdrop on the radio messages that the German armed forces or
certain civilian organizations, such as the Gestapo or Abwehr, sent
amongst themselves as they exchanged information and updates about
the movements of suspects and any arrests they had made.

These messages could sometimes provide some important clues to
what was happening inside the Reich. For example, the level of
German activity was revealing, because a sudden pick-up might indicate that something important was about to happen, while at other
times even just humdrum activity could give away the call signs of
particular military units or reveal details about the inner workings of
the police or other government departments. The listening posts also
allowed the French to intercept the telephotographs—a relatively new
development requiring very expensive machinery—that German stations had started to send between themselves: the French recorded
these on discs that were immediately forwarded to Paris, where they
were assessed by the Bureau's 'Y Department'.

A further function of the listening posts was to monitor some of
Germany's own spying stations. The German security services operated a number of stations that tracked French activity and operations
inside Germany, and tried to recruit agents who could work for them
inside France. One such station, which the Bureau focused on, was
located in Cologne: the Abwehr office here ran an espionage operation
that gathered intelligence about French activity in Saarland, which was
still administered by French officials before it was returned, after a
plebiscite, to German rule in February 1935. This, of course, represented a complex picture of spies being spied upon.[10]

The French operated three main listening posts that monitored
Germany, at Metz, Belfort, and Lille. Each of these had several other
substations from where transmitters and receivers spied upon the
Reich.

Metz was the headquarters of the SR's Regional Office of Military
Studies, which was linked to substations at Luxembourg, Forbach, and
Thionville. Staffed by around fifteen full-time operators, and superbly
located on a hill, about a thousand feet above sea level and about ten
miles to the west of the town, the Metz listening post comprised a

10. Forcade 322.

large room that had direction-finding equipment for fixing the positions of medium frequency wireless stations in Germany. Inside was an enormous map that charted the locations of these stations. The French operated numerous other such sites around or close to the border, notably at Maubeuge, Strasbourg, and Colmar, as well as further south, in the Alps.[11]

However, these listening posts, like so many other intelligence assets of the time, operated on meagre budgets. Living in a constant state of financial crisis that also confronted their British and Czech counterparts, the French intelligence services were forced to rely to an important degree on the information provided by the military attachés who were assigned to their embassies throughout the world.

From these and other sources, intelligence reports about covert German rearmament continued to seep in over the summer and autumn of 1933. Typical of the programme's undercover nature was an aerial transport service that acted as a front for a regular military flying school run by the German navy. This was officially named *Severa*, the Sea Flying Insurance Company that was later rebadged as *Luftdienst*, the coastal flying section of the civilian airline Lufthansa. Although it purported to fly passengers from the Frisian Islands to the mainland, its 135 employees, all officially civilians, were really trainee pilots, observers, and machine gunners for the naval air arm.[12]

Another German ploy was to obtain materials that could have been used either for civilian programmes, as the purchasers claimed, or else for military ends. In July, the Air Ministry noted that 'a number of enquiries from German sources, official and unofficial, have been received by British aircraft and engine manufacturers in the course of the past few months'. This effort to procure dual-use hardware, the report continued, was part of a 'disguised' but 'deliberate attempt to build up the nucleus of a military air force'. One Whitehall report noted the German focus on 'high powered aircraft, for which there is no normal civil use, which moreover are not in use even in German *commercial* aviation. Why were German pilots, at civil aviation schools, being trained on these types of planes, which were now being developed in even larger numbers?' There were other clues to Germany's

---

11. Report on Visit to Paris, 17–19 Apr 1939, HW 62/21 TNA.
12. 'Summary of Breaches of the Treaty of Versailles', 1933 General Staff document AIR 2/1353 TNA.

covert activities. In London, analysts continued to track sharp increases on the Berlin stock market in the value of companies that imported the raw materials, notably scrap metal, copper, iron, cotton waste, that were required for the manufacture of arms. French intelligence first picked up on these increases in July 1933.[13]

Meanwhile, intelligence agents and diplomats were searching hard for clues not just to the quality and quantity of German arms but also about popular attitudes towards their country's rearmament and its relations with the outside world. The feelings of ordinary Germans mattered because even a one-party state, which Hitler's Reich had become within just months of his accession to power, would be reluctant to pursue an aggressive and belligerent foreign policy if there was strong popular opposition. But in these early months of the new political order there was not much sign of any dissension. In July, Basil Newton, a British diplomat who was at this time based in Berlin, noted how '"patriotic fervour is already being whipped up", adding that "it seems hardly possible that a pressure up to bursting-point can be maintained for so long" and that the youth of the nation is equally if not more aggressive' than in 1914.[14]

Other diplomats tried to gauge public opinion and were shocked by what they found. 'The doctrine of hatred of us is very quickly revived' in Germany, wrote a British representative on 9 October, as Hitler brazenly announced an uncompromising line on the issue of international disarmament. And during a visit to Berlin, the former ambassador to Germany, Sir Ronald Lindsay, also saw warning signs of trouble ahead, noting how 'the average German...would very much like to win the next war in order to be in the enviable position of retrieving his losses and of revenging himself for his previous misfortune'. He added that, in contrast to the British, many Germans think 'a fresh war might do some good'. He felt that 'the ultimate objective of German policy is naturally and inevitably the removal of the more galling consequences of defeat... The Polish Corridor, the "Anschluss", "Silesia",

---

13. Hardware—'The Paris Air Agreement', Memo by Sec of State for Air, 27 July 1933, CAB 24/242/50 TNA. Report—'Summary of Breaches of the Treaty of Versailles', 1933 document AIR 2/1353 TNA. Stock market—August 1933 AIR 2/1354 TNA. July 1933—Castellan 267.

14. Soon after becoming chancellor, Hitler appealed for full powers (ie a dictatorship) and on 23 Mar 1933 won a two-thirds majority in the Reichstag that allowed him to pass the Enabling Act that granted these powers. Newton—letter to Simon, 2 July 1933, AIR 2/1353 TNA.

perhaps even the Colonies will all be attacked in their turn.' The new ambassador in Berlin, Sir Eric Phipps, agreed, arguing that soon 'the new German people will be so fanatically patriotic that when the day comes "Germany will only have to shout and the walls of Jericho will crumble." '[15]

In October 1933, as Berlin continued to aggressively confront the Versailles Treaty, Hitler also announced Germany's withdrawal from both the Geneva Disarmament Conference and the League of Nations, which had been sponsoring the negotiations in Switzerland. Alarm bells were ringing louder in foreign capitals. British officials continued to ponder the difficult question of whether they should now support the French government in demanding a formal investigation by the League of Nations into German misconduct. Although Germany was no longer a member, the League still had powers, on paper at least, to take action against any country that undermined 'the peace of nations' and threatened 'external aggression' against others.[16]

But there was a powerful case against doing so. If the League took any effective action, if it was even capable of doing so, then any such move would have hardened feelings in Berlin and deepened divisions with the outside world. The British also feared compromising their intelligence assets. So much of the information about German rearmament emanated from underground agents that any formal complaint to the League would 'seriously prejudice the safety of the sources of secret information'. Alternatively, if the sources were not revealed then the Germans would have simply counter-argued that the charges were groundless. Besides, there was at this stage still hope that the ongoing international negotiations on global disarmament could reap rewards and persuade the Germans to stand down. For these reasons, Whitehall stood apart from Paris, arguing that it would be 'unwise' to 'arraign' Germany with an appeal to the League. It was better to appease Hitler by giving him what he wanted.[17]

15. Hatred—'Material for Deciding British Policy', 22 Oct 1933, CAB 24/243/41 TNA. Lindsay—'The Future of Germany', 9 Apr 1934, CAB 24/248/40 TNA. Phipps— 'The Future of Germany', 9 Apr 1934, CAB 24/248/40 TNA.
16. 'German Attitude', 19 Feb 1934, WO 190/240 TNA.
17. Groundless—HJ Creedy, MI3 Memo, 5 July 1933, AIR 2/1353 TNA. Unwise— 'Germany's Illegal Rearmament', Mar 1934, CAB 24/248/18 TNA.

7

The French and Czechs
Watch the Reich

Throughout the closing months of 1933, more information flowed from the French government into British hands. In October, the Quai d'Orsay informed the British ambassador that Germany was now producing as many as thirty warplanes every day, and that the 'majority' of its motor car factories were now really engaged only in the manufacture of aeroplane machinery. But, whatever the quality of such information, this flow of information was sporadic and also one-sided: there is no evidence that the British intelligence services returned the favour by supplying any information of their own, although in Berlin and elsewhere military attachés shared some information with each other on an informal but sometimes close basis.[1]

In other words, British fears of Hitler's Germany did not at this stage outweigh those of a commitment to continental Europe. The French needed the British more than the British felt they needed them. France's relations with other countries were equally uncertain, for in October 1933 the Polish intelligence service took a step back from its previously close contact with its French counterparts. The reason was that Warsaw was quietly negotiating a non-aggression pact with Nazi Germany, and one secret clause in the agreement foreswore each party from carrying out any espionage on the other's territory. When the pact was signed, in late January 1934, the Polish and French spy services still maintained contact: the following month, for example, the Poles gave the Deuxième Bureau an important document detailing the entire German rearmament programme. But relations had nonetheless

1. Thirty warplanes—FO memo 17 Oct 1933, AIR 2/1355 TNA.

cooled between both spy services and their respective governments. News of the pact confirmed suspicions in Paris that Poland was a greedy, revisionist power—illiberal, anti-Semitic, and pro-German—and that its foreign minister, Colonel Jósef Beck, was a particular 'menace' who was 'arrogant and treacherous'.[2]

The Bureau could no longer count on the Poles to supplement the intelligence that its prize agent, 'Asche', was still providing. But if one star had waned, another now started to shine more brightly, for it was at this time that the French spy service established a close and fruitful relationship with the Czechs.

Like Poland, Czechoslovakia was a natural French ally against the Reich. Less than a year after the Armistice, the French had set up a full-time military mission in Prague to build the Czechs' armed forces, which until 1926 were led by a French general. French businessmen and industrialists also began to invest heavily in this newly created state, and in 1924 the French government signed a treaty of 'alliance and friendship' with President Edward Beneš's administration in Prague. Like the Paris–Warsaw agreement, this was also a loosely defined expression of goodwill and 'concerted action' in the event of any threat to Czech national security, and a more concrete 'Treaty of Mutual Assistance' followed in October 1925.

After Hitler's rise to power, the Czech government had drastically increased spending on its intelligence services. Up until this time the spy service was seriously underfunded, staffed by just twenty officers, and very disorganized and fragmented. Nearly every government department, including the Foreign, Interior, and Finance ministries, had its own intelligence office, and these not only failed to cooperate but even sparred for influence. In January 1933, the Czechs also had 'no network in Germany apart from some informants of low quality', and 'in short, provisions for the conduct of espionage operations were inadequate in every way'. Their limited resources had previously focused on Hungary and Poland, both of which made their respective claims on Czech territory, but this threat was now starting to become overshadowed by the advent of Hitler.[3]

2. 1934—Castellan 82, 478. Beck—Overy and Wheatcroft 9.
3. František Moravec *Master of Spies: The Memoirs of General Frantisek Moravec* Bodley Head (1975) 42–3.

From 1933, the prospect of German aggression towards Czech territory had suddenly become a very real one. In his speeches and writings, Hitler had always openly expressed his ambition to incorporate the German-speaking population of Czechoslovakia into his Reich. These three million ethnic Germans had lived in the Sudetenland, the border districts of Bohemia, Moravia, and Czech Silesia, for centuries. But after the First World War and the dismemberment of the Austro-Hungarian Empire, their ancestral home was placed under the sovereign rule of the newly created state of Czechoslovakia. In the great game of international diplomacy, the Sudeten Germans had been checkmated. German nationalists fumed not just at what they saw as a serious injustice but at the rank double standards perpetrated by the architects of the Versailles Treaty, who had publicly championed the importance of 'self-determination'.[4]

In Prague, a senior officer in Czech Intelligence, František Moravec, began to organize. 'The greatest stress', he wrote, 'should be laid on the active procurement of information. I needed productive agents, networks of them, and to create and maintain them [in] an efficient organization [that] would have to be established.' Although initially cash-starved, his requests for a more generous intelligence budget were suddenly granted in early 1934 without questions even being asked.[5]

Moravec now had the resources to drastically expand and modernize his service. He established a new technical section to set up listening posts, comparable to those that the French had set up at Metz and elsewhere, that deciphered and transmitted coded messages. And he ensured that he had access to the latest developments in secret messages, which could now be written in microdots and exposed by ultraviolet rays.

Building up a network within Czech territory was not so difficult but still had to be done with great care. This was particularly true when there was a very real risk that the Nazis would move undetected across the border and seize his officers or agents and spirit them into the Reich, perhaps because Berlin wanted to arrange an exchange of prisoners or else because they wanted information about what was happening within Czechoslovakia. His worst fears were realized in

4. Speeches and writings—for example, in the Nazi Party's 'Twenty-Five Points' manifesto of 1920.
5. Moravec 32.

1934, when one of his men, Captain Kirinovic, who was based just a few miles from the border, and in a remote region, suffered just such a fate.

Over the coming months, Moravec set up a network of semi-autonomous outposts, always located on Czech soil and invariably very close to the German border but still not quite close enough to make a German snatch operation too easy. He ensured that each was managed by a number of hand-picked and highly trained officers who were up to the job: most of these intelligence officers were in their early thirties, which gave them more emotional maturity than their younger colleagues but more fitness, essential for physically demanding assignments, than the older ones. They were also chosen for their proven patriotism, while preference was also given to married men, who were judged to be less likely to elope to Germany. All acted under cover, posing as journalists, businessmen, and university researchers. And as a further precaution against security breaches, Moravec followed one of the golden rules of intelligence work: to decentralize or 'compartmentalize' each station, operation, and agent, so that no one knew any more than they really had to.[6]

At the same time, he began the difficult and time-consuming task of building up a spy network on German soil. This needed to comprise, firstly, 'sleepers'—trained saboteurs who lived ordinary lives in peacetime but who could be activated in the event of war. They could lie low for years, conceivably decades, living ordinary lives and waiting for a waking order that might perhaps never come. Casual peacetime informers also comprised this network. Like sleepers, these were typically drawn from ordinary civilians—often businessmen or housewives—who appeared to be going about their everyday lives but who were really keeping a close eye on all manner of changes or developments that revealed, or might reveal, that something was afoot. Sudden changes to a railway timetable, for example, could perhaps be a sign of unexpected troop movements, while an acceleration of flying activity could be equally revealing.

Soon the number of active, trusted Czech agents on German territory began to increase, numbering around 100 by the spring of 1934. Each carefully followed their training to spirit information into Moravec's hands, leaving messages, written in code or secret ink, at

6. Moravec 54–6.

prearranged drop-off points: these were carefully selected places that
German counter-espionage agents would not easily be able to watch
without themselves being noticed. When the messages had been
deposited, Czech couriers would undertake closet surveillance of the
sites from afar, to ensure that no trap had been laid, before moving in.
They were then fed back to the Czech outposts, whose officers then
drove them by car or motorbike straight to the agency's analysts and desk
officers in Prague. Again, this network was constantly compartmentalized:
each courier was responsible for only one pick-up point, and would have
nothing else to reveal in the event of capture and torture.

Moravec now had the resources to draw up a clever plan to spy on
the Reich.

In 1934 he and his fellow officers set up a lending bank at Ústí nad
Labem, a Sudeten town that lay close to the German frontier. It was
headed by a bank manager who was really one of his own highly
trained agents, 'a kindly, intelligent [but] a somewhat rugged looking
individual who was given the cover name of "Cut Throat"'.

The idea was simple. Because it was located so close to the border,
Moravec felt sure that the German authorities would give it permission to lend money to German nationals. And because it offered small
loans at an attractive rate of interest, significantly lower than its German
counterparts, he knew that it would equally attract a lot of customers,
including a good many who served in the armed forces and government ministries. Some of those individuals might want to take advantage of the lower rates of interest, which his spy agency was subsidizing,
but others wanted to hide their debts from their fellow nationals by
using a foreign bank. This was exactly the type of client—heavily
indebted with a very poor credit history—that this, very unusual, bank
was looking for.

Moravec did not have to wait long to find such a clientele. The
bank's application for a licence was immediately approved and within
weeks numerous German nationals were applying for loans to a bank
that was covertly owed and run by the Czech intelligence services. To
apply for a loan, each applicant had to complete very detailed questionnaires about his or her personal circumstances, and these were
immediately credit-checked by Moravec's experts, who looked for
well-placed individuals in difficult, perhaps desperate, financial straits.

The Czech spies also concentrated their efforts in Switzerland,
aware of the considerable number of German tourists who went there

on vacation. In particular, Moravec soon struck up a close affinity with the head of the Swiss intelligence service, Colonel Roger Masson, and within weeks Zurich became a hub of spying action.

One of Moravec's ideas was to train a young, multi-lingual Czech intelligence officer, Captain Karel Sedlacek, as a journalist and then provide him, using Masson's influence, with a reporter's job in Zurich, under a false name. This was easy enough to do because so many Czech newspapers were owned by the state, and few editors dared to argue if the government told them to appoint a new member of staff. The main obstacle was that Sedlacek was an atrocious writer, barely able to construct a coherent sentence. But after taking a crash course in writing he was given a job as a Swiss correspondent of a state-run Czech newspaper, *Narodni Listy*, which printed his stories under his new, assumed pen name.

As instructed, Sedlacek carefully watched German tourists, searching hard for those who splashed cash in the most luxurious resorts and night clubs but who did not necessarily have the means to pay for such extravagance. Once he found the right person, he would then have to approach them in an appropriate way, without arousing suspicion. This was no easy task but he felt sure that it would not be long before he would find some prey and swoop.[7]

While his agents were making inroads into the secrets of the Reich, Moravec was also tightening his links with the Deuxième Bureau.

The two agencies had followed their respective governments and begun to work closely together in 1920, when French intelligence officers formed part of the permanent military delegation to Prague and worked, alongside their counterparts in the armed forces, to build the Czechs' new institutions. Both spy services exchanged information about German activity, within the Reich's borders as well as their own, and in 1923 had pooled resources to monitor and foil a number of German espionage operations that were run from Breslau, Cassel, and later Munich. The following year, the Bureau proved its worth when its officers discovered an undercover spy ring that was being masterminded from the German diplomatic posting in Prague: much of this operation was focused on industrial espionage, as the Germans fished for information about the Czech economy in general and about its engineering and aeronautical industries in particular. The French

---

7. Moravec 57–9.

noted that the Germans had been active and highly successful in recruiting agents amongst Czechoslovakia's Sudeten population as well as amongst White Russians who had fled the Bolshevik government and found sanctuary there.[8]

This liaison was a narrowly Czech–French affair, one that the British kept themselves away from. French intelligence officials complained that this was because of British rivalry in the region, driven by a commercial self-interest, although there were other reasons, including a strong British suspicion, bordering on contempt, of the Czechs. Nor were the British involved in the more formal Paris–Prague relationship that began in 1934, when the two allies established a shared office on intelligence matters. Located in Prague, this integrated, joint command was focused purely on Germany and was headed by a Czech general, whose staff included a mixture of officers from both countries. This office and its activities were funded by both Prague and Paris, and in these early days of shared Franco-Czech intelligence-sharing, the relationship appears to have been reciprocal and successful. Such interplay allowed the Czechs to keep up to date with the latest technological developments in radio transmissions and in coding when a leading French criminologist shared his new techniques for exposing secret writing, allowing the Czechs to keep one step ahead of German detection.[9]

While both intelligence agencies exchanged views and summarized some of their intelligence findings, they took immense care not to give away any information that might reveal their sources: just as the Poles kept their Enigma successes to themselves, so too did the Czechs and the French spy agencies keep much under close wraps. Specific details could be revealed only when none of their agents had been directly involved. In 1934, for example, a German plane strayed over Czech territory and crashed, allowing Moravec's men to capture some important material showing that the German police were required to undertake flying courses, as were military and naval officers, in flagrant breach of the Versailles Treaty. This material was passed to both Paris and London because it did not compromise any source.[10]

---

8. Forcade 253.

9. Contempt—Forcade 254; on British contempt for the Czechs, see above Introduction n.13. Liaison—Forcade 254–6; Jean-Arnaud Puig *La SR-SCR et la Tchécoslovaquie entre 1918 et 1937* 84–8.

10. 'Germany's Illegal Rearmament', 18 Mar 1934, Annex II, CAB 24/248 TNA.

Meanwhile Schmidt's value as an intelligence asset was growing in leaps and bounds because, in January 1934, he had been offered a new job in Berlin as a liaison officer between the Cipher Office and the Air Ministry, giving him access to a wider variety of high-grade military secrets than before. Agent HE, as one of the French spy chiefs later exclaimed, 'enabled us to follow step by step the German rearmament, to get intelligence on the highest level of German military policy, to know in advance all the most important projects until the war began'.[11]

But by this stage the experienced officers of the Deuxième Bureau were starting to feel real concern about their star agent's behaviour. His handlers quickly noticed how money went to his head. When they had first met him, in 1931, he had dressed shabbily, true to the spirit of a humble office clerk, whereas now, three years on, he was wearing elegant shirts and suits. He was also taking his wife, Charlotte, on expensive holidays, such as a six-week tour of Czechoslovakia in the summer of 1932 and numerous skiing trips, which doubtlessly made her wonder where he was getting the money from. Agent Asche, his handlers felt, was on a slippery slope and at serious risk of going off-piste. They knew that he would attract the immediate attention of the Abwehr or Gestapo, who were trained to pick up any mismatch between someone's spending and their supposed income: this was the give-away sign that had already cost, and would continue to cost, many agents their lives.[12]

To give him a cover story that would deflect unwanted attention, his handlers instructed Schmidt to set up a plausible cover: the master forgers at the Deuxième Bureau faked a 'bank loan' that he ostensibly used to buy a soap factory whose 'profits', based on sham invoices and sales orders, ventured a plausible explanation for his voluminous amounts of cash. Then a French agent called Guy Schlesser found a clever ruse: he devised a new way of making soap and then set up a fake licence, giving Schmidt the royalties from a fictitious French company that claimed to be using the same processes. Had the Abwehr investigated Schmidt thoroughly at this stage, however, its agents might have noticed that he only rarely visited the premises of his company— his wife spent more time there than he did—and that its organization

---

11. Navarre 55.
12. See for example, Agent A-52 below; and the case of Agent Rodler, Memo 5 Dec 1936, 7NN 2159 SHD ('sa conduite douteuse et ses dépenses ont attiré l'attention').

and procedures were lax to the point of being farcical: staff were often given considerable amounts of paid leave, for example, for no obvious reason.[13]

In the spring of 1934, this single invaluable source provided his handlers with more vital, top-grade information. Schmidt may have also contributed to a dossier on German army strength that the French gave the British in March 1934, and whose contents Whitehall mostly agreed with.[14]

Then, in late May 1934, the French unexpectedly handed over another detailed document, not long after Paris officials had made it clear that they wanted more than just British 'cooperation' to confront Germany and push it towards a disarmament agreement. Once again, this file left the British stunned by the value of what they found.[15]

But, for all his worth, was Schmidt really 'the reliable source'?

Although the Bureau had in fact also acquired 'intelligence from a very good source' that discerned a 'German ambition to build a major air force', most of the information had in fact been obtained not from Agent Asche but from another individual within Nazi ranks. Referred to by Colonel Renondeau as 'the communist informant designated by the letter "L" in my previous correspondence', between 1933 and the spring of 1934 this anonymous source provided the Deuxième Bureau with several thick folders of photographed documents from the German Ministry of Defence. In October 1933, for example, 'L' provided the embassy in Berlin with photographs of the first rearmament programme of the new German Air Ministry, prompting Renondeau to warn his political masters that 'we are on the eve of a complete reorganization of the German military system which will affect not only the armed forces but the entire country as well'.[16]

The identity of this individual, and how he was recruited, remain a mystery but what is not in doubt is that he, or she, suddenly disappeared from view in April 1934. Although French officers had always handled his information with great caution, his loss inflicted a huge blow and meant that they now painfully lacked reliable sources about

13. Soap factory—Paillole *Notre espion* 103. Schlesser—Paillole *Notre espion* 88, Montefiore 26–7.

14. 'The present state of the German Army', 6 Mar 1934, WO 190/243 TNA.

15. 'Cooperation'—Maurice Cowling *The Impact of Hitler* CUP (1975) 68.

16. Other source—Castellan 171, Jackson 60–1. 'L'—Jackson *France and the Nazi Menace* 60–1.

German arms and aircraft production: from this time on, their assessments of Germany's armaments industries were almost always qualified by disclaimers about their accuracy.[17]

'L's document contained details of a highly ambitious Luftwaffe plan to create a force of 500 'first line aircraft' by October 1935. With hindsight, this proved remarkably accurate. This information was based partly on a Luftwaffe programme that had been first authorized in June 1933 and then given extra impetus the following April, when Hitler had secretly ordered a much more ambitious arms programme, creating and lavishly funding a new office, the Central Bureau for German Rearmament, specifically for this purpose. But some of the French claims, such as the proposition that a future German air force would comprise three to four divisions, were wide of the mark and probably drawn, as the cabinet secretary Sir Maurice Hankey argued, from 'conclusions arrived at as a result of a staff exercise carried out in Germany, which envisage the employment of three air divisions'.[18]

The information provoked a furious debate within Whitehall about the likely rate of future German expansion. Although there was a consensus within the British Air Ministry that the Germans had around 338 military planes in service or under construction, compared with a meagre 127 a year earlier, there were now sharp disagreements about what would happen next. Some experts, such as those of the Defence Requirements Committee, thought that Germany would only need five years to properly rearm and acquire relative 'parity' with Britain and France. Others, such as the chief of the air staff, were more complacent, arguing that Germany's output of warplanes would be seriously limited by restraints such as the need for 'efficiency': as the chief of the air staff, Air Marshal Sir Edward Ellington, wrote in 1934, 'a nation so admittedly thorough as Germany will not be content with a mere window-dressing collection of aircraft and pilots'. Hankey also claimed that 'the Cabinet are over-rating the imminence of the German peril. The peril is there all right, but will take more than five years to develop in the military and air sense.'[19]

17. The last surviving communication from 'L' was 'Documents photographiés', written on 30 Apr 1934: 7NN 2593 SHD; Jackson France and the Nazi Menace 93.
18. Luftwaffe plan—Wark The Ultimate Enemy OUP (1986) 40–1. Hankey—31 July 1934, CAB 16/110 TNA.
19. Disagreements—based on information from Group Captain Don in Berlin, Vansittart argued that German 'first line strength was 1,000 aircraft' as early as spring 1934. See

Such scepticism exasperated hawkish figures such as Robert Vansittart, who sighed that 'I have lost all faith in the Air Ministry estimates and consider them dangerous—both at home and abroad.' For Wesley Wark, 'the benefits of this intelligence coup were lost owing to the conservative predictions of the air staff'. Winston Churchill, who was at this stage a backbench MP in his 'wilderness years', was equally infuriated by the apparent complacency of a government that did not share his strong sense of alarm.[20]

Barely five months after sending their last major report, the officers of the Deuxième Bureau provided the British with more devastating information. On 24 October 1934, French intelligence officials informed the British military attaché in Paris about more German plans to expand the Luftwaffe. The German air force was set to expand much more quickly than Whitehall anticipated and was aiming to create 1,300 frontline aircraft, comprising ninety-nine squadrons, by October 1936. Soon French military chiefs would freely admit, for the first time, that they were outgunned by Germany. While they still boasted the largest landed army in Europe, outside the Soviet Union, their large air force was increasingly obsolescent, outsized, and outclassed.[21]

The French intelligence reports later turned out to be accurate, and two years later the Luftwaffe had set up eighty-eight of the ninety-nine squadrons that the French report anticipated. But Germany's secret 'Rhineland Programme' was actually much more ambitious than the report claimed but too ambitious for German industry to adhere to. It was 'a serious underestimate of German intentions'.[22]

Neither the British nor the French could verify all of the claims but were prepared to take them on trust: Whitehall experts found them consistent with the limited information they already had, pointing out that 'this information has been checked by the Air Ministry through its own sources, and the Air Ministry now accept it as an accurate forecast of German air expansion'. Combing through every word of the report, they decided that it was likely to be entirely accurate, showing 'a very

Wark *Ultimate Enemy* 40–1. Ellington—May 1934, AIR 9/24 TNA. Hankey—quoted in RJ Overy 'German Air Strength 1933 to 1939: A Note', *HJ* (1984) 467.
20. Vansittart and Wark quotes—Wesley K Wark, 'British Intelligence on the German Air Force', *HJ* (Sept 1982) 634; *Ultimate Enemy* 39.
21. 1,300 planes—Despatch 24 Oct 1934, FO 371/17695, TNA; Wark *Ultimate Enemy* 42.
22. Wark *Ultimate Enemy* 43.

great increase over the 1934 programme . . . it has been obvious for the past year that Germany has been straining every never to rearm, and to become again both a formidable military and air power'. For the next six months or so, Whitehall relied on the figures provided by the French report to make its own planning.[23]

Germany was emanating a growing sense of menace, and foreign observers were starting to describe the country with a discernible sense of alarm. Germany, it seemed, was in a 'feverish' state. The British air attaché in Berlin described a 'fundamental' change to the German air force and remarked on how the country as a whole had become 'a hive of energy', where 'something very like a war spirit' had appeared. 'A certain purposefulness', he continued, 'is now evident'. Other observers used more extreme terms, commenting on how, 'in the present extremely unusual, almost lunatic, conditions in Berlin', German officials caused serious alarm by making indiscreet remarks to their British counterparts about the scale of German air programme. The British government took note and in July 1934 brought forward the planned date to set up forty new RAF squadrons.[24]

On this occasion, at least, intelligence information had succeeded in changing government policy. But this was very far from being the norm. In his memoirs, Frederick Winterbotham described his 'frustration that the information I was obtaining . . . did not seem to be receiving sufficient attention except by the Air Force Staff'. There was, he continued, an 'apparently deliberate failure to accept or believe any information concerning Nazi rearmament and aggressive intentions'. This, he felt, was partly because of popular pressure: no political party was 'willing to risk the loss of votes by advocating a programme of even limited rearmament'. Stanley Baldwin had quietly planned a

23. Experts—Memo from TGG Heywood, Military Attaché, Berlin, to London, 27 Nov 1935, AIR 2/1355 TNA. Increase—20 Nov 1934, WO 190/281 TNA.
24. Feverish—see for example Lord Londonderry's memo of 19 Nov 1934: 'the Germans are working feverishly to place themselves in a position of armed strength which will enable them . . . to flout foreign opinion entirely. There is not a moment to lose if we are to ever to call attention to the rearmament of Germany,' PREM 1/155 TNA. Purposefulness—'Germany's Illegal Rearmament', 18 Mar 1934, CAB 24/248 TNA. Indiscreet—memo of Lord Londonderry, 26 Oct 1934, PREM 1/155 TNA. July 1934—Wark *Ultimate Enemy* 42.

programme of rearmament until 1935, when he openly put forward the arguments for doing so to the British electorate.[25]

But there was no room for complacency. In the summer of 1934, for example, a double agent working for the Deuxième Bureau sent his handlers in Paris a list of questions given to him by the German spy services. The list included detailed questions about which units guarded specific points along the border, such as Colmar, Metz, Longuyon, and Bitche, and how strong those units were. The Germans could have asked such questions if they had a purely defensive state of mind, and wanted only to prepare themselves for a counter-attack in the event of a French assault. But by the spring of 1934, in its 'feverish state', this was no longer the only possibility. Barely sixteen years after the Armistice, it was no longer unthinkable that Germany could wage an aggressive, unprovoked war against France.[26]

Spying on the Reich had become even more of an urgent challenge.

25. Winterbotham *Nazi Connection* 156–7. A Windham Baldwin, *My Father: The True Story* Allen & Unwin (1955).
26. List—'Questionnaire émanant du SR allemand', July 1934, 7NN 2530 SHD.

8

'The Dark Continent'

Throughout the mid-1930s, British suspicions about the quality of French intelligence reports, and the motives behind them, remained strong. 'There seems no doubt that the French assessment of the German first line is much exaggerated', as Ambassador Phipps wrote from Berlin, while other references to 'exaggeration', 'bluff', and 'humbug' proliferate in high-level governmental correspondence of the time. 'I understand that [the rapporteur of the army budget] has deliberately made his references to German military preparedness as alarming as possible,' as another British official wrote from Paris, 'as he considers that unless the picture is painted in the darkest colours it will fail to command attention.' Even France's top general, Maurice Gamelin, was prepared to commit such excesses, informing the British military attaché in Paris that Germany could put a hundred divisions into the field after mobilization and would be capable of 'attacking in the west . . . from Switzerland to Liège or from Thionville to Holland'.[1]

Other French judgements were similarly exaggerated. Within months of Hitler's rise to power, the Deuxième Bureau had predicted that Germany would be capable of sustaining a two-front war within the space of just two years and that the German army would be 'ready for all types of offensive operations' by the spring of 1938 'at the latest'. And its aviation experts claimed that Germany's clandestine air force would soon comprise a minimum of 800 military aircraft. This evaluation, which did not draw any distinction between 'combat' and 'non-combat' aircraft, was widely off the mark. So too were further reports,

---

1. Phipps—23–4 Aug 1938, FO 371/21710 TNA. British officials—'French Army Estimates', 21 Nov 1934, FO 371/17653 TNA. Gamelin—Jackson *France and the Nazi Menace* 146.

put forward in May 1934, that stressed the 'serious advantage' that Germany already held over France because of the 'mass production of modern heavy aircraft'. These wildly exaggerated figures, and General Victor Denain's 'predictions' that France would be at war with Germany within two years, were essentially a bid to spare the defence budget from draconian budget cuts at a time of economic crisis. This also explains the exaggerated statements made during debates over the military budget in 1935, when French parliamentarians were informed that the size of the Reichswehr had swollen to 600,000 troops—a level that it would not in fact attain until 1939—and that Germany could also field a force of 1.4 million 'well-trained reserves'.[2]

But at the same time the British were hugely dependent upon the French-supplied information and upon the goodwill of the Bureau to get any idea of what was happening inside Germany, even if they did not want to become so dependent upon the French intelligence service that they would be pulled into a more formal alliance of any sort.

Without the French input, the British sorely lacked any reliable intelligence assets inside a highly opaque state. As the British prime minister, Stanley Baldwin, told the House of Commons, it was 'extraordinarily difficult' to get information on a 'dark continent'. In 1935, a French intelligence report complained that running agents in Germany was becoming much more difficult: 'the number of good agents which existed in 1932 is disappearing before our eyes (through arrests)', ran the unhappy conclusion, and were not being replaced by new ones. This meant that 'we no longer receive any truly important intelligence... only fragmentary reports which are often imprecise'.[3]

Much of the intelligence the British gathered at this time was limited in scope and sometimes amounted to little more than guesswork. It was based, in the true manner of most intelligence work, on tiny fragments of information that reached the SIS from a wide variety of sources. It did not even remotely approach the quality and quantity of information that the Bureau's 'very reliable' prize sources—Agents 'L' and Asche—were providing their handlers.

---

2. Spring 1938—Jackson *France and the Nazi Menace* 62. Combat—Jackson *France and the Nazi Menace* 62. Defence budget—Jackson *France and the Nazi Menace* 144. Exaggerations—Jackson *France and the Nazi Menace* 147.
3. Dark continent—Wark *Ultimate Enemy* 42. 1935 report—Renseignement 19 Feb 1935, 7NN 2595 SHD.

Changes in the substance and style of German commerce were amongst these fragments that reached the desks of the SIS. In the summer of 1934, for example, British Intelligence had learned that a number of manufacturers could no longer export some of the spare parts that they had previously supplied without any disruption. The likely reason was that those parts were needed for their rapidly growing domestic rearmament programme. At the same time, word reached London and Paris that the German government was placing large orders for engines built by several leading American firms, such as Curtiss Wright and Hornet, which in December 1934 despatched a very large order of 450 engines, far in excess of what the Germans needed for the supposed size of their air force, to a warehouse in Munich.[4]

While the British and French spy networks were both alerted to, and deeply alarmed by, the sudden increase in German demand for vital raw materials such as specialized chemicals and copper, they were also focusing upon the ways in which civil servants were disguising their exorbitantly high defence spending. The French military attaché in Berlin, Gaston Renondeau, thought that successive German governments had been fiddling their figures since the years of the Weimar Republic. The individual who masterminded this was a financial guru called Hjalmar Schacht.[5]

Schacht not only looked the part of the banker, typically wearing striped trousers, stiff-wing collars, and pince-nez, but knew exactly how international finance worked and therefore how it could be manipulated to disguise illicit activities. Under one of his clever schemes, German industrialists lent money to their government by buying government bonds, known as 'Mefo Bills', that paid interest. From 1934, these loans effectively financed German rearmament with huge sums of around 12 billion reichsmarks but foreign agencies sometimes struggled to see exactly where and how the government's income was flowing. This was because some of the loans were given not to any ministry but to sham organizations that Schacht had set up: officially backed by the government, they gave lenders the security they wanted but at the same time they looked, on the record, like independent companies. As a result, these loans carefully avoided public

4. Castellan 171–2.
5. Raw materials—Castellan 269. Renondeau—Jackson *France and the Nazi Menace* 92.

debate and scrutiny by the Reichstag, which foreign spies would have immediately read or heard about.[6]

Rearmament programmes were also secretly financed in other underhand ways: the construction of new airfields, for example, was funded by a large grant that was secretly diverted from the defence ministry's public budget and then administered by a special branch of the Reich audit office. Intelligence reports also discovered that considerable sums were diverted to rearmament programmes from a government budget to reduce unemployment. Feeling sure that such practices were going on, a British government report noted in March 1934 that 'it is possible for Germany, whether by manipulation of budgetary or extra-budgetary funds belonging to the Reich or to the States, by the use of Nazi Party funds or by suitable diversion of bank credits, to make available very large sums for the manufacture of armaments'. This meant that 'other nations are precluded from tracing such expenditure'. The report saw exactly what would happen, arguing that 'at no very distant date ... Germany [would be] a formidable military factor on the Continent', but Schacht's practices proved too elusive and no foreign governments were able to brandish any proof of what he was doing.[7]

The finance chief and his fellow ministers took other precautions to hide their transactions, typically buying raw materials from foreign markets by using companies that registered and operated abroad, notably in Sweden and Holland, but which were sometimes controlled by German shareholders. Such companies were able to hide or manipulate their order books, or procured materials from countries, mainly Russia and Spain, that were closeted from the prying eyes of the rest of the world.

The Germans practised some other forms of state-sponsored deceptions, for example by setting up a secret state-run technical organization, Fertigung GmbH, that masqueraded as a civil engineering firm. Tasked with supervising the illicit production of aircraft frames and engines, its managers devised some devious ways of evading foreign attention: a common practice was to manufacture or order a spare part not at one single factory, or even several, but at multiple sites. This not

6. Whaley 19.
7. Considerable sums—Arbeits Beschaffungs Program ('Programme for Providing Work for the Unemployed'), 'German Disarmament', AIR 2/1356 TNA. Schacht—'German Industrial Measures', Mar 1934, CAB 4/22 TNA.

only multi-skilled the workforce at those different sites so that 'the potential output of these types is increased' but also made it harder for foreign eyes to notice their arrival, to calculate their quantity, and, in all likelihood, to find their source.[8]

Given their lack of insider information, the British were often forced to make random visits to such sites, driving as close as they could and relying on their powers of observation. In September 1934, for example, a British diplomat made an uninvited visit to Dessau, the site of one of Europe's largest factories, which was run by the engineering giant Junkers. He did not have permission to enter the factory but instead searched for clues from outside.

Driving from Leipzig, he arrived there late in the evening of 21 September and was immediately struck by the frenetic level of activity, commenting in surprise at how 'the main street was far more congested with pedestrians and motorcars than one is accustomed to see in German towns of this size'. Unnoticed by any Abwehr or Gestapo agents, he chatted casually to as many local people as he could, trying to get an idea of when, how, and why these unexpected levels of activity had come about. A municipal architect explained to him that 'the housing problem in Dessau was very acute' because 'in August alone, the population had increased by 700' as more workmen and their families arrived to meet the immense growth in output. The Junkers plant, he continued, 'was working at high pressure in three shifts and was continually having to expand'. The pace of production was so rapid and the shortage of labour so acute that any unemployed people who didn't apply for work there were threatened with fines or even imprisonment.[9]

This mirrored the wider picture of Germany's aircraft industry. The British noted how all of the 'twenty-four known aircraft manufacturing companies and eight known aero engine manufacturing companies...are working to capacity' and their sites had been considerably extended and expanded. A year before, the plant at Siemensstadt had employed 45,000 workers but by September 1934 it had a workforce of 135,000, while the Junkers aircraft factory at Dessau was by this time 'four times the size of the Ford works at Dagenham'. Overall, there were reckoned to be around 150,000 individuals employed on the

8. 'Report on the German Aircraft Industry', 22 Mar 1934, CAB 4/22 TNA.
9. 'Position on German Rearmament', 20 Nov 1934, CAB 27/572 TNA.

aircraft programme, working in several new factories and on much longer hours.[10]

Another itinerant source of information was a highly resourceful and observant soldier, Major Peter Whiteford, who made a week-long visit to Germany in mid-March 1935. Together with the military attaché, he spent some time motoring in the countryside around the capital, not least to locate potential targets for British planes in the event of war with the Reich. Soon the two men noticed an immense amount of construction work close to a military training centre and realized that whole rows of barracks were being built. This was a 'large-scale barrack building programme, which has been in progress for a number of months', he noted. 'It looks as if the German General Staff had in any case decided ultimately to have an army above the twenty-one division mark.'[11]

Scribbling down his findings, Whiteford continued his journey to take a closer look at various other sites that had been built in wood-lands a few miles outside the capital, all of which embassy staff had located by chance when they happened to drive nearby. Unable to get as much information as he wanted, he urged his superiors to arrange for more intelligence-gathering work, arguing that 'reconnaissance [ought] to be carried out by civilians under the cover of walking or motoring tours in Germany; for walking tours it would be possible to make use of the rest houses provided by the German Youth Movement'.

Other undercover agents travelled the Reich to gather intelligence. Given permission to visit a civilian airfield in 1934, the British air attaché noted how 'an ever-increasing numbers of air force personnel are thinly camouflaged as members of the DVS (Professional Pilots School) and wear a blue uniform somewhat similar to our own'. Besides noting a big increase in the number of pilots undergoing training, having personally seen 'between 750 and 800' of these airmen at one aerodrome alone, a technical training school', he also judged that the Germans were placing far more emphasis on night flying than would be expected for civilian pilots.[12]

Like a jigsaw puzzle, various other pieces of information were fitted together to build up a picture of German activity. In November 1934,

10. 'Memo on German Rearmament', 1934, PREM 1/155 TNA.
11. 'Report on a Visit to Germany', Mar 1935, WO 190/321 TNA.
12. 'Memo on German Rearmament', 1934, PREM 1/155 TNA.

the British military attaché discovered from a 'most important and reliable' source, who was probably a highly placed figure in the national energy industry, that 'the average consumption of petrol at each of [Germany's] thirty aerodromes is 35,000 gallons per month'. From this he was able to make a rough estimate of how many planes were based there, reaching a figure of eighteen active aircraft at each airfield, so making a total of 540 planes.[13]

Another, particularly important, indication of covert activity came from Germany's imports. These were considered to be a reliable indication of rearmament because of the limits to Germany's indigenous supplies of raw materials, despite the regime's best efforts to produce synthetic oil and rubber in particular. In April 1934, a report from exiled members of the Social Democratic Party, at this time based in Prague, claimed that there had been very sharp increases in the import of copper, zinc, lead, tin, and nickel amongst other materials, even though Germany was supposedly short of the foreign exchange to buy them. Another source of information was Sir Reginald Wingate, the chairman of the Katanga Mines company in the Belgian Congo, who confirmed that German companies had been buying considerable amounts of copper and scrap metal, as Berlin tried to build a raw material base that it had painfully lacked in the First World War.[14]

Other pieces of information came from casual conversations with the right people. In Berlin, the British air attaché, Group Captain FP Don, discovered that the wives of highly placed Luftwaffe officials would often talk freely. 'The wife of a colonel in the Air Ministry told me that her husband was depressed and miserable,' as he wrote back to London, 'over the halting progress being made in the air force' as a result of general inefficiency and errors. This was entirely consistent with the account given by another fruitful source—an agricultural landowner who knew, from excellent sources, that 'the German statement that they had parity in the air with us was bluff... they were hopelessly behind us in training, ground organization and experience'. Other casual chats with other well-placed individuals yielded all

13. Military Attaché—Memo to Ambassador Phipps, AIR 2/1355 TNA.
14. Shortage—in Dec 1934, the Deuxième Bureau detected a major German effort to introduce synthetic rubber, notably at the Continental Works in Hanover. The French concluded that its quality did not yet suffice, although it had the potential to do so. Castellan 233. Apr 1934—'SDP Memorandum on Rearmament in Germany', 30 Apr 1934, AIR 2/1355 TNA.

manner of clues about Nazi intentions: as early as 1935, for example, a German general let slip to the British air attaché that he knew of plans to invade Russia using the blitzkrieg tactics that were later deployed, to such devastating effect, against France and the Low Countries in 1940.[15]

Such conversations helped foreign observers to get a better understanding of the mentality of both the Nazis in particular and of the German people in general. Major Whiteford, for example, was alarmed by the scale of covert rearmament but took a more moderate line about Nazi ambitions, claiming that they were frequently misunderstood: foreign observers, he claimed, had laid 'too much stress on the aggressive military teaching given to German youth, and did not bring out...the duty of national defence, as opposed to aggression'.[16]

Whiteford also claimed that government announcements and press coverage about Hitler's pronouncements 'were entirely devoid of any aggressive tone. The whole emphasis was laid on the necessity for national defence and security, and on the reestablishment of German honour, now that equality of rights had been achieved by Germany's own action.' He felt even more convinced of this when, soon afterwards, he witnessed an air raid practice, in which thousands of Berliners were forced to take part: while 'we hear a great deal about German aggressive intentions', he argued, but 'after seeing the air raid precautions in Berlin, there is another side to the picture: I can imagine no more effective method of convincing the German people that war is not a pleasant or profitable preoccupation for the civil population, and that no future war will be *ein frischer und* (sic) *fröhlicker Krieg* ("short and sweet") like the pre-war slogan.'[17]

Towards the end of 1934, the Committee of Imperial Defence in London also felt that German intentions were probably benign. 'All indications point to Germany's present preparations being entirely defensive,' argued one Whitehall document, adding that there were 'extensive preparations to evacuate officials and men of military age from the Rhineland in case of a French attack', as well as training other defensive tactics such as in demolitions, delaying tactics, and evacuation. Other British officials concurred, notably the military attaché

---

15. Don and fruitful source—'Germany: Air Strength and Factory Output', 9 Apr 1935, AIR 2/1356 TNA. German general—Winterbotham *Nazi Connection* 108.
16. 'Report on a Visit to Germany', Mar 1935, WO 190/321 TNA.
17. 'Report on a Visit to Germany', Mar 1935, WO 190/321 TNA.

who argued that the Germans were not trained in the 'offensive use of large mechanized formations, and they do not study the attack on fortresses... I suggest that they show there is no intention of using the military forces for a war of aggression for some years to come.'[18]

Other foreign observers felt that Germany's supposed 'fears for its security' really were genuine, rather than a ruse or an excuse to pursue covert disarmament. Lord Lothian felt that 'none of them [the Nazis] is thinking in terms of war for the next ten years. I think Hitler genuinely means peace on its merits. They may have lots of material... but they have had no trained reservists since the war and it takes a long time to train a really efficient mechanized army.' Hitler, he continued, needed an army to 'deal with the Russian enemy ten years hence'. Others pointed to the economic opportunities that rearmament was bringing Germany, creating a plethora of jobs at a time when millions of workers in Britain, America, and elsewhere were out of work: in 1933, unemployment in Britain had reached a peak of around three million, whereas in Germany it was continuing to fall fast by the end of 1934.[19]

But in London, Paris, and elsewhere, there was a growing band of critics who felt a genuine sense of alarm. In Berlin, the French ambassador thought he detected subtle signs of menace, such as Hitler's symbolic use of a replica of Charlemagne's sword, presented to him at Nuremberg in September 1935, and the fact that the tenth anniversary of the Treaty of Locarno was completely ignored by the state-controlled German press. And although he was an instinctive isolationist who argued that 'we must keep out of troubles in Central Europe at all costs', Sir John Simon was prepared to admit that 'with two and a half million people enrolled in the forces... Hitler might be menacing'. He felt that some Germans regarded themselves as 'the predestined rulers of Europe. Nobody who sees inside Germany can doubt this hatred is really being instilled into every German from his or her earliest youth.'[20]

18. Committee of Imperial Defence—set up in 1888, the CID was responsible for research, and some coordination, on issues of military strategy. Whitehall—German Rearmament, Committee of Imperial Defence, Nov 1934, CAB 4/23 TNA. Attaché—Expansion of the German Army, Military Attaché memo, Berlin 23 Nov 1934, AIR 2/1355 TNA.
19. Lord Lothian to Simon, 30 Jan 1935, CAB 24/279/36 TNA.
20. French ambassador—André François-Poncet Souvenirs d'une ambassade à Berlin 1931–8 Perrin (2016) 188. Simon—19 Mar 1934, CAB 10/34 TNA.

At his desk in the Foreign Office, Robert Vansittart continued to play the role of Cassandra, arguing that 'for us, European politics are mostly other people's feuds and grievances... beyond a certain point, the quarrels of Europe are not our quarrels'. And at his country home in Kent, Winston Churchill still felt sure that the Luftwaffe was creating 'an illegal military air force... rapidly approaching equality with our own', which was in fact an entirely fallacious claim. He also felt that by 1937 it would have doubled its comparative strength over the RAF, which proved to be a fairly accurate prediction.[21]

Besides assessing the risk of a conventional attack by Germany's armed forces, the French had another concern for their national safety. This was the danger of a terrorist attack on their own soil by insurgents who were trained, financed, motivated, and perhaps instructed by Berlin. In October 1934, days after the assassination of the foreign minister, Louis Barthou, in Marseilles, this danger became the subject of a police report, which alleged that a number of terrorist attacks on France since 1919 had already been carried out by 'secret German groups'. Since 1933, the authors claimed, several disparate groups had become united under a single command that specialized in stirring up riots, carrying out assassinations, and perpetrating sabotage attacks of 'real audacity' on foreign soil in order to 'dominate European politics by racism' and 'provoke armed conflicts' by 'assisting criminal elements' and *l'action raciste*.[22]

Their track record was, allegedly, an impressive one. Inside Germany, they were said to have carried out attacks against French troops in the occupied Ruhr. But they also allegedly posed a real threat elsewhere, having tried to provoke riots in Upper Silesia and carrying out 'more than 200 assassinations' of people who were suspected of collaborating with the Poles. In 1928, *les groupements secrets racistes* also allegedly set up an underground movement aimed at gathering information and creating unrest in Alsace and Flanders, even fabricating an invasion plan of Holland by the Belgian army and then 'leaking' this false plan to the Dutch government. The French report also claimed that in July 1934 the assassination of the Austrian chancellor, Engelbert Dollfus, was carried out by the same group. Emphasizing that France now confronted

21. Vansittart—Adam Crozier, 'Imperial Decline and the Colonial Question in Anglo-German Relations 1919–39', *European Studies Review* (1981) 208, 225. Churchill, address to the House of Commons, HC Deb, 28 Nov 1934, c857.
22. 'Des groupements terroristes allemands', 21 Nov 1934, F/7/13433 AN.

the same sorts of dangers, it argued that the activities of these groups 'must be followed very closely', both within France and Germany, 'to prevent and avoid events of exceptional gravity'.

But by the mid-1930s, the challenge of spying on the Reich was made even more difficult because of further German counter-measures. For example, the Nazis now had a propensity to locate their new, secret airfields and buildings in forests and undergrowth, leaving spies struggling to see the wood for the trees. One itinerant diplomat discovered this when he detoured as close as he could to an aerodrome that was being secretly built near Neuendettelsau, south-west of Nuremberg. He reported that 'work is being carried on night and day and the whole forest is lit by electricity. A branch railway has been built from the main line to convey the building material right up to the site.' He also detected similar signs of activity at Ansbach, where construction work of a new airfield was ongoing throughout both day and night, although he was unable to get close enough to determine the size and scope of these new projects. And at an airfield near Neustettin, several buildings were constructed underground and covered with soil: this was top secret, and on one occasion the Gestapo hunted down and arrested an engineer who was overheard mentioning its location to an acquaintance at a nearby café. When it was not possible to build a military site in a forest or wood, then the Germans took other measures, siting them underground, planting trees around them, and disguising them as sewers or something similar.[23]

The Nazis also took similar precautions to hide some of their factories. In January 1935, for example, a French spy informed Paris that the Germans were secretly building an underground chemical factory in a forest, located on a mountain slope, outside Teiffing in Bavaria. Around 1,600 workers had been drafted into the town to complete the project, all of whom had been sworn to total secrecy. The German authorities were keeping extremely close watch on all three of the roads that led to the site and issued a special pass to anyone who needed access. The inhabitants of the nearby town were informed only that a factory was being built there.[24]

23. Ansbach—'Position of German Rearmament', 20 Nov 1934, CAB 27/572 TNA. Neustettin—'Le Crime d'Espionnage Commis par une Conversation au Café', 2 May 1935, 7NN 3114 SHD. Underground—Note, 27 Apr 1936, 7NN 3114 SHD.
24. Renseignement, 7 Jan 1935, 7NN 2384 SHD.

Under pressure from the Abwehr, companies also cracked down on industrial espionage. One example was Blohm & Voss, a well-known engineering firm in Hamburg that in 1933 had secretly started to manufacture aircraft, particularly hydroplanes. In January 1934, well aware that its site was of real interest to foreign spy networks, the management issued a strongly worded circular to all employees. 'To give information on the nature and extent of the work is strictly pro- hibited,' ran the warning. 'The staff of the firm have pledged them- selves to secrecy. It is strictly prohibited to take photographs in the aviation works... or to make any drawings.' Around the same time, security was drastically tightened at the naval base at Wilhelmshaven, which the Germans were using to build a new cruiser and several destroyers, to make alterations to the patrol boat *Preussen*, and to com- plete the cruiser *Graf Spee*. The Nazi authorities issued an edict forbid- ding unauthorized planes from flying over or near the base and all visitors, no matter what their level of clearance, were closely watched.[25]

The two giant engineering firms, Krupp and Rheinmetall, had also imposed very high levels of security. In June 1933, for example, the Deuxième Bureau received insider information about this crackdown 'from a proven source who had already provided very important infor- mation'. Although Krupp had 'always had a reputation for harshness, this had grown considerably since Hitler came to power'. The manage- ment there worked in tandem with a specialized unit of the secret police to 'exert a very rigorous level of control, leading to dismissal for even the slightest irregularity', and to carefully scrutinize every recruit, 'looking very closely at their family, past history and political opinions, past and present'. Another source estimated that the workforce at one factory comprised as many as 150–200 Gestapo informers, out of a total of 6,000. And at one Bosch factory in Stuttgart, the Gestapo ran fifty agents who were tasked with watching the staff. Determined not to risk their output of arms, the German authorities also made mass arrests and ordered dismissals from a number of military factories, including Kiel and Wilhelmshaven, of large numbers of workmen whose political sympathies were considered 'doubtful'.[26]

25. Prohibitions—'SDP Memorandum on Rearmament in Germany', 30 Apr 1934, AIR 2/1355 TNA. Edict—Rothermere to Sir Eyres Monsell, 5 Nov 1934, FO 800/290 TNA.
26. June 1933—'Activité des Usines Krupp à Essen, et Rheinmetall à Dusseldorf', 13 June 1933, 7NN 3182 SHD. Informers—'Fabrications de Guerre en Sarre', 8 Jan 1936, 7NN

Anyone who aroused suspicion, or whose espionage was detected, knew what to expect from a regime that took savage reprisals against traitors. Nazi officials threatened German labourers, working on the production of arms, with 'very heavy penalties...for high treason' if they were caught. The German press reported cases of workers who had been executed for economic espionage 'out of sordid egotism or some other low motive to the benefit of a foreign power'. And work-men who were ordered to build some relatively minor defensive posi-tions, alongside some bridges near Baden, were not just hidden carefully from sight behind a barricade but threatened with three months' imprisonment if they even mentioned their work to anyone else.[27]

Nor did the Germans shy away from executing the ultimate penalty. French intelligence officials were horrified by the grisly fate of a young German officer who was beheaded for merely leaking a copy of the evening menu at his barracks: the Deuxième Bureau had asked him to provide this as a starter course, testing his good faith before asking him to do more work on its behalf. And in the space of just ten days, in early 1935, the Nazi authorities condemned two men and two women to death for alleged treason, showing a ruthlessness that then left, as shocked Bureau analysts noted, 'a deep impression on the German people'.[28]

Such ferocity explained why French spy chiefs later felt that they 'probably wouldn't have been able to continue recruiting enough German informers if the war [in 1939] hadn't broken out'. They were forced to admit that such savage German penalties 'will have the effect of increasing the payments that our informers want in return'.[29]

3114 SHD; 'Activité de la fédération illégale', 14 Nov 1935, 7NN 2352 SHD. Mass arrests, Stuttgart—'Activité de la fédération illégale', 14 Nov 1935, 7NN 2352 SHD.

27. Penalties—'Renseignements Militaires', 13 Oct 1933, F/7/13433 AN. German press—*Magdeburger Tageszeitung* 3 Dec 1936. Baden—'Travaux suspects dans la région de Neuenbourg (Bade)', 7 Oct 1936, 7NN 3114 SHD.

28. 19 Feb 1935, 7NN 2595 SHD.

29. Spy chiefs—Navarre 64. Extra pay—'Peine de Mort pour Sabotage Économique', 7 Dec 1936 7NN 3114 SHD.

9

The International Spy Effort

By the spring of 1935, the British and French intelligence services were still focused more on international communism than on Nazi Germany. In a letter written to the Deuxième Bureau on 1 April 1935, for example, Colonel Menzies called for closer cooperation between the two agencies but only on the activities of those Soviet agents and sympathizers who were based in Paris. The SIS had previously been able to intercept their radio messages but now needed the cooperation of the French authorities to continue monitoring them. 'I feel that we must work more closely together in the future', as he told the Bureau chiefs, 'to get a clearer idea of the communist movement'. This emphasis was particularly surprising because by this time Whitehall regarded Germany as 'the ultimate potential enemy'. Others concurred. The chancellor of the exchequer, Neville Chamberlain, described the Reich as 'the *fons et origo* of all our European troubles and anxieties', while a copy of *Mein Kampf* appeared in the Foreign Office library for officials who wanted to gain insight into Hitler's mind.[1]

Even if Germany may still not have been given the attention it deserved, contact and interaction between the two services thrived. Henri Navarre, the head of the SR, recalled that his service's 'closest foreign relationship was with the British, with whom our regular meetings, sometimes held in Paris, sometimes in London, now started to become more frequent. Information was exchanged, its value discussed and methods of work compared.' Navarre was prepared to admit, despite his professional and patriotic pride, how valuable this

---

1. Communist influence—Alexander and Philpott 134–5. Ultimate enemy—DRC, 9th Meeting, note by Sir Warren Fisher, 12 Jan 1934, CAB 16/109 TNA; see Wark *Ultimate Enemy* 28–31. Chamberlain—see Keith Feiling *The Life of Neville Chamberlain* Macmillan (1946) 254.

British input was: 'in the spheres of politics, diplomacy and economics, as well as "action", the British SIS was in our eyes undoubtedly superior'. On counter-espionage, however, the French may have had greater expertise, not least because there were far more foreign agents on French than British soil, given the long and porous shared borders that the Deuxième Bureau had to contend with.[2]

In his memoirs, Frederick Winterbotham described one of his many meetings in the mid-1930s with Colonel Georges Ronin in Paris. 'My liaison over intelligence with my opposite number of the Bureau was extremely close. We knew each other's thoughts and exchanged every bit of information we could about Germany.' His covert visits to the capital would always start at Croydon airfield, where a passenger plane would take off from a grass air strip and land at Le Bourget aerodrome. During his overnight stay, he took his chance to relish a city that he found 'alive and happy' and full of 'traditional gaiety': he always found, for example, that 'the great restaurants in the Bois de Boulogne were full; couture in Paris was at its height and the beautiful women were showing off their latest creations'. Then, the following morning, he would walk to a large, stout green gate, 'not far from the École Militaire', that an aged concierge opened for him. After signing in, he was led to a simple office that was 'furnished with a bare trestle table and some hard wooden chairs, a few filing cabinets and a map on the wall', making his own office in London seem 'positively luxurious'.[3]

The man who greeted him was also in his early forties, quite tall, clean-shaven, and jovial. Winterbotham and Ronin immediately struck up a close rapport and became great friends as they swapped views about Germany's rearmament. In particular, the British visitor was fascinated to observe some of the differences of attitude and behaviour in his French counterparts: he noticed how the Deuxième Bureau enjoyed much greater freedom of action, and that even British agents on French soil 'could get away with anything except murder': in general, he commented, they were 'given much wider authority than our own, which was well circumscribed in London by correct police procedure'. And he noted, too, how the Maginot Line, the vast stretch of supposedly impregnable defences that lined much of France's northern

2. Navarre 73.
3. Winterbotham *Nazi Connection* 136, 144–53.

borders, had created a sense of complacency and a false sense of security.[4]

If the tempo of Anglo-French relations was quickening, it was because the drumbeat of war was still getting louder. Until early 1935, the Nazi leadership had officially denied its rearmament programme, hiding its sheer scale and frantic pace, implausible though its denials generally sounded. The reason for this was that Germany, at this relatively early stage of rearmament, could not afford to provoke any armed confrontation with its neighbours. Its open repudiation of the Versailles Treaty would have risked a pre-emptive strike by the French, whose approach remained consistently more hardline than their British counterparts, or by the Poles: Berlin 'may have been endeavouring to give the impression that Germany is far stronger today than she actually is, in order to counteract any tendency to intervention by the Powers', as the Foreign Office noted in 1935.[5]

Given its high dependency upon the import of crucial raw materials, the Nazi leadership was equally alarmed by the prospect of economic sanctions. They were wise to be, because in October 1933 London was secretly weighing up the viability of economic sanctions against Germany, considering such an option to be an effective threat against a resurgent Reich. To gather more information about Germany's economy, the SIS worked closely with the newly founded Industrial Intelligence Centre (IIC), and recruited a number of British businessmen whose professional work, for companies as varied as Unilever and Eno's Fruit Salts, allowed them to travel to Germany and elsewhere.[6]

But two years after his accession to the chancellorship, Hitler reversed his position and openly boasted about the strength, real or imaginary, of his armed forces. By this time, he judged them not only to be strong enough to deter any possible attack but to threaten his enemies and help him to win what he wanted without a shot even being fired. Up until this time, as a German general later put it, 'Hitler never had any intention of starting a war but he believed he could, through putting over the bluff of rapid rearmament, reach his goal by peaceful means'. The American air attaché, Major Truman Smith,

4. Winterbotham *Nazi Connection* 146.
5. 'Report on a Visit to Germany', 14–22 Mar 1935, WO 190/321 TNA.
6. Oct 1933—'Economic Pressure on Germany', 30 Oct 1933, CAB-24/248/19 TNA. SIS—Andrew 355–6.

thought the same, stating that for Hitler an 'overwhelming military position was a prerequisite to a successful and aggressive diplomacy'.[7]

But just a year before, in February 1934, Göring had made a point of openly telling visitors about the dire state of the Luftwaffe: for example, he informed the *Daily Mail* correspondent, a wealthy, monocled, and gullible figure called Ward Price, that he had only 300 aircraft, most of which were obsolete and militarily worthless, at his disposal. German industry was in such a bad way, he continued, that it would need at least another two years before it could even start proper work on building a new air force. Yet just over a year later, Göring gave Price a journalistic 'scoop' by informing him of the existence of his 'entirely new' Luftwaffe.

It was at this point, in March 1935, when Hitler shook the watching world, and many of his fellow nationals, with shock announcements.

On Saturday 9 March, he proclaimed his ambition to build a new air force that would have 'parity' with those of the Allies. Then, exactly a week later on 16 March, he added that Germany would no longer be bound by the Versailles Treaty. Instead of respecting its limit of 100,000 soldiers, he continued, his regime would reintroduce conscription and expand the army to a strength of 36 divisions, totalling 550,000 men. His confidence had doubtlessly been boosted by the outcome of a plebiscite, held a few weeks before, in the Saar region, whose population voted to return to German sovereign rule after sixteen years under the French. And his anger had then been aroused by the release, just hours before his announcement, of a British government White Paper that called for limited rearmament. The following day, Göring staged a massive fly-past over Berlin, as hundreds of planes, some of which were flown by civilian pilots, roared overhead, deafening everyone and drowning out the words of exclamation uttered below.

These 'Saturday Surprises' concealed a very different truth. In its early years, the Luftwaffe had numerous shortcomings. Many of its officers had recently transferred from the army with little or no training, and much of its equipment was obsolescent or consisted of repainted civilian planes. Its first handbook on tactics and strategy was not even issued

---

7. General Georg Thomas quoted in Kenneth Macksey *Guderian: Creator of the Blitzkrieg* Stein & Day (1975) 58; Henry G Gole *Exposing the Third Reich: Truman Smith in Hitler's Germany* American Warriors Series (2013) 168.

until 1936, and its pilots did not even start to train alongside other branches of the German armed forces for at least a year after its inception. For the first few years, German planes also had poor serviceability and suffered from a high loss rate from accidents. It was not surprising that, amongst many servicemen who were only too well aware of its defects, the air force quickly acquired the derogatory nickname of *Risiko* ('risky') *Luftwaffe*. There were other factors, too, that made the air force far less powerful than Hitler and Göring claimed, and which were enough to bring the sky-high egos of the leadership crashing down to earth.[8]

Berlin now continued to undertake more public relations exercises, and in the summer of 1935 Germany's relations with the outside world entered a new phase that Wesley Wark has called a 'honeymoon period'. Over the next eighteen months, foreign representatives were invited and actively encouraged to visit a wide variety of airfields, military sites, and factories. They were invariably shown considerable hospitality and courtesy before being given a tour of the site followed by some sort of armoured display.[9]

But a lot of the German showmanship was superficial. All of these visits were, of course, carefully stage-managed to cultivate the image of a powerful Germany that was already too formidable to argue with. 'Naturally we were aware of the fact that these officers were expected to furnish their espionage chiefs with reports', as a German officer later noted. There was therefore 'systematic bluff organized at the top level...the visitors had no way of knowing that many of the gigantic hangars they were shown were either completely empty or filled with ancient dust-covered aircraft'. The logic was always the same: in the Nazi mentality, one British report pointed out, 'first and foremost, is force or the capacity to use it. Great reliance is placed in the ability to

---

8. Accidents—RJ Overy, 'German Air Strength', *HJ* (1984) 467. Luftwaffe strength—any of the German planes that were designated as 'combat aircraft' were really just operational trainers with little or no military use. Between 1933 and 1937, nearly two-thirds of manufactured aircraft were 'non-combat' and another 10% were reconnaissance. Until 1938 the Luftwaffe was still using bi-planes. The German air ministry planned on building the Luftwaffe well into the 1940s, expecting to complete its programme around 1944–5. Its reserves were minimal, amounting to just a quarter of first-line strength. See in general Overy *HJ* (1984).

9. 'Honeymoon'—Wark *Ultimate Enemy* 227–31.

attain objectives by the mere threat of overwhelming force. Force is always behind German diplomacy.'[10]

For example, German military demonstrations included large numbers of planes that had been disguised, with a few adaptions and clever painting, as transport aircraft and fighters even though they could never have been used in such a role. Nor were the long aerial processions nearly as impressive as they first seemed, since some of the planes had simply turned around and flown past for a second or even a third time. The Germans tried similar tricks with their land forces: even the crack divisions were short of tanks and had to have extra ones brought in from elsewhere. 'Sometimes we failed to spot these deceptions but at other times it was clear that the parades had been cunningly arranged to mislead us,' as a British attaché later wrote.[11]

In Berlin, attachés worked hard to gauge the public reaction to these developments. 'There were few signs of the intense enthusiasm for the re-introduction of conscription reported in the German press,' observed one British representative. 'There was certainly not the enthusiasm shown for the *Führer* which one saw [for the king] at the Royal Wedding in London.' But some observers nonetheless felt that the omens for the outside world were not good. 'The situation in Central Europe is far less secure and there is a very general fear that Germany, as soon as she feels strong enough, will expand in that direction,' as one British report summarized. While 'it should not at present be assumed that Germany is determined to expand by force of arms in Central Europe.... there is no doubt that she intends to be strong enough to do so, if necessary'. Foreign governments badly needed to get a very accurate idea of the true strength of his armed forces, and what it would reach in the years ahead, in order to judge Hitler's true bargaining power and determine what options, including a preventive war, were open to anyone who stood in his way.[12]

10. German officer—Heinz Riechoff, quoted in Richard Suchenwirth *The Development of the German Air Force 1919–39* Pacific University Press (1984) 190. British officer—'What Should We Do?', Top Secret FO memorandum, 18 Sept 1938, FO 371/21659 TNA.

11. Major General Sir Kenneth Strong *Intelligence at the Top: Recollections of an Intelligence Officer* Cassell (1969) 32.

12. Royal wedding—'Report on a Visit to Germany', Mar 1935, WO 190/321 TNA. British report—'Note on German Rearmament', 6 Dec 1935, WO 190/377 TNA.

But seeing through the superficial veneer, and obtaining a true picture of Germany's capabilities, was no easy task for the British unless they looked to France or any other foreign source. Throughout the mid-1930s the SIS station in Berlin produced 400–500 reports each year but they contained relatively mundane material with limited value. And the SIS not only lacked 'human intelligence' on the ground but also recognized clear limits to the electronic intelligence-gathering that they also used.[13]

British signals intelligence was based at four secret sites—at Montrose, Cheadle, Waddington, and Scarborough—which constantly tracked German wireless transmissions, using the timing of the signals and the speed of the planes to locate new landing grounds and beacons. The experts at these four stations soon became highly familiar with the workings of the German armed forces, knowing such details as the individual call signs of each unit, as well as when and where that unit was being deployed. Efforts were made to discover the call signs of a private landing ground in Bavaria, which British Intelligence believed Hitler and his entourage were using to visit his retreat at Berchtesgaden, although the outcome is unknown.[14]

Equally, they got a good measure of the level of German organization. 'The general efficiency of these German Air Force stations is excellent', judged one of the British operatives. 'The faultless technical arrangements permit the personnel to demonstrate their super skill in manipulation.' He added that 'the excellent standard of manipulation by the [wireless] operators of this new German Air Force surpasses any previously known. The speed at which DF [direction-finding] bearings are obtained and passed to aircraft is remarkable.' Others concurred, pointing out that German wireless transmissions were 'of a remarkably high standard [and] the manipulation of all operators is excellent... the operators show much intelligence in listening through and selecting the precise moment to transmit which will avoid interference to their own stations who are working at the same time. This is rendered easier by virtue of the very short transmissions normally made.'[15]

13. SIS Berlin—Jeffery 279.
14. 'German Air Force', May 1935, HW 2/11 TNA.
15. 'German Air Force', Mar 1935, HW 2/11 TNA.

However, this kind of electronic eavesdropping had real limitations, which the operators themselves openly acknowledged. 'Unlike our own and certain other foreign air forces', as one report ran, 'the German Air Force stations pass extremely few telegrams by wireless and in order to discover the positions or identities of these stations, other evidence than wireless telegrams must be utilised.' Additional sources of information, in other words, were vital.[16]

Besides Agent Asche and 'L', the French intelligence services had also found a number of other sources of information inside Germany. Amongst them were trade union representatives, who not only had first-hand knowledge of what was happening within Hitler's factories but who were, in many cases, viscerally opposed to the National Socialist Party. In August 1935, for example, a Deuxième Bureau report flagged an undercover meeting on French soil, at an undisclosed location 'close to the German border', of twelve union representatives, all of whom were working on Germany's rearmament programme. The topics they discussed were of immense interest to the French spies, including 'the creation of illicit trade unions, with headquarters abroad, in armaments factories; strikes and sabotage inside those factories; the publication of an illegal journal for the companies that had arms factories; and reports from different delegates about German arms and their production'. Not long afterwards, two of the representatives, both working in Mannheim, were arrested by the Gestapo for espionage and illegal activities.[17]

Other reports reached the Bureau of meetings of representatives of banned German unions, sometimes on French soil or in Switzerland, to discuss organizing strikes and spreading illegal propaganda at home. In August 1936, for example, the exiled German Communist Party, which had headquarters in Zurich, took steps to strike up an informal alliance with Germany's embattled Catholics, 'whose own struggle for their faith was just as much the struggle of every other enemy of Hitler and his barbaric dictatorship'. At around the same time, open letters were printed and circulated to these Catholics, urging them to unite

16. 'German Air Force: W/T Activity', AIR 2/1355 TNA.
17. 'Réunion de délégués des organisations illégales des usines allemandes', 21 Sept 1935, F/7/13434 AN.

and rise up against their 'oppressors', despite the best efforts of the police to suppress them.[18]

Viewing them as a possible source of vital information, the Bureau closely monitored the activities, inside the Reich, of Hitler's domestic opponents. This also helped them to gauge the strength and resilience of Hitler's regime: this was a vitally important issue because, if his regime faced meaningful opposition at home, then Hitler was clearly in much less of a position to resist foreign pressure. The Bureau's officers were particularly interested, for example, in a report of dissent within the SS and the SA that reached them in October 1936: when the Gestapo by chance came across information about Communist Party sympathizers in the Reich, they quickly swooped, making arrests, searching houses, and seizing arms—secretly stolen during military exercises—at the homes of some members of the Nazi Party. Another report that caught their interest concerned a group of communist militants, all former officers in the German army and veterans of units that had left-leaning sympathies during and immediately after the First World War. All were put on trial for disseminating anti-Hitler propaganda in Bavaria.[19]

There was another reason why foreign spy agencies were so interested in reports of domestic opposition. If this was financed or organized from abroad, or if this was even seen to be so, then it could lead to heightened tension with the foreign governments deemed responsible. So when, in October 1936, thousands of leaflets were distributed across Germany, calling for 'the German people to unite against 3,000 millionaires', Bureau officers wondered if the campaign had been financed by Moscow and organized by Komintern ('Communist International') agents based abroad. This was part of a wider upsurge in communist agitation inside Germany that alarmed the Nazi authorities, who held high-level meetings to discuss its sources—agitators in the Netherlands, France, and Belgium were considered the culprits—and work out ways of repressing it at home and monitoring it abroad.[20]

18. Unions—'A/S réunion de délégués', 10 Aug 1935, 7NN 2352 SHD. Alliance—'A/S d'un offre d'alliance', 5 Aug 1936; 'Activité du Parti communiste allemand', 23 Apr 1937, 7NN 2352 SHD. Open letters—Activité du Parti communiste allemand', 23 Apr 1937, 7NN 2352 SHD.

19. Gestapo raid—'Opération de Police', 5 Oct 1936, 7NN 2352 SHD. Trial—the units were the Oberland and Aufbruch divisions; Renseignement, 30 Nov 1935, 7NN 2352 SHD.

20. Oct 1936—'A/S de la propagande communiste en Allemagne', 19 Oct 1936, 7NN 2352 SHD. Upsurge—Répression des menées communistes en Allemagne, 18 Nov 1936, 7NN 2352 SHD.

A few weeks later, German communists started to use a transmitter, hidden inside a car that moved around on a daily basis to avoid detection, in a bid to stir up anti-Nazi sentiments inside the Reich. In the course of March, these became daily broadcasts which began between 9.30 and 10 pm, as the speaker urged the German nation to unite and rise up against Hitler to prevent further carnage in Europe. And on 28 April 1937 a more audacious message called for ordinary Germans to come into the streets on May Day. But the Deuxième Bureau noted with alarm that this car was 'close to the French border', although it was not clear if it was on German or French territory. More alarmingly, the transmitter used a shortwave frequency whose details were publicized not just by the underground press but also in the pages of the French communist newspaper *L'Humanité*, arousing fears of German retaliation.[21]

Meanwhile, Moravec's agents had also been busily headhunting potential recruits amongst well-placed Nazi officials and were reaping some significant rewards. For one day in April 1935, Moravec had been contacted by Captain Karel Sedlacek, his undercover agent who had by now been based in Zurich as a journalist for several months. He had some excellent news.

In Switzerland, Sedlacek had certainly had his mountains to climb—headhunting a German traitor was of course always immensely challenging—but he now had a prize in his sights: a senior Luftwaffe officer who was willing to sell secrets.

For long weeks and months, and over successive days and evenings, Moravec's agent had kept close and careful watch on some of the numerous German tourists who made their way in and around Zurich. He quickly discovered the places they frequented—the restaurants, clubs, and resorts, many of which were expensive venues that any visitors would need a sizeable income to enjoy. There he not only listened out for any German speakers but searched for signs that they might be linked with the military. Sometimes someone looked the part, or might have a distinctive bearing that gave the game away. At other times an unusually polished pair of shoes might reflect a military background. Then he looked for indications of lavish spending, and

---

21. Broadcasts—'A/S Poste émetteur communiste allemand', 5 Mar 1937, 7NN 2352 SHD. 28 Apr—'A/S Activité du Parti communiste allemand', 30 Apr 1937, 7NN 2352 SHD.

wondered if the off-duty soldier was spending more money than he could really afford.

A few months before, in November 1934, Sedlacek's efforts began to pay off when he introduced himself to a senior German air force officer. Although at first unfriendly and taciturn, Major Salm had eventually admitted that he needed 'a lot of money' because of his expensive way of life. Although he worked at a high level, as a member of the Luftwaffe's general staff, and had a good salary, he just couldn't make ends meet. Before long, in early January 1935, he declared his interest in the cash payments that this 'journalist' was offering him, supposedly for good stories about what was happening inside Germany.

So important was this new source of information that Moravec soon travelled to Zurich to meet him. Salm was 'the epitome of the Prussian officer', bearing a monocle and a moustache as well as 'a scar on his cheek, so perfect that it looked artificial'. To begin with, he thought that the Prussian was a rather unappealing character but then found, as they got talking and his personality shone through, that he was revising his initial, superficial impression.[22]

Moravec felt that the Prussian was genuine but he wanted to be absolutely sure. Explaining that he and Sedlacek were working for the Czech intelligence services and were not really 'journalists' at all, he gave Salm a significant initial payment as a token of good faith, together with a questionnaire detailing some of the questions that he needed answers to. This initial questionnaire really comprised trick questions. Moravec knew the right answers but needed to match these against Salm's responses: even if Salm's intentions were honourable, he might not have access to the information he claimed.

A few weeks later, Moravec had the information he wanted to see. Salm dropped off a completed questionnaire to an anonymous post office box, as instructed, and it immediately became obvious that he was genuine. Salm was now Agent 52, or A–52 for short, and had become one of Moravec's most highly prized assets. Moravec immediately compiled another questionnaire, promising another very generous payment in return.

Not long afterwards, at a secret rendezvous in Zurich, Salm handed Moravec a batch of documents. The spy chief could barely contain his excitement. Before him, on a table, were the Luftwaffe's most closely guarded secrets, including all the details about its existing strength—its

22. Moravec 60–1.

real strength—as well as its planned expansion over the coming year, together with blueprints, specifications, performance figures, and other technical data. But the price tag was even heftier than Moravec expected because Salm casually demanded a million Czech crowns, which was to be paid in US dollars. But without a moment of hesitation the spy chief nodded his agreement. This document had huge repercussions for the national security of his country, as well as so many others, and his government would be quite willing to pay the price.

The two men met twice more, at the same venue in Zurich, and on both occasions Salm handed over two big files. On each occasion, he demanded, in return, the same enormous fee as before. On each occasion, Moravec paid it, and again did so without hesitation.

Major Salm was by this time a very wealthy man indeed but he was of course playing the most dangerous game. Moravec urged him not to spend lavishly, as he was so inclined to do, and thereby attract immediate attention from German counter-espionage agencies. But it seems his advice was ignored. The following summer, the two men arranged another covert meeting in Zurich and Moravec waited patiently for his star agent, who was usually punctual, to arrive. But, on this occasion, there was no sign at all of A-52. Unknown to Moravec, he had already been arrested and suffered the same fate as Benita von Falkenhayn and so many other traitors to the Nazi regime: imprisonment in one of the most feared places in the Reich, Plötzensee Prison in Berlin, where the executioner's axe fell.

But the Czechs had successfully run A-52 for over a year and shared Major Salm's information with their French counterparts, using the joint command post that they had set up between themselves the previous year and which in late 1935 was still working well. In addition, senior officials from the two departments met twice a year, once in Paris and then in Prague, to exchange information. But the Czechs were by this time becoming disillusioned with their French allies. Although Moravec had initially informed his chief French contact, Major Henri Gouyou, about his breakthrough, he privately regarded the Frenchman as 'well-meaning but bumbling'. And while the French showed a 'hear-no-evil, see-no-evil' attitude which 'seemed to be the norm in Paris' and doubted the authenticity of the material Moravec now offered, the British reacted 'promptly and with vigour'.[23]

Moravec thought very highly of Major Harold 'Gibby' Gibson, the head of the British Intelligence operation in Prague. Gibson, like everyone else, made mistakes—later on, he was severely reprimanded by his superiors for a 'gross error of judgment'—but he was affable and incorruptible, and struck up a good rapport with the Czech spy chief, who now handed him Salm's information. In London it added a great deal of weight to those individuals, in the world of politics, the armed forces, and the civil service, who were demanding that the British should now rearm at a much greater pace.[24]

This realignment in the intelligence world, as Moravec moved away from Paris and closer to his British counterparts, meant that the SIS and the British government were now less dependent than before on the cooperation and goodwill of the Deuxième Bureau to find out what was happening inside Germany.

This made an Anglo-French alliance even less likely. In the weeks that followed Hitler's March announcements, it seemed possible that Britain might finally cede to French wishes and even strike up the alliance that French officials had long wanted. In mid-April, the British prime minister, Ramsay MacDonald, met his French counterpart, Pierre-Étienne Flandin, and the Italian *duce* Benito Mussolini at Stresa, where they agreed to respect the Locarno Treaty, signed a decade before: Western Europe's existing borders, they proclaimed, must stay intact. But any hopes of a British and French alliance were soon dashed by sharp diplomatic disagreements. One source of dispute was a naval agreement that the British negotiated with Berlin without even consulting their French counterparts (Chapter 11). The other concerned Abyssinia, which the Italian army invaded in October. In British eyes, the French behaved in an untrustworthy and unreliable way, as Pierre Laval walked along a diplomatic tightrope in an unsuccessful bid to retain the friendships of both Britain and Italy. The two nations were still separated by clear blue water.

---

24. Mistakes—in Apr 1939 Gibson was severely reprimanded for erroneously telling British journalists about an impending anti-Jewish pogrom in Prague. Memo from Gladwyn Jebb, 17 Apr 1939, FO 371/23007 TNA. Greater pace—Moravec 61.

10

Searching for New Sources of Information

Throughout the 'honeymoon period' that began in the spring of 1935, assessments of Germany's true strength, and its motives, continued to fluctuate wildly. In Whitehall, for example, estimates and predictions of the Luftwaffe's strength varied considerably, as desk officers sparred in a war of interdepartmental, and intradepartmental, rivalry.[1]

Foreign intelligence services needed to obtain a much more exact picture of what was really happening inside the Reich. In one sense, this seemed much easier than before because the German authorities were now inviting foreign guests to visit some of the factories and military sites whose existence they had sometimes not even previously acknowledged. But from an intelligence point of view, these visits rarely rendered any meaningful clues, even to the professional eye, because such trips were so carefully stage-managed and choreographed: the actors were keeping much hidden from the eyes of their audience.

Other countries, further afield than Britain, France, Poland, and Czechoslovakia, potentially had some important information to offer. One such source was the Soviet Union. In May 1935, galvanized into action by the shock announcements that Hitler had made a few weeks before, the Soviets had signed defence treaties 'of mutual assistance' firstly with Paris, and then, a fortnight later, with the Czech government.

---

1. Wesley K Wark, 'British Intelligence on the German Air Force 1933-9', *HJ* (1982) 627-48.

The agreement with Prague included the sharing of intelligence on the Third Reich.

But for the Czechs at least, it soon became clear that the Soviets did not have any information of value to offer. Moravec visited Moscow on several occasions to meet his counterparts and to exchange notes about German rearmament but soon discovered that his hosts knew almost nothing about the Nazis' plans. Although they were keen to find out as much as they could from Moravec, making copious notes about everything that he and his fellow Czech officers told them, they had nothing of value to tell their visitors. 'They revealed great gaps in their knowledge of such data', as he later wrote, adding that he was sure that such ignorance was genuine: 'during a six-day detailed discussion, an Intelligence expert can tell whether the other side is faking ignorance or genuinely lacks the knowledge. The Russians of 1936 did not have the knowledge.'[2]

This may have been because of the prohibitive distance between Moscow and the German border, which may have given the Soviet leadership a false sense of security. Equally, the Soviets did not have a shared border with Germany—Poland stood in the way—and this made it much harder to run agents. It was more likely, however, that the Soviet leadership was preoccupied with suppressing internal dissension and purging its domestic opponents to give any foreign threats the attention they deserved. The leaders of Soviet intelligence certainly were not noted for their longevity: Felix Dzerzhinsky had died suddenly in 1926, supposedly of a heart attack, while his successor, Vyacheslav Menzhinsky, was murdered in 1934, two years before Genrikh Yagod, whom Moravec met in Moscow, was arrested and executed.

Whatever the reason, from Moravec's viewpoint the downside of the Soviet–Czech relationship far outweighed any advantages. This was partly because of the mistrust and suspicion between them, particularly on the part of the Soviets, for whom such feelings were 'a normal state of mind'. But he also began to question the motives of his new allies, and when Moscow proposed stationing 100 of its trained intelligence officers on Czech soil to supposedly help them obtain more information about Germany, Prague immediately dismissed the idea out of hand as an unwarranted intrusion. Even the whiff of such

2. Moravec 69–70.

a deal was enough to arouse strong suspicions amongst the Poles, who soon withdrew their diplomatic representative from Prague in protest. Word of the Soviet suggestion may also have reached German ears and prompted Berlin to step up its drive for rearmament: Nazi officials sometimes privately justified their rearmament programme on the grounds of a supposed Moscow–Prague deal that allowed Soviet war-planes onto Czech soil, using fuel that the Czechs had specially stock-piled for them. Some British experts, who were well aware of the links between Moscow and Prague, felt that their claims were plausible.[3]

The rise of Nazi Germany was also causing concern in the United States, despite the strong isolationist sentiment that was prevalent there. Expressing the trauma of both economic depression as well as the experience of the First World War, such isolationism found strong sup-port across the political spectrum. Its advocates were determined to stop 'the killing of American boys in a struggle over the bean crop in Manchuria', and to end wars against what Senator Homer Bone called the 'megalomaniacs, egomaniacs and psychopaths, who are literally preparing to dip their hands in blood'. So vehement was such isola-tionist sentiment that the Senate had still not even ratified the Treaty of Versailles, and some leading figures regarded the League of Nations as a duplicitous way of pulling their country, and the wider New World, into the affairs of the old: as Senator James A. Reed of Missouri even warned, it would only work in favour of 'black, brown, yellow and red races, low in civilisation and steeped in barbarism'.[4]

However, some American officials in Berlin did have unofficial but close and productive working relations with their counterparts, not-ably the British and French. This was true of Major Truman Smith, who in August 1935 returned to the American embassy in Berlin as military attaché, tasked with acquiring information about the German armed forces and reporting it to G-2, the military intelligence division of the US War Department. Before long, he had close and regular con-tact with the British and French attachés: although there was no offi-cial transatlantic 'alliance' between them, there was a close bond and sense of trust that led to easy, informal exchanges of information.

3. Suspicions—Moravec 71. Nazi officials—'Notes on a conversation with General Wenninger', 6 July 1936, AIR 2/2797 TNA. British experts—'Increased German rearmament demands', 11 Mar 1935, WO 190/306 TNA.
4. Advocates—quoted in M Jonas *Isolationism in America 1933–41* Cornell University Press (1966) 72, 105.

Smith was a good choice for the job, being highly familiar with the country, which he had first visited in 1918 as an infantry soldier, and its language as well as with Hitler and his political party. However, he quickly found that gathering intelligence on the Reich was no easy task. This was not just because of the paucity of accurate information but also because of obstacles closer to hand. Despite the dramatic growth in the quality and quantity of the Luftwaffe, there was a marked lack of interest amongst his fellow Americans in air intelligence. This, as he later wrote, 'was in its early infancy and G-2 treated it as a foster child'. As a result, 'acquiring any information about the Luftwaffe was hard enough but a vastly more difficult task for my office than the similar one posed by the army expansion'. To make matters more difficult, there never had been more than one aviation officer at the embassy, and this meant that 'the gathering of air intelligence concerning the extremely rapid expansion of Göring's Luftwaffe' presented a true challenge. Above all, Smith felt that Washington was not taking the role and strength of the Luftwaffe, and Germany in general, seriously enough.[5]

Other obstacles stood in his way. Although G-2 itself was fairly well organized and staffed, it was also starved of cash, like so many other foreign intelligence services of the time, and 'the special intelligence group in the office of the chief of the Air Corps was small, poorly organized, and given little or no recognition for its work'. In addition, the American ambassador to Berlin, Dr William E Dodd, was at heart a committed pacifist who had little or no interest in military matters, including the gathering of intelligence. Within just a few weeks of arriving in the capital, Smith thought he detected a lack of ambassadorial interest in his own work. Smith's initial impression proved to be right: not once, over the next two years of his service in Berlin, did Dodd ever request any sort of briefing on German rearmament. In addition, Smith's assistant air attaché lacked not only intelligence training but any background in engineering and technical knowledge.[6]

Smith expected to encounter other challenges, since he was no newcomer to this line of work. At their elegant apartment in the Tiergarten district of the capital, Smith and his wife were kept under constant Abwehr surveillance and knew that their phone was tapped,

5. Gole 184–5.
6. Hessen 56, 79; see also General HH Arnold *Global Mission* Hutchinson (1951).

although he wrote later that 'I never let the surveillance interfere with my work or social life, particularly as there was no way to avoid it.' But this did not prevent him building up a good rapport with some big names in the Nazi hierarchy, of whom he wrote some compelling descriptions. Hermann Göring, he argued, 'would have been in his element as a sixteenth century renaissance prince [or] the despot of an Italian city-state of that age' because of 'his will to power, his love of luxury, his desire to be a patron of the arts, his geniality, his readiness to kill anyone who crossed his path'. He held no doubt at all about this latter point, adding that the Luftwaffe chief was 'formidable . . . dangerous and a killer'. Smith was not far wrong about a man who had once ordered his men to 'shoot first and ask questions afterwards' but whose powerful personality frequently overawed those who met him.[7]

Another leading Nazi whom Smith got to know and spent much time with was Erhard Milch, Göring's right-hand man and the secretary of state of the Air Ministry. Smith felt that he was a clever, insightful as well as affable leader, while he described another leading Luftwaffe official and champion pilot, Ernst Udet, as a charming individual and a 'good mixer' with a remarkable myriad of interests that ranged from cartoon-drawing to motorbike racing. He felt, however, that Udet had been promoted beyond his abilities, probably because of his personal rapport with Göring.[8]

Although he was an army man with no close knowledge of aviation, Smith was able to pick up a few clues from some site visits that his high-level contacts arranged: even the most stage-managed show could not always hide everything. In October 1935, for example, he was invited to visit the manufacturing works at Schonefeld, lying to the south-east of Berlin, that were run by the engineering firm Henschel. Smith was amazed not just by the size of the site but by its sophistication and planning. Above all, the installations were carefully planned to minimize the impact of enemy attacks: the hangars were widely spaced and each building had its own power plant, making the task of any enemy bombers much harder. It was in every respect an ultra-modern plant, easily on a technical par with anything the Americans had. This, of course, is what the Germans wanted to show, particularly to a visitor from a country, the United States, that they

7. Gole 197.
8. Gole 197.

feared. But they failed to disguise the fact that this hugely impressive site was manufacturing relatively obsolete planes: Smith was able to deduce that its production lines were really churning out long-outdated biplanes that would be no match for the latest fighters.[9]

But despite Smith's close personal rapport with other military attachés in Berlin, the British and French intelligence services appear to have had very limited input from any American sources of information about Germany. They were instead largely dependent on their own sources of intelligence, the fruits of which they continued to share together without revealing their origins.

Sometimes this information was shared by word of mouth between French officials and British representatives in Paris. One example was a French engineer, representing an aeronautical company, who was granted limited access to a number of Luftwaffe sites and whose observations were fed back firstly to the Deuxième Bureau and then to the air attaché at the British embassy in Paris.

The engineer was a potentially important source because visiting businessmen were not as closely monitored and their visits not as carefully arranged as those ceded to diplomats and VIPs. This individual deduced that German attempts to mass produce aircraft had failed and that many of their materials, including engines and airframes, were 'of a very inferior quality and not comparable in efficiency and fighting value to the aircraft possessed by other countries where slower and more painstaking methods of production are in vogue'. Such troubles, he continued, had prompted the Germans to modify their manufacturing processes. He concluded that 'in spite of its large numbers of aeroplanes the German Air Force will not be a first-class fighting service for at least eighteen months'.[10]

The British and French, and the Poles, also collaborated particularly closely over the supremely challenging task of code-breaking. This interaction had begun several years before when, in 1932, John Tiltman, a senior figure at the Government Code and Cypher School, had visited Paris to share knowledge and swap ideas on breaking Soviet codes with Bertrand's Section D. Bertrand remained in close touch with Tiltman and now showed him photos from Asche's documents,

---

9. Hessen 85.
10. Memo from Group Captain Colyer, 28 Dec 1936, FO 371/20732 TNA.

although the British were unable to help without an updated version of the machine.

There were setbacks in this relationship too. In May 1935, relations between the French and Polish spy services cooled even more when Paris signed a new security pact with Moscow, promising to 'lend each other reciprocal aid and assistance' in the event of 'unprovoked aggression' by Germany. From this moment on, as General Henri Castellan wrote later, 'Franco-Polish military collaboration never returned to the cordiality and trust of before'. On some matters, however, there was still a strong informal contact between specific departments and case officers: in particular, Major Bertrand remained in close touch with his Polish counterparts, making eight trips to Warsaw over the next four years, as they continued their efforts to crack the Enigma Code. Bertrand had been in close touch with Colonel Langer of the Polish Second Department ever since they had first met in December 1931, and the working relationship was close enough to survive the upset of 1935.[11]

By this time, the SIS could hardly dispense with the input of foreign governments, particularly when it was still very short of cash, under-staffed, and its personnel severely overworked. Nor did its case officers have enough cash to lure and bribe prospective agents. In October 1935, a 'most secret' government document on the intelligence services revealed how bad things were. 'The British Secret Intelligence Service has been constantly hampered, by lack of funds, in the performance of its duties,' its authors argued. This shortcoming, it continued, 'has been increasingly felt in recent years, during which other Nations have turned Great Britain's gesture in unilateral disarmament to account by seizing the opportunity to rearm secretly'. It pointed to the main culprit: 'the most glaring case in point has been that of Germany', its authors argued. 'Until the German authorities themselves made the facts public, practically the only sources of information on her rearmament were those available to the Secret Service, and it is a melancholy fact that the march of events has proved their informa-tion correct.'

Concluding that 'a great deal more could, and would, have been accomplished had the Service been in possession of adequate funds', the report also pointed out how the sums allocated to the spy services

11. Castellan 478.

paled into insignificance compared with the costs of maintaining, let alone building, just one Royal Navy destroyer, and the amounts that foreign governments admitted to spending on their own intelligence services. 'Living a hand to mouth existence, with vast areas to cover, it is, as things are, only possible for SIS to scratch the surface. To obtain really inside information means spending big money.' Although there were 'frequent opportunities' amongst disaffected Germans, 'the offer to them of a few hundred pounds a year, which represents the amount usually available, is naturally treated by them with contempt'. Given such limitations, it was 'indeed remarkable that such results have been achieved at all'.[12]

It was not long before the British government relented and increased the intelligence budget but, as Christopher Andrew has written, 'there is no doubt that right up to the outbreak of war SIS was hampered by a shortage of funds. Until 1939 it was unable even to afford wireless sets for its agents'. The Intelligence Service remained severely over-stretched, confronted with numerous other priorities other than the Reich: these included keeping a close eye on events in Spain and Italy, the surveillance of Eire, and dealing with requests from the Admiralty to track the passage of ships, particularly through Scandinavian waters and near the Low Countries. The head of the SIS station in Brussels, for example, was tasked with assessing Luftwaffe strength when he received a sudden and urgent request from the Admiralty to produce naval information.[13]

Nonetheless, the British began to establish their own sources of information that made them less dependent than before on the French intelligence reports. Until now, the SIS had sorely lacked the high-grade information from a well-placed insider comparable to Agent Asche. But as increasing numbers of Germans became more alarmed by Hitler's belligerence, so were well-placed insiders more likely to make their approaches. This had important political repercussions because it allowed the British government to resist French pressure to strike up a defensive alliance.

Not long after the 'Saturday of Surprises', one such approach was made to Frederick Winterbotham, who was at this time acting as a

---

12. 'Memorandum on Secret Service Funds', 9 Oct 1935, CAB 127/371 TNA; Hinsley 51.
13. Andrew 377. SIS Brussels—Gill Bennett *Churchill's Man of Mystery: Desmond Morton and the World of Intelligence* Routledge (2006) 192.

British undercover agent, well connected with Nazi officialdom and, through the influence of William de Ropp, well known in Berlin. In the German capital, a high-ranking Nazi official had heard about Winterbotham and decided to make a direct, and anonymous, approach.[14]

One day in 1935, a letter reached the British Embassy marked for the Englishman's attention, even though he did not work there and did not even have any official connection with it. Winterbotham was at this time living in Britain and only occasionally visited Germany. But the SIS staff knew that it could perhaps be important and immediately forwarded it to him, using their closely guarded diplomatic bags.

Winterbotham was amazed when he opened the envelope and found inside a simple piece of paper, 'about ten inches by eight [which] was obviously a photo of a single page from a book'. Clearly marked *GEHEIM!* ('Secret!'), it was entitled 'The Establishment of Flying Schools' and listed the codenames and exact locations of twenty-five sites throughout Germany. Wondering if it was a hoax or a trap, he scanned the list carefully and cross-matched it against the limited amount of information that he already had obtained. He could quickly tell that at least some of the contents were undoubtedly correct and that the anonymous source, whoever he or she was, was most likely to be genuine.

He had no way of contacting the donor and could only wait patiently to see what would happen next. His patience was rewarded when, a few weeks later, another letter followed in the same manner as before, addressed to and forwarded by the Berlin Embassy.

Inside were more copies from the same document, which Winterbotham called 'Göring's Bible', although this time from different pages. Now, before him, were the details of an entirely new German fighter squadron that he knew nothing at all about. It was, as he later wrote, 'almost too good to be true. It is in fact hard to describe my reaction to these photographs.' There was, however, one condition: heavily underlining his words for extra emphasis, the source insisted that his information, and everything about their contact, should be a British-kept secret and that on no account would the French intelligence services learn anything about it: echoing Neville Chamberlain's views, the source felt that the French 'can never keep a secret for more

---

14. Winterbotham *Nazi Connection* Ch 6 *passim*.

than half an hour'. Despite Winterbotham's close contact and personal
affinity with Colonel Ronin, he was determined to do as the informer
asked.[15]

Several more similar photocopies arrived in the course of 1935, all
providing Winterbotham with more important information. One of
these included details of the Stuka dive-bomber and the special training that its pilots were being given: once again, this tallied with the
accounts he had heard from the young German pilots he had met in
the course of his travels throughout the Reich. But still the source
remained mysterious, even though this second letter gave an address in
the suburbs of Berlin that Winterbotham could use to contact him, or
her, indirectly. The SIS officer could only assume that his anonymous
contact was 'someone on Göring's staff who was either violently anti-
Nazi or extremely greedy'. To begin with, it seemed likely that the
informer was motivated more by conviction, without asking for anything in return. But then, suddenly, the source demanded a big payment
in return for more information. All the earlier leaks of information
had, after all, just been an attempt to whet the appetite of British
Intelligence.

Cash-strapped though it was, the SIS was willing to put up the
money: he needed an eye-watering sum, Winterbotham told his bosses,
but was worth sacrificing other, less important expenses in order to
concentrate on this one: in the words of one of his French counterparts, 'a major source of information has the value of ten lesser ones,
sometimes doesn't cost any more and wastes much less time'. He had
already received six reports in the space of a few months, he continued,
and all had been hugely valuable and proved the informer's worth.[16]

Arrangements were soon made to transfer the funds to this intriguing recipient. One afternoon, an SIS operative, middle-aged, respect-
ably dressed, bespectacled, and moustached, took a train from Hamburg
to central Berlin, bearing two small suitcases which he left in a locker
in the luggage department. He then posted the locker key to the
address that the contact had given them. Within a day or two, another
middle-aged man appeared at the station to pick the luggage up, leaving the station as quickly, quietly, and anonymously as he had first

15. French secrets—Feiling 322.
16. French counterpart—'La Situation de l'Allemagne', 1 Jan 1930; Plan de Renseignements,
    11 Jan 1930, 7NN 2530 SHD.

arrived. Everything had gone smoothly. 'It was the perfectly straight-forward copybook method of transferring payment.' Almost at once, highly confidential, and hugely important, reports continued to flow to London, and by the end of 1938 Winterbotham had acquired at least thirty photocopies of the Luftwaffe's supposedly top-secret plans, all of which helped him to persuade his seniors in Whitehall of the urgent need to undertake a massive programme of rearmament. Stunned, intrigued, and grateful, Winterbotham hoped to meet his source but the opportunity never arose.[17]

Highly valuable, top-secret information continued to flow from other high-level sources. In Berlin, a disgruntled Luftwaffe colonel provided Frank Foley with copies of top-secret documents in return for significant amounts of cash, although these contacts were later broken off. However, impressive though such contacts were, they failed in their most important respect: despite causing alarm in Whitehall, key decision-makers did not initiate any programme of British rearmament until early 1937. Even then, it was very limited, much more so than its critics, like Churchill and Vansittart, demanded.[18]

But such sources of information did allow the British to steer a delicate course of action. On the one hand, they were keeping on close terms with the French, Poles, and Czechs. In particular, the head of the SIS was forced to admit that his cash-strapped organization 'had to depend more and more on French information'. On the other, they had enough information of their own to avoid striking up a closer relationship that could have led towards an alliance. But the rapidly growing German threat would soon be pushing them closer together.[19]

---

17. Winterbotham wrote that the source ceased contact on the outbreak of war in 1939 and failed to turn up to a rendezvous that Winterbotham had arranged in Zurich. He never met this source and, in his memoirs, gives no indication of his identity. *Nazi Connection* 138.

18. Michael Smith *Foley: The Spy Who Saved 10,000 Jews* Hodder & Stoughton (1999) 83; the pro-appeasement ambassador, Sir Nevile Henderson, seems to have ordered the end of the affair.

19. SIS head—Hinsley 51.

II

Spying on the German Navy

One afternoon in the summer of 1931, a young German naval officer finished his shift and cycled out of the closely guarded security zone that surrounded the giant Kiel shipyard, on the Baltic coast, to get home. The guards saw him most days and always let him pass unchallenged, watching him make his way around the barrier.

But if, on this occasion, they had stopped and carefully searched 34-year-old Bruno Rollman, then the guards would have found material of 'considerable importance to German national security'. These included blueprints and negatives of some of the German navy's most precious secrets, including the development of a new torpedo, a type of artificial smoke, and the cannons for a new cruiser, the *Deutschland*. Instead, Rollman now headed straight home with these materials hidden carefully in his clothing, and then, together with his brother, Henri, got ready to contact the French intelligence services.[1]

The Nazi authorities eventually encircled and busted 'the Kiel Spy Ring', raiding a number of houses and making a series of arrests that began in August 1931 and ended four months later. They discovered that Rollman, and several other junior officers and technicians, such as Gustave Gallande and a 32-year-old signalman called Karl Seck, had previously been in contact with French intelligence officers, who had written to them, using false names, from a sham address in Boulogne. They found out, too, that Rollman had been preparing to travel to Belgium to meet his mysterious contact, and had hidden his top-secret information, together with his passport, in a briefcase which he had smuggled into the home of an unsuspecting relative. These traitors, the

---

1. Considerable importance—'La procédure engagée pour trahison', 25 Apr 1932, 7NN 3365 SHD.

Kiel authorities decided, had the potential to inflict 'considerable damage'.[2]

German investigators quickly noticed the personal weaknesses that had driven these men to betray their own country: Gallande was 'a high-spender who spent much of his free nights in bars', while Seck frequented the prostitutes of Kiel, as well as having connections with a female friend in Berlin. They, and others involved in this spy ring, had given themselves away by falling into the same old trap of spending in too lavish and ostentatious a manner, which had been quickly spotted by the highly trained undercover security agents at the naval base. The French spies were of course dismayed by their loss but there was at least a silver lining. As a result of the investigation that followed, they were able to obtain names of other suspects who they thought might have potential as future spies: the Deuxième Bureau was determined to 'focus all the means at our disposal' and 'to undertake a very close but discreet eye' on the base to obtain, above all, 'the design details of a new type of torpedo'.[3]

The Bureau's desk officers had clearly had some success in infiltrating the German Navy, even if it remains unclear just how much information they actually received from the Kiel Spy Ring. And over the next few years, they were successful at finding other sources of information, notably an informer inside the industrial giant Siemens, who told them about the development of a new torpedo, which left no trail in its wake as it headed towards its target. But throughout the 1930s, such successes did not bring London and Paris closer together. On the contrary, both the British government and its intelligence service regarded maritime matters as their own affair and saw no reason to closely cooperate with the French over the issue.[4]

This partly reflected the fact that the Royal Navy was virtually indistinguishable from the status and grandeur of Great Britain as an imperial power. This had been true since at least the time of the Seven Years War (1756–63), when the nation's maritime strength played a vital role in creating, establishing, and defending the British Empire, often at the expense of France. And now a powerful navy was now

2. 'Rapport', 19 Dec 1931, 7NN 3365 SHD.
3. Investigators—Renseignements, 10 Mar 1938, 7NN 3365 SHD. Bureau—'La procédure engagée pour trahison', 25 Apr 1932, 7NN 3365 SHD.
4. Informer—'Constructions et Fabrications pour la Marine', 30 Nov 1935, 7NN 3114 SHD.

vital if Britain was to defend its sprawling empire, particularly against
a coalition of Germany, Italy, and Japan, whose coordinated action
represented the worst nightmare of Whitehall strategists.

But the historic association between Britain and its fleet was not
just a matter of national pride but also one of survival. As an island
power, Great Britain was particularly dependent on the shipped import
of food, oil, and other vital resources in a way that its landed continental neighbours were not. Because it was a geographically much larger
country with several landed borders, France was more able to move
vital supplies over land. Equally, it could ship its imports across much
more diverse sea lanes, stretching all the way from the Mediterranean
as far as the North Sea, than the British had at their disposal. The Royal
Navy, in other words, kept Britain and its empire afloat.

British vulnerability to a naval blockade had become clear during
the First World War. In February 1915, Kaiser Wilhelm had vowed to
sink any ships sailing through British waters, threatening to starve the
population into surrender. His plan was thwarted by the might of the
Royal Navy but British strategists knew that its supremacy was under
constant threat. Above all, the Germans had recognized the potential
of submarines and could use them, in conjunction with aerial cover, to
dominate the North Sea. But by the time Hitler came to power, the
SIS, and other foreign spy agencies, were desperately short of hard facts
about the state of German naval rearmament.

The Admiralty disregarded French intelligence on this matter, however, and this was to some extent understandable. The French only
operated two intelligence-gathering stations that focused on the
Reich's ports and shipyards, one of which was located at Metz and the
other at Dunkerque. In Paris, the Italian navy was instead deemed to
be a much more important strategic threat to French interests than the
German because it had a much stronger presence in the Mediterranean,
threatening the French connection with its fiefdoms in North and
West Africa. For this reason, the most important French naval intelligence post, whose budget was three times greater than the Metz and
Dunkerque stations combined, was the *service de recherches* in Toulon
that kept close watch on Mussolini's ships in the area.[5]

Lacking detailed information about German naval ambitions and
capabilities, French intelligence reports are generally silent or hollow

5. Jackson *France and the Nazi Menace* 35.

on such matters until the late 1930s. In early 1934, for example, the Bureau concluded only that the 'question of submarines (in Berlin) remains provisionally set aside for diplomatic reasons', and despite the gathering pace of German rearmament, none of its monthly or weekly bulletins of that year make any mention of German submarine construction. The Bureau did not even produce clear evidence of a submarine-building programme in Germany until just weeks before the first U-boat was actually commissioned in April 1935.[6]

British disdain towards the state of French naval intelligence became clear during an episode in late 1934, when the Deuxième Bureau obtained some information suggesting that submarines were under construction in the Krupp shipyard at Kiel. On 31 October a French spy chief, Captain Chevalier, informed the British naval attaché in Paris that the Germans were building five submarines on the slipways at the site. Estimating each vessel to be about 100 feet in length, he produced a sketch and photograph of the slipways, although it was too blurred and indistinct to be of any real value.[7]

The French intelligence report was accurate because Hitler and Admiral Erich Raeder had secretly ordered work to start on the construction of six 250-ton submarines, which were concealed inside large huts covering the slipways. But British officials were, quite unreasonably, very sceptical. In Whitehall, a senior diplomat, Robert Craigie, observed that 'the French have had stories of this kind before, and we could not confirm them'. And in Berlin, Sir Eric Phipps argued that 'in the past the French government have been so anxious to prove breaches of the treaty that they have exaggerated, and few of their accusations have proved justified'. The French had mistaken submarines for minesweepers, he continued. In fact, it was Captain Muirhead-Gould, the British naval attaché in Berlin, who had been fooled by the deceptions of the Kiel authorities, who had painted the identification numbers of six new minesweepers on the iron fencing outside the slipways. Although the French were probably attempting to pry further information from the Admiralty—Chevalier's claims were not even mentioned in the Bureau's regular reports, suggesting that they were forwarded to London for a reason other than their supposed value—an opportunity for closer collaboration between the two countries had nonetheless been lost.[8]

Whitehall's protective attitude towards maritime affairs, which it regarded as of limited or no real interest to others, also caused a rift with Paris in the summer of 1935. This disagreement focused upon a naval pact that the British signed with Berlin on 18 June. Desperate for more information about the state of the German navy, Whitehall had been lured to the negotiating table by Admiral Raeder's promises to volunteer 'the fullest information' about his capabilities before striking a deal.

At first sight, the agreement seemed innocuous enough because it placed a clear limit on the size of the German navy, which was now not allowed to exceed more than 35 per cent of the strength of the Royal Navy by the end of 1942. But in Paris, French officials were furious that the British had repudiated the Versailles Treaty without even consulting them: the British, they argued, had betrayed the common front they had proclaimed at Stresa just weeks before. As Robert Vansittart admitted, 'we broke an agreement...that we should only release Germany from restrictions as part of a general settlement' that would include France.'We asked for trouble. The French Anglophobes all came to the surface; our Francophobes carped back.' While the French government was striking a pact with Moscow and seeking to maintain the Versailles Treaty, the British were doing their own thing and openly undermining it.[9]

Any British querulousness may have revealed some bitterness over what they regarded as the diplomatic intransigence of some French officials. 'A year ago, they [the Germans] would have accepted a peace establishment of 300,000 men and equality with France,' wrote one dismayed senior official, 'but French intransigence and our failure to make the French government appreciate the realities of the situation have led inevitably to the German declaration' of March 1935. But whatever lay behind it, the Naval Agreement had created rifts between Britain, France, and Italy just weeks after Stresa. The agreement

8. Craigie—Jackson *France and the Nazi Menace* 136. Phipps—22 Nov 1934, FO 371/17765 TNA. Muirhead-Gould—J Maiolo *The Royal Navy and Nazi Germany 1933–39: A Study in Appeasement and the Origins of the Second World War* Palgrave Macmillan (1998) 29–30.
9. Vansittart, *The Mist Procession* Hutchinson (1958) 527.

therefore represented, in Raeder's phrase, a 'political success' for the Germans.[10]

The Naval Agreement had another unfortunate consequence because Hitler doubtlessly thought that British flexibility was due to his military bluster and threats. During his long hours of after-dinner 'table talk', he mentioned how effectively the British could be bullied into submission. 'I have always been the greatest friend of an Anglo-German understanding', as the German leader later stated, because 'the British mentality ... can only be influenced by force'. And when referring to a meeting with Sir John Simon, Hitler noted that 'only when I assured him that the German air force had reached the strength of that of the English, were we able to express ourselves with mutual respect; thus our naval agreement came into being'.[11]

From a more narrowly military viewpoint, the agreement also represented a major victory for Berlin since it allowed Germany to considerably increase the size of its fleet, and to harbour as many submarines as the British, even though the Versailles Treaty had banned them from having any. But although British admirals were hopeful that a number of new British inventions, notably the 'Asdic' detection system, would give them the edge over enemy submarines in the event of war, they still urgently needed to know more about what Hitler and his admirals were doing.

Before and after the 1935 agreement, the British were desperately short of information about the German navy. They had almost no signals intelligence on the matter, since the Government Code and Cypher School was focused on breaking Japanese and Italian codes, and because the Enigma machine was at this time unbreakable. And in Berlin, Captain Muirhead-Gould relied almost entirely on official German statements because the Nazi authorities denied him the same freedom to visit dockyards that his RAF counterparts were granted to inspect some airfields: they knew, of course, that it was much easier to hide aircraft in their hangars than to conceal enormous ships that were stationary on a slipway during long months, or years, of construction. They relented only in November 1934, when Muirhead-Gould made his first authorized visit to Wilhelmshaven. Just hours before he was due to arrive, a Nazi official informed him that two new capital ships

10. Senior official—'Note on a visit to Berlin', 14–22 Mar 1935, WO 190/321 TNA.
11. DGFP, D, I, p 342.

were being built there but would release no further details, prompting Muirhead-Gould to spend the rest of the winter trying to find out more. He ended up relying upon his 'intuition', which told him that they were being built as battlecruisers or simply as enlarged pocket battleships.[12]

The perilous state of intelligence-gathering on Hitler's navy had become clear in March 1935, when Admiralty chiefs penned a memorandum on 'German Naval Construction'. In essence, this document amounted, in the words of Wesley Wark, to 'a confession of the Admiralty's state of ignorance'. The Naval Intelligence Division couldn't be sure if Germany was already building submarines but did think it was 'possible' that another heavy cruiser, in addition to the one the Germans admitted to, was in the process of being constructed. It was 'probable', the report went on, that the two capital ships at Wilhelmshaven were intended to be 'battleships or battlecruisers', though it gave no details of any sort. Whitehall's state of ignorance became all the more evident when, the following month, Admiral Raeder announced that he was building twelve submarines, catching the Royal Navy by surprise and prompting Whitehall to hasten talks with Berlin in order to prevent further 'surprises'. On naval intelligence, the British were not keeping their heads above water.[13]

But the British did have one high-level informer inside the Reich who kept them well informed, if clearly not intimately so, on the state of the German navy.

In or around the summer of 1919, a naval engineer called Karl Krüger had approached the SIS and offered his services as an inside source of information on the German navy. It is possible, although it remains unclear, that he had appeared on the radar of the British Intelligence station in The Hague because of his affiliations with a Dutch company, Inkavos, that was secretly helping the German navy to develop submarines.[14]

Krüger was more than just an average naval engineer. During the Great War, he had held a senior position as the head of engineering at the Kiel shipyard. Later, in the 1930s, he was elected to the board of

12. Wesley Wark, 'Baltic Myths and Submarine Bogeys: British Naval Intelligence and Nazi Germany 1933–9', Journal of Strategic Studies (1983) 66.
13. Wark 'Baltic Myths' 67; 25 Mar 1935, FO 371/18860 TNA. Raeder—Wark 'Baltic Myths' 67.
14. Maiolo 29.

directors of the Federation of German Industries, before being awarded
an honorary degree by a German academic institute. By this time,
'Dr K.' had also set up a successful business as a consultant naval engineer and won a great deal of business, nearly all of which was based at
the Germaniawerft shipyard in Kiel, with the German navy.

Aware of his abilities and experience as a naval engineer, and keen
to keep a close eye on the state of any future German rearmament, the
British recruited him as a spy, offering to pay him generously for any
information. Throughout the 1920s and early 1930s, he kept the SIS
closely informed of Germany's covert submarine programme, drawing
much of his information from a series of secret experiments that the
German navy undertook in Finland, Spain, and Holland.

Anxious to protect their source, the SIS would have trained him
carefully. Krüger would have to assume, his handlers would have
warned him, that his every movement was being watched and photographed. He would have been told not to put anything in writing, nor
say anything revealing over the phone, nor meet any intelligence
contact unless it was carefully arranged and absolutely necessary. For
the risks he was taking, he would also have been rewarded for his
information: the SIS offered him 'a very handsome bonus', adding that
'a considerable sum would be available for payment to the officer
himself, such sum being dependent on the position he held and the
consequent value of his information'.[15]

Throughout the 1930s, 'Agent 016' sent his handlers a myriad of
reports, including information on the Luftschutzbund, an air defence
organization that he temporarily worked for, and on the state of naval
shipbuilding: one of his most notable feats was to take, in great secrecy
and at huge personal risk, several photos of German destroyers being
fitted out at Kiel. But it was on the pressing question of submarine
construction that Krüger's information was particularly vital.[16]

In March 1935, Krüger had informed London that the Germans
already had ten submarines under construction and were preparing to
build many more. His report prompted the SIS to conclude that there
were 'strong indications' that the Germans were 'already constructing
several submarines'. Muirhead-Gould disputed Krüger's claims but
much of the confusion over this matter was due to the fact that the

15. Jeffery 299.
16. Photos—Jeffery 299.

first flotilla of German submarines really comprised only very small training boats. Then, in the course of 1936, Krüger sent more valuable information about the secret life of the Germaniawerft shipyard. He confirmed British suspicions that the Germans had already built their first submarines, evading detection by assembling prefabricated sections on the slipway and then surreptitiously putting them together. Research was being undertaken 'daily' at Kiel, he continued, notably in a 'specially constructed' workshop where German engineers were trialling a prototype. He was also able to supply information about a new, larger U-boat that the Germans were starting to use but keeping carefully submerged from view: because the Turkish government placed orders for this 740-ton Type IX through Inkavos, Krüger was able to provide drawings of its design.[17]

From his sources, Krüger was able to judge that the German admirals were planning to produce a staggering output of around eighty-seven submarines ever year, vastly exceeding British estimates of annual output only of between four and six submarines. Up to 4,000 workers, working round the clock, were involved in this programme. Krüger was unaware, however, that Raeder had grossly inflated Germany's true capabilities, which were badly hampered by serious shortages of raw materials.[18]

But invaluable though such information was, Krüger clearly had his limitations as an intelligence source. He was not a high-ranking officer within the German navy and, living in Bad Godesberg rather than Berlin, he was not privy to its innermost secrets. He had limited access to just one of several shipyards and after 1934 his reports about the submarine programme were often sporadic. This was because Inkavos was now sidelined from the construction of new U-boats, all of which were placed under constant cover in large huts at Kiel and kept well away from prying eyes.

The British needed much better information because by this time there were growing doubts that the Germans were keeping to the terms of the 1935 agreement. One well-connected Englishman, for example, had learned that Admiral Raeder cheerfully 'admits that the Naval Treaty has already for quite a time been violated. False statistics,

17. Strong indications—Wark 'Baltic Myths' 67. Drawings—Maiolo 105.
18. British estimates—Wark 'Baltic Myths' 87; 'Germany: Submarine Construction', 8 Apr 1936, CAB 104/29 TNA.

according to the admiral, had been given regarding the size of surface and underwater ships, their armaments and protective armour plating.' The Germans, he continued, 'fully intended from the start to carry on at full speed the construction of U-Boats', and were currently building models that were perfectly suited to operations in the North Sea—in other words, against Great Britain.[19]

More indications of Berlin's bad faith emerged. In early November 1936, 'information given under a pledge of secrecy by German interests hostile to the Hitler government' based in Prague gave British officials an alarming, if unverifiable, indication about the true state of German naval rearmament. 'A dockyard for U-boats is being constructed' at Emden, the informants told RH Hadow, and there was 'feverish activity' at Wilhelmshaven where 'the naval base is being enlarged [and] new locks are now larger than those which sufficed during the war of 1914'. The report added that 12,000 labourers were working round the clock to manufacture battleships and torpedoes as well as submarines, and that thirty-six giant cranes had been installed in full working order to deal with the new demands. 'A similar warship', whose details and dimensions were unclear, was also under construction at the Blohm & Voss yard in Hamburg. Eyewitness accounts also emerged, such as the retiring Italian naval attaché who visited Kiel and saw 'the keels of two aircraft carriers and a 10,000 ton cruiser'.[20]

A particular concern for the Admiralty was the German battleship *Bismarck*. Ostensibly sticking to the terms of the 1935 deal, the Germans had informed Whitehall about the battleship's size and tonnage, claiming that it weighed considerably less and was more lightly armed than it really was. The British took the Germans at their word and assumed, quite wrongly, that the *Bismarck* had been designed to confront the Russians in the Baltic and was not suited to challenging the Royal Navy in the North Sea or elsewhere. But snippets of information—including information from a diplomat in Hamburg and the chance discovery that an Italian cruiser was much heavier than the Rome authorities said it was—raised serious doubts about how truthful the Germans were being.

19. The Englishman was Malcolm Christie—see following chapter. Thomas P Conwell-Evans *None so Blind: A Study of the Crisis Years 1930–1939* Harrison (1947) 39.
20. Hamburg—'German Air Bases and Naval Construction', FO 954/10A TNA. Attaché—'Memo from British Embassy', 9 Feb 1936 ADM 116/2945 TNA.

The Germans also deceived British naval intelligence about the *Bismarck*'s sister ship, *Tirpitz*, and the two battlecruisers, *Gneisenau* and *Scharnhorst*, that were also built during the 1930s. Once again Whitehall took the Germans' claims at face value, prompting Admiral John Godfrey to later accept a serious failure of intelligence. He blamed this on a 'simple and unworldly attitude' on the part of the Admiralty, which failed to recognize that the Germans 'lied deliberately and for the [now] obvious purpose of using the agreement [of 1935] to steal a march on us'.[21]

British Intelligence would have done better to pay closer heed to the warnings given by the Soviets. In March 1937, Stalin's ambassador to London, Ivan Maisky, told the British foreign secretary, Anthony Eden, that Moscow had acquired 'disquieting information as to what Germany was doing in regards to the design and character of the ships which had either already been built or were at present under construction'. The Admiralty immediately pressed Maisky for further details, and three months later Moscow provided London with intelligence about the true size of *Gneisenau* and *Schaarnhorst*, although not *Bismarck*.[22]

By this time, the French had also acquired other sources of information, although it is unclear how much of this material they shared with the British. In the summer of 1935, for example, the Deuxième Bureau noted a sudden increase in the hiring of specialist engineers at Baltic ports, to work 'mainly on submarines'. Many of these experts were drawn from factories in Nuremberg, Munich, and Augsburg. The Bureau had also become aware of the top-secret construction of new submarines, 'with a speed of at least 70 miles per hour', at yards at Luerssen and Vegesack near Bremen. And in November that year, a highly regarded *informateur bénévole* informed Paris that the German navy was developing a new generation of torpedoes, which left no visible trail as they shot towards their target, at Eckernforde in Schleswig. Then, in 1937, a source informed the French of a secret German operation to build aircraft carriers: Krupp had organized a work party at Kiel in January 1937 to fulfil an order for four of these carriers, each carrying twenty-five planes.[23] However, such material was not enough

21. Wark *Baltic Myths* 72.
22. Maiolo 94.
23. Torpedoes—'Activité de la fédération illégale', 14 Nov 1935, 7NN 2352 SHD. 1937 source—'Construction de nouveaux navires porte-avions', 20 Feb 1937, 7NN 3114 SHD.

to bring the two capitals close together in an area that the British still regarded as their own.

The British failure to discern the true might of the German navy was not, however, any reflection on 'Dr K.' For all his skill and determination as an intelligence source, he was simply not in a position to find out everything that the Nazi admirals were undertaking, although he continued to try to do so until the summer of 1939, when the German domestic security services had started to close in on him. This may have been because he was betrayed by an SIS defector, Captain 'Jack' Hooper, who attended a secret meeting between the undercover agent and his British handler and who then stumbled across the real identity of the supposedly anonymous visitor. Or it may have been because of an incident the previous year, when he had been seen behaving suspiciously near an airfield. But whatever the reason, the Abwehr's unwanted attention was aroused and he was arrested on 8 July 1939, promptly confessing his guilt.[24]

24. Hooper—MI6: British Secret Intelligence Service Operations, 1909–1945 Nigel West 51. Arrest—Jeffery 299–300; Andrew 608. Krüger is thought to have committed suicide in September 1939.

12

Colonel Z and Other Spies

Early in the morning of Saturday 7 March 1936, soldiers of the German army's Sixth Corps goose-stepped across Cologne's Hohenzollern Bridge and then marched into the towns and cities of the German Rhineland. Soon a huge air armada thundered overhead, deafening those below and creating an unmistakable impression of overwhelming German might. The people of Düsseldorf, Frankfurt, Worms, Cologne, Mainz, and Essen were stunned by these dramatic events but their astonishment soon gave way to jubilation. 'Crowds broke through police cordons', as Piers Brendon writes poetically, 'laughing girls showered soldiers with flowers, church bells peeled, flags flew and bands blared.'[1]

Consisting of the Rhine's west bank and a section, 30 miles deep, that lay to its east, the Rhineland had been demilitarized by the Versailles Treaty, whose architects sought to create a buffer zone between France and Germany, safeguarding both countries from mutual attack and building trust and confidence between them. Although the German government had signed the Locarno Treaty in 1925, pledging to respect these existing borders, few observers doubted that Hitler, who had always vowed to restore Germany's pre-war borders, would soon train his sights on the area: at a Foreign Office meeting in March 1935, for example, a senior official, Ralph Wigram, had argued that 'after she had [acquired] a strong Army, [Germany] would demand the abolition of the demilitarized zone and would try for Memel, Austria and her colonies'. And in January 1936 the Deuxième Bureau noted that 'there was no doubt' that Hitler would order its reoccupation, even if the exact date was unclear. Its experts might have added that

1. Brendon *Dark Valley* 292.

Hitler would be emboldened by the lack of any meaningful response by the outside world to Mussolini's invasion of Abyssinia, and by the domestic political chaos that ruled in France throughout the mid-1930s.[2]

It is likely, however, that few if any of these intelligence reports ever reached decision-makers, even if it is impossible to know in the absence of any ministerial records. The French lacked the same administrative machinery that their British counterparts used to weigh up different reports and then determine how to respond. As Martin Alexander has written, this machinery would have 'ensured smooth coordination and rounded assessment of major geo-strategic options'. As a result, the French were 'structurally unlikely, even incapable, of producing outcomes where all the relevant diplomatic, commercial, financial and military considerations had been maturely weighed, subject to inter-departmental critique, and distilled into an agreed set of policy decisions'. But in 1936 the British, by contrast, established a Joint Intelligence Committee to perform just such a function, and prior to this the Committee of Imperial Defence had performed a similar role since 1902.[3]

Without a centralized and cross-departmental analysis, the French government had little chance of deciding how to respond to Hitler's move. But making matters much worse was the political chaos in Paris. Bureau officers penned a key document on 8 April, circulating it to government ministers just three weeks before parliamentary elections. And when he came to power in early June, as France's first socialist prime minister, Léon Blum and his ministers were much more involved in stabilising their new government, and dealing with the political storms their radical spending plans had provoked, than in matters of foreign policy.[4]

Anticipated though it was, Hitler's move into the Rhineland still horrified French strategists, who feared a surprise German attack on their territory, capable of seizing their industrialized eastern territories. 'When one is master of the Rhine', as Marshal Ferdinand Foch, France's

2. Wigram—'Note on a Meeting at the Foreign Office', 11 Mar 1935, WO 190/305 TNA. Jan 1936—15 Jan 1936, 7NN 2597 SHD.
3. Structurally unlikely—Martin Alexander, 'The Military Consequences for France of the End of Locarno', INS (2007) 566. 1936—Alexander 'Military Consequences' 566.
4. Alexander 'Military Consequences' 568.

commander of the First World War, had once said, 'one is master of the whole country. Without the Rhine, all is lost.' But Hitler's audacious movement was also a further unmistakable sign of his audacity and of the dangers he posed. These fears were heightened by numerous reports that were also reaching Paris of frenetic German efforts to reinforce their grip over the border region: Krupp factories were working tirelessly to manufacture concrete sections of defences that were set up along the Franco-German border by whole armies of labourers, and in a report written on 25 June, Gamelin stressed how vulnerable France had now become.[5]

Hitler's move into the Rhineland plunged Europe into crisis, prompting the Germans to look across the border for any signs of retaliation. A double agent provided the Deuxième Bureau with copies of questionnaires that the Abwehr had asked him to complete just days after the Rhineland occupation. In particular, the Germans wanted him to find out about supplies of petrol to a strategically sited French town in Moselle, very close to the border, to verify the movement of troops from Paris to Metz, and to confirm the existence of military garrisons. Equally, the Bureau searched hard for clues about German activity. French intelligence officers met in secret with underground German union representatives from Mannheim and Goeppingen, who told them that two artillery regiments had arrived at Ludwigsburg from Munich and Augsburg. The Berlin authorities had also suspended all leave for railway workers, who were on constant standby all day and night in case of an emergency.[6]

The continent was a tinderbox. The French needed foreign allies more than at any time since 1918, even if a reliable informant, a 'source within Ribbentrop's entourage', had told the Deuxième Bureau that Germany was not in a position to wage war for at least another two years. In Warsaw, Marshal Rydz-Smigly, the inspector-general of the Polish army, immediately reaffirmed his loyalty to his French allies while regretting the passivity of their response to Hitler's actions. Paris also tightened its links with Prague and soon sent aircraft there to lift

5. Foch—Elizabeth Greenhalgh, *Foch in Command: The Forging of a First World War General* CUP (2014) 477. Gamelin—Adamthwaite *France and the Coming of the Second World War* 41.
6. Petrol—'Renseignement', 26 Mar 1936, 7NN 2530 SHD. Berlin authorities—'Réunion des Syndicats illégaux allemands', 14 Mar 1936, 7NN 2352 SHD.

up the low morale of the Czechs, who feared that they would be the next German target.[7]

But the big diplomatic prize still remained an alliance with Great Britain. A few days before the crisis, on 3 March, the French foreign minister, Pierre-Étienne Flandin, had already told Eden that France would not take any isolated action against Germany without British support, now that 'from the viewpoint of material, Germany is on the verge of surpassing us'. In London, the French ambassador, Charles Corbin, now reiterated these pleas and lobbied the Foreign Office for negotiations. At a subsequent conference, held in the British capital at the end of April, the French delegation asked the British to guarantee sending a token force to support France in the event of a German attack, regarding this as a precursor to a wider alliance, but the British continued to push back. To the despair of General Gamelin, the proceedings concluded only with vague British promises to send two infantry divisions to the continent in such an eventuality. The French were confident of British support only if the Germans attacked them through neutral Holland or Belgium.[8]

One reason for British resistance was that Whitehall was fearful of provoking German retaliation at a time when it still seemed possible that Hitler would sign up to an international disarmament deal. And in 1936 public opinion in Britain, as in France, remained dead set against even the risk of more slaughter, particularly at a time of economic depression. Other, less drastic, options, such as offering Germany colonies in the developing world and economic sanctions, still seemed to be open. 'This country will not support an exclusive Anglo-French military alliance—we may take that for granted', proclaimed the British Labour Party politician Hugh Dalton, on 26 March 1936. For Sir John Simon, 'the British people [do] not contemplate sending their sons to fight on the Continent...and if London was being bombed [they] would not be despatching regiments of soldiers to the Low Countries'.[9]

7. Reliable informant—'A/S Opinion d'une personnalité de l'entourage de Ribbentrop', 6 Mar 1936, 7NN 3114 SHD.

8. Flandin—Adamthwaite *France and the Coming of the Second World War* 38–9. Gamelin—Alexander 'Military Consequences' 568. Confident—'L'appui de l'Angleterre nous serait acquis', Note de 2nd Bureau, 15 Dec 1936, 7NN 2530 SHD.

9. Simon to Baldwin, 25 Mar 1936, PREM 1/194 TNA.

The strength of such isolationist sentiments became clear in the wake of the Rhineland crisis. At the time, not even hardliners like Winston Churchill advocated an armed response to the German move, and calls for military retaliation were voiced only by a few diehards in Paris, including Paul Reynaud, Paul-Boncour, and Georges Mandel. France was not only rocked by political instability but did not have the resources, any more than the British did, to put up much more than a fleeting fight. General Maurice Gamelin, for example, admitted that he did not even have one single armed unit ready for combat, while Stanley Baldwin also argued that any French action would not only bring about 'another great war in Europe' but also 'result in Germany going Bolshevik' in the chaos that would follow another military defeat.[10]

But there were other reasons why Eden and the British cabinet remained deeply suspicious of a formal commitment to assist France. Some influential figures felt that an alliance with France, which was in turn allied with Moscow, would inflame German fears of encirclement and make Hitler feel threatened, prompting him to lash out by starting a preventive war. 'The damned French are at their old game of dragging this country behind them in the policy of encircling Germany,' fumed the former chancellor, Viscount Snowden, as the crisis unfolded. The pact with 'Bolshevism' was in any event considered beyond the pale by figures such as Sir Austen Chamberlain, who wrote, two days after the Rhineland crisis flared, 'there is a great fear of France's entanglements in the East…some of our right-wing politicians feel very much as yours do about the Franco-Soviet pact. They regard it almost as a betrayal of our Western civilization.' Others voiced concern about allying with a country, France, that was 'half-riddled with discontent and communism' and thereby in indirect alliance with the Soviets, whose object was 'to force Bolshevism on a shattered Europe'. Soon, military experts in Whitehall also started to raise serious doubts about whether France was, in any case, a valuable military ally. For the French, these anti-Soviet sentiments gave them a clear choice that was easy to make: 'in the event of conflict', as a French intelligence report argued, 'British support outweighs in power, in certainty, and in

---

10. Baldwin—'Germany', FO 371/19892 TNA. On French calls for a counter-attack, see 'Note par Lt. Col. Buisson', 11 Oct 1935, 7NN 2530 SHD.

constancy that which the USSR can give us. The history of the last war proves this.'[11]

Another reason concerned the availability of intelligence, for by the spring of 1936 the SIS was less dependent than before on the Deuxième Bureau, whose earlier reports on German rearmament had filled such a serious void. This was because the British officers had now acquired a key new source on Nazi Germany. This individual was not a well-placed insider but a British national who was both supremely familiar with the country as a whole and also had a very good array of contacts inside Hitler's regime.

Captain Malcolm Graham Christie was a former RAF pilot whose reputation had soared to great heights during the First World War. He proved to be a brave and daring pilot who flew British agents behind enemy lines before helping to pioneer night-bombing raids over Germany. On one occasion he had even managed to steer his damaged plane away from civilians on the ground and instead crash-landed it into a hangar, at huge personal risk. In the mid-1920s he had started a new career with the British government, taking up an appointment as an air attaché in Washington before transferring to Berlin in 1927. Affable, moustachioed, and invariably courteous and good-tempered, Christie always looked and acted the part. And speaking excellent German, he soon acquired a deep attachment to the country, where he won many good friends and contacts.[12]

On taking early retirement in 1930, when he was still only in his early fifties, he decided to stay in Germany to pursue a business career, acting as a commercial representative for a British exporter and buying a large house close to the German–Dutch border. But as a man of independent means—he had by this time inherited a considerable personal fortune—he had a great deal of time to travel the full breadth of the country in his private car, as well as surrounding parts of Central and Eastern Europe. Well aware, thanks to his professional background, of how German security worked, he was adept at evading unwelcome

11. Snowden—Adamthwaite *Grandeur and Misery* 203. Chamberlain—quoted in Adamthwaite *France and the Coming of the Second World War* 51. France—Maurice Hankey, letters 22 Dec 1936 and 31 Jan 1937. Chamberlain, for example, had a 'hatred of the Russians', Cadogan *Diaries* 53. Experts—'Appreciation of the Situation in the Event of War', 26 Oct 1936, CAB 53/29 TNA. French experts—Patrice Buffotot, 'The French High Command and the Franco-Soviet Alliance 1933-9', *Journal of Strategic Studies* (Jan 2008).
12. Steering plane—*The Times*, 24 Nov 1971.

attention, not least by changing his plans and routes at the last minute, and by staying with friends or in guest houses that escaped, unlike big city hotels and embassies, the unremitting eye of counter-intelligence agents. And throughout this time, he remained in constant and close touch with the SIS, whose officers knew that, given his familiarity with the country and numerous officials, as well as his expertise in aviation, he was always well worth listening to. He was, in the opinion of Robert Vansittart, quite simply 'the best judge of Germany that we shall ever get'.[13]

Christie had recognized signs of danger in Germany as early as 1928 and as Hitler moved closer to power, he detected a significant change of attitude in the country as a whole, although particularly amongst the rulers, that alarmed him deeply. A state of 'unease', he wrote in 1933, had been replaced 'by a sense of self-assurance' and by a strong belief that an organized Germany would be in a position to assert itself and 'withstand the ordeal of modern warfare'. While Britain and France had been traumatized by the experience of the First World War and were desperate to avoid any repetition, he felt that many people in Germany had become hardened to conflict and were willing to risk, or even deliberately incur, more bloodshed.[14]

When Hitler became chancellor and consolidated his grip on power, Christie searched hard to discern the levels of popular support that the Nazi regime really harnessed, wondering if it could just disintegrate or implode. For the moment at least, he thought that Hitler and his government had found widespread support. 'Where discontent exists, it is levelled against persons and methods, and not as a whole against the principles of National Socialism,' he wrote. 'There is no crying over the loss of parliamentary rule and other democratic institutions; on the contrary, a great deal of the work of the Hitler government wins widespread appreciation.' He looked into the country's history and tradition to find an explanation. Concluding that National Socialism was 'in harmony with the spirit of the old Prussian upbringing', he felt that its popular support was therefore 'particularly evident in East Germany' while elsewhere it failed 'to grip as effectively the more calculating and somewhat Latinized minds'. In general, he felt the success of Hitler's

13. Vansittart—'Anglo-German Relations', 22 May 1935, CAB 21/540 TNA.
14. Conwell-Evans 23.

movement reflected its bid to become 'a new religion, a pagan mysticism expressive of the Nazi outlook'.[15]

But there were also times when he noticed unease amongst ordinary Germans, notably at the end of June 1934, when Hitler ordered a murderous purge of some of his political opponents, including Ernst Röhm, the leader of the paramilitary 'Brownshirts'. The events of the 'Night of Long Knives' were particularly bloody and brutal, even by Nazi standards, and, in Christie's opinion, 'undermined public confidence in Hitler in many quarters'. This was because 'the hurried executions and the absence of any recognized form of judicial procedure aroused a feeling of revulsion among the upper classes, and even caused many ordinary citizens to suspect that Hitler had feared to bring Röhm and his associates before a public court of law'. Adding to the sense of unease at this time was a deterioration of governing standards: 'hypocrisy and lip service are rife', he noted after one long journey through the country, 'and will remain so as long as the practice of police spies and informers is approved'.[16]

Over the months that followed, Christie continued to probe more deeply into the mindset of ordinary Germans, with whom he mixed so congenially. And as Nazi attitudes and propaganda seeped deeper into those popular attitudes, he noticed that as a whole they were becoming more aggressive and dangerous than before. 'War is regarded as a highly moral institution,' he wrote in September 1935, and 'youth are being taught...that Germans are supreme and that their main purpose in life is to die for the Reich.' Such observations echoed the warnings of other observers such as Sir Eric Phipps, who wrote in 1935 that 'except that battles are not being fought, Germany may be said without exaggeration to be living in a state of war'.[17]

This highly belligerent mindset spelt trouble for Germany's neighbours. 'The National Socialists require that the government and leaders adopt the same attitude and methods in foreign as domestic policy—Right is everything which benefits the German state,' argued Christie. By 1935 he felt that this spirit of militarism would vent itself against Austria, Memel, or even Czechoslovakia, which the Germans could invade using some plausible pretexts. In such a scenario, he concluded, Berlin did not believe the British or the French would get

15. Conwell-Evans 26.   16. Conwell-Evans 25.
17. 'Germany', 13 Nov 1935, FO 371/18851 TNA.

involved. France, in particular, was judged to be 'very soft and peaceful, and internal resistance to the idea of fighting Germany is likely to occur'.[18]

Although he gathered a great deal of political intelligence, as he carefully probed the opinions and feelings of those in the street as well as amongst elites, Christie's focus was on German rearmament. 'It requires no special intelligence to realize that Germany is rearming pretty thoroughly,' he wrote in 1934. 'Anyone travelling through the industrial districts of the Rhineland and the Ruhr can see the activity for himself; moreover it is an everyday topic of conversation, as it has set idle factories and furnaces going and absorbed the large number of workmen who 18 months ago were unemployed.' By 1935, he esti- mated that the Germans had constructed and put into use as many as 120 airfields, at least two of which, both at Lüneburg Heath, south-east of Hamburg, had hangars and other facilities that had been cleverly positioned underground. Overall, his estimates showed a rapidly rearming Germany that already set up between thirty and forty squad- rons. There was, he concluded, 'a rush to rearm in the air'. And within just weeks of Hitler's announcements of March 1935, he had sent Vansittart a revised and alarming estimate of German strength, prompt- ing the minister to warn that the Germans were already in a position to 'beat the French very easily'.[19]

As he drove freely around Germany, making his own observations and conversing with ordinary Germans, Christie also drew on some other, highly valued, sources of information. He was on close terms with Hermann Göring, whom he had got to know in 1931, when the *Reichsmarschall* was a Reichstag member and acted as an intermediary between Hitler and Hindenburg. Göring was inclined to talk loosely, particularly with a fellow wartime pilot, and during their numerous long chats he admitted that Berlin was 'secretly' producing far more planes than it admitted. 'How many he would not tell me', Christie wrote later, 'but the number was increasing every day and they were excellent planes.' These interactions might have given him a real sense, if not any hard facts, about what was happening at the helm of power in Berlin, but much more valuable was the highly secret information that he acquired from a handful of very well-placed insiders.[20]

18. Conwell-Evans 65, 42.
19. Conwell-Evans 25. Vansittart—22 May 1935, CAB 21/540 TNA. Vansittart was per- manent undersecretary of state for foreign affairs 1930–8.
20. Conwell-Evans 27.

Christie always went to extreme lengths to protect the identity of these high-level sources. In his private papers, he makes coded references to such anonymous and intriguing figures as 'X', 'Dr Y', and 'Z', but he yielded almost no indication about their role and identity: a reader discovers only that 'Fish' had information 'from the highest proven sources', while 'Johnnie' was an ex-German staff officer. However, one of his best sources was an individual he referred to in his notes as 'K', or 'Knight'. His real name was Hans Ritter, an individual with whom Christie shared a particularly close personal rapport. Both men were former wartime pilots and later served in the same professional role, as air attachés, at their respective embassies. Christie himself later wrote that 'during the years that Ritter was employed at the German embassy in Paris, he was in the closest touch with me and supplied me with extraordinarily correct and valuable information'. Other key contacts included Dr Carl Goerdeler, a bitter political opponent of National Socialism whom Christie first met in 1935, and Robert Bosch, whom he described in his letters only as a 'leading industrialist'.[21]

Christie forwarded much of his information and observations not just to Whitehall and the embassy in Berlin but also to Robert Vansittart, who shared his own sense of foreboding about Germany and Hitler while also advocating a similarly hawkish response to any future provocations. Although Vansittart's influence in Whitehall ebbed and flowed, and was set to fall drastically from 1938 when he was 'kicked upstairs' to a less influential position—he was removed as permanent undersecretary in 1938 and became a 'chief diplomatic adviser' to the government—Christie's information always lent his warnings considerable weight.

But his single most important source remained, and still remains to this day, anonymous. Beyond the fact that he was undoubtedly a senior official in the Luftwaffe, the name, rank, and role of 'X' is still unclear, although it is possible that he was the same source that the Czechs had recruited to their own ranks—Major Salm.[22]

In early 1936, Christie forwarded to London a report on Luftwaffe strength, a top-secret memorandum entitled 'Organization of the

21. Christie's sources—Christie Papers 180/1/29, 30 CCCA. Ritter—Christie to Vansittart 15 May 1941, Christie Papers 1/18. See Norman Rose *Vansittart: Study of a Diplomat* Heinemann (1978) 136.
22. Salm—this is the view of Michael Roi in *Alternative to Appeasement: Sir Robert Vansittart and Alliance Diplomacy* Praeger Studies (1997).

German Air Force, December 1935', that X had obtained. Whitehall experts were well aware of Christie's reputation and on his recommendation were willing to comb through every word of the document, even without knowing anything about his source or the authenticity of the material before them.[23]

The memorandum gave detailed information about the existing and projected strength of the Luftwaffe, based on the output of its factories, and revealed a huge increase in its strength: the Germans, according to the report he had sent them, intended to have 3,300 planes by the end of 1938 and create hundreds of new airfields. But some analysts were sceptical, claiming that the document was riddled with 'political unknowns', while the chief of the air staff dismissed it as 'someone's deductions from part of the information at the Air Ministry's disposal...we feel that no useful purpose will be served by continuing these rather fruitless discussions with "X"'. The secretary of state for air, Viscount Swinton, however, was less sceptical and ordered his staff to keep an open mind and ask the mysterious 'X' for more information, using Christie as an intermediary. X replied back to their message, asserting that his information was 'official and correct' and providing more details about the new engines that one of the German models were now starting to use. Yet still some Air Ministry analysts were unsure about these 'unsubstantiated statements'. They demanded more information about who exactly X was and what his sources were.[24]

A few months later, Christie sent another report from the same anonymous source, and this time the Air Ministry viewed the findings in a much more favourable light. It contained, they conceded, 'most useful information'. X's report gave them some very important technical information which they found convincing in every detail. Partly because of the strength of this information, the Air Ministry gradually abandoned its previously optimistic forecasts about what the Germans could and could not do, working instead on the assumption that the Luftwaffe would expand faster and more ambitiously than previously thought likely. As Ralph Wigram commented, 'the cat seems to be out of the bag at last—the Germans are going to have the biggest air force

23. Christie Papers, CHRS/180, 17 CCCA.
24. Ellington—for the Air Ministry's rebuttal, see EL Ellington's memo to Hankey, 22 July 1936, AIR 40/2102 TNA; X's reply—10 Mar 1936, AIR 40/2102 TNA. Wark *Ultimate Enemy* 637.

they can'. He was right: the Nazi leadership had by this time embarked on a four-year plan of frantic rearmament that was designed to equip Germany with the capacity to wage 'total war' by the early 1940s. Christie's contact was now widely acknowledged in Whitehall as 'the most secret and best informed of their sources in Germany'.[25]

Christie was by this time proving his worth not just through his contact with 'X' but also because of the political intelligence he was supplying about what Hitler might try and do next. In particular, he had picked up signs of German interest in the Rhineland several months before the crisis erupted, although his source of this information was and remains unclear. These warnings alone, from such a respected source, should have given Paris and London much time to prepare a response, or at least issue a warning to the German government about the consequences of any such action. Such a protest could have been lodged quietly in Berlin so that Hitler would not have publicly lost face.

In January 1936 the signs of an impending crisis in the Rhineland became harder to ignore, as the German press increasingly raised the issue and tried to whip up public indignation over the matter. When, on 4 March, the British government published a White Paper on defence, which noted the wider trend towards rearmament and argued that Britain now had no choice but to spend more money on arms, an infuriated Hitler ordered his army to prepare to march into the Rhineland, declare its remilitarization, and strike yet another deadly blow at the Versailles agreement.

The quality of Christie's information became clear when, the night before, he had phoned Vansittart with details of the impending incursion and rendered a very accurate figure of how many German troops would move into the Rhineland. His own estimates proved much closer to the truth than those of the Deuxième Bureau, whose officers estimated that the German armed force amounted to 265,000. The truth was that a token force of just 3,000 soldiers, many of whom

25. Technical information—for example, the report stated that the Germans had ceased production of a four-engine bomber and were instead focusing on high-performance medium bombers, and it also gave very detailed information about new German fighters, notably the Me-110, which the British knew little or nothing about: see 10 Mar 1936, AIR 40/2102 TNA. Wark *Ultimate Enemy* 52–5. Wigram—18 Oct 1936, FO 371/19947 TNA; 4 Mar 1937, AIR 2/1688 TNA. Christie's contact—contained within an FO file 'FO source secret X documents on the German air force', AIR 40/2102 TNA.

were brandishing arms that weren't even synchronized to fire, had
moved onto the west bank while another 30,000 had remained on or
close to the eastern side of the river. Such a force could and would not
have stood up to a determined resistance and the Germans even had
orders to retreat if they were challenged by any French soldiers, as
Christie later proved when he produced a copy of a report from
General Fritsch, which ordered an immediate withdrawal of German
troops if the French army crossed the frontier. 'If the French had taken
any action', as Hitler supposedly told his architect, Albert Speer, in the
days that followed, 'we would easily have been defeated; our resistance
would have been over in a few days.'[26]

Besides Christie, Vansittart also had other political contacts to keep
him closely informed of developments inside the Reich. Amongst
them were two brothers, Theo and Eric Kordt, and Ewald von Kleist-
Schwenzin, while another contact was an American, James Mooney,
the head of General Motors Overseas Corporation who was closely
linked to German industry and who willingly helped Vansittart.
Amongst his other sources were figures at the German embassy in
London, whose entire staff, 'with the exception of Dirksen... is
opposed to the policy of the present regime'. These renegades included
Wolfgang Gans zu Putlitz, an aristocrat and first secretary in the con-
sular section who secretly held strong anti-Nazi views, and Jona von
Ustinov, who defected to Britain in 1935 but continued to broker
meetings and contacts between embassy officials and British
Intelligence. Christie is also likely to have introduced Vansittart to
some of his contacts, including Ritter: Vansittart referred to him as 'one
of my sources... in the German Air Ministry' but who his wife remem-
bered as 'a functionary in the German air ministry... very quiet and
nervous and sensitive'.[27]

If Van's 'private detective agency' was now highly active inside
Germany, so too by this time was the independent intelligence service
that the intriguing Colonel Dansey had set up, at Vansittart's request,
six years before.

---

26. Phone call to Vansittart—Christie Papers, CHRS/1/17 CCCA. Albert Speer *Inside the
    Third Reich* Orion (1970) 72.
27. Sources at embassy—this information was from 'a reliable person from German circles
    in Holland'; see Judd to FO, 14 Aug 1939, FO 371/23009 TNA. Vansittart—*Mist
    Procession* 498; Rose 137.

In the summer of 1936, the British diplomatic world had been rocked by a sudden and dramatic announcement that Dansey was being recalled from his posting in Rome, where he had been based as a passport control officer since 1930. The reason for his recall was, supposedly, a serious breach of his duties. No further details were given and rumours abounded that Dansey had been found guilty of siphoning large sums of his budget for his own personal use, leading to his dismissal from his intelligence posting. Not long after, an internal audit seemed to confirm these suspicions, revealing 'irregularities' in the accounts of the Rome passport office.

In fact, Dansey and his boss, Admiral Sinclair, were playing a game of bluff, trying to fool and confuse the Germans who they knew would be watching their every move. Both men had decided to find more audacious ways of keeping one step ahead of their enemy in this deadly game of espionage and counter-espionage. Dansey's apparent 'dismissal' was really just a front that was designed to conceal his next move.[28]

Sinclair and Dansey had in fact determined a clever plan to infiltrate the Third Reich. Until now, Dansey's own intelligence-gathering on Germany had been a loose, informal affair which had been quietly instigated by Vansittart without official sanction. But now, at a time when tensions with Berlin were rising so sharply, Sinclair wanted to do much more. In particular, he had to help British agents evade the Germans, whose skills and cunning were so clear. In particular, he had to assume that the Abwehr had already infiltrated his other overseas stations with the same cunning and ruthlessness that they had shown elsewhere.

The admiral's solution was to create a more organized network that was officially supported and funded by the British state, even if its existence would be known only to very few and its funds would be drawn anonymously from an untraceable bank account. This newly formed 'Z Organization' would then act in parallel with, but quite independently of, the SIS, and potentially replace it in the event of a German invasion of Britain. Everything would be independent of Sinclair's organization, using different safe houses and forms of communication. Agents would be forbidden from contacting British

28. Anthony Read and David Fisher *Colonel Z: The Secret Life of a Master of Spies* Hodder & Stoughton (1979) 173–7.

embassies, consulates, personnel, or anyone else who might betray
them, even if those acts of betrayal were quite unintentional. Given this
unique level of secrecy, Z Organization would be totally compartmentalized and watertight, invisible from German eyes and, barring some
major breach of protocol, impenetrable from the best efforts of Nazi
counter-espionage.

'Colonel Z', as Dansey now called himself, immediately began to
organize his new network, drawing upon the resource pool of informers from Vansittart's own private intelligence service, which the former
permanent undersecretary continued to run independently. But Z
Organization also cultivated its own independent contacts, and added
an extensive list of names to its resource pool. Amongst the most
important was a businessman called Ralph Glyn, a leading name in the
City of London who owned and ran many companies, a great many of
which had investments in German industry. One of Glyn's chief contacts included a businessman, William Stephenson, whom he introduced to Dansey in or around early 1937.

Stephenson, as an SIS report later noted, was a 'Canadian with a
quiet manner [who] evidently knows a great deal about Continental
affairs and industrial matters' and who had 'a thorough grasp' of some
very technical issues. As the owner of the Pressed Steel Company, he
frequently visited German factories and was in a position to quietly
note how much of their output was being directed into the manufacture of arms. He was able to feed this information back to Dansey,
together with copies of the accounts and invoices of those companies,
and concluded that German military spending amounted to the
equivalent of around £800 million. Dansey forwarded such information not just to Sinclair—his only known direct contact with SIS—but
also to the newly created Industrial Intelligence Centre, as well as to
Winston Churchill, fuelling all his suspicions about the gathering
storm that he felt sure would soon break. Stephenson also appears to
have organized what became a secret organization within a secret
organization—the 'British Industrial Secret Service'—that gathered
information on German industry. Its agents used numerous commercial covers, including a travel agency in Highgate and the Duveen art
dealing business in central London, to gain access to the Reich.[29]

---

29. Stephenson, commercial covers—Bennett *Churchill's Man of Mystery* 193–4;
    H Montgomery Hyde *The Quiet Canadian* Hamish Hamilton (1962) 15–16.

Jewish businessmen and women, watching the growing Nazi persecution of their co-religionists with growing concern, were a particularly voluminous source of information and support. One such supporter was a 43-year-old Hungarian Jew called Sandor Kellner. Using an assumed name, Alexander Korda, he set up his own film business that was soon to rise to worldwide fame with a string of major commercial successes. A passionate Anglophile who was keen to make his personal contribution to his adopted country, Korda provided Dansey's agents with perfect cover, employing them in a variety of different roles, training them at his studios in Denham, and then providing them with professional accreditation that gave them a passport to travel to any place, in Germany and elsewhere, where they had some plausible excuse to do so: one Z operative working in this role was a young university graduate called Andrew King, who was in his mid-twenties when he was recruited by Dansey and who acted as an overseas representative for London Films, headhunting for future stars, searching for scripts, and scouting for locations in Austria and Switzerland.[30]

Z Organization also reaped considerable benefits from the support of two larger than life brothers, Solly and Jack Joel, whom Dansey had met during his travels in South Africa in the 1920s. Both men had been born and raised in East London before sailing to Cape Town in their early twenties, hoping to find a golden future by working with family members to search for and exploit precious metals. It was a shining success, and both men were self-made millionaires by the time they reached their thirtieth birthday. Dansey now contacted them, appealing to their sense of patriotic duty for their British homeland as well as to their hatred for the Nazis, and found that they were willing to spend considerable sums to help him fund his new intelligence-gathering operation.

Numerous other individuals were now playing a part in Z Organization. Amongst them were Dansey's former wartime comrades Sigismund Payne Best, who owned a pharmaceutical and chemical agency in Holland that distributed its products widely within Germany, and Rex Pearson, who worked for Unilever in Switzerland. Others included a Conservative MP, Frank Nelson, numerous journalists for leading newspapers, and oil magnates such as Calouste Gulbenkian

30. Andrew King—Obituary, *Daily Telegraph*, 15 Nov 2002.

and Henri Deterding of Royal Dutch Shell. All of these individuals either gave Dansey's agents cover for travel throughout Germany or else acted on his behalf.[31]

Dansey watched and ran this growing network of informers from his carefully disguised office. Located at the top of an eight-floor suite in Bush House in Aldwych, central London, it was situated over a mile away from the SIS headquarters, at Broadway. He knew that he would not be noticed there because his rooms officially acted as the export office of the Joel Brothers' diamond business, which was based in the adjacent suite. And Dansey always used a side door, unknown to all but very few, that allowed him to slip in and out totally unnoticed.

Z Organization, in other words, seemed like something out of a John Buchan novel, and in the very few records that survive there is certainly much romance and intrigue. There are stories, for example, of a well-known British artist who toured Germany, secretly sketching and painting airfields and other military installations, in the same spirit in which Lord Baden-Powell had made his own undercover spy mission there decades before. But the truth was that such 'intelligence' did not give any foreign spying agency a clear idea of what was really happening at those carefully concealed sites, which only aerial reconnaissance or insider information was in a position to do. By this time, however, the RAF sorely lacked resources and expertise in aerial reconnaissance, badly lagging behind French expertise, and it could have made highly profitable use of the significant sums of money that Dansey had given this artist, and other operatives, to tour Germany.[32]

This leads to an awkward question. Despite its undeniably romantic appeal, how much did Z Organization actually achieve? When, in July 1939, SIS officers met and spoke with one of their top sources of information, William Stephenson, they discovered that some of Dansey's 'sources' were in fact British Intelligence officers who had sold information to his agents in order to supplement their poor pay. The value of Dansey's network remains unclear.[33]

31. Read and Fisher 174.
32. On the RAF's aerial reconnaissance, see Hinsley 11, 27–8.
33. Stephenson—Bennett *Churchill's Man of Mystery* 194.

13

The French Step Up
Their Operations

In December 1936, the German ambassador in Paris, Count Johannes von Welczeck, wrote of 'the downright hysterical nervousness that has been evident among the public here for several days'. In the capital, he continued, there were 'crack-brained rumours circulating regarding the inevitability of a war, simultaneous military attacks on France from the east and the south planned by Germany'. Such fears were expressed not just in the streets but also in political debate, where mainstream politicians such as the foreign minister, Yvon Delbos, even claimed that 'Europe is on the edge of a general war' and felt that there was 'a risk of saying "goodbye" to French independence'.[1]

Events in Spain were fuelling these grave French insecurities. Civil war had broken out there in the summer of 1936, as the nationalist forces, led by General Franco and strongly supported by Hitler and Mussolini, fought the left-leaning republicans. The conflict weighed heavily on French hearts, arousing deep fears of encirclement by a fascist alliance comprised, if Franco won victories in the field, of three countries. It seemed a very real possibility that the Italian and Spanish navies would then be able to dominate the Mediterranean, cutting the French mainland and its territories from North Africa and sub-Saharan Africa. This would deprive France of many of its resources, much of its manpower, and a great deal of its prestige as an imperial power. 'If Spain is hostile towards France, then that would open up, to German and Italian advantage, a new theatre of operations that would threaten our borders along both the Pyrenees and in Morocco,' as a Deuxième

---

1. Adamthwaite *France and the Coming of the Second World War* 45.

Bureau report argued. 'The scope and scale of any such effort [to open up a theatre of operations] should be determined as early as possible.'[2]

As the fighting raged, the French Special Services kept close vigil, initially assigning two officers to monitor the war from two radio stations, one at Bayonne and another at Perpignan, while more listening posts were also soon created in Morocco. This included stations at Rabat and Tangier, both of which were run by the French military attaché at the consulate, while a post was also set up at Oran in Algeria.[3]

In French eyes, the events in Spain made a bad situation worse because their fears had already been heightened by a major rift between France and Italy. The two countries had both been signatories to the Locarno agreement and thereafter remained on good terms, subsequently signing, in April 1935, the Stresa agreement that bore testimony to their mutual goodwill and cooperation. In Paris, Italy seemed a natural partner and ally against Hitler's Germany. For his part, Mussolini deeply resented Nazi designs on Austria, which he regarded as lying within Italy's sphere of influence, and had vowed to defend it from Hitler's advances: he had moved his troops close to the border in 1934, for example, when Austrian Nazis assassinated the chancellor, Engelbert Dollfuss, in Vienna. But relations between Paris and Rome had subsequently deteriorated, partly because Paris failed to support the Italian invasion of Abyssinia in 1935, and partly too because of Mussolini's strong military support for Franco. Tension between Rome and Paris then erupted in October 1936, when the *duce* struck up an alliance with Hitler.

The emergence of a Rome–Berlin axis was a heavy blow to French defence chiefs because it meant that Paris could no longer rely on Italian friendship. In the event of a war with Germany, French generals would have to move fourteen divisions, about a fifth of their total strength, to the Alps and North Africa to guard against an Italian attack. But if Italy remained neutral, then they would be free to concentrate those extra numbers along the Franco-German border.

What made things even worse, in the eyes of French strategists, was Belgium's declaration of independence in March 1936 and its renunciation of a defence pact with Paris, which it had signed in 1920. With a single stroke of a pen, the Belgians denied French generals the chance of moving through Belgium to help fend off a German attack further south.

2. 'Plan de Renseignements', 29 Mar 1939, 7NN 2530 SHD.   3. Navarre 43.

Plate 1. The Treaty of Versailles (1919) was formulated at the Paris Peace Conference after World War 1. Pictured here, at the conference, are (from left) David Lloyd George, Vittorio Orlando, Georges Clemenceau and Woodrow Wilson.

Alamy: D95YEC

Plate 2. Hitler in Munich in the 1920s.
Alamy: 2BH9G1W

Plate 3. Key units of the German navy assemble at Kiel in 1934.
Alamy: P66WCM

Plate 4. Göring with Charles A. Lindbergh and his wife.

Library of Congress: 2002712457

Plate 5. Great Britain's top diplomats – The 1st Earl of Halifax, on the right, with Sir Alexander Cadogan.

Alamy: 2BW24HB

Plate 6. Sir Stewart Menzies, later head of the SIS, pictured here in the 1920s.
Getty: 3140523

Plate 7. Sir Robert Vansittart, a senior British diplomat before and during the Second World War, and a strong critic of the appeasement of Nazi Germany.
Alamy: 2BW8DMN

Plate 8. A Luftwaffe display at the Nuremberg Rally in 1938. The Nazis used these displays to intimidate their opponents, and project an exaggerated image of their military strength.

Not long afterwards there was a minor war scare that mirrored but also added to the existing sense of crisis in Paris. Over the summer of 1936, the Deuxième Bureau detected a sharp increase in tension along the Franco-German border, as if the Nazis were preparing for war. The intelligence signals were varied: German spies close to the border or inside France were given a special phone number to call and new codes to use 'in case of an emergency'; large caches of arms were suddenly transported to town halls, railway stations, and customs offices near Baden and in the Palatinate, while anti-aircraft batteries were installed around Munich and other cities.

Changes to railway timetables were also revealing. The Bureau had long recognized the importance of the railway to German military movements and worked hard to obtain insider information: now a well-placed informer on the railway network witnessed a sudden inflow of aluminium and other raw materials that the German war machine would need in the event of conflict.[4]

Such reports gave extra resonance to the highly pessimistic, and typically overblown, assessments of German capabilities, matched against a strong sense of French vulnerability, that echoed in the governmental offices of the French capital. The new aviation minister, Pierre Cot, deliberately manipulated intelligence information to create this impression and lend extra weight to his arguments for an alliance with Moscow, proposing to add a military dimension to a vague 'mutual assistance pact' that had been signed the previous year. In June, he argued that 'Germany is moving towards a (first-line) force of 3,000 aircraft; for our part, even with an enormous effort, it would be difficult for us to surpass one-third of this number.' And in a memorandum to Yvon Delbos, for example, he emphasized that German industrial power dwarfed that of France and argued that 'this vital realization ... must dictate our policy'. Cot, felt some British officials, was 'a remarkable liar' who led them to brand French information as 'misleading'.[5]

---

4. See for example 'Trafic de la gare de Lauterbourg', 24 Nov 1936, 7NN 3114 SHD. In a 1932 document, the Bureau had noted 'the extreme importance the Reich attaches to transport issues' and its own efforts to find out more: 'A/S RW et Chemins de Fer', 30 Sept 1933, 7NN 3182 SHD.
5. Delbos—Jackson *France and the Nazi Menace* 198–9. Cot—Jackson in ed. Alexander and Philpott 129.

The loss of Italy as an ally forced Paris to look to London with even more needy eyes, but as France was gripped by a growing sense of vulnerability, relations between the two countries had become more complicated than ever. This was a result of the Abyssinian Crisis. On the one hand, this issue created a deep cross-Channel rift about how to sanction Italy because the British advocated a much harsher line than the French: the two countries pulled further apart, as the British accused the French, who were always half-hearted about sanctions, of duplicity and unreliability while Anglophobic Frenchmen fumed at their old adversary who was depriving them of forging an alliance with Rome. But on the other hand, France needed Britain more than ever, and on 10 September Laval unsuccessfully asked the British to promise 'collective security' in Europe—a euphemism for a commitment to France to compensate for the loss of Italy as an ally.[6]

In the immediate wake of the Rhineland crisis, a close dialogue between the two intelligence services often flowed. In Paris, the British air attaché, Group Captain Douglas Colyer, and his French counterpart shared information about Luftwaffe activity in the different parts of Germany that they had agreed to monitor between themselves. Although very few accurate records remain, the diaries of Colonel Rivet, the head of the SR, show that he travelled to London in February 1937 for a three-day trip and held several meetings with British Intelligence officers, while Menzies from October 1936 made three journeys, each of two days' duration, to Paris. But such cooperation was sporadic and traditional rivalries and suspicions, exacerbated by disagreements about how to deal with the Spanish Civil War, quickly resurfaced instead.

French dismay at the lack of cross-Channel cooperation emerges from a report written by General Victor-Henri Schweisguth, the deputy chief of the French general staff, in November 1936. Based on reports from the French military attaché in London, he commented on the negative influence of the City of London, where he felt there was strong sentiment in favour of 'peace with Germany', and concluded that in the country generally there was 'complete disinterest in the affairs of central Europe'.[7]

6. Accusations—Adamthwaite *France and the Coming of the Second World War* 35–6.
7. Forcade 211.

The same suspicion of Great Britain's motives, and of the SIS in particular, is evident from the Bureau's reports about British Intelligence 'agents' suspected of being sympathetic towards Nazi Germany. In the summer of 1936, for example, it noted with alarm that a British military attaché, Colonel PT Etherton, had arrived in France en route from his diplomatic posting in China. Etherton, who had made a name for himself by becoming the first man to fly over Everest and by undertaking aerial reconnaissance of South America and Arabia during and after the First World War, was placed under constant watch by undercover officers. He was in touch, the French spies emphasized, 'with a number of Germans, notably Richthofen, the cousin of the great aviator, who is currently on an assignment in London [and] who has also recently visited Hitler'. The intelligence report argued that this 'would be well-suited to German propaganda and would suggest that, for England, an alliance with Germany is preferable to one with France'.[8]

Another 'British agent' who aroused French suspicions at around the same time was a journalist called Sefton Delmer, who had arrived in France in 1933, when he was 37 years old, as a correspondent for the London *Daily Express*. His previous posting had been in Berlin, where he reported on the rise of Hitler and worked hard to build close contacts inside the Reich. Bureau officers had doubts about him, noting that he was 'full of pro-German sentiments [and] speaks very warmly of Germany and its Chancellor but seems less enthusiastic about France', adding that 'he seems to agree with German propaganda and seems to think that, for England, an alliance with Germany is preferable to one with France'. Because they felt sure, quite unjustly, that he was a British agent, there was a clear hint about where London's true loyalties might lie.[9]

A few years before, the French had held similar suspicions about Georg Bell, a young German national who was closely linked to Hitler's one-time friend and comrade Ernst Röhm. The Deuxième Bureau felt sure that he was 'one of the principal agents' of the SIS and kept Bell under close surveillance during his travels in France and Portugal. But their surveillance and files reveal no evidence of any such link, although Bell did have some acquaintance with a British fascist, John De Santi, whom the SIS denied having any association

8. 'A/S du Colonel Anglais Etherton', 29 July 1936, 7NN 3250 SHD.
9. Bureau officers—'A/S du nommé Delmer', 3 Apr 1935, 7NN 3250 SHD.

with. French intelligence reports about Bell were also littered with factual errors—claiming, for example, that the Nuremberg-born man who had served in the German army in the First World War 'was a Scotsman who settled in Germany after 1918'.[10]

. But if the French were able to obtain more high-grade intelligence from supremely well-placed sources, such as Agent Asche, then they would have more leverage not just over the SIS but over a British government that would be forced to admit its dependence on the French. More specifically, the greatest prize of all would be to get hold of inside information that clearly demonstrated Hitler's fears of an Anglo-French alliance.

By the summer of 1936, the Bureau certainly had more intelligence successes against Germany to boast of. Quite apart from running their star agent, Hans-Thilo Schmidt, its officers were also undertaking successful reconnaissance of key sites in Germany, allowing them to obtain information about closely guarded secrets such as the new Solothurn anti-aircraft gun, manufactured by Rheinmetall. The French also led the way in covert aerial photography, using hidden cameras in passenger planes to undertake surveillance of a number of sites around Munich, Salzburg, Donauschingen, and Villingen. This also enabled them to discover that the Germans were now switching production of their war materials further inland to safeguard them against attack. Unlike the SIS, French spies also had information flowing from a number of Belgian sources. Despite Belgium's neutrality, unofficial contacts between the French and Belgian spy services continued, and the Belgians turned a blind eye to the Bureau's outposts in Belgium. 'The local population, notably in Wallonia and Brussels, were well-disposed to the French', as Henri Navarre noted, 'and we were quite easily able to recruit informers among them'.[11]

But during and after the Rhineland crisis, the Germans continued to tighten their domestic security. In the course of 1936, the French lost touch with thirty-two agents who were working undercover in Germany, of whom at least nine were known to have been detected and arrested while the rest may have evaded capture but been deterred, by the strength of German countermeasures, from continuing with their covert work. Other agents, whose loyalty had never previously

10. 'Assassinat de Georg Bell en Autriche', 22 Apr 1935, 7NN 3250 SHD.
11. Quoted in Alexander 'Did the Deuxième Bureau Work?' 321.

been in question, were suspected of betrayal, forcing their handlers to make difficult judgements about the reliability of any information they may have still been sending.[12]

In particular, the Germans continued to drastically tighten their security along the border. As they searched for political dissidents and smugglers as well as spies, the German border guards made meticulous checks on visitors' permits and passports, subjected them to prolonged questioning about the purpose of the trip, carried out very thorough body searches, and imposed draconian penalties on anyone who broke their rules.

Once inside the Reich, an undercover spy faced all manner of obstacles, noted the Deuxième Bureau, since 'all military sites, including barracks, aerodromes and fortified zones are under heavy guard and surveillance'. In addition, the German police, whose style and ethos were 'remarkable aggressive', carefully watched the roads and railways as well as making frequent and close inspections of the hotels and guest houses where visitors were staying. Germany, the report concluded, was a state ruled by fear, where 'someone can be arrested if they have aroused the slightest suspicion, condemned for the slightest reason and executed without delay'. In short, '*la répression est féroce*'. The very high risk of detection by such a formidable adversary meant that the Bureau was very reluctant to employ any French nationals who volunteered their services: even if they had a legitimate reason to visit the Reich, some 'do not realize the risks they would be taking'. Equally, informers demanded higher payments to make up for the growing risks to their safety.[13]

Compensating for the loss of a growing number of agents was a demanding task. 'Germany is currently in a state of siege', complained French spy chiefs in early 1937, as they bemoaned the failure of their case officers to find new recruits inside the Reich, despite their best efforts to do so. The Bureau had previously relied heavily on German expatriate workers in France, who on their return home could some-times produce quality information, but by 1936 their number had started to sharply tail off. This may have been partly because there were by this time far more job opportunities at home but it was also because

12. 32 agents—Forcade 129. See for example the case of Agent Rodler, Memo 5 Dec 1936, 7NN 2159 SHD.
13. Réunion des Chefs de Poste, 18–20 Jan 1937, 7NN 2502 SHD.

of heightened security measures, as the Nazis restricted travel permits and demanded a convincing reason for someone to leave the Reich. The number of foreign visitors to Germany, including visits by French nationals, had also started to diminish significantly, and in May 1937, an alarmed Colonel Rivet also complained to his bosses about how difficult his recruitment task was, adding that it was much harder because there were just a few hundred French expatriates in Germany.[14]

The sheer difficulty of recruiting agents meant that, on many matters, the Deuxième Bureau 'had no source of particular importance' and all of its newly recruited agents were instead 'dedicated but relatively insignificant individuals from areas close to the border'. This created huge gaps in its knowledge. Its officers knew little, for example, about the state of German fortifications along the border, relying only on information from insiders 'of average importance': one such informant was a source, most likely to have been a workman, who was based at Istein, where the Germans had just started to build an ambitious 'West Wall' designed to fend off any French attack.[15]

There were some successes, however. Alerted to the scale of German work along the border, the French prepared to undertake covert photographic reconnaissance along a stretch of territory between Rastatt-Karlsruhe and Otterbach. At the same time, the French spies set up a number of new garrisons close to the border, confident that their presence would enable them to 'make contact with defectors of interest, facilitate research and recruit well-placed informers'.[16]

French security chiefs also set up a series of border posts where their officers could question anyone who crossed from Germany into France, regarding such individuals as 'one of their best sources of information' about the Reich: these *postes d'examen* and *centres interrogatoires* were also based at ports, railways stations, and airports as well as along the border. The Bureau also carefully watched German exiles who were living on French soil, although how much information it obtained from them remains unclear. Many of these figures were members of, or loosely affiliated to, the exiled Social Democrat Party, whose leadership had in 1933 moved firstly to Prague and Karlsbad and then later, in 1938, to Paris: through its loose network, the SDP

14. Nazi restrictions—Réunion des Chefs de Poste, 18–20 Jan 1937, 7NN 2502 SHD.
    Rivet—Réunion des Chefs de Poste, 18–20 Jan 1937, 7NN 2502 SHD; Forcade 309.
15. Istein—Réunion des Chefs de Poste, 18–20 Jan 1937, 7NN 2502 SHD.
16. Réunion des Chefs de Poste, 18–20 Jan 1937, 7NN 2502 SHD.

exiles had a steady and copious flow of information about what was happening inside Germany but its veracity was always open to question and the organization itself was felt, with good reason, to be ridden with Nazi spies.[17]

One exile who particularly attracted French interest was the brother of the famous German writer Thomas Mann. Heinrich Mann had fled Germany in 1933 and helped to set up an international 'Centre for German Refugees' that had representatives in Prague, Paris, and Geneva. Placed under constant surveillance at his home in Nice, it became clear that he had good information about what was happening inside Germany, mostly obtained through contacts and intermediaries in Switzerland. Hoping to find more information, French operatives closely watched all the meetings he organized and attended, such as a conference at the Lutetia Hotel in Paris in late September 1935, when around fifty anti-Hitler activists met to discuss forming a common front, to highlight and campaign for victims of Nazi persecution in concentration camps, and to vow to 'overthrow Hitler and to restore democracy in Germany'.[18]

Another exile of great interest was Georg Bernhard, the editor of a Paris-based newspaper for fellow refugees, *Pariser Tageblatt*, and a member of 'The Jewish Union Movement' that was set up in Paris in November 1935. Dedicated to promoting pan-Judaism and protecting Jewish interests, it met twice a week at the Café Mephisto under the leadership of a Dr Dallman. Infiltrating or dealing with these exiles, however, was challenging: all were deeply fearful of *agents provocateurs* and of Gestapo threats and therefore eyed outsiders warily. This was certainly not an unreasonable fear, and the Bureau compiled lengthy reports about *les mouchards* ('snitches') who could sometimes reap handsome rewards for such duplicitous work, or else regarded it as their duty to find traitors to Germany. Willi Baumann, for example, was a Gestapo agent who spied on refugees in Czechoslovakia and craftily lured them back into the Reich. Others, like Erich Anton, had been known to snatch emigrants from Copenhagen and spirit them into Germany. Such risks demoralized these exiles particularly from

---

17. Border posts—'Feuille de Renseignements', 14 Mar 1934, 7NN 2486 SHD. SDP—Marlis Buchholz and Bernd Rother *Der Parteivorstand der SPD im Exil: Protokolle der Sopade 1933–1940* Dietz (1995). See also Introduction, footnote 2.
18. Nice—'Ludwig Mann', 11 Feb 1936, 7NN 3083 SHD. French operatives—'Congrès des Réfugiés', 7 Jan 1936, 7NN 3083 SHD.

the mid-1930s, as Hitler's regime won huge popularity at home, crushed domestic opposition, and won some plaudits abroad.[19]

Some of the challenges, dangers, and difficulties of obtaining reliable information inside Germany were described by Paul Stehlin, the French air attaché who arrived in Berlin in the summer of 1936.[20]

To begin with, Stehlin was struck by the courtesy and helpfulness of his German hosts. Since he was on remarkably amicable terms with both Göring and Milch, the Frenchman was able to get permission to fly a small training aircraft, lent to him courtesy of the German government. This was supposedly to allow him to undertake 'training flights' and to reach every corner of this sprawling country for the various events and meetings that an air attaché was allowed to attend. Under the informal agreement he struck with Göring, Stehlin would outline the course of his forthcoming journey with air traffic control but was otherwise given huge freedom to undertake his 'training flights' wherever and whenever he wanted. He knew that, by doing so, he could make careful observations and get a strong sense of the normal humdrum of activity in and around the main roads, railways, and the military bases.

But although he had good friends in extremely high places, Stehlin was nonetheless subjected to a great deal of surveillance from the domestic security services, and not long after arriving in the capital he was nearly caught in a 'honey trap'.[21]

Invited to an official function one evening, he met a German woman of considerable charm and finesse. Assertive without being pushy or overbearing, she struck up an easy rapport with him and soon they were spending more time in each other's company, in the restaurants, theatres, and other bright lights of Berlin. Initially very cautious and reserved about discussing any political matters, she gradually wanted to know more about his professional interests. She was keen, a bit too keen, to make her way to his flat 'to get an eye on my documents and correspondence' and he was suspicious when she declared her antipathy towards Hitler and National Socialism, and offered to

19. Fearful—'Renseignement', 9 Nov 1935, 7NN 3083 SHD. Anton—Liste noire communiste, 9 Dec 1935, 7NN 2352 SHD. From mid-1930s—'La Stimmung des Émigrés', 30 Sept 1936, 7NN 3083 SHD.
20. See in general Paul Stehlin *Témoignage pour l'histoire* Robert Laffont (1964) Chs 3–5.
21. Stehlin 47–8.

put him in touch with anti-Nazi figures. Hyper-vigilant and trained in intelligence, he recognized the signs of a trap.

He felt sorry for this young woman, who was probably not being paid well for work which, in his view, did not befit her talents. Very possibly, she was not even sympathetic to the Nazi cause. But he none-theless had little choice but to foil her efforts. Her efforts to seduce him, he felt, were below the belt. Together with a colleague at the embassy, he devised a way of warning her off, and warning off her handler, without causing anyone unnecessary trouble.

Since he had her address and phone number, he arranged for his colleague to phone her from a public call box just outside her flat. As a native German speaker using a bad line, the Frenchman sounded quite plausible as a rather irate Abwehr officer who was instructing her to cancel her meeting with Stehlin and return to the office immedi-ately. Sure enough, the young *fräulein* left her flat and walked to the Abwehr office in central Berlin, wholly unaware that she was being followed by the Frenchman who had just phoned her and watched her leave. And as she entered the Abwehr office, Stehlin and his colleague had the proof they needed about who she really was. The next day Stehlin politely told her on the phone not to resume contact: her boss was wasting his time as well as hers.

Even on supposedly neutral territory, foreign intelligence officers had to tread with real care. And the importance of doing so became clear when French intelligence officers were suddenly contacted by a senior Nazi officer who offered to sell them, for a high although quite reasonable price, insider information about the German armed forces.[22]

Although the approach seemed genuine enough, Colonel Rivet was wary because the German insisted on meeting them in Denmark, ostensibly because it was safest to do so on neutral soil. Rivet knew that a good many Danish police officers and security forces were sympathetic to Germany, although he allowed the meeting to go ahead provided that two of his most experienced officers, Henri Navarre and 'Rex' Lemoine, undertook the mission and went together.

The two French officers travelled to Copenhagen and checked in at the same hotel. They did so by following the basic rules of their training by working independently and feigning no knowledge of, or

22. Navarre 66–7.

acquaintance with, each other. Then, as Rex lurked unnoticed in the background, Navarre made his way into the hotel lobby at the prearranged time and found his contact waiting for him in an armchair. They chatted to relax the situation before the German told Navarre his rank, although not his name, and gave him details about the documents he could sell, showing him extracts of several pages to prove that he was genuine. But he didn't feel safe handing over the documents here, continued the Nazi officer. They could meet the following morning, perhaps in a bar or café, and he would hand them over in exchange for the money that the French had promised.

The French spies were puzzled and alarmed. Why did the German think it was safe to pass on some extracts at the hotel but not the entire documents? Meeting in a café or a bar was also much more dangerous, because there were far more people around to eavesdrop and listen, and far less time to cover up and disappear if things went wrong. But there might have been a lot to lose, and Navarre reluctantly agreed to meet the next morning, carefully discussing with Rex how best to take precautions.

The following morning, with precise timing, the anonymous German arrived at the café, carrying a briefcase that contained a bulky document. Navarre was waiting for him and the two men got straight down to business. The Frenchman played for time, wanting to get a better sense of what was unfolding, and explained that he wanted to ask a number of specific questions before taking things further forward. But as they talked, 'Rex' suddenly walked into the café and made a prearranged gesture to signal that danger was afoot. Keeping careful watch outside, he had spotted several Danish policemen who were poised to raid the café and arrest his fellow officer on some criminal charges.

The Germans had set a trap by tipping off the Danish authorities, and they had come within a whisker of succeeding. Had the two French agents been caught, they would have faced prison sentences on charges of espionage or handling stolen material, and perhaps even been deported to Germany. With moments to spare, Navarre had stopped everything in its tracks and escaped.

On other occasions the Gestapo also tried to lure French intelligence officers into the Reich on false pretences. On one such occasion, in 1936, a German civilian called Hermann Brester arrived in France, ostensibly in search of work, and soon contacted the Deuxième Bureau to offer his services as a source of information. He was in fact an undercover Gestapo agent who had been carefully briefed to give the French false information about his homeland, to gather as much information as he could about the workings of French intelligence, and then to lure the French officer who was dealing with his case, Captain Durand, into the Reich. Brester gave Durand the name and address of a German officer who was supposedly willing to help him and who, he continued, had deposited a packet, stuffed with highly classified documents, at Trier's railway station. But as he listened to these fictions, Durand sensed a trap. Brester was arrested and given a prison sentence for spying.[23]

Not all agents who gathered intelligence on Germany in the 1930s were so lucky. In 1936, the Nazis sentenced six spies to death, upon whom befell the same grisly, barbaric fate that Major Salm suffered— beheading. Of these, four had worked for the British, whose network in Germany was badly shaken by a series of arrests. In June, for example, Abwehr operatives captured Gustav Hoffman as he took illicit photos in Magdeburg. Hoffman later confessed to working for British Intelligence and said he had been recruited by the SIS station at The Hague, providing the Abwehr with an important lead. The SIS station in Holland then suffered a further blow when it was betrayed by another of its agents in 1936.[24]

The Germans had now discovered the importance of Holland as a British staging post for intelligence-gathering operations inside the Reich.

Holland's importance partly reflected the growing strength of German domestic security and counter-espionage, which forced both the British and French spy services to rely on their Dutch and Danish stations to recruit and run agents. Not only were such operations safer but there was no shortage of potential recruits amongst an expatriate community of German-speaking Dutch and Danish nationals who could move easily across relatively porous borders. This resource pool grew from the early 1930s, as an increasing number of political exiles and activists fled Germany and into Holland, where they made contact with a charitable organization, International Red Aid (IRA), which provided food and shelter to political refugees.

23. 'Affaire Bertholet', 7NN 2524 SHD.   24. Jeffery 277.

The Deuxième Bureau's files cite several typical examples. Paul Maas was a German Communist Party activist from Münster who had fled Gestapo harassment and made his way to the Dutch border, where he was met by a sympathizer who led him by foot across the border near Enschede. Mathias Klingen had been a German Communist Party leader from 1926 until November 1933, when he had disappeared from his native Düsseldorf and headed for Amsterdam, where he found food and shelter from International Red Aid. And Hermann Rodewig had helped to set up an anti-Nazi group that masqueraded as 'a Skiing Club' before the Gestapo swooped and broke it up; he slipped into the Netherlands, using an escape route that went through Aix-la-Chapelle and Maastricht. Another key crossing point, which the IRA's activists used frequently, was near Hengele.[25]

There was another reason why the Netherlands were so important to both Britain and France. Over the preceding few years, the Germans had used Rotterdam to import some crucial raw materials, moving them into the Ruhr along a series of inland waterways. Chief amongst these materials was iron ore, which was shipped from the Swedish port of Lulea during the summer months and the Norwegian port of Narvik in the winter. British experts, working at the Industrial Intelligence Centre, knew that the German economy was hugely dependent on these imports and in 1937 estimated that the Reich would soon need to import around nine million tons of this single resource to sustain its rearmament programme. This dependency would be of vital importance in the event of war because the Royal Navy could impose a naval blockade and cut the Reich's economic windpipe. In the meantime, the SIS and the Deuxième Bureau wanted to keep a very close watch on Rotterdam's port facilities, tracking the arrival of these raw materials.[26]

Both countries were also well aware that, in the event of a war against them, the Germans would be tempted to strike through the Netherlands, where they could establish air and naval bases against Britain. For this reason, both the SIS and the Bureau carefully monitored the Dutch–German border for signs of any changes. In January 1935,

25. Maas—'A/S Méthode employée par certains communistes allemands pour se rendre en France', 21 May 1937, 7NN 2352 SHD. 'A/S Mathias Klingen', 24 Oct 1938, 7NN 2352 SHD. 'A/S Hermann Rodewig', 24 Oct 1938, 7NN 2352 SHD.
26. 1937 paper—'Germany: Reserves of Raw Materials', 28 Jan 1937, FO 371/20714 TNA; Wark *Ultimate Enemy* 175.

for example, a French spy discovered a series of hidden transmitters hidden along the road between Xanten and Goch that could signal to spy planes flying overhead, as well as secret artillery bases in the Reichswald, near Kleve, where long-range guns could be trained against any army moving across the border. The following year, the Bureau also detected covert German efforts to build fortifications in Effeld forest, near Viersen, as well as other sites.[27]

For the moment, the SIS was so well networked in Holland that it did not need any helping hand from the French, who had few unique sources of information in the country to boast of. Despite its neutrality, the Dutch government was on close and cordial terms with London, not just because of their historic defensive ties against France but also because of the City of London's vast investments in the country. This meant that the Dutch would sometimes turn a blind eye to SIS activities within their own borders, or even actively assist them: French spies noted, for example, that the SIS chief there 'liaises directly with the head of the Dutch intelligence service, who has promised to help him in any way he wishes. Conversely, there was considerable anti-French sentiment in parts of Holland, reflecting centuries of religious antagonism and war.[28]

The SIS office in The Hague was located at the embassy's passport office, at Nieuwe Parklaan in Scheveningen, and was initially organized and led by Major Hugh Dalton. For a while, much of his work was focused on monitoring the exodus of German Jews, many of whom used Dutch ports to make their way to British-controlled Palestine: fearing that uncontrolled Jewish immigration would spark a revolt amongst the Arab population, the SIS kept a close eye on the numbers of these German émigrés. Dalton, however, was embroiled in a scandal when he was caught embellishing funds and committed suicide on 4 September 1936. The French, meanwhile, ran several operations against Germany from their embassy.

At this time there was no cooperation in Holland between the British and French spy services, although the Deuxième Bureau knew the identity of some of Britain's key agents and did its best to keep tabs on them. One such agent was a Dutch army officer by the name of

27. Jan 1935—'Travaux allemands à la frontière hollandaise', 7 Jan 1935, 7NN 3114 SHD.
    Covert efforts—'De la frontière germano-hollandaise', 22 Apr 1936, 7NN 3114 SHD.
28. French spies—7NN 395/101 SHD.

Adrianus Vrinten, who kept the Bureau informed about his work for
the SIS. From 1933, Vrinten had become focused much less on communist activity and international arms dealing and much more on
monitoring developments in Germany. French intelligence officers
noted that Vrinten 'frequently travels to Germany to take part in Nazi
Party meetings and events. Over the past two months or so, he has
been entirely focused on such activities.' The French may have been
aware that Vrinten kept a roster of all the agents run by the Dutch
office: these amounted to a tally of fifty-two full-time agents, as well as
numerous casual informers, almost all of whom were based inside
Germany.[29]

The Bureau was almost certainly unaware, however, of the growing
presence in The Hague of Dansey's Z network. This was run by Captain
Sigismund Best, an old wartime acquaintance of the colonel who had
first visited Holland during the Great War and subsequently stayed
there, marrying a Dutch woman and setting up an import–export
business that allowed him to hide his ongoing although informal association with British Intelligence. Although he cut a very flamboyant
and distinctly British figure in the Dutch capital, sporting a monocle,
bowler hat, and rolled-up umbrella, he was a trained intelligence
officer who knew exactly how to conceal his spying activities, hidden
just as much from the SIS as from the Germans.

The contacts between London and The Hague stepped up sharply
at the beginning of 1936, when French intelligence detected secret
discussions between the two sides about the prospect of a German
invasion of the Low Countries: defenceless before a prospective
German onslaught, the Dutch considered allowing British planes to
use its military airfields, although the French were concerned that the
sheer speed of a German attack, coupled with inevitable delays of
communication, would render such an agreement valueless. But within
just months, the Abwehr and Gestapo had smashed the SIS network in
Holland, dealing a devastating blow to British operations against Nazi
Germany.[30]

But by this time Nazi counter-intelligence also had numerous
prisoners in its grip who had been recruited by these Danish and
Dutch stations, and it did not hesitate to extract as much information
from them as it could.

29. Vrinten—7NN 395/101 SHD.   30. Forcade 241.

SIS operations in The Hague were blown in 1937, when Dalton's replacement, Major Monty Chidson, recruited a young Dutchman, Folkert van Koutrik, who was secretly working for the Abwehr. The Germans had now infiltrated the SIS station in The Hague. Making matters more difficult for the SIS was the fact that, despite Dutch neutrality and its close ties with the authorities, there were by this time numerous pro-German sympathizers within its government and the ranks of its police and intelligence services, where fear of communism outweighed fear of Hitler and his Reich.[31]

The relationship between the Dutch government and both the Deuxième Bureau and the SIS was by this time strained. The Dutch authorities were now giving them 'virtually no assistance', reported the French at the end of 1936, although shortly afterwards Dutch intelligence did provide their French counterparts with a dossier detailing the names and details of German refugees in their country. Now that their Dutch operations had been compromised, the British and French instead shifted their attention to Copenhagen. But resources were very stretched, recruits hard to find, and the Germans extremely vigilant.[32]

The Nazis had dealt British Intelligence a very heavy blow. The SIS now had more reason than before to seek help from its French counterparts if it was to make any real inroads in the closely guarded Reich.

31. Koutrik—West 49; sympathizers—Forcade 239.
32. Dutch dossier—Forcade 239.

14

British Intelligence Watches
the Reich

In June 1937, the Deuxième Bureau provided the British government with more intelligence information, the source of which was once again almost certainly Agent Asche.

The material was an analysis of some military exercises that the German armed forces had carried out the previous year, and it described some of the different ways in which the Luftwaffe could be deployed in the event of war. However, if the French wanted the document to land a 'knock-out blow' on the British and persuade them of the indispensability of their intelligence service and the benefits of an alliance, then their effort failed. Before forwarding it to the prime minister, Sir Maurice Hankey added a note, stating that it contained nothing new, while some weeks later the British air attaché in Berlin also personally witnessed the German army's exercises and his own statements confirmed what the French said.[1]

If the French saw their document as a political bombshell, then it had missed its target. In the summer of 1937, British Intelligence still had enough of its own sources of information on Germany to keep the Deuxième Bureau at arm's length even if, by this time, the British and French air ministries had formally agreed to exchange information about Germany.[2]

Some of this information came from an anonymous visitor who in April had arrived, unforeseen, unseen, and unnoticed, at the British embassy in Zurich and posted a letter addressed to the 'Officer

---

1. 'German Air Force', CAB 104/32 TNA; Wark 'Baltic Myths' 63.
2. Jackson in Alexander and Philpott 139.

Commanding the Military Section of the Intelligence Service'. Signed in simple, clear handwriting by a 'B. Jones', the author wrote complimentary words about Britain and claimed to be able to obtain highly classified Luftwaffe documents for an undisclosed fee. Frank Foley took over the case and used the only means which the letter gave—an anonymous post office box in Germany—to contact the mysterious messenger. Over the next few months, 'Mr Jones' provided British consuls in Germany and Switzerland with several documents before suddenly disappearing in February 1938.[3]

Meanwhile, more detailed information continued to reach London from Malcolm Christie's equally enigmatic source, 'X'. The Air Ministry experts remained intrigued by this anonymous individual, guessing that he was probably motivated 'by a desire to harm the present regime in Germany' rather than by any financial motive, and wanted to know if he had any vested interest in exaggerating the facts and figures he was sending them. 'It would assist enormously in assessing the authenticity of his figures if we were allowed to know something of the source himself and his means of access to German state secrets,' as one report noted, 'but all information of this nature has so far been withheld.'[4]

Then, in May 1937, after weeks of waiting, Christie forwarded another report. This was the third compilation that X had sent to the British, 'one of which had proved correct and the second of which was then on the way to fulfilment. It also proved correct.' And now this third report, as Maurice Hankey wrote to Air Marshal Ellington, confirmed 'your worst anticipations'. This was because it provided Whitehall with the full details about a new German expansion plan 'of greatly increased magnitude', which aimed at creating 360 squadrons by the end of 1939. This was a staggering figure, well beyond anything the British had anticipated. The source gave details about the sites and structure of the newly reorganized and expanded air force, and their anticipated deployment in wartime.[5]

Admitting that all of X's earlier reports had previously provoked considerable disagreement amongst them, experts at the Air Ministry now quickly accepted the report as entirely genuine and accurate.

3. Jeffery 298.
4. 'Notes on Germany's Air Force Programme', 31 May 1937, AIR 40/2043 TNA.
5. Wark *Ultimate Enemy* 60.

'Subsequent events', they concluded, 'have proved that the substance of his reports was undoubtedly correct...and his information can be relied upon as trustworthy. We have no hesitation in accepting the present report as genuine. It cannot be doubted that this writer is in possession of a great deal of accurate and valuable information.' They now accepted that the Luftwaffe would soon comprise 360 squadrons, despite the Ministry's original estimates that 'there was to be a pause in the creation of new units'.[6]

Some days later, on 11 June, Whitehall officials used Christie as an intermediary to obtain more information from this source, sending a questionnaire that asked for clarification and further details, as well as asking him to account for certain discrepancies in his earlier document. These supplementary questions were varied in scope, ranging from the strength of the war reserve and the output of flying schools to the design and use of gun turrets. Several days later, they received some answers that seemed to confirm the accuracy of the earlier reports, and once again the Air Ministry pleaded for more information. But X now disappeared from view and no more was heard from him. If he had now been captured and executed, then his work had not been in vain because it spurred British defence chiefs to draw up and press ahead urgently with a plan to drastically beef up the RAF.[7]

By now, British Intelligence was also obtaining information from other visitors who made their way to a number of German industrial sites in the course of 1937. During the summer, for example, a British engineer and industrialist, Roy Fedden, made a tour of Germany that William de Ropp, who was always able to arrange trips and meetings that helped sell the Reich to the outside world, had arranged on his behalf.

Fedden knew, of course, that the Luftwaffe's 'open doors' approach had much superficial window dressing but his visits gave him a good idea of the technical advances that the Germans had made since Hitler came to power. 'The aircraft production factories...are extensive, modern, highly organized plants', he judged, 'of which we have nothing comparable in this country', where industry was 'obsolete and inadequate' by comparison.[8]

Of particular interest were the 'shadow factories' that his German escorts and minders wanted to keep hidden from view. Despite their best efforts, he was able to discern that each of the four main parent companies in the Reich—BMW, Junkers, Mercedes-Benz, and Siemens—operated two separate self-contained 'shadow factories' that were located close to, but hidden from, a main site that they worked in tandem with. Of these 'shadow' plants, he was only allowed to visit BMW's operation at Eisenach. He was struck, above all, by its virtual invisibility from the air, consisting as it did of just five individual buildings, all of which were carefully located in a dense pine wood, and each of which had only two storeys, whose roofs were camouflaged. And because the shadow factory had its own separate power supplies, it could keep operating even if the main plant was attacked and knocked out of action.

Fedden was also much impressed by another aspect of the German arms industry. This was the 'tremendous seriousness and enthusiasm of everybody connected with this industry in Germany'. The German government was doing everything it could, he emphasized, 'to improve the social standing and technical mentality of their staff'. By contrast, nowhere in Great Britain was there a comparable 'personal touch and obvious bond between the employees, the management and the owners'. Such an impressive emphasis on social conditions and welfare, he concluded, would be of real benefit to the factories and their output. Writing to Winston Churchill on 5 October, he concluded that 'I am absolutely shattered at the tremendous progress of aircraft and engine production in Germany, not from a technical aspect so much as in quantity and organization. What they are doing is quite astounding.'[9]

Other visiting experts were even more taken aback by German prowess. In October, Fedden forwarded a very troubling report written by an individual who admitted to being 'profoundly concerned' by what he had seen first-hand during successive trips to Germany. The Germans, this source argued, had already long surpassed the British in both the quality and quantity of their arms output. The Reich had raced so far ahead, judged this informant, that 'the declared British

8. 'German Air Force', CAB 104/32 TNA.
9. Martin Gilbert *Winston S. Churchill: The Prophet of Truth* Houghton Mifflin (1977) 871.

plan of having an Air Force which is on a basis of parity with Germany by April 1939 is quite out of the question'. Even more serious, he continued, was the state of British aircraft which he deemed to be 'completely inadequate…unsuitable and restricted' compared with Germany's. Unless the government faced up to this dire reality then there was 'not the least chance of our ever approaching parity with Germany'.[10]

But German industry still had its limits, notably its dependency upon, and shortage of, imported raw materials. In September 1937, for example, British Intelligence learned from sources within these industries that 'the great Rheinmetall firm, manufacturers both of armaments and consumption goods in a very large way, and which until recently had experienced no difficulties in obtaining steel for any purpose, was [now] living from hand-to-mouth with stocks only sufficient for 10–12 days', forcing the firm to defer some private and export work. Some of these shortages were due to 'administrative blunders' as well as domestic demand. One source of information on these shortages was the metals market in the City of London, which indicated the size of the German strategic reserve of crucial materials such as rubber, aluminium, copper, and ferro-alloys. The SIS also received other information that denoted technical obstacles confronting the German arms industry: 'reports have been received from many quarters', went one such assessment, about 'a falling-off in the standard of excellence of German work in many spheres' because so many relatively unskilled labourers had been so 'hurriedly pressed into service'.[11]

In Berlin, the new British military attaché, Colonel Frederick Hotblack, also noted that a severe shortage of crucial metals and food supplies was constraining German ambitions. 'The Achilles Heel is the purchase of metal for armaments abroad. This depends on many factors which cannot be foreseen,' such as poor German harvests and on the global availability of the raw materials. One consequence was that while the German generals had regained their prestige 'more quickly than the most optimistic had estimated, they are nevertheless extremely anxious not to jeopardize this happy situation' by getting involved in a

10. 'Precis of Reports on Visits to Germany', Oct 1937, CAB 104/32 TNA.
11. Sept 1937—'Rate of Output of Arms', 20 Nov 1937, FO 371/20732 TNA. Shortages—Wark *Ultimate Enemy* 178. Metals market—'Rate of Output of Arms', 20 Nov 1937, FO 371/20732 TNA. SIS—'Rate of Output of Armaments in 1937', 20 Nov 1937, WO 190/379 TNA.

protracted conflict. He added that the top brass thought highly of the British and French armed forces and their willingness to fight, whereas the Nazi Party hierarchy was relatively contemptuous.[12]

Whitehall also needed Hotblack's opinion about the ambitions and plans of the Nazi leadership. Was the general staff 'obsessed with the idea of a concentrated attack on France, as Hitler advocated in *Mein Kampf*?', Whitehall asked Hotblack. 'Or alternatively are they paying more attention to the possibility of a campaign on Germany's Eastern frontiers?', pursuing a policy of *Drang nach Osten* ('Drive to the East'). Others had asked and tried to answer this vital question, and shortly before he left Berlin to take up the ambassadorship in Paris, Sir Eric Phipps argued that the Germans would move both east and west, prompting Eden to ask his spy service to assess Hitler's likely intentions.[13]

Unknown to the SIS and to the watching world, Hitler knew exactly where he wanted to turn, having spent the past few months secretly drawing up war plans that gave terrifying substance to his semi-coherent ramblings in *Mein Kampf* about acquiring 'living space' in the east for his fellow nationals. After finalizing these aims in a speech before his generals on 5 November, they were subsequently summarized in a highly confidential document by a Wehrmacht officer, Colonel Friedrich Hossbach. But despite private talk about 'vassalizing' central Europe, Hitler and his entourage gave nothing away in public.

Wholly unaware of the Hossbach memorandum, Hotblack looked for clues to German plans. Basing his views on his conversations and observations, he felt that the Germans were likely to look eastwards, arguing that 'Herr Hitler and the Army both consider expansion east-wards to be essential, and that it is hoped that such expansion will at the most lead to minor wars, such as the three German "wars of unity" of the 19th century'. The composition of the German army revealed nothing, however, since it was 'organized with a view to the possibility of fighting both in the East and West, though there is a tendency to give more consideration to a campaign in the East'.[14]

12. Hotblack—'German Military Preparations', 6 Sept 1937, FO 371/20733 TNA. Top brass—'German Military Preparedness', Aug 1937, FO 371/20733 TNA.
13. 25 Apr 1936, CAB 24/262 TNA; Cowling 145.
14. 'German Military Equipment'; 25 Jan, 11 Feb 1937, FO 371/20733 TNA.

Some months before, in January 1937, several further clues to Berlin's plans had also emerged when British Intelligence discovered that the Germans were showing particular interest in winter warfare. 'I hear from reliable sources that the German General Staff are particularly anxious to study "winter warfare"', noted Hotblack, arguing that Berlin had instructed German attachés in Scandinavian countries to make 'special efforts' to obtain information on this matter. It was, he continued, of 'the greatest importance' to ensure that German army transport would be able to cope with 'the difficult conditions on Germany's eastern frontiers, and will not be tied to the good roads which are available in Germany itself'. Hotblack found other unmistakable clues elsewhere in Germany: during a trip to Bavaria in early 1937, he came across Alpine troops who were 'specially equipped to operate in the snow and in mountains', and saw motorized units that were also perfecting their expertise in driving in icy conditions. Field-Marshal Werner von Blomberg also informed Hotblack that such moves helped to redress a much-needed balance because landowners had previously denied the army permission to train in the mountains, depriving the country of an Alpine Corps.[15]

Hotblack also closely tracked the fluctuating and complex state of public morale and popular opinion. He thought he detected a 'lack of united devotion to the regime at home', which was one factor that 'will increase the General Staff's unwillingness to incur the risk of a long and general war'. This relative disunity was the result of a generational divide, comprising 'anxiety with regard to the future' amongst older age groups while 'the younger generation were almost unanimous in their delight in the progress which was being made in Germany'. He also found a 'marked fall in British popularity' at around this time, probably because determined and persistent Nazi propaganda was making an impact. At the same time, there was a continued reverence amongst many ordinary people for the armed forces, and he commented on a visit to a German army exercise where soldiers 'appear to have been received everywhere with great enthusiasm by the civil population, who gave up to them more accommodation than was actually demanded'.[16]

15. Greatest importance—'Winter Warfare', 18 Jan 1937, FO 371/20733 TNA. Blomberg—Hotblack to Phipps, 16 Feb 1937, FO 371/20733 TNA.
16. Public morale—'German Military Preparations', 6 Sept 1937, FO 371/20733 TNA. British popularity—'German Military Equipment', 25 Jan 1937, FO 371/20733 TNA. Reverence—German Manoeuvres 1937, 12 Oct 1937, FO 371/20732 TNA.

Obtaining more specific information, however, remained very difficult. For example, the International Motor Show in Berlin promised to be a useful source of information but at the last minute the Nazi authorities suddenly and unexpectedly withdrew some of the army's latest vehicles from the show. And although military attachés had previously been invited to watch some German army exercises, in 1937 they were suddenly kept away from 'the most important manoeuvres' that were due to take place in north-east Germany. 'The efforts to maintain secrecy', as Hotblack wrote to the newly appointed ambassador in Berlin, Sir Nevile Henderson, 'are in no way being relaxed and camouflage names are being used to cover the organization of new military formations.' In particular, 'great secrecy is being observed on the subject of reserve divisions, and an opportunity has not yet occurred for estimating the fighting value and state of preparedness of these units for war'. The best way of avoiding this security, he continued, was to cultivate friendships with senior German officers. 'The art of secrecy is being so highly developed in this country', wrote Colonel Hotblack, 'that it is now essential to lose no opportunity of meeting Germans on friendly terms if information on current affairs is to be obtained'. He urged British officers to arrange more visits to Germany since such trips gave 'the opportunity of mixing freely with Germans in high positions and of picking up information which subordinates cannot or will not give'.[17]

There were other subtle indications of what was going on in Germany and in the minds of its leaders. In particular, in the winter of 1936–7 some astute observers detected a quicker tempo within the country, as if it was being prepared for war: although they were unaware of it, Hitler's Four-Year Plan, initiated in August 1936 to prepare Germany for full-scale 'total' war by 1940, was making its presence felt. Such a tempo was discernible in February 1937, for example, when, in bitterly cold weather and in conditions of total secrecy, thousands of civilians, all men aged between 35 and 45, were suddenly called up and sent to army training camps. This chilling news only came to the attention of British observers when the local press made an oblique reference to the affair, prompting Hotblack to comment on how 'this training of the population in secrecy is only one of the ways in which

17. Hotblack to Henderson, 14 June 1937, FO 371/20733 TNA. Secrecy—'The German Army', 15 July 1937, FO 371/20733 TNA. British officers—Memo from Berlin 13 Oct 1937, FO 371/20732 TNA.

the German population … is being trained for the role which it should play in the event of war'. He added that the general staff 'consider that this training will greatly increase Germany's total military strength in comparison with 1914'.[18]

By the latter half of 1936, the British were not only obtaining a limited amount of information from their own sources, such as Hotblack, but were also building closer relations with countries, other than France, that were also in a position to monitor the Reich. Relations between the SIS and the Czech intelligence service, for example, were improving markedly at the same time that Franco-Czech relations were distinctly cooling.

In June 1936, the Czechs stopped forwarding intelligence information to Paris and closed down their joint intelligence command, set up with the Deuxième Bureau two years previously, replacing it with the independent, separate, and informal liaison that existed before. This partly reflected Czech concern about a number of security breaches committed by a French liaison officer, Commander Pierre Gouyou, who sometimes failed to encrypt reports that he sent back to Paris, despite protests and remonstration from his superiors. This was no minor matter, since by this time the Germans were intercepting signals traffic between Paris and Prague.[19]

Another reason was that although Moravec's men had provided Paris with a good deal of information, they had received very little, if anything, in return, perhaps because of French fears about Prague's links with Moscow. In the first few months of 1936, for example, Czech spies gave the Bureau information about a wide variety of developments inside the Reich, ranging from the increase in security around its border customs, the movements of armoured vehicles, the output of arms factories, and developments in the construction of new railways. But they received far less information from Paris. Visiting Prague in November 1937 to assess the situation, General Gauché found that the cooperation and trust of earlier days had melted away. Soon Moravec was pulling away from his French counterparts, noting 'their lack of interest and intentional underestimating of the gravity of the situation'.[20]

18. Hotblack, 'German War Preparations', 26 Feb 1937, FO 371/20733 TNA.
19. Gouyou—Forcade 257. Signals—in 1938 Schmidt told the French that the Abwehr was intercepting these signals. See Paillole *Notre espion* 133–4.
20. French fears—Moravec 121. Gauché—Forcade 259; Moravec 122.

At the same time, Moravec and his fellow spies were turning towards London. 'The Czech [intelligence] services hold the British [SIS] in high regard,' noted Gouyou in a confidential despatch in November 1937. The British were equally impressed. Czech intelligence on Germany was 'both extensive and efficient', wrote Brigadier Stronge, the British military attaché in Prague. Equally, his counterpart in Berlin also had very close links with his Czech counterpart, Colonel Hron, whom he considered to be 'one of my most useful and trusted colleagues'.[21]

In early 1938, Whitehall authorized Major Harold Gibson, still the head of the SIS station in Prague, to liaise directly with Moravec to gather more information about German targets. Although Gibson had close contact with his Polish counterpart in Prague, Major Kwiechsky, this did not obstruct his work with Moravec, and this Anglo-Czech collaboration immediately proved fruitful. In March, Gibson reported that the Czechs had provided him with information on German movements in Austria that were 'more detailed and exhaustive than anything I could have hoped to obtain through independent agents'. At the same time Czech contacts assured him that nothing would get in the way of 'our collaboration'.[22]

This growing relationship between the SIS and Prague now proved its worth because the Czech spies were experts at agent-running inside the Reich. Some of their most useful recruits were smugglers, who were of course highly familiar with much of the border territory between the two countries. Most were also open to generous cash bribes, together with guarantees of immunity to prosecution by Czech customs officers. In 1936, for example, an undercover Czech intelligence officer called Alfred Hauke approached two quarry workers called Ferdinand Bienert and Dolní Polná, aware that both moonlighted as smugglers: Hauke offered them a generous cash sum in return for details about German military deployments along the River Neisse. As native German speakers who blended easily into the local area, Bienert and Polná were able to chat to local people near the

21. Gouyou—Forcade 259–60. Stronge—Memo of 23 Jan 1936, sent to Henderson B Braddick; see Braddick *Germany, Czechoslovakia and the Grand Alliance in the May Crisis 1938* University of Denver (1969) 26. Hron—Strong 31.
22. Gibson's links with the Poles were noted by the Deuxième Bureau. See 'Agents de l'intelligence service en France', 27 Jan 1936, 7NN 2229 SHD. Collaboration—Jeffery 307.

Neisse and found it easy to buy drinks for off-duty soldiers, who talked easily and told them what they wanted to know.[23]

Moravec ran hundreds of these 'walkers', who regularly crossed the border and who would leave photos and letters, bearing important information, in pre-assigned 'letterboxes' on Czech soil before heading back into Germany. The challenge for the Czech spy service was verifying such a welter of information. To prove that their informers weren't simply inventing their 'information' or glossing it up, the Czech spies asked for proof that they had really visited the places they claimed, and asked for receipts and even postcards as evidence.

Above all, however, Moravec had by this time acquired another hugely valuable intelligence asset.

The story of 'Agent 54' began in March 1937 when a thick blue envelope, marked 'Very Secret' and addressed to the 'Head of the Czech Intelligence Services', arrived on Moravec's desk. The envelope bore no return address and the only indication about its origin was the postmark, which had been stamped in the frontier town of Chomutov. Consisting of three closely typed pages, the letter 'offered the services' of its author and summarized the topics on which he could provide very precise information, listing them in nine numbered paragraphs. These were wide-ranging and included 'German mobilization plans' and 'armaments' as well as covert Nazi activity on Czech soil. It was signed by 'Karl', who gave details only of an anonymous post office box in Chemnitz as a source of contact, and who requested a face-to-face meeting in the city, stating that he would hand over the documents in return for a very considerable cash payment of 100,000 reichsmarks.[24]

Although Moravec received numerous letters making such offers, he had a strong sense of what was and was not genuine. Most were written by fraudsters and he could spot their giveaway signs within the first paragraph or two, or even the first sentences, of their letters. But he knew instantly from the tone and content that this was genuine. Even the way it was phrased, with very precise sentences and in an 'official' tone of voice, suggested that the author was a trained intelligence professional. And the information he offered was of paramount importance at a time when tension between Berlin and Prague was rising so sharply.

23. Karel Pacner *The Czech Intelligence Services* Themis (2002).
24. Moravec Ch 5 *passim*.

The only downside was the proposed meeting-place. 'Karl' wanted a rendezvous in Chemnitz, which was on German soil, close to the border but nonetheless far too risky for even the most highly trained and experienced Czech intelligence officer to visit. Moravec replied quickly, despite the reservations of some colleagues who sensed a trap, and proposed meeting on home ground.

Within just a few days he received a reply. Karl was willing to cross into Czech territory and meet in the tiny Czech town of Kraslice, just a few hundred yards from the border. Even this venue was dangerous enough because Kraslice lay in the heart of the Sudetenland, where pro-German sentiment was rife amongst a local population that was known to be actively but secretly assisting undercover German agents. It was, admitted Moravec, 'virtually enemy territory'.

Moravec worked out a way of approaching this dangerous initial encounter and wrote to Karl with his suggestions. Again, his contact quickly wrote back, saying that he would appear, as agreed, late at night, entering the town square from a specific place at exactly 11 pm, and that he would identify himself by stopping in front of the church and setting his watch as he stood by the clock tower. Moravec decided to go alone and meet him, while a number of his officers, all acting undercover, would lurk in the background, out of sight, just in case it was a Nazi trap.

They arrived in the town centre well before the appointed hour, approaching it cautiously and taking up carefully selected positions that would guard them against any nasty surprises. At this late hour, a deathly, almost ghostly, hush had descended upon the tree-lined streets of this frontier town, which was lit only by a few gas streetlights.

The clock struck eleven but silence quickly fell. No one appeared. Still the spies waited. Still there was no sign of their mysterious visitor. Just silence.

Another half-hour passed and they were on the verge of giving up and aborting the whole operation when a middle-aged man, holding two suitcases and some packages under his arms, suddenly and silently appeared out of the dark and stood at the venue, adjusting his watch. Moravec and his men felt a surge of relief and excitement. Within minutes, the man was in a car, alongside Moravec and two of his men, and being driven to a safe house a short distance away.

Before them, in the sanctuary of the safe house, stood a German man of medium height and build, with short brown hair and blue eyes.

Although slightly bow-legged, he had a distinctly military bearing and seemed curiously relaxed at such a supremely tense moment. Over coffee and then brandy, Karl gave the suitcases to Moravec's fellow officers, who got to work examining their contents. Then he began to talk.

His visitor, who did not reveal his real name and never did so in the course of his career as an agent for Czech Intelligence, told Moravec his story. He wanted to marry his Serbian girlfriend, he explained, but was too short of money to do so. He added that she hated the Nazi regime, and he himself had never been a supporter of Hitler and his cause in any case. 100,000 reichsmarks was a lot of money, he admitted, but he could and would get far more documents in the future.

After the Second World War it emerged that his real name was in fact not 'Karl' but Paul Thümmel and that his story about a Serb girl-friend and a looming marriage was entirely fictional. He was already married and, it appears, quite happily so. And it seems unlikely that this highly placed and highly decorated German intelligence officer had any motive other than sheer greed. Creating an entirely fictitious identity and personal story probably just helped him to ease his conscience.

Moravec was sceptical about Karl's supposed motives. 'Spies, being human,' as he later wrote, 'often invent a better-sounding motive if their sole reason for betraying their country is money.' But otherwise his visitor sounded quite convincing. From his knowledge and style, Moravec could instantly tell that, as he suspected from the introductory letter, Karl was not a soldier but an intelligence expert. To add weight to his claims, he was carrying some documents that were of priceless value to Moravec. Amongst them was the Nazis' Frontier Defence Plan, showing the exact deployment of Hitler's forces around the Czech border, and some documents revealing how the Nazis were orchestrating unrest amongst the Sudeten Germans in Czechoslovakia. Even more alarming was proof of a high-level mole inside the Czech government, who had leaked top-secret information to Berlin.

Throughout the course of this initial meeting, the Czech spies continually probed their visitor for more information, just to make entirely sure he was who he claimed to be. They asked him about the meaning of certain abbreviations and references that were used in the documents, well aware of what the right answers were. Each and every time they heard the answers they wanted to hear, as Karl responded effortlessly and accurately with the same unruffled calm.

From Moravec's point of view, this traitor to Germany was entirely genuine, a superb intelligence asset who could, and did, provide extremely valuable information. After four hours of discussions, Moravec agreed to pay the money, here and now, if Karl could promise to provide more information, as well as surrender the documents before them. Karl agreed. He would arrange regular meetings with Moravec, always on Czech soil, and use coded letters and postcards, sent to a residential address in Prague, to let Moravec know when he had information ready. In the event of an emergency, he continued, he would use secret ink. And in a clear indication of his professional training in intelligence work, he said that he would use the latest methods of encryption to do so.

It was now nearly dawn and, as the daylight started to break, the Czech spies drove Karl back to the market square in Kraslice, where he silently slipped out of the car. He was now a wealthy man although, no longer bearing the heavy suitcases, he was also lighter in pocket.

'Karl' had now become Agent 54, or A-54, and within weeks was providing Czech Intelligence with further top-quality information. In July, at a meeting in Chomutov, he informed Moravec that the German armed forces had been wargaming an attack, codenamed *Operation Green*, against Czechoslovakia. So sophisticated were the plans, he added, that the Nazis had even built several exact replicas of key Czech fortifications, allowing their elite units to work out and rehearse ways of seizing them. Karl also told them that Berlin intended to stir up unrest amongst the Sudeten population and then take 'names at random from the telephone book to publicise them as martyrs to Czech brutality'. The Nazis would then seize on the subsequent Czech reaction and use it as an excuse to launch an outright attack, launching lightning strikes at several specific, carefully chosen points along the border, just north of the town of Kraliky, and then splitting the Czech army into two helpless halves. The German generals estimated that all of this could be done, and the whole of Czechoslovakia taken, in a matter of just days. Moravec was stunned by the quality of the information as well as the audacity of the German plan, and within hours had informed the Czech government, Gibson, and Colonel Louis Rivet, who became Bureau chief in 1936.[25]

25. Telephone book—Robert Kee *Munich: The Eleventh Hour* Hamish Hamilton (1988) 144.

Soon A-54 revealed more details about the sheer scale and daring of the Nazi plans to take the Sudetenland. He told Moravec that he had been tasked with setting up a network of secret transmitters inside Czechoslovakia that German agents, all Czech nationals, could use to keep in close contact with their puppet masters in Berlin. The plan was that, when a signal was given, these agents would undertake acts of sabotage and violence that would incite anti-Czech feeling amongst the Sudeten Germans and stir up demands for independence or political union with Germany. 'Karl' not only told Moravec the whereabouts of these transmitters but also provided details of the secret codes that German units would be using in the event of hostilities.[26]

Events were marching to the drumbeat of war.

26. 'Annexe aux statuts du M.', 1 May 1936, 7NN 2682-1 and 'Report on Czechoslovak intelligence by Colonel H. Kühnmunch' (chief of the Belfort SR station), 1 Apr 1938, 7NN 2622 SHD; Jackson *France and the Nazi Menace* 28.

15

The 'Spies' Who Never Were,
1937–1938

In the closing weeks of 1937, the British and French intelligence services suddenly moved closer together, starting a new phase of their long and complex relationship.

This was a sudden shift because relations between the SIS and the Deuxième Bureau had been cool and distant just weeks before, when Colonel Menzies had travelled to Paris to meet Rivet and other senior members of the Bureau. During this October visit, in contrast to the letter he had penned in April 1935, Menzies's attention was focused on Germany and the threat it posed. But if the French had entertained high hopes about the purpose of his journey, they were disappointed. During his brief visit to the capital, Menzies had spent little more than an hour with his French counterparts and did so only after an initial meeting with the British air attaché, as though he was more important and meeting anyone else was just a formality.

Nor did Menzies provide Rivet with any confidential information, instead claiming only that the SIS had no material to share because there were so many gaps in its knowledge about Germany and its armaments. Instead he made a series of predictions, none of which were in any way original, about Hitler's next moves. The Nazis, he argued, would probably seek to annex Austria and then act against Czechoslovakia, adding that neither British nor French public opinion would support war against Germany over these conquests. Such support, he concluded, would not be forthcoming even if their armed forces were ready for conflict against Germany which, he added, they weren't at this stage. Rivet's report on the visit was brief and terse, and mentioned the way in which Menzies had 'thrown his views around carelessly and without conviction'.[1]

But within just two months there was a noticeable turnaround, as the SIS actively sought closer ties with Rivet's organization, calling for more frequent meetings and exchanges of information. In early January 1938, as they reviewed developments over the preceding year, the heads of the Deuxième Bureau praised *les résultats tangibles* of their improved liaison with London, as well as the 'favourable contact with particular people' within the Polish, Dutch, and Czech secret services. And a few weeks later, General Gamelin was prepared to acknowledge 'considerable progress' in the relationship between the SIS and the Bureau, noting 'the first meaningful, direct collaboration between representatives of the two bodies' that had 'yielded considerable results'. Soon, the War Office in London would be providing the French military attaché in London, General Albert Lelong, with regular intelligence updates about Nazi Germany, which he used to compile detailed reports that he sent back to Paris. Meanwhile in the French capital, the British military attaché, Colonel William Fraser, forwarded War Office assessments directly to Gamelin.[2]

This interaction continued. On 19 January, Winterbotham had also made another trip to Paris to share information about the Luftwaffe while the British air attaché in Paris, Group Captain Colyer, provided Rivet with a number of photographs, plans, and prospective targets that he had requested. More high-level meetings and exchanges were subsequently held: at a conference in Paris on 3–4 March, the British and French drew up plans to jointly compile dossiers on German industry, assessed vulnerabilities and weak points in the Nazi war machine, and staked out different parts of German territory where each would focus their respective resources.[3]

These discussions then led to more formal Franco-British negotiations on defence and cooperation that were held in London at the end of April between the prime minister, Édouard Daladier, and the foreign secretary, the 1st Earl of Halifax, the newly appointed foreign minister who inexplicably judged Hitler to be 'very sincere' and bizarrely compared Göring to 'a modern-day gamekeeper at Chatsworth'.

1. Compte-Rendu de visite de Menzies, 19–20 Oct 1937, 7NN 2701 SHD; Jeffery 289.
2. Jan 1938—SR Réunion des Chefs de Poste, Jan 1938, 7NN 2693 SHD. Gamelin—Forcade 215. Fraser—Jackson in Alexander and Philpott 142.
3. Forcade 213–15.

Relations between London and Prague had by this time also taken a step closer. Shortly before, in early March, Moravec and ten of his fellow officers had flown to London to share a treasure trove of information with British officials.[4]

The British government and its spy services had moved closer to their French counterparts for a number of reasons. One was that some startling intelligence information had—allegedly—fallen into the hands of the Deuxième Bureau, clearly showing that Hitler's plans were no longer defensive, designed to fend off foreign attack, but unmistakably aggressive. This, at least, was the claim of Paul Paillole, a senior officer of the Service de Renseignements throughout the 1930s.[5]

Paillole claimed that, early in the morning of 6 November 1937, a French journalist in Berlin by the name of Georges Blun had unexpectedly received a dramatic phone call. The message was brief in the extreme: 'Uncle Kurt has died.' Blun knew exactly what the message meant and within minutes he had headed off to a prearranged meeting place.[6]

Like many other journalists in the German capital, Blun was an informer, although not a paid agent, of the French intelligence services. The message on the phone was a distinctive call sign that immediately identified one particular agent: Hans-Thilo Schmidt. Agent Asche had agreed to use this to signal that he had information of the highest importance at his disposal and would meet at a specially chosen rendezvous—the waiting-room at Charlottenburg railway station in the city centre—to pass it on. Blun arrived there soon afterwards, confident that they would not attract unwanted attention at such a venue and at the height of rush hour. He then surreptitiously picked up a package that Schmidt, sitting alongside, left behind as he got up to leave.

Schmidt's package contained a summary of Hitler's speech of 5 November, detailing his plans of aggressive conquest. The Nazi jackboot was ready to stamp on the face of whole swathes of Europe according to a precise timetable: Austria would fall in the spring of 1938; Czechoslovakia in autumn 1938; Poland in autumn 1939; and then northern France in the spring of 1941. Schmidt's brother had heard about Hitler's plans from Colonel Hossbach, and then, trustingly,

4. Halifax—Forcade 214; Adamthwaite *The Making of the Second World War* 63.
5. Gauché 34.
6. Paul Paillole *The Spy in Hitler's Inner Circle* Casemate (2016) 90.

told him what the *Führer* had said. Within hours, the information had been passed to André François-Poncet, the French ambassador in Berlin, and then went straight to the highest levels in Paris.

If this account is true, then it is inconceivable that the Bureau would not have shared such shattering, top-grade information with London, even though it would of course have continued to closely guard its source. The repercussions on British security of a German invasion and occupation of any area of France and its northern coasts were of course self-evidently enormous, just as in 1793 and 1914 the mere threat that a hostile enemy power would dominate the North Sea led to a British declaration of war. The British would have had no choice but to strike an immediate alliance with Paris, or at least build much closer relations.

But there are reasons to suppose that Paillole's account hugely exaggerates the value of any such information that Agent Asche provided: François-Poncet's telegram of 6 November was just brief and only mentioned 'problems' in the Reich's supply of raw materials, while the diaries of senior figures in Paris, such as Colonel Rivet, render only a quick reference to the agent's material.[7]

Instead, events in the Far East provide a more convincing explanation for the closer embrace between the SIS and its French counterparts. In July, the Japanese attacked China, sending shockwaves of alarm in London, where the Imperial navy was viewed as a rapidly growing threat to the security of the British Empire. 'We cannot provide simultaneously for hostilities with Japan and Germany,' as Chamberlain had previously written. At the same time, British and French ships were being targeted by Italian submarines as they traded with Spanish Republican ports. 'There were limits to our resources both physical and financial,' as the prime minister told the Committee of Imperial Defence on 5 July, 'and it was vain to contemplate fighting singlehanded the three strongest powers in combination.' By this time Italy also seemed to be moving closer to both Germany and Japan, and in November, two months after he had visited Berlin, Mussolini joined the Anti-Comintern Pact that Hitler and the Emperor Hirohito had signed the previous year.[8]

7. Adamthwaite, 'French Military Intelligence and the Coming of War' 192 in Christopher Andrew and Jeremy Noakes (eds) *Intelligence and International Relations 1900–45* University of Exeter (1987) 31.
8. CID 5 July—Paul W Doerr *British Foreign Policy 1919–39* Manchester University Press (1998) 209; Chamberlain—Adamthwaite *The Making of the Second World War* 63–4.

But there were other reasons why the British and French intelligence services were moving so much closer together. Until February 1938, when Joachim von Ribbentrop ended his term as the German ambassador in London, Hitler had entertained high hopes of striking an accord with Britain that would allow him a relatively free hand to pursue his ambitions on continental Europe. But Ribbentrop's failure to win this agreement infuriated the German leader, who now vowed to ignore British interests and press ahead regardless. In November, as he termed Britain and France as 'our enemies who both hate us', Hitler ordered his navy to make long-term preparations for conflict—a clear sign that he was preparing for war with Great Britain, as a naval power, in particular.[9]

In addition, by late 1937 both countries were overestimating the military strength of the Third Reich. Amongst politicians, this overstatement would help create and sustain the cause of appeasement, as figures like the foreign secretary, the 1st Earl of Halifax, Neville Chamberlain, and the British ambassador in Berlin, Sir Nevile Henderson, argued that satisfying Hitler's demands was more likely than a policy of threats and deterrence to lead to *détente* with Germany. These overestimates also drove the SIS and the Bureau closer together.

This image of German power was projected by a distinctive mindset. In London and in Paris, many an imagination was gripped by worst-case scenarios. Fears were widespread that, in the event of war, the Luftwaffe would inflict a devastating 'knock-out blow' against undefended big cities, killing huge numbers of civilians. It was significant, for example, that when he flew to Germany to negotiate with Hitler in 1938, Neville Chamberlain looked down at London and imagined the mass destruction caused by German bombs. And in Paris, General Joseph Vuillemin declared that, in the event of war, Germany was capable of wiping out his own air force in a matter of just fifteen days.[10]

These fears now started to grow markedly. This was essentially because foreign intelligence services, despite their successes, still lacked a clear picture of Germany's true strength. In September 1937, for example, the Air Ministry had admitted to an 'alarming shortage' of

9. Ian Kershaw *Hitler: 1936–45 Nemesis* WW Norton & Co (2000) 100.
10. Mindset—see in general Wark *Ultimate Enemy* Ch 3 *passim*. Chamberlain—24 Sept 1938, CAB 27/646 TNA; Wark 'Baltic Myths' 65–7. Vuillemin—15 Mar 1938, DDF 1932–9, Vol 8 No 446.

information about the Luftwaffe, and called for the creation of a specialized technical department with the expertise to properly assess
German capabilities. At the same time, the War Office was regularly
complaining that the SIS was failing to meet its growing and urgent
need for accurate information about the Reich, while the Air Ministry
dismissed its intelligence as 'normally 80% inaccurate'. Such criticisms
forced Sir Alexander Cadogan to mount a spirited defence of British
Intelligence.[11]

On such a relatively blank canvas, it was easy for the Germans to
paint a picture of their own making, or else for others to do this on
their behalf. But this image was largely superficial, undertaken by a
regime that remained true to its origins: born and raised in the rough-
est streets of the Weimar Republic, its guttural instincts were those of a
strutting street fighter that bullied its enemies with threats, fear, and
intimidation.

In truth, Hitler was bluffing the outside world with remarkable success, creating a muscular image that disguised a lightweight. While
German factories were producing far more planes than ever before,
these raw production figures in fact revealed little meaningful information because they potentially showed replacements of existing
planes rather than additional capacity. Many of the Luftwaffe's 'air
squadrons' really existed only on paper or were considerably under
strength because of a state of disorganization. Widening this gulf
between theory and practice was the fact that, at any given time, a
significant proportion of planes were being repaired or serviced, and
often by ground staff that had limited technical expertise. All of these
different things—the mediocre quality of the ground personnel,
including air traffic control, the limited numbers of reservists and
reserve aircraft, which the British hugely overestimated, and the shortage of staff officers to train for military operations—help explain not
only the Luftwaffe's high rate of accidents but, more generally, why
'production figures' were superficial.[12]

Another serious limitation was the quality of German aircraft. The
'combat aircraft' produced by German factories, as Richard Overy has
concluded, were in fact often 'little more than trainers' or advanced
trainers. Between 1933 and 1937, around two-thirds of Germany's total

11. Sept 1937—Wark *Ultimate Enemy* 65. Cadogan—Hinsley 55–6.
12. On paper—RJ Overy, 'German Air Strength 1933 to 1939: A Note', *HJ* (1984) 466.

production was made up of non-combat planes, and even in 1939 these comprised nearly half of the total, while another quarter was composed of 'auxiliary bombers' that were not a serious military threat to any enemy. 'Many of the aircraft that the German air force counted as first-line', he continues, 'were of relatively poor performance and of doubtful military utility.' As a result, until 1938, Germany's air power was 'a paper tiger, ineffective as a fighting force until the new generation of aircraft that arrived at the end of the 1930s and until sufficient crews had passed through the training schools'. Before 1939, when the Germans started to mass produce their best planes, the Luftwaffe posed 'no real threat to Britain' and even then was not prepared for the events of 1940.[13]

A few experts saw through the superficial German picture. In December 1936, for example, a French businessman, working for a defence manufacturer called Societé Ariel, visited the British air attaché in Paris and informed him about a visit to Germany made by an acquaintance who worked for a leading French defence company. The visitor was sure that German production methods were a 'failure...the material with which their air force is consequently equipped is of a very inferior quality and is not comparable in efficiency and fighting value to the aircraft possessed by other countries where slower and more painstaking methods of production are in vogue'. He added that 'German aero-engines have been found as unsatisfactory as have the air frames, and new types of engines have to be designed...the German air force will not be a first-class fighting service for at least eighteen months'. But such voices were easily drowned out by the more influential.[14]

One reason why the intelligence services were starting to exaggerate German strength is that they were seduced, quite unconsciously, by the appeal of a contemporary media star who, by late 1937, had started to tell the outside world exactly what the Nazis wanted him to say.

They were seduced because many people viewed Charles Lindbergh as something he wasn't. He was not a high-value intelligence asset with unique sources. And he was not an expert analyst, with a great knowledge of engineering and industrial processes, who was qualified

13. Overy 'German Air Strength' 467, 469.
14. Memo from Group Captain Colyer, Paris to London, 28 Dec 1934, FO 371/20731 TNA.

to predict how far and fast the Nazis would produce aircraft. Nor, for that matter, was the individual who invited him into the intelligence game against Nazi Germany—the American attaché in Berlin, Major Smith, who was an army man with no real expertise on aviation matters. Lindbergh was doubtlessly amazed by the weight that many people attached to his words, admitting on one occasion that he 'was not a military expert'.[15]

But the superlative terms in which Smith described his fellow American help explain why Lindbergh exerted such a remarkable but unwarranted influence over so many contemporaries.

Lindbergh, felt Smith, was 'a genius, an explorer and adventurer worthy to stand alongside Columbus'. He was, it was true, a highly driven man. Lindbergh had made himself into a household name a decade before when, in May 1927, at the age of just 25, he made history by undertaking the first non-stop, and the first solo, flight from New York to Paris, carrying out this feat in a single-seat monoplane called *The Spirit of St Louis*. Not only was this a real landmark in the history of aviation, one that spurred huge interest and investment in the future of air travel, but it was also a remarkable triumph of personal resilience and daring, since he had covered 3,600 miles in the course of his 33-hour journey. Overnight 'the Lone Eagle' became one of the most famous people in the world, as newspapers splashed his name, cameras rolled, and the highest honours and decorations, including America's Medal of Honour, poured in. He received hundreds of letters every day from fans across the world, forcing him to hire a team of clerical staff to deal with the deluge. The reputation of 'America's most popular personality' had soared to extraordinary heights.[16]

The great man and his diminutive wife Anne had at this point retreated from the public gaze, trying to live a quieter life away from the glare of media scrutiny and even disguising themselves when they left home in a bid to avoid unwelcome attention. But the hyperbole and exaggeration continued to follow him. When, in March 1932, his infant son was kidnapped from their home in New Jersey and murdered, the media termed the tragedy, shocking and appalling though it was, 'the Crime of the Century'.

15. Adamthwaite *France and the Coming of the Second World War* 240.
16. On Lindbergh's fame, see Memo from the British Embassy, Washington 27 Dec 1935, FO 115/3408 TNA.

But his name still cropped up from time to time in the pages of the national press. And when, in May 1936, Smith saw a newspaper article about a trip that Lindbergh had made to several French aircraft factories to see first-hand the latest developments in aviation, he wondered if his fellow American would do the same in Germany.

Smith felt sure that the Germans would welcome any association with Lindbergh. Given his worldwide fame, Nazi propagandists would view any visit as an endorsement of their regime and exploit it to the full, particularly before the forthcoming Olympics in Berlin. A visitor as eminent as Lindbergh bestowed a certain amount of recognition and respect in the eyes of the world, and also curried favour from the world's most powerful nation. Smith now made some initial enquiries to his key contacts in the Luftwaffe, asking them if they would be interested to host the great American, and within almost no time he received a positive response. Smith decided to write Lindbergh a handwritten and personal letter, one that appealed to his strong patriotism. The approach worked and Lindbergh duly made his first trip to Germany at the end of July 1936.

Over the course of their ten-day trip, the Lindberghs met many leading figures in Nazi Germany, including the Hohenzollerns, Hermann Göring, and Ernst Udet, and attended an honorary lunch with numerous German and American guests. Smith hoped that the Germans would do everything they could to impress their highly esteemed visitor as they toured the various military sites that Lindbergh was invited to view.[17]

With Smith at his side, Lindbergh's tour had started at some of the airfields in and around Berlin, where he saw first-hand many different types of German aircraft, including the Ju-87 and the ground attack plane, the Stuka. Döberitz airfield, just outside the capital, was home to an elite fighter group whose standard of German flying he judged to be only 'of mediocre quality', even if its infrastructure and buildings were very modern and impressive, while the personnel all had an excellent attitude. However, he was particularly taken aback by the quality of some other sites he then visited, notably a research facility at Adlershof, south of the capital, which was headed by a noted aeronautical scientist, Dr Seewald.

17. Hessen 94–109.

The following year, Smith invited Lindbergh back to Germany to make another intelligence-gathering trip. The aviator immediately accepted the invitation from his good and trusted friend, and arrived on 11 October to start a two-week journey.

Overall, Lindbergh made four trips to the Reich. Soon he was given relatively unrestricted access to numerous sites and demonstrations, and he paid visits to the Focke-Wulf factory in Bremen, where he saw an experimental helicopter, and to the Henschel, Daimler, and BMW factories, where he flew several planes. He made his fourth and final trip to the Reich in 1938, when Hermann Göring awarded him a Nazi medal, the Service Cross of the German Eagle, that not only attracted a great deal of publicity but also provoked a great deal of criticism that severely damaged his reputation.

Smith and Lindbergh now worked together on a detailed intelligence report, amounting to four pages, that Smith sent back to the G-2 headquarters in Washington. This 'General Air Estimate' reached some startling conclusions. Germany's air force had made enormous strides over the past few years, it argued, and had already surpassed France in its quality and size. Soon, the author continued, it would surpass British capabilities. The Germans already possessed a vast air fleet of around 10,000 warplanes and it was rapidly expanding at a rate of between 500 and 800 planes every month. At the same time, Smith's report included a great deal of very detailed information about the design of the planes and their engines, as well as how the pilots and crews were trained. Given the importance of these findings, Smith did everything he could to seize attention at the highest levels of power in Washington, writing his report in a provocative style and strongly highlighting Lindbergh's own contribution.[18]

Smith's report attracted a great deal of interest in Washington, and G-2's officers responded by asking a lot of very detailed questions. For the first time since 1935, the attaché felt that he had finally succeeded in drawing attention to the dramatic growth in the size and capabilities of the Luftwaffe, and to the prospective threat that Hitler's Reich posed, just as Lindbergh's visits to Germany had also attracted a great deal of wider American interest there. Soon a number of prominent personalities of the American aviation world also made their own 'veritable pilgrimage' to Germany, including figures such as Glenn Martin,

18. This was the General Air Estimate of 1 Nov 1937.

Laurence Bell, Igor Sikorsky, who provided a good deal of information on Focke-Wulf's experiments with helicopters at Bremen, and James Kindelberger, president of the North American Aviation Company. A number of G-2 officers, academics, and test pilots also paid visits to Germany in the course of 1938.

But all this 'intelligence' had one enormous, glaring flaw. Lindbergh, for all his expertise, had no precise way of verifying the output of German factories. Although he could of course venture his personal opinion on the quality of specific planes and pilots, and about the specific sites he visited, it was not clear why any of his 'estimates' about German strength had any particular value or merited any real attention.

The truth was that his 'estimates' about the strength of the Luftwaffe, with its huge and rapidly expanding air fleet, bore no resemblance to what was really going on. At the time of the Munich crisis, the Luftwaffe's actual strength was 3,315 aircraft and monthly output was less than 300 planes. Nor did these raw numbers state anything about the quality of those planes or of the pilots, their reserves, and back-up. On each and every count, the Germans, for all their dramatic advances over the preceding few years, were not nearly so impressive. Lindbergh, who later acquired a reputation for covertly harbouring pro-Nazi sympathies, certainly helped Hitler and Göring by creating a sense of awe about German military might that would help Berlin to intimidate the outside world.[19]

Smith would have passed many of Lindbergh's findings over to his British and French counterparts in Berlin, with whom he liaised constantly and closely and who would have seized upon such information because it was becoming much harder to obtain. This was partly because the earlier period of goodwill between Berlin on the one hand and Paris and London on the other, when these countries had exchanged visits and shown their visitors considerable courtesy and hospitality, had drawn to an end in late January 1937, after Air Vice Marshall Christopher Courtney had led a mission to Germany and been deliberately deceived by General Milch, a 'slippery figure' in the eyes of the Air Ministry. This had created an intelligence void that

19. Of these 3,315, only 1,246 were serviceable bombers: see Whaley 26. On the outbreak of war, Luftwaffe strength was 3,541—see Wark *Ultimate Enemy* 59.

Lindbergh's observations, particularly of closely guarded sites that British visitors had always been barred from seeing, seemed to fill.[20]

Some experts were always highly sceptical of the value of Lindbergh's reports. Air Marshal Sir John Slessor, a member of the air staff in 1938, felt that the American was 'a striking example of the effect of German propaganda'. And in London the Labour Party's Hugh Dalton pointed out that the American 'had flown the Atlantic but knew no more about military aircraft than our own Amy Johnson'. But these sceptics could not stop Lindbergh from exerting a curious grip over so many contemporaries. In the course of 1938, Lindbergh toured several Western capitals to air his deeply flawed views before highly influential circles, causing deep alarm amongst leading figures such as the French foreign minister, Georges Bonnet: as the British ambassador noted, Bonnet was 'very upset' after listening to Lindbergh 'and said peace must be preserved at any price'. Across the Atlantic, the aviator's wildly exaggerated figures also seduced Franklin D Roosevelt, who estimated that annual German aircraft production stood at 40,000 planes, more than twelve times the actual number of combat aircraft: the upside of this was that the president was willing to divert 20,000 planes from American production lines to Britain and France, prompting him to proclaim that, in the event of war, Chamberlain would feel that 'he had the industrial resources of the American nation behind him'.[21]

Lindbergh had thrown paint onto a sheet of paper and watched, doubtlessly with some bemusement, as onlookers hailed him as a great artist. Like Jerry Sosnowski and William de Ropp, his views and 'intelligence' were assigned far greater importance than they merited, even if he did not deliberately deceive his audience.

This represented a wider flaw in the efforts to gather intelligence on Germany. Such efforts were increasingly falling into the hands of private, parallel networks, run by figures such as Vansittart and Colonel Dansey, that were drawing on a wide variety of sources. Although this produced a great deal of information, there was an obvious downside: such networks lacked the structured, methodical approach to the institutionalized handling of 'intelligence sources' whose value and veracity

20. Courtney—23 June 1937, FO 371/20734 TNA.
21. Slessor—Adamthwaite *France and the Coming of the Second World War* 240. Dalton—Adamthwaite *France and the Coming of the Second World War* 240. Bonnet—14, 16 Sept 1938, FO 800/311 TNA. Roosevelt—'The correspondence of Arthur C. Murray, Note of conversation between Roosevelt and Murray', 23 Oct 1938, British Archives Online.

was open to question. Lindbergh's 'intelligence', for example, made its way straight to the highest levels of government before it had been assessed by in-house experts.

This equally afflicted Z Organization. For example, it relied heavily upon the testimony of refugees who may have hoped for a reward in exchange for 'intelligence', no matter how dubious or fanciful, or who may have wanted to hype up the German threat to try and provoke a war against a regime they hated. Winterbotham, for example, was highly critical of the information that such refugees provided, citing the example of one individual who reported the construction of an airfield in an area that he knew was in fact just a swamp. This reliance upon dubious sources may explain why Z Organization, despite its romantic appeal, deserves to be seen in a very sceptical light: 'what it achieved', as its deputy, Commander Kenneth Cohen, later admitted, 'was very limited'.[22]

Equally, Vansittart later admitted that some of his key sources were not as wholesome as he had wanted to believe. Of Theodor Kordt he wrote that:

I gradually discovered that what he really wanted was a German maximum without war with *us*. His real game was to get a free hand in expansion east, and expansion to the limit, including Russia…Kordt was riddled with the notion of expansion. Otherwise he was a decent, humane man, and emphatically not a Nazi.[23]

And of Carl Goerdeler, a former mayor of Leipzig and a well-connected critic of Hitler, Vansittart's doubts also grew. He later admitted that the German was 'merely a stalking horse for German military expansion…although Dr Goerdeler may from time to time be able to furnish interesting pieces of information on the internal situation in Germany, he is not only worthless but suspect as an intermediary for a settlement'. Earlier, however, he may have looked away from their shortcomings and instead exaggerated the importance of his 'intelligence sources' in a bid to cling to his position as permanent undersecretary when

22. Winterbotham—Read and Fisher 186. The French also felt that 'refugees tend to mistake their own desires for reality': Renseignement, 18 Sept 1935, 7NN 3114 SHD. Cohen—Andrew 382.
23. Rose *Vansittart* 136–8, 222.

Anthony Eden, who was appointed as foreign secretary in 1936, started to ease him out of office.[24]

This fundamental failing of every parallel network and private intelligence agency helps to explain why the British and French governments seriously overestimated the strength of German might and, in the spring of 1939, wholly misjudged Hitler's ambitions towards Poland and Romania. In each case, these misjudgements had disastrous consequences.

But while the two spy services moved closer together, Whitehall still resisted an alliance with France: if London struck up such an alliance, it was argued, then Britain would have to honour the French commitment to Prague. In November, Chamberlain warned the visiting French foreign minister, Yvon Delbos, about 'the state of opinion in England [where] there was a strong current against Great Britain running the risk at any price of being involved in a war for Czechoslovakia, a distant country, with whom England had little in common', particularly when 'the public considered that the Sudeten Germans had not been fairly treated by the Czechoslovak government'. Equally, the top brass was sceptical of France's value as a military partner: although 'France was our most important friend', as the cabinet advised on 8 December, 'and was strong defensively... the French Air Force was far from satisfactory'. Soon after, the British chiefs of staff dismissed any suggestions of joint planning with France on the grounds that 'the very term "staff conversations" had a sinister purport and gives an impression... of mutually assumed military collaboration'. The two old adversaries were still a long way apart.[25]

24. Goerdeler—7 Dec 1938, FO 371/21659 TNA; Goerdeler was mistrusted by some officials in the FO: 'the latest expression of his views does not inspire confidence in his judgment. He sounds rather bewildered', as one official wrote on 30 May 1939: FO 371/23006 TNA.
25. Delbos—'Anglo-French conversations', 29–30 Nov 1937, DDF 1932–9, 2nd series, Vol 7 No 287. Cabinet—Cabinet Memo, 8 Dec 1937, CAB 23/90A TNA. Chiefs of staff— Peter Jackson, 'French Security and a British "Continental Commitment" after the First World War: A Reassessment', *EHR* (Apr 2011) 351; DBFP II series, Vol 19, 853–7.

16

Watching *Anschluss*

The British, French, and Czech spy services were pulling together to find out more about a growing threat that, for all their successes, still remained highly opaque in the spring of 1938. 'We are working in the dark', as an intelligence chief in Whitehall admitted to Admiral Sinclair. Britain's most valuable single source of intelligence, Christie's anonymous informant 'X', had by this time disappeared, but his information had in any case only ever had a limited scope: he had revealed much about the Luftwaffe's capabilities and plans but said nothing about numerous other military and political matters. On these wider issues, there was a dearth of information.[1]

In narrowly military terms, for example, the SIS needed to know much more about the number of reserve planes the Luftwaffe could count on, and where its squadrons were based: one highly classified British report, for example, noted that 'very few' German bomber bases 'have been located, and it will probably call for extensive photographic reconnaissance to identify them in war, since the Germans pay a great attention to camouflage'.[2]

On a wider political level, the SIS still sorely lacked insider information about Hitler's plans and about the personalities, agendas, and rivalries within the ruling elite that surrounded him. In June 1938, for example, Major Malcolm Woollcombe of the SIS admitted that his political intelligence about the Reich was very limited, built 'on a very narrow basis' that had only two 'solid' sources. One was William de Ropp, who was the origin of 'at least 70%' of his political intelligence about Germany. 'If for any reason we lose him, it is obvious that our

1. Sinclair—21 June 1938, AIR 2/1688 TNA.
2. 'List of German Landing Grounds', 14 Dec 1938, AIR 40/1155 TNA.

supply of XP [political intelligence] will...be very seriously affected.'
But de Ropp's value as an asset was open to question. The other source
was a 'first-class' Baltic German who was based in Italy but who nonetheless had information from friends and family living in Germany.
Woollcombe urged his officers to 'find more first-class alternatives' to
these two individuals because 'sources of this type, having real access to
"the goods", are few and far between'.[3]

At least, by this time, the SIS had more resources to count on: in
April 1938, Sinclair told the Deputy Chief of the Air Staff that it was
'not a question of money, as we now have ample funds with which to
take advantage of an opportunity which offers, or any circumstances
that may arise, in which money may help'. But other government
departments, responsible for the evaluation of intelligence information,
remained cash-starved at a time when the British government was
harvesting very meagre tax revenues from its highly depressed economy: the coffers of the Air Ministry, for example, remained severely
malnourished, prompting the officer in charge of its German section
to admit that his department 'lived from hand to mouth'. As a result, it
became difficult to recruit and retain top-quality staff, forcing the
director of air intelligence to make a desperate plea to the War Office
for the loan of several experienced analysts. This was equally true in
France, for in 1938 the budget of the French army's secret intelligence
service was no larger, in real terms, than it had been twenty years before.[4]

The chronic lack of good-quality information became clear in the
summer of 1938 when a senior SIS officer, Commander Reginald 'Rex'
Howard, asked departmental heads to summarize what they knew
about Germany's armed strength. Menzies commented that 'the results
are disappointing in that we have no military sources of any standing
and have to rely on numerous small fry', while Winterbotham added
that 'the results are not very good but I am hopeful'. Captain Russell,
responsible for naval matters, stated that while some of his intelligence
was good—this was a reference to Krüger's information—it nonetheless had only limited scope, since he had no source who was a serving
member of the German navy. And Admiral Charles Limpenny, head of
the Economic Section VI, reported that although he had 'excellent'

---

3. Woollcombe—Jeffery 308–9.
4. Sinclair—Jeffery 295. Desperate plea—21 June and 10 Sept 1938, AIR 2/1688 TNA.
   French budget—Navarre 41.

information on Germany's construction of new vessels, he knew almost nothing about its fleet air arm. In general, there had been 'very little' information 'in regard to production figures and numbers of hands employed in individual factories' over the previous eighteen months, and there was a 'serious lack of information' on land armaments.[5]

But by this time the Germans were maintaining extremely tight internal security. In April 1938, Sinclair informed the deputy chief of the Air Staff that 'no one was more fully alive to the importance of obtaining information as to German Air Rearmament than the SIS but the fact of the matter is that during the last twelve months or so things have become very difficult indeed in Germany'. Robert Vansittart also noted how by this time 'intelligence was becoming increasingly hard to operate in Germany, because informants died slow and horrible deaths if detected. Money was no longer enough for the risk of vastly improved tortures.' British undercover agents felt that because of the risk of 'murder, persecution and extreme penalties of the law', intelligence work had 'become most restricted'. Making matters harder still was the risk, real or imaginary, of Nazi infiltration into Whitehall: 'the Germans profess to be able to learn what they want from the British Secret Service and boast that they have their men in it', as a young British journalist told his intelligence contact. 'They have shown friends of mine a report from British officials in Berlin to Government departments in London which has been photographed and sent to the Berlin war ministry.'[6]

On the ground, the Nazis had also taken further steps to hide some of their key sites. In the mid-1930s, they had even tried to disguise some of their aeroplane factories, although given their sheer size such a task was neither practical nor particularly successful: when the vast Junkers factory at Dessau was painted green, for example, some observers wondered if it had thereby become more conspicuous. And at one important factory, the Germans had installed machinery that could emit smoke, 'with the object of covering the whole site with an artificial fog-bank in emergency' if it came under attack, although the effectiveness of such a tactic remains unclear. A number of Air Ministry reports also noted the Germans' extensive use of camouflage. 'Barracks and

5. Jeffery 300.
6. Sinclair—Jeffery 295. Vansittart 499. Journalist—Colvin to Lloyd, 13 Apr 1939, Lord Lloyd Archive GLLD 19/19 CCCA.

smaller buildings are situated within the woods, hangars along the edge and painted green to simulate their background', ran one report, adding that the Nazis had also started to lay out dummy paths and hedges, although this practice was not yet widespread.[7]

Some British reports did not conceal their admiration for these tactics. By 1938, noted one analysis, most of the German air bases were well camouflaged, using 'varnish of appropriate colours' to hide 'large number of underground installations such as petrol tanks, ammunition dumps and command posts'. Often located in woods and nearly always some distance from roads or any other vantage points, they presented a very elusive intelligence target. Their buildings and infrastructure were also widely dispersed within their individual sites. Hangars, which were often built with a very low section to make them harder to spot, were usually sited along the outer edge of the aerodrome, while workshops were placed at some distance from the aerodrome. 'Distributed over vast areas, and in certain cases, with secondary landing grounds established in peacetime but cleverly concealed, well dispersed, carefully camouflaged and, to a certain extent, very well protected with efficient means of active anti-aircraft defence', noted British analysts, 'these aerodromes would be . . . difficult to reconnoitre, sometimes hard to identify and frequently difficult to attack'.[8]

The Nazis devised other ways of deceiving their enemies. Some buildings, such as photographic darkrooms and processing labs for aerial reconnaissance operations, were disguised as farmhouses, while they also made extensive use of netting, consisting of wood and grass, to render their planes almost invisible from above. The Luftwaffe also used carefully crafted canvases to create silhouettes of dummy aeroplanes that looked very convincing from even a low altitude, while anti-aircraft guns, defending such sites, were positioned to avoid casting a giveaway shadow. British analysts judged such tactics to be highly effective, although they noted that, as the size of the Luftwaffe continued to grow, it would get harder to hide the planes because 'the typical German forest consists of comparatively small pine trees grown close together and is not ideal for concealment from above', particularly when 'aerodromes are sited at the edge of woods'.[9]

7. 'Notes on the German Air Force', AIR 10/644 TNA.
8. 'List of German Landing Grounds', 14 Dec 1938, AIR 40/1155 TNA.
9. 'Germany's Air Force', Oct 1938, AIR 10/1644 TNA; 'Importance and Vulnerability of the German Aircraft Industry', AIR 9/99 TNA.

In Paris, Colonel Rivet shared the same sense of exasperation and despair as his British counterparts:

Under Hitler, Germany was subjected to the most severe type of surveillance and repression that the country had ever known. The entire state apparatus, from top to bottom, was geared towards internal security, and this saturated everyone's daily life, in every way. The German Army shared these traits of the utmost secrecy. Hitler's strategic decisions were known only to a handful of his inner circle, and even then only when preparations to carry them out had already been made.[10]

Inside the Reich, Britain's incoming military attaché, who arrived in Berlin in early 1938, also quickly noticed the obstacles and dangers of gathering intelligence. Colonel Noel Mason-MacFarlane was no newcomer to espionage operations but nonetheless found Nazi Germany to be a formidably difficult place in which to operate. East Prussia was by this time largely out of bounds to foreign nationals, while security was particularly tight in the vicinity of the Austrian and Czech borders. Soon, all foreign military attachés were barred from visiting whole swathes of border territory, including the entire Rhineland. The reason was simply that the Germans wanted to hide the construction of new fortifications, comprising 'the Siegfried Line', that were intended to defend the Reich against a French attack: a huge labour force and enormous quantities of concrete and ready-made fortifications were being moved into the area, all of which would have been immediately noticed by any outsiders and yielded vital clues about the state of progress, or the lack of it.[11]

For his own sake as well as for the safety of others, 'Mason-Mac' also had to be very careful whom he met with, given the high risks of being noticed or covertly followed: 'I was a marked man,' as he wrote later. 'Contact with me would have met with swift retribution at the hands of the Gestapo.' As a result, he sometimes tried to keep his personal contacts to a minimum and instead searched for strands of information from unlikely sources. Intelligence-gathering in a police state, he felt, was 'largely a question of getting around and picking up and piecing together scraps of information from widely scattered sources'. On one occasion, for example, a family member had come

10. Navarre 48.
11. This decree was issued on 30 July 1938; see Henderson to Halifax, 1 Aug 1938, DBFP III series, Vol 2, 1938, No 562.

home and casually mentioned seeing a new insignia on a German uniform, denoting the formation of a new unit. And he was also taken aback when a German doctor announced that he was unable to treat Mason-Mac's gallstone because of a sudden shortage of morphine and other drugs, which had been unexpectedly diverted to the armed forces.[12]

Such challenges also became clear in the summer of 1938, when the SIS sent an undercover agent, an RAF officer codenamed 'Agent 479', on a motoring holiday in Germany to carry out covert surveillance of airfields.[13]

Accompanied by 'a suitable [female] secretary', who was given a crash course, en route, in basic spying techniques, and driving an expensive Wolseley car, he did all he could to avoid arousing suspicion but found it very difficult to obtain the information he wanted. The location of the airfields was 'quite unlike anything' in his homeland, not least because agricultural fields nearly always lay between the road and the airstrips, making any access difficult and surreptitious access impossible. As a result, Agent 479 'seldom got close enough to get numbers' of planes or any other details. The two spies were also unnerved by the strength of German security: they were stopped and searched several times by agents who 'turned the car inside out' before following them for several days. The spies responded by making 'wild dashes all over the country' which either 'shook them off or they lost interest'.

After spending three weeks in the Reich, and travelling over 2,000 miles, Agent 479 finally abandoned his mission and headed home, mainly because his companion was showing signs of personal stress. The SIS praised his report for its 'considerable value' because it had succeeded in 'discovering the exact positions of aerodromes, which we had previously been unable to get'. The same agent was clearly not one to give up easily and went back to Germany a few months later before returning home with more 'valuable information'.

Such agents were not, however, in a position to obtain information or insights about Hitler's ambitions and actions, which were becoming more belligerent. And as if in perfect step with the timetable laid down

---

12. Ewan Butler *Mason-Mac: Life of Lt. Gen. Sir Noel Mason-Macfarlane* Macmillan (1972) 69. Papers of Mason-Macfarlane, PP/MCR/C5, IWM.
13. Jeffery 299.

in the Hossbach Memorandum, he was by this time training his sights on Austria.[14]

A union (*Anschluss*) between Austria and Germany had long been a dream of many nationalists who wanted to create a Reich that united all German speakers: nearly a century before, in the political turmoil that swept through much of Europe in 1848, revolutionaries had made a determined push for just such a pan-German nation. These nationalists were dismayed when, for all President Woodrow Wilson's noble and ebullient talk about 'self-determination' during the Paris Peace Conference in 1919, the Treaty of Versailles had nonetheless created an independent Austrian state out of a defeated Habsburg Empire, despite strong support amongst its six million German speakers for a union with its northern neighbour.

For Hitler and his followers, *Anschluss* quickly became an article of faith, worshipped at the Nazi shrine: the *Führer* described it as his 'supreme task' and gave it pride of place in his manifesto, the 'twenty-five point programme', of 1920. But for other Nazis, notably Göring, who felt as strongly about the issue, this was not just a matter of racial nationalism: Austria also possessed voluminous natural resources, notably a skilled workforce that was capable of making an important contribution to his Four-Year Plan, and large deposits of iron ore in the Austria district of Styria.

In late 1937, the Nazi leadership saw an opportunity. This was because a strident opponent of *Anschluss*, the Italian leader Benito Mussolini, who saw himself as the 'protector' of an independent Austria, was not only distracted by his invasion of Abyssinia but also heavily embroiled in the Spanish Civil War, strongly assisting General Franco's nationalist forces. On both of these military and political frontlines, he needed Berlin's support.

The British and French governments had long been aware not only of Nazi ambitions towards Austria but of various acts of provocation that were intended to realize them. In 1933, for example, the British cabinet had discussed Nazi involvement in 'extensive terrorism, dropping seditious leaflets from German aeroplanes over Austrian territory and persistent subversive broadcasting inciting the Austrian people to

---

14. AJP Taylor has argued that 'Hitler's exposition (in the Memorandum) was in large part day-dreaming, unrelated to what followed in real life': *The Origins of the Second World War* 169.

resist the present government', in blatant violation of the Versailles Treaty. In London, such ambitions were viewed largely with resignation: 'I almost wish Germany would swallow Austria and get it over,' as Cadogan recorded in his diary on 14 February. 'What's all this fuss about... when we can't do *anything* about it?' In Paris, by contrast, the looming annexation was viewed as 'an act of war likely to bring into question the status quo of Central Europe'. Either way, all foreign governments wanted to know when Hitler would move and assess the way in which his annexation was undertaken.[15]

The source about the timing was once again Malcolm Christie, who in February 1938 was tipped off about a speech that Hermann Göring had given before a highly select audience comprising top generals. Göring, who was inclined to throw his weight around, wanted to get heavy. Berlin's aim, the *Reichsmarschall* had argued, was to seize Austria and then dismember Czechoslovakia while it had the chance. At that point, the rest of Eastern Europe—Poland, Hungary, Yugoslavia, and Romania—would soon fall under the sway of German economic might. Nazi Germany could thereby realize an old dream that had lived in the imagination of Germans, and before them of the Prussians, over the ages—a dream of *Mitteleuropa*, economic hegemony over central Europe. This would happen of its own accord, Göring continued, although it would do so more quickly if Berlin actively assisted fascist parties in seizing power. Soon Germany would have forged a federal union, an ever closer union encompassing a huge swathe of central Europe.[16]

Meanwhile, the Bureau had its own sources on the matter. In Vienna, Mme Madelaine Bihet-Richou, an expatriate teacher who gave French language classes to a disaffected Austrian military intelligence officer called Colonel Lahousen von Vivrement, acted on its behalf: with a strong dislike of the Nazis but a good rapport with his tutor, 'Agent MAD' gave extremely useful material about German designs on his homeland, based on his own insider information, and continued to do so, as a senior Abwehr officer, after the outbreak of war. And in Berlin on 3 March, Paul Stehlin warned Paris about another sudden and drastic change of tempo, while the British embassy also received an urgent

15. 1933—CAB 23/76/20 TNA. Paris—quote from a French memorandum to the British government, 18 Feb 1938, FO 371/21791 TNA.
16. Conwell-Evans 124–5.

call from Donald St Clair Gainer, its representative in Munich: he had suddenly seen huge numbers of troops and vehicles making their way along the Bavarian roads towards the Austrian border.[17]

German armoured movements on such a scale represented a rare intelligence-gathering opportunity for foreign spies that was too good to miss. And astonished that the Abwehr hadn't jammed his phone line to block Gainer's message, Mason-Mac quickly got to work.

Energetic, passionate, and reckless in style, the new military attaché had quickly made his mark in Berlin. Sporting a keen interest in fast cars, amateur dramatics, and poetry, this decorated veteran of the First World War had previously worked as a defence attaché in British India, Hungary, Austria and, Switzerland, where he had impressed his superiors: MI3, the intelligence and section of the War Office that dealt with central Europe, felt that 'he combines a first-class brain with a remarkable flair for intelligence work. He has a keen sense of humour and is an excellent linguist. Full of mental and physical energy and with great initiative, he should go far.' And with his aptitude for foreign languages, he was, 'the closest thing to a professional intelligence officer the British Army possessed'.[18]

But clever and able though he was, 'Mason-Mac' was not, however, a perfect source of intelligence information. Some people questioned his judgement and a good number of his reports were widely off the mark. As a student at Staff College, for example, his teachers noted that his judgement was only 'fairly good, rather immature and lacking balance'. Perhaps this was because he was inclined, as he freely admitted, 'to look out for trouble'. And quick to feel anger,—a future field marshal felt that Mason-Mac was 'quite capable of pulling a knife or pistol on me'—his heart at times doubtlessly trumped his mind. Equally, he had a professional background, like Truman Smith, in artillery and was not qualified to pass weighty judgements about more specialized issues, or indeed about events in particular places, that he was unfamiliar with. Such shortcomings, and the curious 'hybrid' status of every military attaché, help explain how and why some of his intelligence assessments about

17. Bureau's sources—Gauché 54. Vienna—Navarre 56–9. Rivet's diaries also make references to 'Madelaine' and Agent MAD. Stehlin 76.
18. MI3—Butler 61. Aptitude—Wark 'Three Military Attachés' 600.

the Third Reich, in the crucial days of the appeasement crisis in 1938 and in the following spring, were so badly flawed.[19]

He did not lack energy and enthusiasm, however, and within almost no time he was behind the wheels of his Ford V-8 coupé, roaring southwards along the German roads through Leipzig towards the Austrian border. He needed not only to find out what was happening but to obtain as much information as he could about Germany's armed forces while they were there, before him, rather than confined behind the high walls of their barracks.

It was not long before he came across German armoured columns that were moving southwards 'in very considerable strength'. On the afternoon of 11 March, he sent an urgent telex to Henderson, reporting 'well over 3,000 armed police' on the Berlin–Leipzig road. One indication of the size of the deployment was the presence of large numbers of reservists, who always wore distinctively yellow boots. Noting the names and emblems of the individual army units, he searched hard to find out more about how they were organized and to gauge their numbers. But by the time he arrived at the border, Schuschnigg had capitulated to the Nazis, effectively bullied into submission by an intimidating and very real threat of German attack. Austria had fallen without even a shot being fired, and German troops and planes were now pouring across the border, at the invitation of the new government, while the outside world watched helplessly.[20]

Stunned by the sheer speed with which developments had unfolded, Mason-MacFarlane crossed the border into Austria. In the chaotic hours that accompanied, and followed, regime change in Vienna, one of his first destinations was Aspern aerodrome, which was a scene of frenetic activity as hundreds of German planes flew troops and supplies into the capital. Driving through the gates without being challenged, he was able to see first-hand the strength and organization of the Luftwaffe. He was impressed by the co-ordination of the entire operation, as the planes took off and landed in a constant, uninterrupted stream, without any glitches or disruption. And after memorizing as much information as he could—to take notes would have attracted immediate

19. Staff college—Butler Ch 1. Field marshal—this was the view of Lt-Col (later Field Marshal) Gerald Templer, Butler 100–1.
20. Henderson to Halifax, 11 Mar 1938, DBFP III series, Vol 1, 1938, No 1012. German troops—there was 'no way to prevent Hitler from swallowing Austria', as Camille Chautemps explained to Bullitt. Adamthwaite *The Making of the Second World War* 79.

and very unwelcome attention—he left the aerodrome just as a plane carrying General Kurt von Tippelskirch, who the previous day had earnestly assured him that the German army would not attack Austria, touched down.[21]

In this unsettling and often dangerous political lacuna, which always exists between the demise of an existing state and the establishment of the new, Mason-MacFarlane was now able to make his way around the capital with relative freedom. He wanted to know more about the state of public opinion, wondering if the Nazis really did command the high levels of support there that they claimed and that others said they had noticed: a few days before, for example, the American correspondent William L Shirer had been 'swept along' in the streets of Vienna 'in a shouting, hysterical Nazi mob'. The attaché did not have to search for long to find the truth behind his words, since there was 'obviously a quite substantial measure of support for National Socialism', whose propaganda 'had made many more converts throughout the country than most people were inclined or willing to believe'. There was, he continued, 'no sign anywhere of overt hostility towards the Germans...and no lack of outwardly enthusiastic crowds'.[22]

Mason-MacFarlane next moved fast to get in touch with one of his best contacts in the Austrian capital, identified in his correspondence only as 'Tommy K'. This was the head of the SIS station, Captain Thomas Kendrick, who ran the Passport Control Office. Kendrick had been a chief source of information about the Austrian Nazi Party, and Mason-MacFarlane urged him to get out of the country immediately, before German counter-espionage agents became organized. There was a real risk, he continued, that the Gestapo might know of him or his whereabouts, or capture and torture someone who did. To his dismay, however, 'Tommy' stayed put.

But Mason-Mac was right in thinking that the German secret police would waste no time in swooping on anyone they suspected of opposing Nazi rule: during the night of 12–13 March alone, for example, they arrested 21,000 such suspects. Amongst them was a high-level informer, codenamed 'Du Terrier', who had previously provided the Deuxième Bureau with inside information about the state of high-level

21. Papers of Mason-Macfarlane, PP/MCR/C5, 13 Mar 1938, IWM.
22. William L Shirer *Berlin Diary: The Journal of a Foreign Correspondent, 1934–1941* Knopf (1941) 97. Papers of Mason-Macfarlane, PP/MCR/C5, 13 Mar 1938, IWM.

Austrian politics. Canaris had personally accompanied the advance German units so that he could personally seize the files of the Austrian intelligence service and question its head, Colonel Erwin Lahousen.[23]

In the weeks that followed *Anschluss*, however, Abwehr activity did not stop more Allied operatives from making their way to Austria to gauge as much information as they could. In the third week of March, the British air attaché, Squadron Leader John Vachell, also posed as a member of the general public, although he had diplomatic papers to prove who he really was if the need arose. Soon he was able to slip into six of Austria's eight aerodromes and build 'a fairly comprehensive picture' of German activity. His observations were of course 'superficial', he admitted, but 'it is possible that a visit of this nature affords a truer indication of actual conditions than can be gained from visits to units arranged officially, when there is probably a certain amount of window-dressing'.[24]

Like Mason-MacFarlane, Vachell was very impressed by the level of German organization, noting that 'the move of so large a force at such short notice was a very notable achievement'. Although a basic war plan would have been worked out in advance, he emphasized that 'the move itself came as a surprise', and that some of the units had been given just a few hours' notice. 'No less impressive', he continued, 'is the achievement of building up such an apparently efficient weapon as the German air force in such a short space of time.'

Vachell had witnessed first-hand how the Nazis subjugated every aspect of society to war with an efficiency that also impressed but also shocked the French. But crucially, he took a much dimmer view of the state of the German air force. The Luftwaffe, he felt, was 'by no means ready for war' and was not likely to be ready for at least another twelve to eighteen months. In addition, 'the most noticeable feature of the German air force units', he wrote to Henderson, 'was the number of obsolete, or at least obsolescent, aircraft'. The more impressive and modern planes were outnumbered by the ageing, inferior ones. Although press photos tried to convey a different picture, he saw 'no more modern bomber than the out-of-date Junkers-52 and more than half the German aircraft I saw in Austria were of that type'. Most of the Luftwaffe units were smaller than he expected, he continued, since

---

23. 'Du Terrier'—Réunion des Chefs de Poste, 18–20 Jan 1937, 7NN 2502 SHD.
24. Vachell to Henderson, 3 Mar 1938, CAB 104/32 TNA.

they comprised just nine planes instead of the anticipated twelve, and he was sure that Hitler's rearmament plan 'has not progressed as fast as we had believed'. In addition, the Luftwaffe was also very slow to phase in more efficient ways of refuelling their planes, relying on requisitioned civilian tankers instead of the camouflaged petrol tank lorries that the RAF had long been using.

But Vachell's measured judgements represented a rare voice of moderation and were drowned out by the more influential but much more alarming reports of individuals such as Charles Lindbergh, whose views were at this time still being circulated widely in both London and Paris. 'The *Führer*', as Colonel Fraser wrote from the British Embassy in Paris, has 'found a most convenient ambassador in Colonel Lindbergh, who appears to have given the French an impression of its might and preparedness which they did not have before.' As a result, he continued, 'Hitler is convinced that the threat of his air force is suffi-cient to keep the French, and consequently ourselves, quiet under all circumstances'.[25]

The undue weight given to Lindbergh's reports was both a symp-tom and cause of a profound pessimism that prevailed amongst many British and French observers. As Wesley Wark argues, Nazi Germany represented a blank screen upon which outsiders easily projected their fears and insecurities, conjuring an imaginary Goliath. From the end of 1937 in particular, the governments and intelligence services of these countries seriously overestimated Germany's strength.[26]

Sir Warren Fisher articulated this gloomy mindset in April 1938 when he wrote to Neville Chamberlain and warned him, in a clear reference to Hitler, that 'for the first time in centuries our country is (and must continue to be) at the mercy of a foreign power', blaming the 'incompetent' Air Ministry for misjudging the true strength of the Luftwaffe. For Henderson, the Luftwaffe posed 'a real and very imme-diate peril' because it was 'immensely powerful and far superior to our own'. And in Whitehall, the Air Intelligence Directorate hugely exag-gerated the bombing capabilities of the Luftwaffe, estimating that it could drop 600–700 tons of bombs every day on British cities for weeks on end, including 3,500 tons in the first day of hostilities alone. Such a massive assault, they continued, would cause as many as

25. Fraser to Phipps, 21 Sept 1938, DBFP III series, Vol 2, 1938, No 507.
26. See in general Wark *Ultimate Enemy* Ch 3.

50,000 civilian casualties in the space of just twenty-four hours: 'even the air staff', Wark writes, 'did not entirely believe in its own "calculus of destruction"'.[27]

In fact, these 'predictions' were very wide of the mark and saturated with errors: the overall figure was nearly three times greater than the actual tonnage dropped in the Blitz campaign against Britain in 1940–1, and the estimate for the first day of hostilities was more than five times greater. Nor did British and French experts know, for example, that in August 1938 the Germans had only 378 fully trained bomber crews, although they should have been aware that most of the German bombers, notably the Junkers 86, were obsolescent and had made unimpressive performances in the Spanish Civil War.

The French, in particular, considerably overestimated the German army. In a major assessment undertaken in the spring of 1938, for example, the Deuxième Bureau very considerably overstated the number of reserve-type divisions and the size of the German field army. This error was not a purposeful exaggeration, intended to secure increased expenditure on the military, but the result of meagre information. In December of 1937 and again the following February, Daladier admitted to parliamentary bodies that accurate information about such vital factors as armaments production and stocks of strategic raw materials was still very patchy. French Intelligence also estimated that German factories were producing more than 1,000 planes every month, more than double the actual figure.[28]

But the Bureau's political intelligence, on the question of where the Nazis would strike next, was closer to the mark. Days after the *Anschluss*, Colonel Gaston Renondeau, the French military attaché in Berlin, had warned his colleagues in Paris about a pending operation against the Czechs, who had now become highly vulnerable to a German attack. Then on 6 April 1938, French intelligence officers received a highly classified report stating that 'staff headquarters of the army corps stationed at Munich are currently preparing a mobilization plan against Czechoslovakia'. The report emanated from a source who

27. Henderson—DC Watt *How War Came: The Immediate Origins of the Second World War, 1938–1939* Pantheon Books (1989) 86. Wark *Ultimate Enemy* 67.
28. Daladier—Jackson *France and the Nazi Menace* 281.

was 'top secret and completely reliable', prompting Rivet to immediately inform Daladier.[29]

The source proved to be correct. The spectacular success and extraordinary ease of the Nazi operation against Austria had created an enormous wave of popular support for Hitler and his regime to ride upon, whetting the Nazi appetite for further conquest. The *Führer* felt increasingly confident, even invincible, and blessed with the support of Providence. Now Hitler not only wanted to 'liberate' the three million German Sudetens, currently ruled by the government in Prague, but also to seize as much Czech territory as he could. *Anschluss* had extended Germany's border with Czechoslovakia by 240 miles and, as General Jodl commented, the Reich's southern neighbour had now 'become enclosed by pinchers . . . and would fall victim to any attack before any effective assistance would arrive'.[30]

29. Renondeau—16 Mar 1938, 7NN 2601 SHD. 'French Military Intelligence and Nazi Germany 1938–9', Young 'French Military Intelligence' 274. Apr 1938. Rivet—Paul Paillole *Services Spéciaux* Robert Laffonte (1975) 107. The identity of this informant remains unclear.
30. Braddick 3.

17

Intelligence and the Sudeten Crises of 1938

In Paris, pressure for an alliance with Great Britain was growing. 'More than ever', General Gamelin told Daladier in late March, 'it is essential that we have England with us.' And on 15 March, the French foreign minister and former prime minister, Joseph Paul-Boncour, had urged the British to 'declare publicly that, if Germany attacked Czechoslovakia and France went to the latter's assistance, Great Britain would stand by France'. Soon, a high-level committee in Paris published an official paper on 'Franco-British military cooperation', emphasizing French vulnerability to a German attack and urging the government of the day to pressurize Britain into providing more support, including the provision of substantial expeditionary force in the event of a crisis.[1]

But despite Hitler's annexation of Austria, there was still strong suspicion in London of any alliance with France, which was seen as greatly overextending Great Britain's overseas commitments without adding any clear benefits in return. Speaking before the House of Commons just over a week later, Chamberlain announced that he could not guarantee British support for France in the event of a confrontation between Prague and Berlin. This was partly because, in the words of Sir Thomas Inskip, 'it seemed certain that Germany could overrun the whole of Czechoslovakia in less than a week', rendering any such British commitment meaningless.[2]

---

1. Gamelin—Jackson *France and the Nazi Menace* 293. Paul-Boncour—Phipps to Halifax, 15 Mar 1938, DBFP III series, Vol 1, 1938, No 81. Official paper—Adamthwaite *France and the Coming of the Second World War* 231.
2. Sir Thomas Inskip, 18 Mar 1938, CAB 27/623 TNA. Inskip was the minister for the coordination of defence.

Just over a week later, Daladier arrived in London, hoping to moderate this uncompromising line in the event of a crisis over the Sudetenland. Because Paris already had a defensive pact with Prague, Daladier emphasized that, if Hitler attacked his eastern ally, he would go to war against Germany even without British support. But despite the prospect of a German counter-attack that would overrun France, British delegates refused to commit more than two divisions, and even then only 'if the government of the day decided in favour of sending such a force'. Daladier was crushed.

But the SIS nonetheless continued to liaise closely with its French and Czech counterparts. 'My collaboration with British Intelligence was already long-standing and close,' as Moravec wrote. 'In the field of intelligence, we had never stopped exchanging information and technical data.' And in the spring of 1938, such contact became all the more indispensable because Moravec's spy service had succeeded brilliantly in infiltrating Germany's armed forces.[3]

The Czech foreign intelligence service had already obtained details of German plans to attack Austria from its highly prized source, Agent 54, while another of its undercover informers in German ranks, code-named A-53, also confirmed the details. Given the importance of the information, and the quality of his source, Moravec had immediately travelled to Paris to warn the Deuxième Bureau of Hitler's plans, emphasizing that his agents had also picked up unmistakable signs of German preparations for war and a sharp increase in German espionage within his own country. But at this conference he came to the 'reluctant and astounded conclusion' that the French were suffering from a 'blind defeatism', created by a desire to avoid war at all costs, and that in return they were giving the Czechs very little information about Germany essentially because they had very little to give. The French authorities, he concluded, were guilty of a 'lack of interest' and 'intentional underestimating of the gravity of the situation'. It is quite possible that the senior Bureau officers shared his exasperation since Colonel Rivet had immediately informed Daladier about Moravec's information but there is no evidence that he received any response.[4]

But despite his misgivings regarding the French spy services, these three spy services still worked together in the weeks that followed *Anschluss*, during what became known as the 'May War Scare'. It was

3. Moravec 145.   4. Moravec 121–2.

at this very tense moment that Hitler was seen, by the outside world, to back down before an apparent threat of joint action by the three countries. And their respective intelligence services were instrumental in creating this apparent, although entirely non-existent, 'threat'.

The story of the 'May War Scare' began when the three services received numerous intelligence reports about a massive and imminent Nazi attack on the Sudetenland. Although the origins of these reports remain mysterious, the most plausible explanation is that the Czechs panicked, overreacting to news of German manoeuvres. Wherever and however these reports started, they were without substance: German activity on the ground was no different from usual, and reconnaissance by the military attaché revealed 'no definite indication of any troop concentration or any unusual movement'. They were based either on misunderstandings, exaggerations, or outright lies that spread like wildfire in such a supremely flammable environment.[5]

But Major Paul Thümmel, 'A-54', was instrumental in creating, as well as defusing, tension at this difficult hour. As reports of Nazi troop movements poured into Prague, he had sent Moravec an urgent message, requesting a meeting on Czech soil at very short notice. Hours later, at a secret location close to the border, he told his handlers what he knew: the Germans, he explained, were preparing a campaign of sabotage and agitation against Czechoslovakia that was designed to culminate in a coup in the Sudetenland on the eve of forthcoming elections, scheduled for 22 May. Considerable quantities of weapons, ammunition, and explosives were already being smuggled across the border while German sympathizers, led by a charismatic and politically inflexible former gymnastics teacher called Konrad Henlein, were waiting for a codeword, *Altvater*, that would be broadcast on radio and would be a signal to start an insurrection. At this point, Henlein would allege Czech atrocities against his 'martyrs' and call for German intervention to 'protect' them.[6]

A-54's warning, and Moravec's swift response, was based on false premises. Although Henlein may have planned an uprising, the Germans

---

5. Overreaction—Strong thought that the Germans concocted the incident: see *Intelligence at the Top* 33. However, Brigadier Stronge, the British military attaché to Prague, felt that the incident was 'trumped up' by Prague for its own purposes. See Braddick 26 and Tim Bouverie *Appeasing Hitler* Penguin (2019) 204–10. German activity—Henderson to Halifax, 23 May 1938, DBFP III series, Vol 1, 1938, No 287.
6. Moravec Ch 9 *passim*.

had no plans to intervene. However, when on 20 May German radio broadcast the codeword, Beneš met with his cabinet in an emergency session and immediately imposed martial law on the Sudetenland, crushing any nationalist hopes of an insurrection.

Thümmel was taking considerable risks in bringing his handlers this information. Returning from one such covert meeting with Moravec, he was driven back late at night to the Czech–German border by three plain-clothed Czech intelligence officers. This was an area where Henlein's followers were operating in organized and armed gangs, ruling much of the region by night and sometimes by day. As they approached the border, the spies were confronted by armed guards who had put down a roadblock in their path and then fired a series of shots, deafening at close range, to warn them to stop.

As a trained intelligence officer, Thümmel could stay calm and think quickly under pressure. Seizing the moment, he coolly got out of the car and approached the gunmen. His three fellow passengers could hear him talking to them and slipped back the safety catches on their rifles, bracing themselves for a gunfight. But to their relief, and astonishment, they saw Thümmel walk back to the car while the roadblocks were pulled aside.

After the car had pulled away, A-54 told them what he had done: he had informed the gunmen that he was a German intelligence official and explained, quite truthfully, that the three men in the car were his agents. He also knew a closely guarded password that allowed them to get through the roadblock and allowed his three fellow travellers to return afterwards.[7]

At this very tense hour, the Allied intelligence services now orchestrated a coordinated response to dissuade Berlin from unleashing an attack that Hitler never intended to make.

Closely informed of events by the SIS, Halifax sent a message to Ribbentrop from London on 22 May, making 'the most serious of warnings' if Germany undertook any move against the Sudetenland, while Bonnet publicly affirmed French allegiance to Prague. At the same time, the three agencies reiterated these warnings in a number of prearranged telephone conversations between London, Paris, and the rest of Europe, speaking on lines that they knew the Germans were bugging. And from his home on the Dutch–German border, Christie

7. Moravec 131.

also made a carefully timed late night phone call to a Sudeten German leader, Dr Walter Brand, who he knew was in the company of Reinhard Heydrich, the Gestapo chief who had Czech responsibilities: a 'British mobilization order', ran Christie's message, 'is already lying on the desk'. At the same time, the SIS and Deuxième Bureau released statements to the world media emphasizing the 'countermeasures' that London, Paris, and Prague were taking. All of these carefully choreographed steps were the fruition of close liaison between the three agencies. In fact, the British government had consistently vowed not to enter a war 'caused by German aggression against the Czechs', and at the end of August was still refusing to even consider such an option.[8]

Hitler had never contemplated attacking the Czechs at this stage because his generals warned him that their army was not strong enough to confront both Czechoslovakia and France, let alone the British, at the same time: between them, the French and the Czechs could field ninety-seven divisions, more than double the size of the German army. Details of this gloomy assessment were posted to senior army officers throughout the Reich and fell into French hands. But Hitler was still determined to use force against the Sudetenland as soon as the moment arrived, and the May Crisis made him even more determined, infuriated as he was by the apparent loss of face, before a watching outside world, that he felt he had suffered.[9]

As Hitler privately spewed out his bloodcurdling determination to 'smash' Czechoslovakia, foreign spy services searched for signs that the Germans were mobilizing and for clues to the true strength of their armed forces. This was challenging, not least because of deliberate German efforts to deceive them: when in mid-July, for example, the British heard that the Luftwaffe's top pilots in Spain were being recalled to Germany, and that all of their leave had been cancelled, they dismissed such reports as 'calculated indiscretions [that] represent a policy of deliberate bluff'. But other sources of information, known to be reliable, painted a different picture.[10]

8. Halifax also told Ribbentrop 'not to count upon this country being able to stand aside if from any precipitate action there should start a European conflagration'. In a speech on 24 Mar, Chamberlain had been 'unable to give the prior guarantees' to the Czechs but cautioned that 'if war broke out, it would be unlikely to be confined to those who have assumed such obligations'. Statements—Braddick 21. British government—Jackson *France and the Nazi Menace* 292.

9. Assessment—Gauché 54. More determined—Bouverie 208.

10. Indiscretions—Henderson to Halifax, 18 July 1938, DBFP III series, Vol 1, 1938, No 507.

At the end of July, the SIS detected 'disturbing signs of military preparedness' to strike Czechoslovakia after the summer harvests, when Germany was in a better position to withstand an economic blockade, and before the summer of 1939, when Nazi strategists expected the British and French to have rearmed. Other worrisome information, which came from various sources, included reports of an acceleration in the construction of the Siegfried Line; the mobilization of the Railway Protection Troops (*Bahnschutz*); the stockpiling of oil, which was noticed by a Berlin-based British representative closely connected with SIS; and the building of a 'special filtering plant' for cleansing oil at the experimental stations at Rechlin and Aldershof. The SS had also reportedly taken responsibility for the control of much of Germany's borders, while some senior German officers had sent their families to live in Switzerland. As signs of German preparations mounted, the Bureau put its local intelligence-gathering stations on high alert and exchanged more information with both the Czechs and the Poles.[11]

Then, on 10 August, Malcolm Christie received a phone call from a Belgian contact, who was the head of a worldwide industrial concern in Germany. The contact gave a clear warning. 'The Nazi Party is in full war cry,' went the message. 'Mobilization, which begins next week, aims at giving the troops practice with their new equipment and tactics.' In London, British Intelligence also picked up signs of 'feverish' German preparations for war and predicted an imminent outbreak of violence against Czechoslovakia, after Berlin had created 'a situation in which she will not appear in the role of an aggressor but rather as the protector of her nationals living in a foreign country', perhaps by 'contriving an insurrection'.[12]

Some other clues came from personal observations, or even from casual conversations. French spies in the Rhineland noticed that the German authorities were suddenly taking 'draconian measures' such as expropriating land without warning, and ordering farmers not to take their vehicles on the roads at times when military convoys and construction workers, who were busily building fortifications, might be using them. And it was to find similar clues that Major Kenneth

---

11. Worrisome information—Halifax to Henderson, 22 Sept 1938, DBFP II series, Vol 1, 1938, No 1014. SS—Strang to Henderson, 21 July 1938, DBFP III series, Vol 1, 1938, No 530. Bureau—'Note sur la mobilisation des Centres de Renseignements', 24 July 1938, 7NN 2486 SHD.

12. 'Germany August 1938', WO 190/644 TNA.

Strong the deputy military attaché in Berlin had set off to drive around Germany, on the lookout for signs of mobilization.[13]

One of his first ports of call was Königsbrück, the site of a major German camp 20 miles north of Dresden, which the Nazis would certainly use in the event of any action against the Czechs. Since his car had a German number plate, Strong knew that he could probably evade the domestic security services long enough to gather some useful information.

He drove as close to the base as he could and then wandered a short distance from his car, looking out for any signs of preparation for war. He did not have to wait long, for every few minutes trains steamed into nearby sidings to bring a rush of soldiers and supplies. Making his way back to the car, he was alarmed to find an armed German infantryman waiting for him, although to his relief the friendly young man only wanted a lift back to Dresden to bid his girlfriend goodbye before hostilities began. The conversation that followed was informative, for the hitchhiker talked freely, telling his British driver about the war plans against Czechoslovakia. He and his fellow soldiers had been told to expect heavy fighting and casualties, chatted the garrulous passenger, and the German army faced a chronic shortage of petrol that could cripple its fighting capabilities.[14]

But useful though they were, such tiny pieces of information did not fill the big gaps in the Allied picture of Nazi Germany. Sharing intelligence was now all the more important. In June 1938, Commandant Guy Schlesser, the head of the Service de Renseignements, visited London to exchange information with his British counterparts about German agents operating within their borders, while the following month Menzies wrote to Rivet, emphasizing that he was 'ready to collaborate' against Germany. At the same time, Menzies arranged a meeting in The Hague between French officers and the SIS head of station, Major Richard Stevens. The French shared information about German infiltration of France and were in return very keen to establish closer relations with the SIS station in Holland, because of its importance in infiltrating agents into Germany. Soon afterwards, Stevens reported that he had been received by the French with 'the utmost kindness and frankness', adding that their offer of 'reciprocal cooperation' was

---

13. French spies—'Concernant l'État d'Esprit dans le Palatinat', 1 Aug 1938, 7NN 3129 SHD.
14. Strong 55–6.

'absolutely genuine and without *arrière-pensée* [ulterior motive] of any sort'. Sinclair thanked Rivet for the 'extraordinarily kind reception which you gave to Stevens during his few days in Paris', adding that the SIS officer had 'come back more French than British. I trust that the collaboration which will be arranged in Holland will prove of value to both our services.'[15]

But an internal Air Ministry report, published in August 1938, illustrates the desperate shortage of information about the 'ultimate enemy'. 'There is at present a scarcity of information concerning the enemy's reserves of airframes and engines,' bemoaned the report, 'and we have nothing to indicate where such reserves, if they exist, are stored.' Unfortunately, it continued, 'Germany has a large and increasing reserve but all efforts to discover where it is located have so far been fruitless.' Amongst the possible locations were factories, aerodromes, depots, and parks.[16]

Another priority for aerial intelligence was pinpointing Germany's most vital factories. The British were sure that the Reich possessed six ball-bearing sites but only knew the whereabouts of four of these. And of the fourteen factories manufacturing specialized units for aero-engines such as crankshafts, casings, and bearings, the British had information on just six, and only the 'approximate location' of the other eight. 'We can only consider them as practical targets until available information is adequate to assure their identification by crews,' ran another report. An Air Ministry document also noted how estimating 'the production of the JU-86...has given rise to special difficulties for the rate of output of machines is only known—and that approximately— for the Dessau factory'.[17]

Making matters much harder was the fact that, by the summer of 1938, the Gestapo had also started to put more pressure not just on German civilians but also on foreign diplomats and representatives suspected of agent-running. On the morning of 17 August, for example, its agents struck a heavy blow against British Intelligence when they arrested the head of the SIS station in Vienna, Tommy Kendrick. At the time of his arrest, according to a subsequent report in *The Times* of London, Kendrick was 'partly through or near territory where German

15. Jeffery 291.
16. Report, Bomber Command memo, Aug 1938, AIR 9/99 TNA.
17. Air Staff Report—Bomber Command memo, Aug 1938, AIR 9/99 TNA. Other report—4 Oct 1938, AIR 40/1155 TNA.

manoeuvres were understood to be in progress'. At the same time, the Gestapo swooped on several of his operatives. Kendrick was interrogated for three days before being ordered to leave the country, together with several other office staff members from the British passport office. This prompted another SIS officer, Kenneth Benton, to burn all his papers since he was 'afraid that the Gestapo might just come in and search the whole office, so everything that could be burnt was destroyed'. These aggressive German tactics prompted the SIS to recall its representatives elsewhere in both Germany and Czechoslovakia, including the highly experienced station chiefs Frank Foley and Harold Gibson.[18]

Such precautions proved wise. Some months later, a British diplomat allegedly 'committed suicide' in Czechoslovakia but was reputedly shot dead at his desk by German agents. Another lived 'under perpetual surveillance by the Gestapo . . . and all foreigners regard themselves as potential candidates for a concentration camp'.[19]

Because of such a shortage of crucial information at an increasingly tense time, foreign governments were vulnerable to Nazi traps. And at this carefully timed moment, as fears of another pan-European conflict once again reached a crescendo, Berlin renewed its efforts to mislead the watching world by portraying a vastly overhyped image of its armed forces. When, in August 1938, Milch and Göring invited the head of the French air force, General Joseph Vuillemin, to visit the Luftwaffe's bases, they were playing an ace card in their ongoing game of propaganda, designed to intimidate the French, and British, and make them bow to Berlin's demands.

The French air attaché, Paul Stehlin, knew exactly what game the Nazis were playing. In front of Vuillemin, he commented later, they put on display 'a pageant of German military power that was calculated to kill any French intention to use its admittedly weak air force, even though it was the only way that Czechoslovakia could be given immediate aid'. The general was certainly stunned by what he saw. '*Je suis écrasé!*' ('I'm floored!'), muttered the Frenchman, after witnessing an astonishing aerial display. Milch and Göring had every reason to feel pleased with themselves because Vuillemin later stated that the Luftwaffe

18. Kendrick and Benton—Jeffery 301.
19. The diplomat was Walter Neumark, the British vice-consul in Brno; see 'Czechoslovakia', 14 June 1939, FO 371/23009 TNA; see also Parliamentary Questions 20 March 1939, HC Deb 20 March 1939 vol 345 cc885-91. Gestapo—Kennard to Halifax, 30 July 1939, FO 371/23009 TNA.

could wipe out the French air force in less than two weeks. Stehlin was sceptical but did not have the rank and influence to question Vuillemin.[20]

But, like Lindbergh, Vuillemin was not qualified to pass any more than a superficial judgement about the capabilities of the Luftwaffe. He had made a name for himself in the First World War, partly as a flying ace who had downed an impressive number of enemy planes, partly too as a pioneer of night flying. His reputation proved enduring for in 1936, in a bid to bolster the confidence of the French public as the German threat grew, he was offered the role of chief of the air staff. But his appointment was puzzling because he had none of the specialized knowledge of aircraft engineering and design, or of the industrial processes, that would have qualified him to properly assess German capabilities. For the same reason, his impressions of the Luftwaffe were superficial, even though they attracted a great deal of attention. Not for the first time the French and British governments attached too much weight to relatively insignificant sources.

The truth was that although the Luftwaffe had a clear edge in both quantity and quality, the British and French air forces would have prevailed over the Germans if they had worked in tandem with the Czech air force, and certainly with the Soviet in addition. Once again, however, such public relations exercises had a disproportionate impact and influence. This was because they operated in a void that the British and French intelligence services were still unable to fill with reliable and accurate data. And it was partly, too, because they told advocates of the policy of appeasement what they wanted to hear: it was better to give Hitler what he was asking for and hope for the best, their thinking ran, than stand up to him and go to war.

The Frenchman had fallen into a trap but this was a particularly unfortunate moment to become ensnared by German propaganda. Meeting the British prime minister at his mountain retreat at Berchtesgaden on 15 September, Hitler had proposed self-determination for the Sudeten population in Czechoslovakia but then, in a further conference in Bad Godesberg on 23 September, he had toughened his demands. German troops had a right to immediately occupy the Sudetenland, the Nazi dictator now insisted, even before any plebiscites were even held. 'It's awful,' sighed a demoralized Cadogan, as news broke

20. Pageant—quoted in Telford Taylor *Munich: The Price of Peace* Doubleday (1952) 719–20. Stunned—Ernst Heinkel *Stormy Life* Dutton (1956) 180–1.

of Hitler's revised demands, 'I've never had such a shattering day, or been so depressed and dispirited.'[21]

It was at this pivotal moment that more erroneous intelligence assessments reached decision-makers in London and Paris. One French report was based on a conversation between Stehlin and a Luftwaffe general, who had boasted that Germany had amassed 2,000 bombers and dive-bombers along the Czechoslovak frontier. All of these, he continued, had been assigned precise objectives and all were supposedly ready to take to the air at the Führer's command. These figures provided by the Luftwaffe officer were hollow boasts but were wrongly judged to be 'perfectly admissible if one takes into account the quantity of material which must have accumulated as a result of the uplift of the German aviation industry this past summer'. As a result, the figures were accepted without question by the Deuxième Bureau and written into an extensive report which the Air Ministry prepared on the Munich crisis.[22]

Another highly influential but quite flawed report was once again made by an individual who was not qualified to pass an emphatic judgement, and whose words were given much more weight than they merited.

The source in question was the energetic Mason-Macfarlane, who had volunteered to travel from Berlin to Prague to show the Czech authorities a copy of the ultimatum that Hitler had laid down at Bad Godesberg. His journey was long, arduous, and, at times, very hazardous: finding that long stretches of the Czech roads were blocked by pro-German Sudeten militias, the attaché was forced to walk for hours through dense woodland, sometimes in the dark and on occasion under hostile rifle fire from Henlein's followers.

On his arrival in Prague, he discussed the military situation with the British attaché, Colonel Stronge, who had ventured an upbeat assessment about Czech military capabilities. Puzzlingly, Mason-Mac—who was in any case an expert only on artillery—had only been on Czech territory for a few hours but had already made up his mind about the capabilities of its armed forces. He 'stoutly maintained', wrote Stronge,

21. Cadogan Diaries, 24 Sept 1938, 104.
22. Jackson France and the Nazi Menace 303. This led to seriously inflated estimates of the size of the Luftwaffe. An assessment prepared for Guy La Chambre in late December that put the first-line strength of the German air force at 4,170 aircraft. Significantly more than 3,000 of these aircraft were considered to be modern types.

'that the morale of the Czech army was poor, and would not listen to any denial'. The following morning, Mason-Mac communicated these views to London by telegraph and on his return to Berlin continued to argue that the Czech army was in a poor state and would not put up much fight. 'I gain the impression', he informed Sir Nevile Henderson on 26 September, 'that Czech morale is not very good, certainly if forced to fight alone.' Mason-Macfarlane and Henderson now flew back to London, where the attaché briefed the prime minister and reiterated his views. This was a crucial moment because Chamberlain was about to fly to Munich to meet Hitler and finalize the future of Czechoslovakia.[23]

Bizarrely, Mason-Macfarlane had passed a similarly critical judgement about the Czechs months before he had even arrived on their territory. On 9 May, from his office in Berlin, he had argued that French and Czech 'confidence...that the Czech army will be able to resist any possible German offensive...is misplaced...and artificial'. Such confidence, he continued, was 'designed to bolster up morale, and to induce the French, and possibly ourselves, to think in terms of the possibility of successful preventive hostilities more seriously than we might otherwise do'. Henderson—described by Piers Brendon as 'obtuse enough to be a menace and not stupid enough to be innocuous'—immediately despatched his report back to London, without explaining why, as an attaché based in Berlin, he was able to venture any judgement at all upon the state of the Czech armed forces.[24]

The truth was that President Beneš's thirty-five divisions were considerably stronger than the attaché realized, boasting some excellent equipment and dug into some very well-prepared positions. They could, very conceivably, have defended their territory against a German invasion force for a few weeks. Hitler and his generals were not in a position to assume an easy victory, and this meant that an Anglo-French threat of intervention was likely to have prompted them to back down.[25]

23. Stronge—'there are no shortcomings in the Czech army', Stronge to Newton, 3 Sept 1938, CAB 21/949 TNA. Stronge—Wark 'Three Attachés' 604. To Henderson—CAB 27/646/101 TNA.

24. Mason-MacFarlane quoted in Henderson to Halifax, 6 Apr 1938, DBFP III series, Vol 1, 1938, No 196; 'Innocuous'—Lewis Namier *In the Nazi Era* Macmillan (1952) 162.

25. Few weeks—Peter Jackson, 'French Military Intelligence and Czechoslovakia', *Diplomacy and Statecraft* (1994) 98.

The Czechs' true capabilities had been drawn to Whitehall's attention just months before, when Basil Newton had written to Halifax, informing him of Stronge's much more positive impressions: 'given the necessary breathing space', Newton had written, the Czechs 'will have prepared a system of fortifications strong enough to offer very serious resistance to an eventual German attack'. At the same time, a number of other reports that emphasized German vulnerability, from much more reliable and better-informed sources than Mason-Macfarlane, were mysteriously overlooked or underplayed. Mason-Mac's hasty and superficial impression carried weight at this crucial diplomatic moment, despite Stronge's best efforts to contradict them and Cadogan's scepticism about Mason-Mac's credibility as a source of information. His instructors at staff college had been right all along about his judgement, which was probably rendered even more erratic as a result of the regular shots of morphine that he was taking to ease the pain caused by several car accidents.[26]

Other erroneous intelligence reports undermined the case for standing up to Hitler over the Sudetenland. As international negotiations over the Sudetenland reached a critical point, the Bureau continued to give the Siegfried Line more credit than it deserved, arguing that it was a formidable barrier against an advancing French army, even though it was still being built. In the spring of 1939, some visitors felt that the fortifications consisted 'in some cases simply of some concrete wrapped round an old barn. Even the local people seemed to see through their flimsiness'. In general, British Intelligence judged that their French counterparts overestimated German numbers by around one-fifth.[27]

26. Newton to Halifax, 6 Apr 1938, DBFP III series, Vol 1, 1938, No 129. Other reports—in August 1938, the War Office reported that if Berlin was not 'successful in staving off French and British intervention, it is possible that Herr Hitler would avoid forcing a situation which might be fraught with the gravest danger to Germany', particularly when the general staff in Berlin 'have no illusions regarding the outcome of a European war at the present stage of preparedness of the German Army'. Above all, the report continued, Germany was economically vulnerable to a naval blockade: 'Strength of the Germany Army in August 1938', WO 190/644 TNA. Cadogan and Stronge—Wark 'Three Military Attachés' 604. Stronge gave an upbeat assessment in his memo of 13 Sept 1938 CAB 21/949 TNA. In his diaries, Cadogan asked 'what does he [Mason-Mac] know about it?', 27 Sept 1938, Diaries 107.

27. Siegfried Line—Adamthwaite 'French Military Intelligence' 192. Flimsiness—British Consul, Cologne, to Whitehall, 21 Apr 1939, FO 371/23008 TNA. Overestimates—Strong 58; Patrice Buffotot, 'La Perception du réarmement allemand par les organismes de renseignement français de 1936 à 1939', Revue Historique des Armées 262 (2011) 176; Douglas Porch The French Secret Service Farrar Straus & Giroux (1995) 147.

Such pessimistic views were seized on by advocates of appeasement. In Paris, General Gamelin made the most of them in his discussions with Daladier and Bonnet, while they also reached London at a time when ministers were already 'frightened out of their wits' by the prospect of war, entrenching the pro-appeasement views of ministers such as Halifax and the diplomat Sir Horace Wilson.[28]

In the bitter war of opinion, these erroneous, pessimistic judgements proved victorious. Like besotted lovers, the architects of appeasement saw what they wanted to see: for example, the French air attaché in Berlin, Paul Stehlin, noticed and condemned a tendency to mistake gossip for 'intelligence', and noted how some ministers would search for and select 'less pessimistic' reports, whatever their source, if information from official channels was not to their taste. In London, Chamberlain 'wobbled around all over the place', while in Berlin, Sir Nevile Henderson also lapped up such reports, writing back to London that:

the Germans, if they do not intend to commit an act of aggression on us, propose to use their air force as a big stick to enforce a *Pax Germanica*. There is no doubt in my mind that Hitler's intransigence and readiness to embark on war was solely due to the conviction that Germany as a result of Göring's efforts possessed 1) an air force which in quantity and quality far surpassed anything which France and England could put up and 2) an immeasurably superior ground defence.[29]

In one sense, their fears were quite understandable. At this time, the British were still very short of modern anti-aircraft guns and searchlights, and had only five squadrons of their most up-to-date fighter, the Hurricane, while the rest comprised obsolescent biplanes. Radar, which two years later was to play such a pivotal role in the desperate battle to save Britain from German invasion, was still in the process of being developed. But while Chamberlain conjured images of mass casualties in British cities, ordered the mass distribution of gas masks to British civilians, and arranged for the evacuation of children from London, he was unaware that the German air force was not capable at this stage of inflicting any such 'knock-out blow'. He did not know that

---

28. These were a conversation between Gamelin and Chamberlain and a telegram from Phipps. Cadogan *Diaries*, 27 Sept 1938, 107.
29. Stehlin 162. Chamberlain—Bouverie 272; Henderson—11 Oct 1938, FO 371/21710 TNA.

just a week before, on 22 September, a Luftwaffe chief had informed Göring that his force simply did not have any such capability.[30]

In Paris, Vuillemin's sombre message also reverberated. The prime minister was certainly not one to disregard intelligence reports. Having served as an intelligence officer in the First World War, Daladier was inclined to spend a great deal of time reading despatches and reports and listening to briefings from officials of the Bureau, regularly giving parliament and civil servants detailed evaluations of German power. But he shared the pessimism that exerted a grip much more widely across the political spectrum. False intelligence, in other words, had entrenched pacifist sentiment: 'all that is best in France is against war, almost at any price', as Phipps argued at the height of the crisis, adding that a more aggressive British approach risked splitting the two countries and 'turning against us'.[31]

During the Munich conference, Vuillemin continued to send Bonnet 'fresh, pessimistic information' about French capabilities, or the lack of them, and his views were invoked by the French delegation at the summit to justify the abandonment of Czechoslovakia. But at this time neither the British nor the French representatives were given any precise and impartial details about the Luftwaffe's ability to strike their homelands: the issue was once again left entirely to the imagination.[32]

---

30. 'British Intelligence on the German Air Force and Aircraft Industry 1933–9', Wark *HJ* (1982) 627–48.

31. Pessimism—see for example the political activist Anatole de Monzie, a committed pacifist whose views found sustenance from the air chief's sombre reports. 'The most bitter experience of the past few weeks', as he wrote at the time of Munich, had been the recognition of Germany's 'terrifying' air superiority, which meant that 'whatever happens it would be folly to go to war'. The French air chief, de Monzie continued, 'had laid the foundation for this viewpoint after his Berlin visit'. Joseph Caillaux, the chairman of the Senate finance committee, also made a very French allusion to the consequences of the 'heavy air bombardment of factories round Paris', which he felt might be 'the cause of another Commune'—a reference to the Paris Commune of 1871, a mass and bloody insurrection which followed in the aftermath of the defeat of France by Prussia. For Guy La Chambre, the air minister, 'the safest place for the next two years in France would be a trench'. For General Henri Dentz, French cities would be 'in ruins' in the event of war over the Sudetenland—Phipps to Halifax, 22 Sept 1938; DBFP III series, Vol 2, 1938, No 1034. Phipps to Halifax, 2 Sept 1938; DBFP III series, Vol 2, 1938, No 1076. Days later, Phipps was noting 'a complete change' in French public opinion: DBFP III series, Vol 2, 1938, No 1106. See OH Bullitt *For the President* Houghton Mifflin (1972) 297–8.; Adamthwaite *France and the Coming of the Second World War* 108.

32. Vuillemin—Adamthwaite *France and the Coming of the Second World War* 239.

On the ground, meanwhile, intelligence operatives were doing their utmost to keep a close eye on German troop movements in case Hitler broke his word by sending soldiers into the Sudetenland before any settlement had been reached. It was at this point that Kenneth Strong and his counterpart at the Italian embassy were given permission by the Nazi authorities to drive around Germany. Although they were escorted as they did so, Strong was able to seize his chance, trying to commit as much information as he could to memory.

Strong was able to pick up details and changes about the organization of the German armed forces. He thought that they had rectified some of the organizational shortcomings that he had noted at the time of *Anschluss*, and this meant that 'the morale and efficiency of the German army now seemed to be at its highest point'. The Germans whom he met and saw were, he noted later, 'lost in a sort of euphoria. I have seldom known military enthusiasm so high or confidence in the future greater than it was amongst the men... with whom I spoke.' He was also able to verify and memorize its order of battle and 'fill in many gaps in our information' while also getting a good sense of the characters of all the leading officers, including Leeb, Reichenau, Bock, and von Rundstedt, who were all later given high command. This trip was, for Strong, 'one of the most rewarding intelligence-gathering operations that I have ever experienced'.[33]

Strong verified that the troops were doing as they should, and not straying over the border. On this occasion at least, Hitler had kept his word. But the Nazi leader doubtlessly knew that he did not need to send his troops into the Sudetenland before an agreement had been reached at Munich. He would have sensed weakness and vulnerability in Chamberlain and Daladier before they surrendered to all of the stringent demands that he had laid down shortly before at Bad Godesberg: under the agreement, Germany would take over not just the Sudetenland but also important Czech hubs of communication, industrial centres, and some key fortifications. Beneš, who was not even invited to the Munich conference, was left with just a rump of a state.

Chamberlain returned from the Munich Conference claiming 'peace for our time' but for Winston Churchill it represented a 'total and unmitigated defeat' because the prime minister had given Hitler everything he had asked for. Meanwhile Hitler, who had been

determined to attack Czechoslovakia but who had lost his nerve in the
face of determined Anglo-French threats of war, brazenly stated that
the Sudetenland would be his 'last territorial ambition in Europe'.[34]

The British and French intelligence services can hardly be accused
of causing the disastrous policy of appeasement, which was of course
the product and reflection of so many influences, most notably the
strong public reaction against the risk of another pan-European conflict so soon after a 'Great War' that had engulfed an entire continent,
killing and maiming millions: in September 1938, for example, the
French public was overwhelmingly against war with Germany. But the
overestimation of German power did entrench, rather than undermine, the mindset of those who wanted to avoid war at almost any
cost and who were reluctant to confront Berlin. In Paris, for example,
the Deuxième Bureau's reports further clouded General Gamelin's
poor judgement. The general who had once argued, at the London
Conference in November 1937, that 'even Romania is a better asset
than the Russian army', was also guilty of seriously overestimating
German strength. And Mason-Macfarlane's reports equally played into
the hands of arch-appeasers such as Henderson and Chamberlain.
'When I left the meeting', as Mason-Macfarlane later wrote about the
briefing he had given the prime minister and general staff in September,
'I was left with the impression that the members of the cabinet were
less concerned with supporting the Czechs than with avoiding war at
all costs.' He did not explain, however, why he had given them such
questionable information that played right into their hands.[35]

By the time Chamberlain returned home from Munich, he had
taken a big step out of the state of isolation that Great Britain had
entered into after 1918. On 19 September, he had given a commitment
to the security of Czechoslovakia, despite the misgivings of his defence
chiefs and despite his own earlier admission that 'you only have to look
at the map to see that nothing that France or we could do could possibly save Czechoslovakia from being overrun'. A week later he had
publicly pledged Britain's support for the French in the event that they
were drawn into war to defend the Czechs or any other country.

34. Churchill—Piers Brendon *Churchill: A Brief Life* Pimlico (1984) 132.
35. Sept 1938—'War would now be most unpopular with France', noted Phipps on 24
    Sept 1938. 'All that is best in France is against war, almost at any price.' Cadogan *Diaries*
    104. Nov 1937—Adamthwaite *France and the Coming of the Second World War* 235.
    Mason-Mac—Butler 84.

Despite Cadogan's misgivings about France's true intentions—' "active hostilities" probably meant a squib offensive [to bring us in] and then retirement on the Maginot Line to wait for your "Kitchener armies" ', as he wrote—the two countries had moved closer together, not least in resisting 'a considerable tendency to recrimination between certain quarters' in both France and Britain over the outcome of the Munich agreement.[36]

36. 19 Sept—in March, a report of the chiefs of staff had concluded that 'neither Great Britain nor France could render any direct assistance to Czechoslovakia, and the only method of rendering even indirect assistance would be by staging offensive operations against Germany', which they judged France to be incapable of. In September, they argued that 'no pressure . . . could prevent Germany from overrunning Bohemia'. See Cadogan *Diaries* 64–5; 108. Cadogan—FO Memo, 28 Sept 1938, FO 371/21592 TNA; Cadogan *Diaries* 26 Sept 1938, 106.

18

Predicting Hitler's Next Move

In the wake of the Munich agreement, relations between the Czech intelligence services and their French counterparts plunged to a nadir. Because the Czechs had a formal defensive alliance with France, they felt a strong sense of betrayal at the outcome, much stronger than the feelings of disappointment that they harboured towards Chamberlain and the British. General Louis-Eugène Faucher, the Frenchman who had set up the Czech armed forces in the early 1920s, now wrote of the 'violent indignation' in the country provoked by the betrayal of Czechoslovakia by France and tore up his own French passport in disgust. The long-standing collaboration between the Czech spies and the French was now 'in limbo, neither formally liquidated nor fully operative', wrote Moravec. Many of his colleagues were even returning their French service medals to Paris, 'often with unflattering comments', and he himself felt intensely bitter 'towards a country I had once admired so much for its courage'. British diplomats were well aware of this rift, noting that 'the Czechs regard the French as beneath contempt' because of their 'unanimous and callous indifference'.[1]

The sense of betrayal was heightened by the fact that the remnants of Czechoslovakia were now surrounded by overwhelming German forces and also under immense pressure from within, as pro-Nazi activists stepped up their efforts to destabilize the Prague government. Deeply aware of being watched closely by German undercover agents, Moravec knew that he could not afford to make any false moves.

---

1. Faucher—Peter Jackson, 'French Military Intelligence and Czechoslovakia 1938', *Diplomacy and Statecraft* (1994) 82. Moravec 144–5. British diplomats—'Situation in Germany', Memo by W W Astor, 21 Nov 1938, CAB 104/43 TNA.

But if relations between Paris and Prague were now considerably cooler, then so too had the Polish government become even more estranged from the British, French, and, if it were possible for matters to become even frostier, the Czechs. Both the French and Czechs had been strongly suspicious of the Polish government before the Munich crisis: in April, the French military attaché in Warsaw had commented on the 'very mistrustful' attitude of his French and Czech counterparts towards Poland, which they felt 'was flirting with Germany whilst having an alliance with France'. Equally, officials at the French Foreign Ministry had at this time thought they noticed 'clear parallels between German and Polish diplomatic action towards Prague', and felt sure that the Poles would exploit Czech vulnerability when Hitler threatened Prague. During the Munich crisis, such fears seemed prescient because Warsaw issued its own ultimatum to Beneš, demanding the cession of the Teschen region, which he had been powerless to resist.[2]

Instead of adding their voice to the Anglo-French condemnation of Hitler's claims, in other words, the Poles had stepped aside and pursued their own independent, duplicitous line. Daladier told the American ambassador in Paris that 'he hoped to live long enough to make Poland pay for her greed', while the British condemned Colonel Beck for his 'vanity' and 'ambition to pose as a leading statesman'. The Polish ambassadors in London and Paris immediately noticed the 'cold and hostile' atmosphere and 'obvious ill-will' around them.[3]

Meanwhile, although they had no other potential partners to choose from, the British still refused the full embrace of the French. In November, Chamberlain was alarmed by intelligence reports that Hitler was contemplating an attack on the Low Countries that would herald an assault on Britain but he nonetheless rejected Daladier's calls for high-level talks between the general staff of the two countries. Such was the mistrust between the capitals that, in a letter of 1 November to the British ambassador in Paris, Halifax even wondered if France might conclude a non-aggression pact with Germany or, more dangerously, might 'contract out of Europe altogether', leaving Britain to face Hitler alone. Soon, the British ambassador in Paris warned him that 'there is a certain element of opinion in France which

2. Firebrace to Chilston, 18 Apr 1938, DBFP III series, Vol 1, 1938, No 151.
3. Overy and Wheatcroft 9.

would hesitate to come to our assistance in the event of England being attacked alone'.[4]

Equally, the British chiefs of staff dismissed suggestions of joint planning with France by observing that 'the very term "staff conversations" has a sinister purport and gives an impression ... of mutually assumed military collaboration'. However, there were stronger reasons than ever before to reconsider this position. Striking up an alliance with the French would stop them from retreating and leaving Britain isolated. Soon the British cabinet had agreed that 'the strategical importance to the British Empire of Holland and her colonies is so great that a German attack on Holland must, in our opinion, be regarded as an attack on our own interests'.[5]

The SIS and the Deuxième Bureau were moving closer together, pooling some of their resources as they worked towards the same end. In January, Godfrey visited the Bureau's headquarters in Paris alongside Dunderdale, who wrote later that 'their impression of Captain Godfrey was a very good one and I am sure that they will do everything for us after his visit'. Godfrey also met his French counterparts, Rear Admiral Raymond de Villaine and Admiral François Darlan, who gave him details of how their warships secretly tracked enemy vessels, using insider information drawn from informers based at foreign ports. Led into a complex of underground tunnels in the centre of Paris, the guest was also shown the French navy's protected teleprinter communications that networked all of its bases across the world, a network in which London was now included.[6]

Two weeks later, a French delegation made a return visit to London to meet with Stevens and Menzies, who proposed stepping up the SIS counter-espionage operations in Holland, leaving the French with more resources to concentrate on Belgium and Luxembourg. Soon

---

4. Halifax to Phipps, 1 Nov 1938, C12819/85/18, FO 371/21673 TNA. British ambassador—FO Minute, 21 Jan 1939, FP 371/22972 TNA.
5. British chiefs of staff quoted in Peter Jackson, 'French Security and a British "Continental Commitment" after the First World War: A Reassessment', *EHR* (Apr 2011) 351. Britain isolated—Fraser to Phipps, 4 Jan 1939, FO 371/22915 TNA. British cabinet—this was partly because Dutch ports offered Germany control over the North Sea but also because 'the destruction of Dutch authority in the East Indies would weaken our position throughout the Far East'. 'German Aggression Against Holland', 25 Jan 1939, CAB 27/624 TNA.
6. 'Mission to Paris, Jan 1939', *The Naval Memoir of Admiral JH Godfrey*, Vol 5, 15–16, 119, privately published memoir (1964–6).

Dunderdale had also started to work with the French to develop joint mobilization plans in the event of war with Germany. Menzies briefed the French on his plans, which included proposals to recruit more agents from Abwehr stations inside Germany and from within customs offices and police stations in neighbouring neutral countries, such as Switzerland and Belgium. He also expressed his doubts that Germany was capable of fighting a protracted war, noting that 'three very good agents living on the other side of the Rhine, who have given me perfect intelligence during the last period of tension, have confirmed this viewpoint'. In addition, the two organizations collaborated with a number of double agents who were based in the Low Countries, notably a Belgian, codenamed 'Agent Li 270', who provided the SIS and the Bureau with German questionnaires on the French aircraft industry.[7]

These meetings also gave both parties a better idea of each other's capabilities. The French team felt that their British counterparts were missing the well-placed double agents that the SR had proved so capable at running, and that they were weighed down by a cumbersome legal system that deprived them of the powers they needed to be effective: this mirrored the observations of the French made by SIS representatives such as Winterbotham, who was surprised at the French spy services' relative freedom. The French were also alarmed by the lack of security at the SIS station in The Hague, noting its improvised nature and its vulnerability to a high level of German activity that was working with relative impunity.

There was one other factor that was by this time driving both countries closer into each other's arms. Towards the end of 1938, British Intelligence had become increasingly aware of a rapidly growing German interest and presence in West Africa, posing a threat to the British and French colonies there. 'German penetration of the African coasts is being carried out in a remarkable fashion,' as one report noted, 'for behind a commercial or industrial screen, political infiltration is being started which might, at a given time, be used to support military action.' Given the lack of information about the state of Germany's navy, it seemed possible that Hitler and his admirals did have the maritime strength to realize such goals.[8]

7. Jeffery 292.
8. Report—'German Activity in Africa', 1 Oct 1938, AIR 9/93 TNA.

This heightened Nazi interest was ostensibly an effort to win back the territories, or a comparable amount of land, that Germany had lost at Versailles. It was to this end that, inside the Reich, General Franz von Epp was organizing 'propaganda' and the 'formation of skeleton colonial units at the former German colonial school in Witzenhausen and the new colonial school in Ladeburg'. During the Munich crisis, British Intelligence also discovered that von Epp had discussed the issue with Hitler and had subsequently expressed his view that 'the Cameroons would be returned to Germany by April 1939'. Earlier in 1938, the Germans had taken a harder line, before the issue had gone quiet.[9]

But Whitehall was sure that Berlin was forming 'an excellent screen behind which a military and political activity can be prepared quite quietly, ready for wartime', in British Gambia, the Bissagos Islands, Liberia, the Cameroons, Togoland, and South West Africa. This included the building of a '"naval-string" that could connect German centres set up on the West African coast' for harbours and air strips.

France's own colonies in the region were equally threatened by the Nazis. 'A certain activity has been reported', noted the British, 'in the districts near French Guinea—construction of roads converging on our colony, construction of an aerodrome with cemented runway at Saniquelle, a carriage road from Saniquelle to Monrovia … the German trading houses are stated to have a number of agents out of all proportion to the turnover of the factories'. And this meant that the interests of the two imperial powers were closely bound. To defend its West African colonies, the British government needed support from the French. In the British Cameroons, for example, there was a strong and vocal German expatriate population 'who could in case of war effect the sabotage of telegraph-lines, roads and bridges'. They posed the risk that a putsch 'effected in cooperation with the German colony in the French Cameroons, might be aimed at cutting the strategic routes by which we could get help from French Equatorial Africa'.

Of particular strategic importance were the Bissagos Islands, positioned along a key sea route and making 'an excellent natural base for

9. In early 1938 Hitler had originally stated his ambition to restore Germany's pre-1918 colonies or their equivalent, which included 'a large compact area' in West Central Africa. After *Anschluss*, German colonial leaders talked of more ambitious goals to help sustain Germany's need for raw materials. 'Most Secret Memo', 15 Nov 1938, CAB 104/43 TNA.

submarines and cruisers'. Because intelligence reports had noted keen German interest in these islands, Whitehall decided that it would be 'urgently necessary' to keep a watch on them. But again, French cooperation was necessary to do this. 'Owing to difficulties of approach, it seems that this task would fall primarily to the Air Force which, starting from the coasts of Senegal (a French colony) or French Gambia, could easily discern traces of naval or military occupation.'[10]

At around the same time, while Chamberlain, Hitler, and Daladier had been determining the future of Czechoslovakia, French and British spies were also working together on an ingenious plan to watch Germany from the skies.[11]

This plan was concocted by Frederick Winterbotham and Georges Ronin, who had hit on the idea of hiding the most up-to-date aerial cameras in a civilian aircraft that would have an excuse to fly through German air space, and even over its most closely guarded places. Although a joint venture, this was an area of French expertise, since the Deuxième Bureau had made considerably greater use of covert aerial reconnaissance than the RAF: after their withdrawal from the Rhineland in 1930, the French air force had flown over the area in a bid to keep track of developments, despite drawing official protests from the German authorities in the process.[12]

The Bureau now offered Whitehall the full use of its modified aircraft and flying strips close to the border with Germany. The chief challenge was obtaining permission from the German authorities to fly over the Reich, as well as headhunting a pilot who would not only fail to arouse any German suspicions but also be brave enough to undertake such a hazardous journey: there would be a strong risk of detection and arrest on charges of espionage, or else of an 'accident' if the Germans detected the true purpose of the flight.

In the autumn of 1938, Winterbotham had approached someone who was admirably qualified to help. Alfred Miranda was an American arms dealer and businessman, based in New York, who was well connected across the world. He immediately knew the right man for this demanding job. A decade before, Miranda explained, he had attended the New York Motor Show and met an affable and outgoing Australian

10. 'German Activity in Africa', 1 Oct 1938, AIR 9/93 TNA.
11. Winterbotham *Nazi Connection* Ch 13 *passim*.
12. 'Au sujet d'avions militaires', 28 May 1931, F/7/13428 AN.

pilot by the name of Sidney Cotton. The two men had struck up a
good rapport and shared a love of fast cars: in 1934 Miranda had even
lent Cotton a sports car that the Australian had then used to drive from
Washington to Miami. Cotton was now engaged in promoting the
most up-to-date type of colour film, known as Dufaycolor, and often
flew all over the world to promote it. This company was struggling to
build its clients and revenues and, like so many other recruits to the
intelligence services, Cotton was open to any generous cash offers.[13]

Within days, Cotton was talking to a middle-aged man 'with grey-
ing hair… and a quiet air of discretion'. Over several meetings and
expensive dinners, the SIS officer emphasized the urgency of the situation and explained what Cotton could do to help: if he could fly over
carefully chosen parts of Germany, then he could use a concealed camera to photograph high-value targets. So useful would this information
be, Winterbotham continued, that the French government was willing
to pay every expense. The plane itself would need to be acquired from
outside Europe to avoid arousing German suspicions, particularly
when Nazi agents were keeping close watch on the activities of
French aerodromes. Given the importance of the mission, and relish-
ing the prospect of some adventure, Cotton nodded his agreement.
But he added that he wanted to use a particular American plane, a
Lockheed 12A.

Winterbotham knew that German Intelligence could well have
informers inside British customs who could cast an evil eye upon any
imports of weapons or vital raw materials. To avoid detection, he
arranged for the Lockheed to be taken apart and shipped across the
Atlantic in several large crates. On arrival in Southampton,
Winterbotham quietly waved the containers through customs before
moving them to an isolated hangar at Heston aerodrome. The plane
was then reassembled and, through the influence of the SIS, flown to
France without any of the usual customs checks that any Nazi infiltra-
tors might easily have undertaken or learned about. The plane had
arrived without encountering any unwelcome turbulence.

Eventually, after a great many delays, Cotton was ready to get the
operation under way, assisted by a co-pilot and engineer called Bob
Niven, a 'tall, zestful and enthusiastic' former bus driver from Calgary.
The two men flew in a private aircraft from Heston aerodrome in west

13. Sidney Cotton *Aviator Extraordinary* Chatto & Windus (1969) Ch 12 *passim*.

London—where, just months before, Chamberlain had trumpeted the Munich agreement as 'peace for our time'—to an airfield outside Paris. Here they were met by a senior officer in the Deuxième Bureau who was 'short and compactly built, with the physique of a boxer', as Cotton wrote later. Colonel Pépin certainly punched above his weight, telling them with the 'manner of the lecturer, precise and pedantic, without a glimmer of humour', about what lay ahead and explaining the risks they were taking.

The following day, Pépin explained, a specially adapted camera would be fitted into an aperture that had been cut into the floor of the plane's cabin. The camera, a huge and bulky piece of equipment measuring about five feet in length, would then have to be smuggled into the hangar and fitted on the plane in the utmost secrecy, when they were sure no one was watching, because of the high risk of Nazi infiltration within the base. Then a highly experienced French navigator would join them and lead them along a carefully charted flight path around Mannheim: there had been reports of several new airfields and factories in this vicinity, he explained, and because it was so close to the French border it was essential to find out what the Germans were doing there.

Pépin told them his plan for evading detection, explaining that they would have to leave at a very precise moment, at exactly eleven o'clock, because that was the same time that the daily civilian passenger plane left Strasbourg for Mannheim. Their best chance was to confuse German air traffic control, who would hopefully mistake their own flight for the passenger plane. If, in a worst-case scenario, they were detected and forced to land, he concluded, then they would have to ditch the camera over water or a forest and then claim to be the innocent victims of navigational error.

Despite some hair-raising incidents, notably being approached by a German fighter that disappeared as rapidly and mysteriously as it had appeared, Cotton's first flight went to plan, and over the next few days he and his two co-pilots made several more such journeys, flying above the Siegfried Line and along the Swiss border, on each occasion without incident. But however good the quality of the photos, there were huge areas of the Mannheim region that he was not able to photograph: it was simply too extensive and the opportunities too fleeting, and to make any more journeys would push their luck. But Cotton got a further chance some weeks later, when quite unexpectedly he received an invitation from a German acquaintance, now working in the film industry, to fly over to Berlin to promote Dufaycolor. The Germans' interest may well have been aroused by the quiet intervention of the SIS, which had used its contacts and influence to generate commercial interest and publicity for Cotton's company.[14]

Winterbotham nonetheless suspected a trap, wondering if the Nazis had discovered the truth about his flights over Mannheim, but Cotton was willing to take the risk and flew to Tempelhof aerodrome. He felt confident that his cameras, concealed in the wings and operated by switches on the dashboard, were now much harder to find. Nonetheless, on landing he quickly found, to his immense relief, that he was received as an honoured guest and not as an enemy spy. Amiable and outgoing, he was able to strike up a good rapport with his German hosts and, as an Australian with a very strident accent, he did not arouse their suspicions.

Cotton got his chance when the Nazis, very impressed by his Lockheed plane as well as by his knowledge of the film industry and contacts within it, subsequently invited him to attend an international air show at Frankfurt. Soon after arriving, a senior German army officer, Albert Kesselring, asked Cotton to take him for a test ride, and the Australian tried his luck. Using his best acting skills, and conscious that a very tempting reconnaissance target was only about 50 miles away, he exclaimed that he had 'a favourite aunt who always raved about the beautiful Rhine at Mannheim'. To his surprise the ploy worked, and the following day he took his guest into the skies above Mannheim, flying at low altitude, just 2,000 feet, over several new air-fields and installations, all the time thanking his non-existent aunt. As they passed over one installation that was, from their vantage point, very obviously a new military site, Cotton could not resist a bit of irony, shouting out to his passenger that he was 'not supposed to see that', as the German laughed in response.[15]

When the air show was over, he was ordered to return to France following the same closely mapped flight path that he had made his way along. But once again he had a stroke of good fortune because he departed in heavy cloud, and this meant that he could easily stray off course and just claim that he had lost his way. He immediately headed back towards the Siegfried Line and followed much of its course, in

14. Winterbotham *Nazi Connection* 241.   15. Cotton 130.

German air space, all the way as far as Aachen before heading towards Brussels. Cotton's mission, using German-made cameras to covertly film top-secret German sites, had been a spectacular success. For the SIS and the Bureau, Cotton was now a film star.

The Australian's presence in the Reich may well account for another intelligence success at this time. Perhaps won over by his charm, one of Cotton's business contacts in Berlin, a German civilian who worked for the same company, managed to obtain detailed information about a new type of acoustic mine that the Nazis had now developed: detonated by the motion of the propellers of passing ships, this mine posed a significant threat to Allied shipping, but the insider's information now allowed the Admiralty's experts to take preventive measures.[16]

Meanwhile, other intelligence operatives on the ground were doing their best to gather information. By the spring of 1939 this was an even harder task because the Germans were hiding their military preparations more effectively than before. By late 1938, for example, German units had removed the numbers from their military uniforms that had previously allowed the British to identify them; similarly, armoured vehicles no longer bore identifying numbers. Only an occasional slip enabled foreign observers to find out such specific details: on the eve of a major ceremony in Berlin, for example, Colonel Strong saw that an official had mistakenly chalked the names of entire units, comprising almost the whole German army, on the pavements where they were due to stand the next day. Memorizing as many details as he could of this 'real bonanza' before writing them down in the safety of the embassy, Strong departed just as a Nazi official discovered the mistake and ordered some street cleaners to scrub the markings away.[17]

Sometimes ominous signs appeared in unexpected places, and in early 1939 the French military attaché in Berlin, General Henri Didelet, noticed that iron lamp-posts and fencing for lawns and cemeteries were suddenly disappearing from the city's streets, a clear indication that Germany's war economy was preparing for war by stockpiling valuable materials. And in February, Mason-Mac returned to Vienna to search for just such signs of impending military action.

At first sight the Austrian capital seemed quiet and the British attaché could not hear any 'dreadful note of preparation' indicating any sign of imminent war. But to get a better idea, he walked and drove

16. Winterbotham *Nazi Connection* 241.   17. Strong 40–1.

past several German barracks and depots. He looked out for, but could not see, the most obvious sign of action—the highly distinctive yellow boots of the reservists—although from the road he did get numerous glimpses of 'transport of all kinds being loaded up'. But by 13 March he felt it was 'reasonably clear that operations were imminent', particularly when he drove outside the capital and, a few miles outside, saw a great many anti-aircraft guns being dug in. Apart from their state of readiness, he also managed to establish the units that were involved and, as he drove along the icy Austrian roads, he was also able to observe how efficient and organized the German army had become. A year before, he had noticed how many of its vehicles had skidded off the roads and tracks but now no longer noticed any such losses.[18]

Mason-Mac and other foreign spies were also trying to gauge the feelings and attitudes of the German people towards the likelihood of outright war. They knew that the leaders even of a state as totalitarian as Nazi Germany could not afford to go to war if it would result in mass protests, strikes, and riots. In October 1936, for example, the Deuxième Bureau noted how the Gestapo had tried to suppress 'an upsurge in popular alarm about the price increases and famine that war would cause'. So seriously did the Nazi authorities take this, the report continued, that Heydrich had ordered his security chiefs to find out who had started this 'particularly dangerous and subversive propaganda'.[19]

The importance of public opinion had also become clear after Hitler's conference with Chamberlain and Daladier at Bad Godesberg in September. Although Hitler himself had taken a highly belligerent position over the Sudetenland, he had suddenly backed down and instead called a four-power conference at Munich. This was largely because Mussolini intervened and persuaded him to negotiate, but Hitler had also been taken aback by the brazen hostility of some Germans towards the threat of conflict. This had become clear during a military parade in Berlin on 27 September, when crowds of ordinary Germans had shouted *Heil Chamberlain!* An unnerved *Führer* had exclaimed in private afterwards that 'I can't lead a war with such people' and ordered newspaper editors to 'psychologically prepare the German people'. And a stunned William L Shirer, who witnessed the spectacle, also commented on the fact that 'it has been the most striking demonstration against war I've ever seen'.[20]

Such negative reactions were a sign of a wider 'war psychosis' that appeared to have afflicted a great many ordinary Germans at this time. Until now, Hitler had won several foreign policy victories—the Saar, the Rhineland, and Austria—without a shot even being fired. But now the prospect of war with Britain, France, and Czechoslovakia over the Sudetenland had seemed a very real one. In his diary, the propaganda minister Joseph Goebbels noted this public malaise, while informers working for the exiled Social Democratic Party reported that 'people are afraid that it will come to war and that Germany will go under in it'.[21]

Getting a 'feel' for public opinion meant talking as much as possible to ordinary Germans in every walk of life, whilst at the same time trying to evade Nazi surveillance. During the Munich crisis, one British diplomat 'heard nothing but admiration and gratitude for Mr Chamberlain but heard no expression of enthusiasm for the *Führer*'. He noted, instead, the drastic change that had come over the majority of ordinary Germans, who just a year or so before had been overwhelmed with joy and gratitude towards their leader for restoring German pride. An American official in Cologne also informed him that many factory workers were strongly opposed to Hitler and, more generally, to the prospect of conflict: at an agricultural machinery factory near the city, workers were even planning to mount a demonstration against war. This echoed reports that reached French Intelligence in January 1939, when there were outbreaks of strikes and protests in the mining region of Alsdorf: the SS broke up the demonstrations and arrested 165 workers, opening fire on the protesters.[22]

Other members of the public told the British diplomat about strong anti-Nazi feelings prevalent amongst ordinary Austrians and predicted more uprisings in Vienna if war broke out. 'The general opinion among people with whom I talked, both German and others', he concluded, 'was that in the case of war, the Germans would have followed Hitler's

20. Unnerved—Hans B. Gisevius, *To the Bitter End* Da Capo Press (1998) 325; Brendon *Dark Valley* 463–4. Shirer 117.
21. Evans *The Third Reich in Power* 675.
22. British diplomat—'Notes on Germany and Central Europe', FO 371/21659 TNA. French reports—'Mouvement d'opposition de mineurs allemands', 14 Jan 1939, 7NN 2352 SHD.

orders, but with little heart for the adventure; and that after a few months' experience of war conditions they would have turned against the Nazi regime.' The source added that:

The German people were however greatly alarmed at the possibility of war; and this alarm has not contributed to the popularity of the regime. For the moment they seem strangely ungrateful to their *Führer* for the brilliant diplomatic successes of Austria and Sudetenland. They can only think of him as the man who nearly involved them in war for a cause in which little personal interest was taken in Germany.[23]

French spies detected similar sentiments. In September 1938, the Bureau judged that 'Germany will enter into a conflict of loyalties which are, beyond any doubt, very unsettling and which can only worsen if the war drags on for some time and especially if serious losses are incurred.' Another report noted that the general population was 'profoundly troubled' by the military preparations and that, although the people would follow Hitler into war, there was 'no enthusiasm amongst either the troops or the public'. The French minister in The Hague, Baron De Vitrolles, also emphasized the 'fear and hatred of war amongst the German people as a whole'. During the final weeks of August, Daladier, Gamelin, and senior ministers in Paris received daily briefings on public morale in Germany that had been sent from the embassy in Berlin and from the network of French consulates inside the Reich.[24]

But foreign intelligence officers also noticed other attitudes, prevalent amongst some German officers, that were rather more alarming. Over dinner one evening in September 1938, a group of rather inebriated Wehrmacht officers told a French military attaché that anyone who did not share the Nazi Party's commitment to expanding Germany's borders deserved to 'disappear'. Their attitude, noted the alarmed Frenchman, revealed 'a brutal, worrying and heart-breaking aspect of the German mentality'. It was a sign of things to come.[25]

But if there was much pacifist sentiment amongst ordinary Germans, by early March 1939 there were equally clear signs that Hitler and his generals were prepared to ignore it and reach for their rifles. The question

23. 'Notes on Germany and Central Europe', 18 Sept 1938, FO 371/21659 TNA.
24. De Vitrolles—Jackson *France the Nazi Menace* 354.
25. 20 Sept 1938, 7NN 2601 SHD.

for the intelligence services was very simple to ask but extremely hard to answer: where would they aim?

In the short term, the most obvious next goal was the 'liquidation' of Czechoslovakia. Although Hitler had won so much Czech territory at Munich, the remnants of the country were still a tempting Nazi target. This was mainly because of its resources—minerals as well as armaments and industries—but also because if Hitler intended to move east and attack Poland, the Ukraine, or the entire Soviet Union, then he would probably want to capture the rest of Czechoslovakia first.

But Hitler was unpredictable. Towards the end of 1938, reports 'from a number of secret and other sources' emerged that Hitler was planning to attack the Ukraine over the year ahead, and that preparations for such a strike had already started. But he could have chosen to seize the Lithuanian city of Memel, where 150,000 ethnic Germans lived, or perhaps Danzig, with more than twice that number. The Ukraine then seemed to be a likely target, since it would offer him foodstuffs and access to the Mediterranean. Or he could also have targeted the Polish Corridor or, much more ambitiously, Poland in its entirety, while Switzerland, which was the home for several German-speaking cantons, was also at risk. But some wondered if the Nazis were really planning to invade the Balkans, tempted by the vast quantities of Romanian oil or the Hungarian wheat that the Reich urgently needed. More radically still, he could even have struck next in the west, invading Holland before attacking Britain, towards which by the summer of 1939 Hitler's invective had become increasingly vituperative. Other rumours were flying, including reports that 'the Germans hope with the Italians to make a drive in Africa from Abyssinia through Tanganyika towards the Belgian Congo'. Everything seemed possible.[26]

26. 1938 reports—'Information regarding German designs on the Ukraine', 16 Jan 1939, FO 371/22961 TNA. Ukraine—this was the view of Lt Col de Vitrolles, for example; see Colyer's memo of 19 Jan 1939, AIR 9/93 TNA. Belgian Congo—'Message from CE', 31 Jan 1939, FO 1093/86 TNA. The Germans tried to spin these rumours about Abyssinia by 'arranging for postcards written by their troops in Spain to be sent to Abyssinia for despatch from there. This is apparently to give the impression that there are now German troops in Abyssinia.'

19

Intelligence and the
Anglo-French Alliance

Foreign intelligence services searched desperately for clues to Hitler's next move but were extremely short of sources of information. 'We cannot know whether Hitler will decide to go East...or whether he will deal with the West first', as one cabinet paper pointed out. Confronting them by this stage was not a lack of intelligence information but an excess of it, for by early 1939, as Admiral Godfrey discovered after his promotion in January, 'there were so many authentic rumours about Germany's intentions that, whatever happened, someone could say "I told you so."' Vansittart's replacement in the Foreign Office, Sir Alexander Cadogan, also found that he was 'daily inundated by all sorts of reports'.[1]

It was inevitable, in such a situation, that some empty rumours would become confused with accurate intelligence, and this helps to explain what became known as the 'January War Scare'.

In November 1938 and again in January 1939, both the SIS and the Deuxième Bureau received a series of reports strongly indicating that Hitler was planning to strike in the west. The Germans, according to these sources, would attack either both Britain and France or, as many of them concluded, strike just at Britain alone, moving through the Low Countries to set up air bases from which to raid London. All sorts of other terrifying eventualities suddenly loomed large in the imagination of British leaders. It seemed possible that Berlin would encourage the Italians to attack France, tying down French resources that would

1. Cabinet paper—'Possibility of a German Attack on the West', 19 Jan 1939, CAB 27/627 TNA. Godfrey Vol 5, Part 1, 7. Cadogan—Cadogan *Diaries* 158.

leave German forces free to launch their own devastating assault in the north. Or Hitler might strike up an alliance with Japan, urging its leaders to seize whole swathes of the British Empire at just the same time that he moved westwards.

The source of the SIS information was a diplomat, Ivone Kirkpatrick, who was based at the British embassy in Berlin. Shortly before he was due to leave the German capital and return to London, Kirkpatrick had received an unexpected letter from 'a former civil servant close to General Beck', asking him for an immediate, private meeting. Nothing, ran the letter, could safely be said over the phone or communicated by telegram, since the Nazis had broken British ciphers. Hours later, during their face-to-face encounter, the elderly German relayed his dramatic message. Hitler, he claimed, had ordered preparations for a sudden, surprise, and massive aerial attack on London, and wanted everything to be ready—aircraft, airfields, bombs, and targets—as soon as possible. And 'drunk with his resounding successes, thirsting for more political adventure and confronted with growing economic and domestic discontent', the *Führer* was ready to launch his attack within just a few weeks.[2]

Kirkpatrick later called this a 'sensational and rather lunatic little episode' but nonetheless rushed to the Foreign Office in London, where his story created a minor panic: within hours the cabinet had discussed this 'top secret intelligence' and ordered anti-aircraft defences to be set up all across central London, while the Committee of Imperial Defence ordered preparations for an attack to be stepped up urgently.[3]

But the 'intelligence reports' were in fact based on rumours that the Deuxième Bureau had deliberately fed to London, hoping to trick the British into a formal alliance: now that Hitler had emasculated its Czech ally, Paris needed London more than ever. The French spies provided Ambassador Phipps and his military attaché, Colonel William Fraser, with a steady flow of reports about a pending Nazi attack in the west, and on 30 January the Quai d'Orsay had sent an urgent despatch to London with 'information suggesting that a German action, if initially oriented towards eastern Europe, could be directed either suddenly or in conjunction with Italian ambitions, towards the west,

2. Ivone Kirkpatrick *The Inner Circle* Macmillan (1959) 136–9.
3. 'German Military Activities', FO 371/22958 TNA.

that is to say Great Britain, France, Belgium, the Netherlands, and Switzerland'. But the Bureau never took these 'warnings' seriously and remained convinced that Hitler would strike first in the east: the diaries of General Rivet, for example, do not even mention a possible German attack in the west. Instead, the communications to London were, in the words of Robert Young, 'a carefully orchestrated scare tactic' intended to lure Whitehall into a closer military relationship with France. Ironically, this tactic may have been conceived not in Paris but in London, where the British chief of staff, Sir Henry Pownall, instructed Fraser to advise the French to intensify pressure on the British government for a military alliance.[4]

Some other sources of information appeared to confirm these reports, including SIS contacts within the propaganda ministry in Berlin and several German news agencies, which had offices in London, as well as a number of informants who were in close touch with the Nazi foreign minister, Joachim von Ribbentrop, and the president of the Reichsbank. The very dubious nature of these sources should have made the SIS extremely wary of falling for a plan of deception that was intended to throw the British off the trail. But the information carried weight because it coincided with other reports, stating that Hitler was 'consumed by an insensate hatred of this country' and with an intense German press campaign depicting Great Britain as 'Public Enemy Number One'.[5]

Halifax immediately presented Kirkpatrick's reports to the cabinet and put forward a Foreign Office document on 'Possible German Intentions', outlining Hitler's alleged plans for a pre-emptive strike against London that was allegedly due to start on 21 February. The report provoked a mixed reaction. Halifax himself and several other ministers were sceptical about the claims but they were overruled by others who argued that the intelligence source had previously proved himself to be reliable. He was equally unsure about striking a closer relationship with France, which he argued 'might be attacked from more than one quarter', as he told the cabinet, 'whereas we were only

4. Robert Young *In Command of France* Harvard University Press (1978) 222–3; Jackson *France and the Nazi Menace* 326. Pownall—Peter Jackson and Joseph A. Maiolo, 'Intelligence in Anglo-French Relations', in Alexander and Philpott 144–5.

5. Deception—Basil Collier, 'Hidden Weapons: Allied Secret and Undercover Services in World War' 41. Press campaign, 'Insensate hatred'—Memo from Gledwyn Jebb, 19 Jan 1939 CAB 27/627 TNA.

liable to be attacked by Germany, and the obligations of mutual assistance in the event of attack would not, therefore, be equal'. Again, he was overruled and the cabinet decided to act quickly to defend Belgium and France in the event of a German attack on the Netherlands.[6]

The previous November, Chamberlain had refused Daladier's request for staff talks but the British now approached the French and asked to start them, to the delight of Gamelin and other senior figures in Paris who felt sure that London was about to make a general commitment to defend their country. On 23 January, the Foreign Policy Committee, heavily swayed by Halifax, decided that an attack on Holland would amount to a provocation of war and three days later the British cabinet agreed to enter high-level staff conversations 'tantamount to an alliance' with the French and to send an expeditionary force to the continent in the event of a war. The two intelligence services now followed their respective governments and became closer than at any time since 1918, making a coordinated and formal effort to share information about Nazi Germany.[7]

In effect, the British were now in the process of striking up an alliance with France. This mirrored a wider shift of public opinion that the French military attaché in London thought he noticed. There was a 'clear hardening of opinion towards the Axis', Albert Lelong had written the previous month, 'and a strong current of sympathy for France'. He concluded, on 15 December, that 'at last one sees a widespread recognition of the need for close Franco-British collaboration in the face of further aggression'.[8]

On 6 February, Chamberlain took one further step forward, telling the Commons that any threat 'to the vital interests of France … must evoke the immediate cooperation of this country' and promised 'immediate cooperation in the event of a threat to her vital interest from whatever quarter'. This was not just because he wanted to defend France, from both Italy and Germany, but also because Halifax wondered if France would support Britain if Hitler attacked the British alone. So strong was the anti-war lobby in France, focused around the foreign minister Georges Bonnet, that in such an eventuality it seemed quite possible that a French government could instead choose to

6. FO document—19 Jan 1939, CAB 27/627 TNA. Closer relationship—25 Jan 1939, CAB 23/97/2 TNA.
7. Jackson and Maiolo 'Intelligence in Anglo-French Relations' 146.
8. Jackson and Maiolo 'Intelligence in Anglo-French Relations' 143.

remain neutral: Chamberlain's promise would help his supporters in Paris to win the argument. As the British general staff argued, 'any effective French support … is likely to be contingent on our intervention on land on the Continent'. There is also 'circumstantial evidence' that General Gamelin, in a bid to win British support, had orchestrated a campaign in Paris to exaggerate the risk of French neutrality—'of giving up the unequal struggle (to make) the best terms she could with Germany'—in the event of a German attack.[9]

In fact, there was no truth behind the 'intelligence reports' and a groundless war scare had needlessly sent shockwaves of alarm through western capitals. At this time Hitler and his generals had no plans to attack the Low Countries or any other western target, and such plans were not determined until much later, after the fall of Poland in September 1939. The Luftwaffe had in fact only been carrying out exercises to practise an attack on London but had no instructions to carry one out. Mistrust of, and tension with, Germany, in other words, had become significantly heightened by 'intelligence reports' that were fundamentally flawed.

The true sources of this false information were in fact to be found not in a general's armchair in London or in the corridors of Parisian power but in Berlin, where they had been concocted by a number of senior figures who were bitterly opposed to Hitler, and who wanted to stop the apparent rush to war. Their likely aim was to prevent war by provoking Britain into rearmament and an alliance with France.[10]

The SIS and the British government had become aware of this group of dissidents some months before, when Professor T Philip Conwell-Evans, a British academic based at the University of Königsberg who had close contact with both the British and German governments, had met Erich Kordt in Berlin. Kordt was linked to a group of disaffected German top brass, notably General Ludwig Beck, the head of the German general staff, and Admiral Canaris, who were prepared to defy Hitler but who needed, or so they claimed, clear British support if their resistance was to gain traction. If Great Britain made a firm and public declaration of support for the Czechs, Kordt had quietly explained in the weeks before Munich, then it would sway

9. 6 Feb—'Great Britain and France', Hansard HC Debates, 6 Feb 1939, Vol 343. Gamelin—Imlay 105, 107, 111.
10. Bouverie 313.

the balance and the coup would have enough support to go ahead: the imminence of war against Britain and France would cause so much consternation amongst ordinary Germans that the conspirators would be sure of their support.

More information about this group had emerged over the summer when a string of visitors arrived, unexpected and uninvited, at Mason-Macfarlane's office in Berlin. One was a Nazi officer by the name of Silvius von Albedyl, who told the attaché about the true scale of discontent within the German high command, while three days later a well-connected former German soldier, Victor von Koerber, gave a similar account of the true scale of dissension. Other reports came from the French, whose ambassador, André François-Poncet, reported bitter disagreements between Hitler and General Beck.[11]

Soon afterwards, Canaris arranged for another of his fellow conspirators, an aristocratic landowner by the name of Ewald von Kleist-Schmenzin, to talk directly to the British. On 18 August, using a false identity and passport, Kleist was taken in an Abwehr car to Berlin's Templehof airport, where he skirted past customs and passports. Hours later he touched down at Croydon airfield, accompanied by an SIS officer, HD Hanson, who arranged for 'the civilian in the grey suit' to pass through customs unchallenged.

Kleist pleaded his case to several implacable opponents of the Nazi regime, including Vansittart, Lord Lloyd, and Churchill. 'In the event of the generals deciding to insist on peace, there would be a new system of government within forty-eight hours', he explained. 'Such a government, probably of a monarchist character, could guarantee stability and end the fear of war forever'. But he was unable to secure the backing of Chamberlain, who was still convinced that he could bargain with Hitler, dismissing Kleist-Schmenzin and his 'friends'. 'I think we must discount a great deal of what he says', Chamberlain concluded, even though Halifax wished to declare British support for the Czechs and told the cabinet, on 24 September, that if Hitler went to war, 'the result might be to help bring down the regime'. But Cadogan, wary of Kordt's suggestion about making any such broadcast, declined.[12]

---

11. Koerber—Wark 'Three Attachés' 602. 3 Aug 1938—FO 371/21667 TNA. François-Poncet—17 Sept 1938, 7NN 2523 SHD; Young 'French Military Intelligence' 282.

12. Kleist—'Note of a Conversation at Chartwell', FO 800/309 TNA. Friends—Cadogan *Diaries* 6–7 Sept 1938, 94–5; 5 May 1939, 178. Cadogan—19 Aug 1938, FO 800/309 TNA.

Now that the British government had ignored these pleas, the German resistance to Hitler was probably trying another tactic—deliberately falsifying 'intelligence reports' that would mislead the British and French governments, pushing them closer together. The tactic worked.[13]

In the weeks that followed the Munich agreement, it is likely that Hans Ostler was the source of these intelligence reports. Clever, devious, brave, calculating, and sophisticated, Ostler had all the hallmarks of a successful spy but also of a traitor: viscerally opposed to Hitler, National Socialism, and the prospect of war, he had the courage and every motive to carry out a very honourable act of treason by deliberately leaking misleading information about Nazi plans. Less than two years later, in May 1940, he went on to do the same by warning the Dutch government of an imminent German attack, knowing that his exaggerated statements would help stir the Dutch into last-minute action.

In fact, Hitler had decided not to strike in the west but instead attack Bohemia and Moravia, which comprised the remnants of the Czech state, and to conquer what he called the *Untermenschen* ('sub-humans') who lived there. And the first foreign agent to find out the details of his plans was once again Moravec's master spy, Agent 54.[14]

In early March, Moravec had received an urgent message from A-54, once again requesting an almost immediate meeting. The Czech spymaster had heard nothing from his best agent for some months and had wondered if he had been captured, or else been forced by German surveillance to stay under the radar. Nor was Moravec able to trace him, since he still had virtually no hard facts about this mysterious although supremely well-informed source, being quite unaware of 'Karl's' true name or where he worked: Moravec could only guess, and did so correctly, that he was an officer in the Abwehr and that he was based at Chemnitz, close to the Czech border. But now, after such a long silence, this enigmatic man once again stood before him, standing to attention as he was accustomed to doing. And 'with his customary efficiency', worthy of a German officer, he now reeled off his latest report.

The Nazi spy was certainly the bearer of great news, although, in a meeting that lasted less than half an hour, his message was only brief

13. 19 Aug 1938, FO 800/309 TNA.   14. Moravec Ch 12 *passim.*

and to the point. A large German force, he told his audience, was bracing itself to storm Czech territory in just a few days' time, on 15 March, and install a puppet government that would be ostensibly under the 'protection' of Berlin. He urged Moravec and his men to leave the country immediately and destroy or remove their key documents because the Germans would round up all senior Czech intelligence officers and prise information out of them. And he needed reassurance that all the files about his own self, and the information he had passed on, were destroyed too: even if Moravec had no hard facts about him, the Germans would search relentlessly to pinpoint such a high-value source. With that, Agent 54 was finished. He was driven back to the German border, alongside a single plain-clothed Czech officer, and Moravec never saw him again.

This was a desperate situation and Moravec immediately informed the cabinet and general staff as well as Major Gibson, who promised to press the British government to make a diplomatic intervention and urge Berlin not to make any move against Prague. But to his dismay, his pleas to Paris fell on deaf ears, and Moravec also found that many senior figures in Prague were refusing to believe the information. It was almost as if such news, like every trauma, was simply too bad to accept.

Within just days, 'Karl's' warnings had proven, once again, to be entirely prescient, chiming perfectly with the increasingly shrill alarms that other intelligence sources, notably those of Vansittart, had been uttering over the preceding weeks. On 14 March, President Emil Hácha made a last-ditch journey to Berlin to plead with Hitler to spare his country but he was faced with such vitriolic threats—Göring swore to reduce Prague to 'ruins'—that he collapsed on the floor and had to be revived by Hitler's personal doctor. He succumbed to such bullying tactics and in the early hours signed the ultimatum that was thrust brutally before him. Within almost no time, Hitler's legions were marching, unopposed and once again without a shot being fired in protest, across the border towards Prague.

The Czech state had proved too tempting for Hitler to resist. It offered a perfect base from which to attack more ambitious targets further east and, above all, it had numerous resources to boast of. A huge bounty of Czech weapons fell intact into Nazi arms, enough to equip twenty German divisions, as well as three vast industrial complexes, at Pilsen, Prague, and Brno. Rumours also abounded of Czech technical innovations, 'far in advance of anything of the sort in existence', that could now fall into German hands. In addition, the country possessed considerable quantities of gold and other precious metals, as well as a skilled workforce, that would steel the German war machine. The Nazis could have kept Hácha's state untouched, luring it into an economic union with the Reich from which it would have been unable to escape, but in the end the temptation of making a single, rapacious swoop proved too much, despite the immense political cost of doing so.[15]

Appeasement had failed and Hitler had broken his word: the Sudetenland was not, as he had promised less than six months before, his last territorial demand in Europe. The German Reich was now unarguably expanding beyond any reasonable limits, outside the areas where ethnic Germans lived. In Birmingham on 17 March, Chamberlain conceded that Hitler was no longer trying to restore Germany to its rightful place, which the Versailles Treaty had taken away, but 'to dominate the world by force'. In Berlin, Henderson despatched a furious cable, denouncing 'the cynicism and immorality of the German action [that] defied description' and condemning Hitler who 'has gone straight off the deep end again'. The rest of Europe braced itself for confrontation. 'War', as George Orwell wrote, was 'in the air you breathe.'[16]

Shortly after two o'clock on the afternoon of 31 March, two weeks after the Germans had seized control over Bohemia and Moravia, Neville Chamberlain rose in the House of Commons to make a dramatic statement before his fellow parliamentarians.

The prime minister looked frail and unwell but spoke with some vigour. Although negotiations were ongoing, he announced, he and the members of his cabinet had agreed that, if Poland's 'independence' was threatened and its armed forces resisted any foreign attack, then both Britain and France 'would feel themselves bound at once to lend the Polish Government all support in their power'. The two governments, he continued, 'have given the Polish Government an assurance to this effect'. The House was stunned by the announcement but cheered.[17]

---

15. Technical innovations—this was a 'silent aeroplane engine, invented by a Czech called Dr Cebe', as well as a 'new pharmaceutical invention, suitable for treating wounds', 'Czechoslovakia', 10 June 1939, FO 371/23009 TNA.
16. Henderson—Watt 167. George Orwell *Coming Up for Air* Victor Gollancz (1939) 193.
17. Hansard, HC Deb, 31 Mar 1939, Vol 345 cc2415–20.

Although the French were much more wary and sceptical, and Halifax only consulted with Paris after the announcement had been made, London and Paris were soon anchored to the same commitment that now led them down a road to war six months later.

The logic of this guarantee, however, was and remains very open to question.

Because of the geographical distance, it was unclear why or how either country was in a position to actively assist the Poles, particularly when any German campaign against them was likely to be too swift to offer any such opportunity. The only foreign power that might have been able to defend them was the Soviet Union, whose armed forces could react quickly to a Nazi onslaught: without an alliance with Stalin, as David Lloyd George argued, 'the demented pledge' to Poland represented 'the most reckless commitment that any country has ever entered into'. As Halifax had warned some months before, such a commitment was being made 'on behalf of a State which we were unable effectively to defend'. And just the day before, British and French delegates, undertaking staff conversations between the two countries, had admitted that neither 'could render direct assistance to a victim of German aggression' if war broke out in the east. Chamberlain, however, deliberately suppressed any military advice that was critical of any commitment to Poland.[18]

Nor was it even self-evident why Britain needed to take any such position. The fate of Poland did not directly impact on the security of Great Britain, whereas a German invasion of the Low Countries, or of France, much more clearly did. Not surprisingly, Hitler doubted the sincerity of Chamberlain's commitment to Poland, and often appeared certain that the British would back down in the event of a German invasion, allowing him to fight a 'localized' war against the Poles alone. Daladier also wondered why the British were making a guarantee to a country that had proved duplicitous during the Munich conference, exploiting Czechoslovakia's vulnerability to seize some of its territory instead of standing steadfast against Hitler: just a few weeks before, information had reached Vansittart that the Poles might even unite with Germany against Russia. Other critics, such as the British top brass, noted that a guarantee to Poland, or Romania, could spark a pan-continental war of cataclysmic destruction over a relatively minor, local, insignificant matter, such as the future of Danzig.[19]

The guarantee also had other very corrosive effects. Now that they had won the commitment they wanted, the Polish leaders, such as the foreign minister Colonel Józef Beck, saw no reason to make some of the compromises that might have avoided war in the summer of 1939. They now resisted British and French pressure to defend Romania against German attack and failed to compromise over the fate of Danzig, which was, and had long been, a key German demand. Hitler had long insisted upon the incorporation of this independent 'free city' into his Reich, arguing with justification that most of its 400,000-strong population were culturally and ethnically 'German'. Later in the year, in early August, Chamberlain could not stop Warsaw from overreacting to a minor customs dispute with the Danzig authorities, as the Poles proclaimed that they would consider any direct challenge to their treaty rights to be a provocation of war. But they could scarcely have found any better way to concoct a provocation of Hitler's anger.

News of the Polish guarantee also aroused deep suspicion in the Kremlin, as Stalin wondered why he and his London ambassador, Ivan Maisky, had been kept in the dark until just minutes before Chamberlain made his Commons statement. In Moscow, a furious Litvinov shouted at the British ambassador, Sir William Seeds, as he vented his rage about the futility of Anglo-Soviet talks that had now been 'summarily dropped', while also echoing Hitler's own doubts about the substance behind the British 'commitment'. Stalin now became more amenable to the diplomatic advances of a German leader who now needed to protect his eastern borders if he was to face the British and French armies in the west.[20]

Chamberlain's announcement also immediately created rifts at home. Deeply critical of his position, London newspapers such as *The Times* and the *Evening Standard* sought to undermine his commitment by exposing loopholes in its wording: the British would only fight, the newspapers pointed out, if Polish 'independence' was threatened, not its 'integrity'. A German attack on Danzig, for example, would not

---

19. Hitler's doubts—Volker Ullrich *Hitler*, Vol 2: *Downfall 1939–45* Vintage (2021) Ch 1. Vansittart—'Germany: Internal Affairs', 12 Jan 1939, FO 371/23005 TNA. Top brass—3 Apr 1939, CAB 53/47 TNA.
20. Litvinov—Watt *How War Came* 216.

provoke the British into war because it would not threaten Poland's independence. The articles helped to stir up a public debate and on 3 April prompted the Foreign Office to make a public statement, rebuking attempts to 'minimize' Chamberlain's promise. In Whitehall, Cadogan argued that it was a 'frightful gamble' while Sir Horace Wilson feared that the prime minister had 'gone off the deep end'.[21]

The logic of Chamberlain's guarantee to Poland is discernible only in the context of overwhelming political pressure at home to 'do something' about Hitler. But arguably he could have done this by sticking to the looser, vaguer commitment that he had made to Czechoslovakia almost exactly a year before when, on 24 March 1938, he had decreed that he was 'determined to uphold' its interests but stopped short of making a formal guarantee. Later on, prior to making his commitment, he had instead reiterated his faith in a looser commitment to Poland, one that would constitute a warning to Berlin and keep Hitler guessing. If Chamberlain had also made some belligerent gestures, such as mobilizing the Royal Navy and appointing Churchill to the cabinet, then such a warning might have served its purpose, sending a clear message to a German leader who put much more emphasis upon action than words (see Conclusion). Privately, he and his fellow cabinet members should have recognized that there was nothing they could do to save Poland without Soviet support.[22]

Why, then, had Chamberlain made this deeply questionable 'Guarantee' to Poland? The role of the intelligence services, and of the 'spies', real or supposed, who caused panic, plays an important part in the story.

21. Public statement—Watt *How War Came* 186. Wilson—Robert Crowcroft *The End is Nigh* OUP (2019) 154.
22. Political pressure—Crowcroft 154–5. Looser commitment—Aster 81. Soviet support—on 6 July 1936, the cabinet had 'suggested [that] our policy ought to be framed on the basis that we could not help Eastern Europe. We ought, however, to resist by force any attempt against our own Empire or Flanders.' This, as RAC Parker has noted, is as close as the British government ever came to granting Germany a free hand in eastern Europe. *Chamberlain and Appeasement* Palgrave Macmillan (1993), 69.

20

The 'Spies' Who Caused Panic

In the weeks that preceded Chamberlain's commitment to Poland, a series of intelligence reports had also reached Whitehall that described noticeable changes in German public opinion.

The reports emanated from several British diplomatic posts, within the Reich and beyond, and were all based on the eyewitness accounts of respected sources. In Berne, officials passed on information about the 'misery' and 'violent dissatisfaction at the regime, including the Nazi leaders' that an informant had discovered in Berlin, prompting him to 'fear an internal upheaval'. In Vienna, amidst 'well authenticated reports of dissensions and even strikes', the consul felt that 'the political situation in Austria is now as uncertain and as strained as it has been at any time since *Anschluss*'. Such agitation, he continued, unnerved the Nazi minority, which was 'feverishly trying to stabilize its position by a display of 'ruthlessness' which will break the spirit of the opposition', and had prompted the Gestapo to become 'extremely active' and undertake a 'steadily mounting' number of arrests: one strike, at a laundry factory in Vienna, was broken up by Nazi henchmen who sent ten of the thirty-strong workforce to a prison camp and the remaining twenty into the ranks of the German army. But an Austrian informant 'could not believe that so much dissatisfaction could in the long run be controlled'.[1]

Rumblings of discontent were also noted in Hamburg and Munich, where there was 'a very great change in atmosphere … growing distrust of internal conditions and the policies of the regime'. One consul commented that 'from every side there are reports of increasing

1. Memo from British Legation, Berne to Strang, 9 Jan 1939, FCO 371/23005 TNA. Austrian informant—Memo from British Legation, Vienna to Ogilvie-Forbes, 27 Feb 1939, FCO 371/23005 TNA.

discontent…the Ides of March are awaited with the utmost anxiety and foreboding for the first time', while 'the women particularly can be heard voicing their grievances openly in shops and public places'. Soon there were also rumours of mutiny amongst German soldiers stationed in the Vorarlberg, and of passive resistance amongst factory workers in Bavaria, where some coal mines were only producing a fraction of their maximum output.[2]

In Whitehall, this political intelligence reached the desk of Frank Roberts, a relatively junior but highly regarded and influential official who was tasked with keeping an overview of developments inside Germany. 'These reports from Vienna, Munich and Hamburg', he judged, 'all tell the same story of growing alarm and outspoken discontent with the regime and its leaders.' But crucially Roberts thought he saw what might follow. Hitler, he continued, would see 'the necessity for taking radical counter-measures to cope with this discontent [and] the moral to be drawn from these reports is that an adventurous foreign policy is now a vital necessity for the Nazi regime, but that if we stand firm, the state of public opinion in Germany should act as a powerful break on extreme courses'.[3]

This echoed the view of other diplomats on the ground, such as John Carvell in Munich, who felt that 'there are those who regard another adventure in the sphere of foreign affairs as inevitable as it is the only means whereby the regime can distract attention from the internal situation'. In London, Cadogan also concurred, arguing that 'there can no longer be any doubt that there is great dissatisfaction in the German population…and the risk is that Hitler may be impelled to a wild adventure'. In Paris, Bureau officers also wondered if the unrest was a sign of a resource shortage that would spur the regime to further territorial conquest, perhaps encouraged by disgruntled industrialists. And in Berlin, Mason-Mac argued that Hitler would resort to 'some foreign excursion' to distract his people from domestic troubles and was preparing at 'full throttle' for imminent mobilization.[4]

2. Ides of March—memo from British Legation, Munich, 6 Jan 1939, and from British Legation, Hamburg to Ogilvie-Forbes, 15 Jan 1939, FCO 371/23005 TNA. Mutiny—Memos from British Legation, Berne to Strang, 26, 27 Jan 1939, FCO 371/23005 TNA.
3. 'Situation in Germany', 20 Jan 1939, FCO 371/23005 TNA.
4. Carvell—Memo from British Legation, Munich, 6 Jan 1939, FCO 371/23005 TNA. Cadogan—'Situation in Germany', 20 Jan 1939, FCO 371/23005 TNA. Paris—Young 'French Military Intelligence' 291. Mason-Mac—Memo of 2 Jan 1939, FO 371/22960 TNA.

Such reports could only serve to hype the extreme state of tension and nervousness that pervaded London and other foreign capitals in early 1939. Something had to be done urgently to stop war. But where would Hitler strike? Spies, diplomats, and politicians continued to search for clues.

In the story of how and why Chamberlain made his dubious commitment to Poland, which was followed soon after by an Anglo-French commitment to Romania, the intelligence services play an important part. But this was a role enacted not just by the SIS or the Deuxième Bureau. It was instead also played by an *ersatz* ('substitute') spy service that provided, inadvertently or not, false information about German intentions. Its story thereby provides another reminder of the dangers posed by private intelligence services, and how easily such parallel networks can arise, and be given excessive credence, when any state is confronted by an opaque regime that yields such meagre clues about its plans and capabilities.

The commitment to Poland was made, as Halifax later wrote, 'at very short notice to meet an immediately critical situation' in which 'without our pledge the whole position in East Europe might have been irretrievably lost'. And instrumental in creating this impression—of 'an immediately critical situation'—was a 26-year-old British journalist called Ian Colvin, who arrived in London two days before the prime minister made his Commons statement.[5]

Colvin had been based in Berlin in 1936 as a correspondent for Reuters before joining a newspaper, the British-owned *News Chronicle*. His abilities were not in question. A fellow journalist regarded him as a 'brilliantly intelligent and clever man' who had been trained by his father—also a journalist and a 'past master'—in the art of cultivating friendships and contacts amongst highly placed people'. He also had a taste for adventure—a diplomat noted his propensity for 'indulging in activities most dangerous to himself and possibly to the embassy too—and he doubtlessly went looking for danger even if there was none to be found.[6]

But Colvin was not without his faults. Like any opinionated individual, he heard what he wanted to hear and was therefore vulnerable

5. Halifax to Pares, 27 July 1939, FO 800/309 TNA.
6. Fellow journalist—'Notes on Interview with Mr Harrison of the BBC', 16 Jan 1943, HS 9/337/9 TNA.

to falling victim to false rumours that suited his agenda. And there was no doubt where those loyalties lay, for by 1938 the *News Chronicle* had become a strong and very vocal critic of Chamberlain's policy of appeasement. Like his editors, he pushed for a much more hawkish line against a country that he felt sure posed a serious threat to the outside world. In his private correspondence, he argued that 'the word peace is little used' in Germany, where 'its frequent utterance is interpreted as a sign of weakness in the democracies and unwillingness to fight'. This meant that 'if the Germans are to be dissuaded, they must be faced with a very firm warning at the right time, a warning made before the world... only preparations of a definitely military nature by Great Britain can convince Germany that the politeness of the British is not a sign of weakness'. Sharing such convictions, Colvin supplied Winston Churchill with information about what was happening inside the Reich. And a few weeks after Chamberlain made his guarantee to Poland, a senior British diplomat complained about his 'tendencious [*sic*] ... and objectionable reports' that presented 'a serious handicap to Anglo-German press relations'.[7]

A few years later, during the Second World War, Colvin's faults were brought to the attention of British Intelligence when he proposed travelling to Sweden to make indirect contact with highly placed opponents of Hitler. 'It seems fairly clear why the various secret departments have declined the services of Colvin,' as one MI5 report noted. 'It is apparently a habit of his to intrigue with higher authorities behind the backs of his own chiefs... this is most undesirable.' He was 'an intriguer and not loyal to anyone but himself' 'who was constantly plotting behind the back' of a fellow journalist 'to get his job'. And like many brilliant men, Colvin was viewed as 'an obstreperous gentleman' who was apt to go 'too far with his ideas'.[8]

7. *News Chronicle*—for example, on 17 Mar the paper denounced Hitler's 'naked aggression' and criticized the prime minister's weak response in the Commons, which it said had enraged British public opinion. The paper called for a 'Peace Front' in order to confront Hitler's next act of aggression with the prospect of immediate war. Private correspondence—Note to Lloyd 7 Mar 1939, Lloyd Papers, GLLD 19/19 CCCA. Churchill—Foley on Colvin, 11 Jan 1943, HS 9/337/9 TNA. Senior British diplomat— Ogilvie-Forbes to London, 3 Apr 1939, FO 371/22989 TNA.

8. MI5 briefing, 16 Jan 1943, HS 9/337/9 TNA. Intriguer—MI5 briefing on Colvin, 12 Dec 1942. 'Obstreperous', 8 July 1943, HS 9/337/9 TNA; 'Notes on Interview with Mr Harrison of the BBC', 16 Jan 1943, HS 9/337/9 TNA.

These insights help to explain why, in his private correspondence, his 'predictions' were invariably anti-German and dramatic yet frequently wide of the mark. On 9 February, for example, he claimed that the Nazis had plans to undertake 'an African expedition via the Italian colonies' and make diversionary attacks in Egypt as well as advance into Angola: but this rumour about Africa was groundless, for which he deserved a black mark.[9]

Equally, Colvin saw an invisible German hand in untouched places. He argued, for example, that a number of terrorist bombs in Great Britain in early 1939 were subsidized by secret German funds. Such attacks would continue, he claimed, because they were 'part of Hitler's policy of shaking British self-confidence and making internal trouble'. In fact, the Nazis had no known involvement at all in a series of very insignificant bombings in London at this time. Colvin also made some very dubious claims about Colonel Jósef Beck, who he claimed 'was firmly in the Germans' pocket'. Dismissed by Sir Howard Kennard as 'ridiculous', Colvin's claim is difficult to reconcile with the offer of an Anglo-Polish alliance made to Halifax by Beck's ambassador in London, Count Raczynski, on 24 March 1939. But it did lend credence to fears that Poland could cut a deal with Nazi Germany unless Chamberlain did so first.[10]

Almost as soon as he arrived in London from Berlin, Colvin made his way to the Foreign Office and claimed, on arrival, to be in possession of hugely valuable information that had all the makings of a journalistic scoop but which he instead wanted to keep private. Soon he was taken directly to see Sir Alexander Cadogan, who had overall responsibility for secret service operations abroad.

Cadogan had a sceptical eye and was not susceptible to panic. He was widely considered as 'not only intelligent, efficient, imperturbable, loyal, economical in language and thoroughly conventional, [but] also "sound" in judgment, and reserved but not without charm'. He now listened intently as the young reporter, whom he judged to be 'a nice young man—rather precious', spilled out his story.[11]

9. Note to Lloyd 9 Feb 1939, Lloyd Papers, GLLD 19/19 CCCA.

10. Terrorist bombs—Note to Lloyd, 28 Feb 1939, Lloyd Papers, GLLD 19/19 CCCA. Beck—Note to Lloyd, 23 Mar 1939, Lloyd Papers, GLLD 19/19 CCCA. Count Raczynski—Colvin *Chief of Intelligence* Victor Gollancz (1951) 78.

11. Widely considered—'Sir Alexander Cadogan', *Oxford Dictionary of National Biography* OUP (2004), 413. Cadogan *Diaries* 164.

According to a 'reliable source', the visitor explained, the Germans were on the verge of undertaking a major attack against Poland, occupying almost the entire country and leaving only a narrow buffer zone between Polish and Soviet territory. A food supplier had also been suddenly ordered to provide just the same quantities of rations to the Germany army that it had supplied the previous September, when an attack on Czechoslovakia was imminent. The contractor was told to deliver them to 'forward dumps in an area of Pomerania that formed a rough wedge pointing towards the railway junction of Bromberg in the Polish corridor'. This suggested an 'attack on the Polish Republic in twelve hours, three days, a week or a fortnight'. More action would soon follow, he continued, because Hitler planned on seizing Lithuania and striking up a pact with Stalin that would leave him free to seize whole swathes of the British Empire.[12]

Cadogan was startled by what he heard but sceptical, writing in his diary that 'I was not entirely convinced. I am getting used to these stories'. However, he immediately took Colvin to meet Halifax.[13]

The lofty foreign secretary, who at nearly 6´ 5´´ towered over his visitors, was not one to easily fall for tall stories. But nor did he look down on his visitor with condescension, listening to the 'hair-raising details' of Colvin's story and wasting no time in taking him, with Cadogan at their side, to meet the prime minister, who was at this time getting himself ready to meet the king and queen for dinner at No 10. In the surreal circumstances of the moment, anything seemed possible: just days before, on 15 March, Frank Roberts had reiterated his warning that in Germany, an 'increasing failure in home affairs [points] to an external adventure as the most likely expedient to still growing criticism of the regime'.[14]

Chamberlain immediately harboured his doubts about Colvin's claims, many of which he found 'so fantastic as to doubt [their] reliability'. But they helped to swing the balance, pushing the prime minister into action to defend a country that seemed to be on the verge of being invaded. The prime minister, under huge domestic

12. In a letter to Lloyd on 23 Mar, Colvin had said that 'Hitler will shortly annex Lithuania...then the sequence will go Estonia, Latvia, Finland'. Lloyd Papers, GLLD 19/19 CCCA.
13. Cadogan *ODNB* 164–5.
14. 'Dresden Political report', 10 Mar 1939, FCO 371/23005 TNA. Roberts's remark was written on 15 Mar.

pressure to be seen to 'stand up to Hitler', now 'agreed to (the) idea of an immediate declaration of support of Poland, to counter a quick putsch by Hitler'.[15]

Halifax arranged for a parliamentary question to be tabled the following day, asking about British preparations for an imminent attack on Poland, while Chamberlain personally wrote an urgent telegram, calling for united action to defend Poland, that was immediately cabled to Paris. Another telegram offered Warsaw support, falling short of the alliance that the Poles wanted but nonetheless making an offer that a stunned Beck immediately accepted. Had Colvin not appeared on that Wednesday evening, then it is quite possible that the prime minister might have pulled back from making a commitment while it was still possible to do so without serious loss of face and honour.[16]

But the prime minister had in fact been right to harbour serious doubts about the journalist's 'intelligence information'. With hindsight, of course, his information about the Nazi designs on Poland and Lithuania were entirely accurate. But the dates and timetable were quite wrong.

Colvin's source appears to have had first-hand knowledge of a directive that Hitler gave his commander-in-chief, General von Brauchitsch, on 25 March for *Operation Case White*, the German invasion of Poland. But crucially, the directive of 25 March specified no date for any proposed attack: Hitler and his generals never planned to invade Poland until much later, and they did not even pencil in a proposed date for the attack, 1 September, until several days after Colvin met Chamberlain.

Colvin's own intentions may have been sincere enough but his sources were feeding him with false and misleading information. His chief source, or perhaps Colvin himself, had deliberately concocted the details, inventing a timetable that did not exist in order to create a strong sense of alarm in London and Paris, thereby panicking both into making a commitment to defend Poland. The only motive for

---

15. Fantastic—Watt *How War Came* 184. Immediate declaration—Cadogan 164–5. On the domestic political pressure to stand up to Hitler, see Crowcroft 154–5.

16. Telegram—Watt *How War Came* 185. Colvin's appearance—Cadogan's diary reveals that moves towards making a guarantee were already under way and Colvin's arrival 'precipitated' the announcement. However, without Colvin's influence, the prime minister could have delayed or even cancelled it. Cadogan *Diaries* 29 Mar 1939, 164–5.

wanting to create such a commitment was to deter Hitler from attacking Poland and to stop Europe descending into war: Britain and France needed to threaten war, ran the calculation, in order to avoid it.

This strongly suggests that Colvin's sources lay in the growing ranks of Hitler's opponents within the general staff, particularly the Prussian aristocracy, that had come to the attention of the British and French the previous summer. Having failed to lure Chamberlain into making a public commitment to Czechoslovakia, they were now trying the same approach to secure a guarantee to Poland. And as Hitler became more aggressive and confident, so too were the numbers of these disaffected Germans growing. By this time, they included Ernst von Weizsacker, a state secretary at the Foreign Ministry in Berlin, and two generals, Walter von Reichenau and Gunther von Kluge, as well as Hjalmar Schacht. At the German embassy in London, Wolfgang zu Putlitz passed confidential information to Vansittart, using his valet as an intermediary. But Colvin's main source was probably Ewald von Kleist-Schmenzin, whom the British Embassy considered to be 'usually well-informed' and 'in a position to obtain accurate information'. However, some of his earlier reports were inaccurate, such as a report the previous November that the German army was poised to strike at Prague.[17]

Colvin may well have picked up on these stories as early as the end of December, when British diplomats in Warsaw noted 'a lot of wild talk... about war on Poland next spring'. These more measured voices judged that 'it is impossible to form any decisive conclusions as to what may happen this spring, and how far Germany may go in putting a pistol to Beck's head'. But Colvin, because of his personal convictions, more readily confused 'wild talk' with intelligence.[18]

Whatever or whoever his exact sources, Colvin had made several such warnings prior to that March afternoon, when his false prophecies made such a tumultuous impact within the corridors of decision-making in London. His first known warning about a German attack on Poland came on 27 January, when he had noticed an increase in Nazi activities and argued that an invasion was imminent. He reiterated these 'warnings' throughout February and March, stating that Hitler would also attack the Baltic states. 'German military preparations',

17. Ogilvie-Forbes to Halifax, 29 Nov 1938, DBFP III series, Vol 3, 1938, No 386.
18. Warsaw—Sir H Kennard to Sergent, 27 Dec 1938, FO 371/23015 TNA.

he had written, 'indicate an attack on Poland in March.' But while Colvin sent these reports to a contact, they do not appear either to have been forwarded to Whitehall or else to have made any impact if they were.[19]

Why, then, did Colvin's claims, which were unsubstantiated and based on unknown sources, carry such undue weight on that March afternoon? And why was such a young and unknown British journalist given such immediate and unchallenged access to the highest levels?

Colvin benefited from his curious, hybrid status. On the one hand, there is clear evidence that he was acting as an intelligence agent for a private spy network that was linked to, but not part of, the British state. But on the other hand, because this was a parallel agency rather than an 'official' governmental organization, its informers and sources of information were not subjected to the same checks and were therefore much more likely to be unreliable. This allowed Colvin to resemble and then to be treated as something—as a reliable source of high-level information—that he simply wasn't. And when, on 23 March, he had written to his private spymaster and asked him to 'arrange for me to meet some of your friends' on his arrival in London a week later, his wishes were granted.

The spy master who ran this private intelligence service was a formidable British aristocrat and diplomat by the name of Lord George Lloyd. Described by DC Watt as 'one of those uncontrollable *lusi naturae* ('curiosities') the British elite throws up from time to time', Lloyd had had a distinguished and varied career by the time Hitler came to power, having served as a member of parliament before the Great War and subsequently in the Middle East, alongside TE Lawrence 'of Arabia', and in British India. After a spell as British high commissioner in Egypt in the late 1920s, he returned to Britain and began to watch developments in Germany with a growing sense of alarm.[20]

With considerable personal wealth and a wide array of contacts across the globe, Lloyd was in a position to establish and run his own private intelligence network, comparable to the network of Robert

---

19. March attack—for example, on 28 Feb he wrote to Lloyd that 'the dispositions of food that have been made lead me to expect an aggressive military move against Poland by the end of March or rather, at the end of March', Lloyd Papers GLLD 19/19 CCCA.

20. *Lusi naturae*—Watt *How War Came* 90. On Lloyd in general see L Atherton, 'Lord Lloyd at the British Council and the Balkan Front, 1937–1940', *International History Review*, Vol 16 No 1 (Feb 1994) 25–48.

Vansittart. But his real asset was his chairmanship of a newly created government body, the British Council, which had been set up in 1934 'to create in a country overseas a basis of friendly knowledge and understanding of the people of this country'. The British Council was from the start closely linked to prominent critics of appeasement, including Lloyd himself who, as its head, had enormous freedom 'to travel where he wished, see whom he wished and virtually do as he pleased in the service of his country'. In particular, he worked hard to improve relations and create closer links between Britain and Romania, orchestrating King Carol's visit to London in November 1938, and he also travelled to Rome in early 1939 in a bid to gauge Italian public opinion during and after a visit by Neville Chamberlain.[21]

Although he was one of Lloyd's key agents inside Nazi Germany, Colvin was untrained in intelligence matters and was easily manipulated by the growing resistance to Hitler. In addition, his 'intelligence reports' about imminent German designs on Poland were not passed from desk to desk, along and up an established hierarchy whose very purpose is to check and verify such claims, in the way that the SIS or any other governmental intelligence service deals with such unverified claims as those he bore on that March day. Instead, he was able to immediately access the key decision-makers, such as Cadogan, Halifax, and then Chamberlain, who then rushed, or even panicked, into making an almost immediate decision to support Poland.

In the exceptionally tense circumstances of the moment, when every European capital was seething with rumours, when stories of Hitler's 'towering rage' grew and when, on 23 March, more anti-aircraft guns and searchlights appeared in and around central London, such a reaction is of course fully understandable. Reports had been filtering in, from reliable sources, of German preparations for war: in mid-February, for example, 'the director of a very well-known international manufacturing company, who has just returned from visiting his company's factories in Germany', gave some very alarming indications of these preparations. Halifax felt compelled to write that everyone in Whitehall was 'moving in a mental atmosphere much like the atmosphere with which a child might be surrounded in which all things were both possible and impossible, and where there were no rational guiding rules'. But because so many of those rumours were

21. Enormous freedom—Watt *How War Came* 182.

contradictory, and included, for example, numerous scare stories about a German attack in the West, these leading figures merit criticism for making such a rushed commitment to Poland.[22]

However, Colvin's ability to immediately win such an audience, and to win it over, did not just depend on his 'information'. He also made his claims about German mobilization at a particularly volatile moment. In particular, they coincided with at least two other reports, from quite different sources, that echoed the same fallacious information and thereby gave him more credibility than he deserved.

One of these sources was the ubiquitous British military attaché in Berlin, Colonel Mason-Macfarlane, who had also visited the German–Polish border at around the same time. Earlier in the month, on 3 March, Mason-Mac had informed London that the German army was starting to stockpile food in east Pomerania and that this would be completed by the end of the month. Then, on 29 March, he had filed a further report that seemed to confirm Colvin's claims, referring to a number of arms caches that were being set up in east Pomerania, and to the claims of 'well-informed army and SS sources' who seemed to be referring to an attack on Poland. This crucial report reached Whitehall just hours before Ian Colvin arrived in London.[23]

But even if Mason-Macfarlane's claims are taken on trust, they proved nothing. In the spring of 1939, the German army had arms dumps in numerous places as it prepared for every eventuality, including self-defence against a surprise enemy attack, in such a tense and uncertain time. And his unspecified 'well-informed sources' were likely to have been referring only to exercises of the sort that every army regularly undertakes.

Instead, the timing and content of the attaché's report, which reached London at such a pivotal moment and coincided perfectly with Colvin's arrival, strongly suggest that he had a private agenda. So too does Mason-Macfarlane's professional record. Six months before, he had made some negative comments about the Czech armed forces that supported the cause of appeasement. But he was subsequently galvanized into action after Hitler's occupation of Bohemia and

22. Mid-Feb—'Industrial Mobilization Preparations', 13 Feb 1939, FO 371/22301 TNA. Halifax—D Gillard *Appeasement in Crisis: From Munich to Prague* Palgrave Macmillan (2007) 84.

23. 3 Mar—Minute by Col Mason-MacFarlane, FO 371 22958, C2882/13/18 TNA. 29 Mar 1938, FO 371/22958 TNA; Wark 'Three Military Attachés'; Butler 94–5.

Moravia, fighting his case for an Anglo-French alliance with Poland and other eastern states, and arguing in favour of a preventive war before the Germans had any opportunity to incorporate and exploit the huge arms booty and natural resources they had seized in Czechoslovakia. He claimed, without detailed knowledge of the complexity of the topic, that the Reich was vulnerable to an economic blockade, a suggestion that experts in London lambasted. Germany's position was 'extremely unsound', he concluded, and 'there is every reason why we should do our best to produce a situation leading...to war' rather than 'wait until autumn [when] Germany will have a breathing-space'. He also alleged that he entertained his own plan to assassinate Hitler, taking a long-range shot from a window at the British embassy in Berlin: if he ever did more than daydream about such an eventuality, he was clearly acting beyond his remit by even harbouring such an idea. Here was a perfect example of the curious hybrid status of the military attaché, who was a spy and a diplomat without being either (see Chapter 5).[24]

Such maverick behaviour did not go unnoticed in London, where Cadogan referred to his telegram of 29 March as a 'rather hysterical outpouring'. Equally, such a maverick figure, who was clearly so capable of acting beyond his station, would have seen little or nothing wrong with deliberately manipulating governmental opinion to suit his own ends. It is possible that he armed Colvin with vague but exaggerated claims and encouraged him to fly to London to pitch his story directly to the senior decision-makers: as Colvin made his journey, Mason-Mac then filed his own despatches in a bid to add weight to a non-existent story. The two men had previously had close contact in March 1938, when Colvin had informed Mason-Mac of his secret meetings with Ewald von Kleist-Schmenzin, noting that the attaché was almost the only person he could confide in about this contact. The attaché was prematurely recalled to London a month later—a clear sign that his actions had caused alarm in Whitehall—but by this time it was too late for opponents of the Polish Guarantee.[25]

If Mason-Mac's 'intelligence reports' about German plans reinforced the atmosphere of panic in which the guarantee to Poland was born,

24. Germany's position—Butler 94–5.
25. Hysterical outpouring—Minute by Sir A Cadogan, 31 Mar 1939, FO 371/22958 TNA. Secret meetings—information to the author from Clare Colvin, trustee of the Ian Colvin archive, 4 Feb 2021.

then another such influence was the American ambassador in Warsaw, Anthony J Drexel Biddle Jr. Just ten days before, on 20 March, Biddle had sent a report to the American ambassador in London, Joseph P Kennedy, claiming that Ribbentrop had not only won Hitler's ear but was 'now pressing for immediate action against Poland, pointing out that Great Britain and France will fail to support Poland and that this failure would serve to alienate American opinion from France and Great Britain'. His source was allegedly a 'German journalist who has a connection with an American press agency in Berlin and on previous occasions been reliable'. A senior American diplomat, Herschel Johnson, then showed this telegram to Sir Orme Sargent. However, in Berlin, Sir Ogilvie Forbes dampened speculation, writing on 31 March that he 'had no confirmation that Ribbentrop is pressing for immediate action against Poland'.[26]

But the deep sense of alarm in London, which culminated in panic at the end of the month, had not been set in motion by the alarming reports forwarded by Biddle and Mason-Macfarlane. Nor was the groundwork laid merely by information about protests and dissatisfaction inside the Reich. It was instead partly perpetrated by another individual who also claimed to have 'intelligence information' about German plans but who in fact peddled uncorroborated claims, rumours, and, in all likelihood, deliberate lies. At this desperate hour, one so easily became confused with the other.

Virgil Tilea was a well-dressed and affable 43-year-old Romanian diplomat who had arrived in London the previous year as a representative of King Carol. He was a good choice for the role, speaking excellent English and being highly familiar with his host country, having once studied at London University. But for all his attributes, he was inclined to be excitable and lacked the level-headedness required for any senior diplomatic role, particularly at a time as tense as the spring of 1939. And during the afternoon of 17 March, he had called firstly on Joseph P Kennedy and then on Halifax in a state of real trepidation. He had just received the deeply alarming news, blurted out the Romanian, that his homeland was on the verge of being attacked by Nazi Germany, which badly needed Romania's vast deposits of oil and

26. Herschel Johnson—Memo from Sir Orme Sargent, 29 Mar 1939; Memo from Kennard, 31 Mar 1939, FO 371/23015 TNA. Telegram from Sir George Ogilvie-Forbes, 31 Mar 1939, FO 371/23015 TNA.

which had just presented a series of demands as an ultimatum. Within hours, Tilea was reiterating his story to Cadogan and numerous other diplomats, from several other countries, across London. The next day, the story was splashed all over the headlines.

Tilea later claimed that his actions were the result of a single telephone call he received early that morning from someone in Paris. But if this rings true, who called?

Some accounts claim that this call was made from Bucharest, where a government official was providing intelligence information about German plans. Others have wondered if an enigmatic businessman, Max Ausnit, was implicated, as he tried to tie London and Bucharest together to suit his own commercial ends. Whatever the truth, the 'intelligence information' was ungrounded and nothing more than empty rumour. The Germans were not about to attack Romania and had no plans to do so. In Paris, the Romanian representative admitted that his 'young colleague' in London was involved with matters that were 'some weeks old', although it would have been more accurate to say that 'intelligence' was being manipulated for political ends: both men had been trying for some weeks to persuade the two governments that Berlin was trying to 'enfeudalize' Romania and that they should openly support Bucharest to stop this from happening.[27]

Tilea's approach, likely to have been based on a ruse, now had some effect as London and Paris worked with the Poles and Soviets to float proposals to 'offer joint resistance' if the security of any European country, including Romania, was threatened. More generally, Tilea had considerably heightened tension in London, tension that easily spiralled into panic.

In early April, for example, a further series of 'intelligence reports', almost certainly leaked by the Abwehr, led to another war scare, as the Admiralty ordered its ships onto a war footing. Once again, the 'intelligence' had turned out to be based on hollow rumour. 'The recent scares', as Cadogan wrote later, 'have not originated principally with the SIS agents in Germany but have come to us from other sources.' This was making him, and others, highly sceptical about the value of any of the information that was reaching London from these 'other sources', even though they sometimes had value: in February, for example, Professor Conwell-Evans had provided Vansittart with extremely accurate information about Hitler's ambitions to annex Czechoslovakia, although Cadogan was very sceptical about the professor's value as an intelligence source.[28]

By this time, the French capital was also racked with an extreme nervousness, allowing all sorts of rumours and false reports to thrive. In early April, a string of false intelligence reports reached Daladier that pressurized him into making a commitment to Romania on the same grounds as the British commitment to Poland: such a promise to Bucharest, it was argued, would deter Hitler and prevent war. On 3 and then 7 April, he was informed that the Germans were about to make an imminent attack on France, using mechanized divisions based in Prague while the Italians were planning a simultaneous assault on Gibraltar. There were other reports of Nazi attacks on London, Poland, Danzig, Egypt, and Yugoslavia, as well as a Turkish invasion of Syria and a Spanish assault, across the Pyrenees, into France. The Nazis, it seemed, would soon be everywhere.

'The involvement of French intelligence' in these reports, as DC Watt has asserted, 'when coupled with the overestimation of German strength, does cast considerable doubt on the balance and competence of French sources, if not on their loyalty'. It was in such a state that, on 11 April, the French cabinet made its own guarantee to Romania, and two days later Chamberlain announced that the British government was doing the same. The prime minister had reluctantly made the same commitment in order to preserve Anglo-French unity.[29]

---

28. Further series—Watt *How War Came* 390. Cadogan to Henderson, 28 Feb 1938, FO 800/270 TNA. Sceptical—21, 24 Feb 1939, FO 371/23006 TNA.

29. Watt *How War Came* 212.

21

Signals from the Reich

Growing cross-Channel collaboration was not whole-hearted, for in other parts of the world there remained a considerable amount of competition, rivalry, and mistrust between the two powers. This was particularly true in the Middle East, where the French feared the encroachment of the 'Anglo-Saxons' on their territories in the Levant. Local Deuxième Bureau officers closely monitored the movements of British diplomats in places such as Turkey's Hatay province, alleging in February 1939 that London's representative there was sending 'briefings against the interests of France' to Turkish ministers. Suspicions of 'Perfidious Albion' remained strong in Paris, where many French officials were very wary of British betrayal. Daladier told William C Bullitt, the American ambassador in Paris, that 'he fully expected to be betrayed by the British', particularly when he considered the prime minister to be 'a desiccated [*sic*] stick, the king a moron; and the Queen an excessively ambitious woman'. He felt, continued Bullitt, 'that England had become so feeble and senile that the British would give away every possession of their friends than stand up to Germany and Italy'.[1]

The two countries each had an arm around the other but were still not quite in a full embrace. Chamberlain continued to refuse making a formal alliance with France, telling Daladier that there were clear limits to what his country could do on the continent, despite Churchill's calls for a 'grand alliance' between the two neighbours to contain Hitler. But both countries knew that they needed each other. 'We could only defeat Germany in a war', as a French War Ministry document ran, 'if we were assured, in every conceivable way, of total British support.' Equally, the British government showed a much greater will-

1. Hatay—'Activité Britannique', 14 Feb 1939, 7NN 2534 SHD; Bullitt 309–10.

ingness than before to avoid any disagreement with Paris, giving a nod of approval not just to its insistence on a guarantee to Romania but also to French demands for the introduction of conscription in Britain, which began on 27 April.[2]

In particular, after Hitler's annexation of Bohemia and Moravia, the British and French intelligence agencies worked closely together, with *une intensité accrue*, to get a clearer idea of where Hitler might strike next. They did this along with their Polish and exiled Czech counterparts, while on the outer fringes of this network were the Dutch, Yugoslav, and Romanian spy services, with which the SIS and Deuxième Bureau had a 'fruitful collaboration'.

Such collaboration was vital not just to gain insight into Hitler's mindset but also to fill gaps in their knowledge about German capabilities: in early 1939, a Bureau report again highlighted 'considerable gaps in our knowledge…about German war materials' which had to be filled, including over matters such as the armed forces' organization, strategic doctrines, and locations. During the war scare of September 1938 in particular, there had been *grosses difficultés* in tracking the movements of armed units as they moved through the Reich, and although some 'excellent pieces of information' had reached them over the preceding year, these had been 'too few' in number. The Bureau also needed to make *un gros effort* to find out more, in particular, about German units deployed close to the border with France, and headhunt informants within their ranks.[3]

The lack of reliable intelligence partly reflected the fact that, in addition to the extremely tight layers of security that protected the secrets of the Reich, any effort to gather information on Hitler's plans continued to face several other major obstacles. For example, even when he had formulated the details of his next move, which he often did at the last minute, the *Führer* shared them only with a select few. When on 23 May, for example, he made a key announcement, stating that 'there is no question of sparing Poland and we are left with the decision to attack it at the first opportunity', he did so only before a handful of hand-picked individuals, all of whom were sworn to total secrecy.[4]

2. Document—Young *In Command of France* 22.
3. 'Liaison avec les SR Étrangers', 7NN 2693 SHD.
4. Those individuals were Göring, Raeder, Brautisch, Halder, Kenel, Milch, Bodenschatz, Schniewind, and several staff officers.

But in the months that preceded the outbreak of war, other obstacles made the task of intelligence-gathering harder still. In particular, it had become entangled not only with the activities of Ostler and other domestic opponents of Hitler, who were still deliberately feeding foreign governments with false leads, but also with the Reich's internal political rivalry, as its leaders vied and jockeyed for influence over Hitler. In particular, there was an intense and highly acrimonious rivalry between Ribbentrop, who had assured Hitler that Britain and France would not honour their commitment to Poland in the event of a German invasion, and Göring, who wanted to avert the wider war that he felt sure such an invasion would trigger. Although the *Reichsmarschall's* machinations remain unclear, he doubtlessly encouraged and perhaps organized a series of misleading leaks of information as well as a number of private peace initiatives by a wide variety of intermediaries. His motives doubtlessly changed over time, but one such ambition was to mobilize British and French support for Poland in a bid to prove Ribbentrop wrong and discredit him in the eyes of Hitler.[5]

Wherever and whenever the *Führer* struck, Britain and France would have to pull together, and at the end of March 1939 top brass from the two countries met in London to start staff conversations that would allow both armies to fight an effective campaign together against Germany: they were held in secret, as the French delegation arrived at Victoria Station not just untrumpeted but, wearing civilian clothes, unnoticed. But this was not the only source of high-level collaboration: one other vital source of information was German signals traffic, which the British, French, and Polish experts were scrambling to intercept and decipher.

The SIS had got a first-hand idea of French capabilities in the middle of April, when a delegation made a further visit to Rivet's headquarters in Paris to exchange information and discuss closer collaboration. Rivet and his men showed their guests 'remarkable hospitality', as one of the SIS officers commented. 'Nothing was too much trouble and their insistence on paying for everything embarrassed us to

---

5. Rivalry—'Ribbentrop, Hitler, and Himmler are the three leaders desiring war', Memo of 22 May 1939, FO 371/23006 TNA. 'Particularly fierce are the relations between Göring on the one side, and Himmler–Ribbentrop on the other', 9 Jan 1939, FO 371/23005 TNA.

the extreme.' After talks in Paris, the French spies took their visitors on a tour of some of their listening posts, close to the German border.[6]

The Deuxième Bureau was at this time in the process of setting up a new listening post, purely to intercept short-wave transmissions, at Chartres. This was an impressive new investment but the British agents were disappointed by the meagre resources that the French spies currently had at their disposal. 'The station at Metz has been thoroughly starved,' they recorded on their return home. 'The personnel and equipment available are but a fraction of that required to take full advantage of the magnificent geographical situation of what should be the most important French Y [signals intelligence] station.' Much of the equipment, they continued, 'was out-of-date', the main exception being an American-made receiver, and the main d/f (direction finding) set was of 'fairly ancient design'. In general, this was largely because the 'military Y work is not taken seriously by the French higher authorities but Bertrand and his staff are very keen'.[7]

Resources aside, the British also noticed the technical shortcomings of the listening posts at Metz and elsewhere that they were taken to see. 'The system of control is far from efficient, in so far that there is no direct line of communication between any of the stations,' ran their subsequent report. 'All four stations are having to rely on the public telephone lines for inter-communication. It was understood that direct lines could not be allowed in peace on the grounds of expense, although special lines were reserved in time of war.' The SIS men also noted that there was 'much duplication and consequent loss of other available material through lack of efficient means of inter-communication and cooperation'. In general, 'the standard of operating did not appear to be very high and some of the soldier operators appeared very young and inexperienced', while messages were not transcribed in a reliable and effective way, and some were doubtlessly missed altogether.[8]

Despite the shortcomings of French signals intelligence, the SIS agreed to cooperate more closely with Rivet's men and to exchange more information. Using a simple code, they would now start to regularly pass messages on the telephone. Under this arrangement, Rivet

6. 'Report on Visit to Paris', 17–19 Apr 1939, HW 62/21 TNA.
7. 'Report on Visit to Paris', 17–19 Apr 1939, HW 62/21 TNA.
8. 'Report on Visit to Paris', 17–19 Apr 1939, HW 62/21 TNA.

promised to send London a daily report on the signals intelligence that his stations had picked up over the preceding twenty-four hours, and to have this report ready by a certain time on each afternoon. The information, which would be transmitted by telephone using a special code, started to flow on 15 May.

But this collaboration was vastly outsized by the dramatic progress that British, French, and Polish codebreakers were now making as they continued to work together to crack the German 'Enigma' machine.

Unknown to the British and French, the German section of the Biuro Szyfrów, the specialist codebreaking team in the Polish Second Department, had cracked the Enigma code years before, in or around 1933. This astonishing feat was achieved partly by a cryptanalyst and businessman called Antoni Palluth, who had set up and run a Warsaw-based communications company. Palluth and a few hand-picked members of his staff had managed to build replicas of the Enigma machine, using a specially designed, and carefully hidden, workshop on the factory premises to do so. Basing their design on the model that the customs staff had inadvertently come across in 1929, they were able to finish their work in just six months. What was missing at this early stage was a close knowledge of how the Germans had wired the machine's wheels and discs, connecting the machine's plugboard and wheels in order to scramble a message into code. But in the course of 1933 an outstanding mathematician, Marian Rejewski, made breakthroughs that then enabled the Biuro Szyfrów to decipher around three-quarters of German traffic. This breakthrough was made possible partly by the supremely valuable information that Schmidt had obtained for the French.

The Poles had made this breakthrough by exploiting a serious, almost elementary error that the Germans made: the Nazis decided that the machine's 'message setting'—the position of the wheels when the first letter of a message was enciphered—should be enciphered twice in succession before being sent at the beginning of each message. But this, as Hugh Montefiore has written, was a 'terrible mistake' since a basic rule of coding is not to repeat anything unless it is absolutely necessary: it easily betrays a pattern that an eavesdropper can immediately detect. Here was the 'Achilles' heel' of the Enigma machine, one that the Poles continually exploited throughout the 1930s.[9]

9. Montefiore 44–5.

Warsaw had deliberately kept this technical breakthrough a closely guarded secret because word might inadvertently get back to the Nazis, who might well have infiltrated other foreign intelligence services. Equally, such an accomplishment was a supremely valuable bargaining-chip, one that could not be used lightly, to win favours from foreign powers. But that moment was fast approaching: after Hitler's seizure of the Sudetenland and then Prague, rumours of a Nazi attack on Poland increased, particularly when, on 28 April 1939, Berlin rescinded its non-aggression pact with Warsaw.

There was also another reason why the Poles were now willing to consider working with the British and the French on the German codes. From 1936, the Germans introduced much stronger security procedures, making a number of technical changes to Enigma that even the best cryptanalysts struggled to keep pace with. In particular, the machine had three coding rotors which occupied three places, and the operators always changed these settings every month until October 1936, when they started to change them every day. The change was sudden and unexpected, and totally flummoxed the top Polish experts. It was at this point that the French had asked the British for more assistance, although at this stage the Poles could still read most of the German traffic.

Shortly after the Munich crisis, the Germans had once again changed their procedures, perhaps because they were anticipating conflict in the near future. This was a change to the 'ground setting': until now, all German operators set their machines to a prescribed initial position before they got to work. But in September 1938, the Enigma's 'ground settings' were now changed not every morning but for each individual message, and there were nearly 18,000 different ways in which the operators could change these settings. Polish intelligence had already been tipped off in advance about these changes by an informer inside the signals section of the Luftwaffe but they were nonetheless still powerless: their replicas of the machine could not now work because they relied on all messages being sent on the same daily settings. In Warsaw, experts admitted that it was now much harder to decipher the huge number of Enigma messages that they intercepted every day.[10]

10. Informer—Turing 88.

By this time, Anglo-French cooperation on the German codes was already close. On 9 September, two of Britain's leading cryptanalysts, John Tiltman and 'Dilly' Knox, sent Rivet a list of technical questions about Enigma that they hoped the French could answer: the fact that they had sent this letter before the Germans had introduced further modifications reveals just how far ahead the Nazis were now pulling of the Allied spies. The French were completely unable to answer the questions but did now send a great deal of highly confidential information across the Channel, much of it bearing signals intelligence that the Poles had obtained and passed on to Paris.[11]

Bertrand wrote later that the French sent around 925 intelligence reports to London between September 1938 and August 1939. Referred to by the British as the 'Scarlet Pimpernels', the reports were always presented in an immaculate and distinctive style, typed in a purple ribbon and numbered, in red ink, with a characteristically French font. Stamped *Très Secret* in brazen red, they were then signed, on receipt, by Commander Dunderdale, who used the codename 'Dolinoff'. The SIS praised the French reports, which were deemed of 'very great interest' and 'very considerable value', while another document refers to the way in which the work of British codebreakers 'was enormously enhanced' by French input.[12]

Then, on 21 October, Alastair Denniston, the head of the British codebreaking centre, invited Bertrand to a meeting in London to exchange ideas about Enigma and the technical modifications introduced by the Germans. The proposed agenda included a presentation by one of his staff members on how, in the view of British experts, the Germans were operating their coding machine, followed by an analysis of intercepted German signals. But although the French were unable to answer the questions that Tiltman had posed, Bertrand promised to do his best to get some further information. On 5 December he wrote to Denniston, stating that 'he had found someone who believed he could get access to any army Enigma machine and asking his British counterpart to send a list of questions, specifying what he needed to know. Bertrand's source was Agent Asche, although of course he gave

11. HW 25/12 TNA.
12. Dolinoff—HW 65/9; 25/10; 43/78; 25/12 TNA; Turing 90–1. SIS—Turing 87.

no hint of the existence of any such spy to anyone outside a very tight circle in Paris, let alone outside its borders.[13]

It was this point that Bertrand suggested a follow-up meeting with the Poles, who were forced to turn to Britain and France for help. 'A collaboration with Warsaw on technical areas', as Rivet wrote to Menzies on 14 December, 'could offer common advantages... bring together representatives of each service with a view to putting forward the results of current researches on radio traffic... thinking that this occasion could be the prelude of a deeper collaboration, both in peace and war.' They would not do anything, in other words, to reveal their supremely confidential sources of information. This involved, however, 'keeping the sensitivities of each party paramount'.[14]

By the time this meeting took place, in January 1939, the Germans had also created even more layers of complexity in their formidable Enigma machine. In December they added two more wheels, or 'rotors', to the machine that enabled Enigma to produce nearly one million different rotor combinations, vastly more than before. Its operators could choose which three of those five rotors would produce the codes and then put them into the machine in different ways, leaving foreign eavesdroppers scrambling to work out what the Germans had done.

Two weeks later, they once again changed the wiring on the machine's plugboard. In a single stroke, years of painstaking Polish codebreaking work was rendered useless. The plugboard on the machine would now have between fourteen and twenty connecting cables, which would mean that only six of the twenty-six letters in the alphabet would remain unchanged, instead of the previous twelve. Colonel Langer was forced to concede that his men could now no longer read German codes: the German section of the Biuro Szyfrow, the specialist codebreaking team in the Second Department, could now read only a fraction of German messages, having previously deciphered as much as three-quarters. The Poles surrendered: they would need foreign assistance to regain their ground, particularly when they were cash-starved.

In mid-January, representatives from the three agencies met in Paris to discuss the Enigma challenge. The British, represented by the cryptanalysts Hugh Foss, Alistair Denniston, and Alfred 'Dilly' Knox,

13. Agenda—Turing 91. Source—HW 65/1 TNA; Turing 92.   14. Turing 92.

exchanged some ideas with Lt-Col Gwido Langer and his associate, Maximilian Ciezki, and their French counterparts, although all were very guarded about giving away too much information. Dennison showed the French and the Poles a technique, developed by Knox, to reverse-engineer the wiring of Enigma's rotors, while the French offered to obtain any information the British needed about how the rotor was wired and the plugboard connected. By the time the meeting drew to a close, it had largely served its function, building trust and introducing the codebreakers to each other rather than exchanging information. The British, never inclined to give praise easily, even grudgingly acknowledged French expertise, described by Dennison as 'quite capable'.[15]

The three agencies now made more frequent exchanges, each using abbreviations that became famous during the wartime years: Paris was represented with the letter 'X', London 'Y', and Warsaw 'Z'. Then, on 30 June, Gwido Langer proposed another meeting. This time he wanted to invite his counterparts to Warsaw and give them an honest assessment of Polish capabilities in a bid to win closer cooperation. Without this, there was simply no hope of breaking Enigma. Above all, Langer wanted to talk more to Knox, a highly gifted intellectual whose prowess at translating Greek verse matched his affinity for breaking German codes.[16]

At the end of July, a British delegation, comprising Knox, Denniston, and a naval codebreaker called Commander Humphrey Sandwith, left London to make a two-day journey by boat and train across Germany to the Polish capital. After checking in at Warsaw's best hotel, The Bristol, on Tuesday 25 July they were collected by car and taken to a secret location to meet the French delegation, made up of Bertrand and Henri Braquenie, and their Polish hosts.

This meeting-place was the enormous listening station at Pyry, outside Warsaw. Only opened a few years before, the Jedynka mast was not only vastly expensive but the most powerful antenna in the whole of Europe, capable of picking up signals as far away as Iran and Manchuria. One of eight listening stations in Poland, it allowed Langer and his men to keep close tabs on German movements, even if many people questioned why so much money had been spent on such a resource at

15. HW 65/3 TNA; Turing 114.
16. 'Conference between X and Y', 15 May 1939, HW 61/21 TNA.

the expense of so many other pressing priorities. Close to hand, in the Kabaty woods, was a top-secret bunker where signals experts from the Polish Second Department had moved in 1937. And it was to this closely guarded site, codenamed 'Tornado', that the codebreakers were taken on that July day in 1939.

During the conference that followed, the Poles stunned the British and French by announcing that they had cracked Enigma years before, using their own versions of the machine to determine the vital internal wiring. Their astonished guests were now shown several replicas of the German machines, as well as the Bombe, which was a very basic computer that could move through millions of possible permutations at a very rapid rate.

Langer and his colleagues now vowed to be transparent about everything they had learned, and even decided to send one of their replicas of the Enigma machine to both Paris and London. Some of the visitors had mixed feelings, sometimes filled with a strong sense of fury toward the Poles for keeping their achievements to themselves: not only was this deceitful, in their opinion, but the French knew that some of their own agents, notably Schmidt, had unnecessarily risked their lives trying to get hold of information that the Poles already had. But none could hide their admiration, and on his return, Knox sent a letter of gratitude to his hosts, together with a depiction of a horse race—an acknowledgement that the Poles has won the race to crack the code.

On 16 August, a boat-train pulled into Victoria Station, where a splendidly dressed Colonel Menzies was waiting, dressed for a celebratory dinner. Bertrand also appeared, flanked by Dunderdale and another SIS officer. Bertrand was escorting a large wooden box containing an imitation of the Enigma machine, donated by the Poles and forwarded from Paris by diplomatic baggage. The Poles had given a huge boost to the British effort to break Enigma, and probably reduced the time it eventually took by at least a year. The first fruits of this cooperation came just four months later, and by the following spring Allied intelligence was deciphering hugely valuable Enigma traffic.[17]

Electronic eavesdropping did not, however, help British and French spies and diplomats to gauge the state of German public opinion which, in the summer of 1939, had become more a pressing priority

17. HW 25/16 TNA; Turing 124.

for foreign governments. They needed to know the level of popular support for a war against the Allied powers, while a closer understanding of popular attitudes inside the Reich would also help them to focus British propaganda.

Over the Easter holiday, for example, Group Captain Vachell left his desk in the capital and spent four days driving around Bavaria to get a better idea of what ordinary Germans were thinking and feeling. In general, he felt that, in this area at least, Nazi propaganda had been 'singularly unsuccessful and the fact that one was British ensured a cordial reception'. At cafés and restaurants, ordinary Germans were 'not hostile but friendly' and 'pleased to see an Englishman', showing a benevolent interest when they saw him reading a British newspaper and introducing themselves. In Vienna in particular, 'the Englishman is assured of a very hearty welcome which I imagine it will take a vast amount of propaganda to change'. And as he travelled through Graz, he was often asked by passers-by if he was a Berliner but his reply 'that I was an Englishman at once produced a far more cordial attitude'. The 'natural enemies' of local people, he summarized, were Czechs and Italians 'but the British are definitely popular in Bavaria and it will require either considerable time or some startling event to change that attitude'. Not all of his counterparts elsewhere in Germany were quite so enamoured, and in Hamburg a diplomat felt that the effect of anti-British propaganda was 'noticeable', although others concurred with Vachell.[18]

The RAF man was less sure, however, about the long-term effects of Nazi propaganda. 'The hatred of England which is being taught in schools is having a great effect on the younger generation.' Such a constant barrage of images and messages, which was 'presented to children at their most impressionable age, must have a very important effect and will be well-nigh impossible to eradicate'. This meant that, even if the Nazi regime 'achieves nothing else [it] must succeed in producing a whole-hearted hatred of Great Britain throughout the coming generation of Germans'.

18. Vachell—'Effect of Anti-British Propaganda', 29 Apr 1939, FO 371/23008 TNA; Memo from Hamburg Consulate, 6 July 1939, FO 371/23009 TNA. In Dresden, the British consul also felt that such propaganda would eventually have an impact 'if it is persisted with'; Memo, 23 Mar 1939, FO 371/23006 TNA. However, in Bremen it was felt that 'there is little sign of anti-English feeling', memo of 6 Apr 1939, FO 371/23008 TNA.

Others, visitors and native Germans alike, shared the Englishman's concern about the effects of Nazi indoctrination on children. One British businessman, who regularly visited the Reich throughout the 1930s and kept Whitehall closely informed of his findings, noted how German professionals of his acquaintance were starting to arrange, 'by means of beer evenings', ways of 're-establishing sympathetic relations with their children, who they felt were completely alienated by the absorption of Nazi doctrines'. Such parents, he concluded, were 'generally in favour of cooperation with England' and wanted 'to get rid of the extremists'.[19]

A few weeks later, an undercover, anonymous agent also travelled through the Reich to report on these popular attitudes as well as to look for any signs of preparation for imminent war. He noted that, in the spring, the government had ordered all schools in Wiesbaden and many other towns to clear rooms for food storage, and the gym of one particular school was stuffed full of wheat. The government also commandeered marquees, which the armed forces would need, while some reserve officers had also been called up for extra training: there was a 'great increase in frequency and number of training periods for reservists'.[20]

Nonetheless, the visitor reported on a 'general feeling of disquiet' at the heightening international tension and the 'growing fear' amongst ordinary Germans that their leaders would lash out at the outside world if they felt threatened. In particular, he discovered that 'reports of Austrian indifference and Czech hostility [were] believed to be causing much anxiety at Party headquarters'.

He also detected other signs of popular disquiet with the regime. There was, he felt, a 'growing indifference to propaganda' and also some signs of industrial unrest, including 'discontent among railway workers [and] reports of secret strikes for better conditions having taken place in the spring'. He also saw signs of a 'growing disgust at corruption among lesser party officials', some of whom were reportedly 'lining their pockets in anticipation of a possible internal collapse'. This 'disgust', he continued, became clear from the number of officials who were stepping back from their party duties. Because there was so much negative sentiment in the country, there was also 'increasing

19. 'Interview with Mr Langmead', 7 Feb 1939, FO 371/23005 TNA.
20. 'Report from Germany', 12 June 1939, HW 62/21 TNA.

doubt, in military circles as well as among civilians, about the reliability of reservists in the event of war'. This, he continued, may have been partly because of anger about the government's hostility towards the traditional churches.

These reports were consistent with a number of other intelligence reports that reached London and Paris in the late spring of 1939. 'The German people as a whole do not want a prolonged war', as Halifax had told the cabinet, and 'there are in fact many forces militating against the "will to war"... and those forces may prevail.'[21]

Such information also helped British officials to get a more nuanced idea of the limits and scope of their own propaganda towards Nazi Germany, a task that became more pressing throughout 1939. 'British broadcasts in the German language', which were 'listened to with avidity', as a Whitehall official wrote, were the nation's 'most potent weapon today'. For example, one of Chamberlain's broadcasts, in which he accused Hitler of breaking his word of honour, 'carried conviction [since] German loyalty is an ancient boast' that badly wounded the Nazi leadership, inflicting a 'blow... to Herr Hitler's prestige'. The BBC also had a strong following 'because it is and is known to be straight news, with no propaganda', whereas the French broadcasts in German had completely defeated themselves by being violent, propagandist, and mendacious.[22]

In Whitehall, throughout 1939, Sir Orme Sergent and Rex Leeper tried to tailor just the right propaganda message to ordinary Germans. They concluded that the most powerful messages would carefully differentiate between the interests of Germany and those of its regime, and contrast the 'overreaching and wasteful stewardship of the Nazi Party' with the 'prosperity and peace' that 'cooperation and stability' with the outside world would bring. Most Germans, they felt, had a strong sense of 'moral truth' that was currently being suppressed but which effective propaganda could bring out. Getting across such a message, however, was not easy: 'to convey these ideas by words under the guise of "news", it would be necessary that they should be presented in the form of speeches by public men and to a less extent by articles in the press'. A few weeks later, another assessment proposed

21. 25 Jan 1939, CAB 23/97/2 TNA.
22. Chamberlain—British consul, Frankfurt, 22 Mar 1939, FO 371/23006 TNA. BBC—Memo by WW Astor, 24 Nov 1938, CAB 104/43 TNA.

targeting British propaganda, in the event of conflict, at Hitler's true war record, 'which differs widely from the story now being sent to every German home, that Hitler was a desperate warrior. If we can discredit Hitler he will cut and run', as one informant advised Whitehall.[23]

But despite the relentless focus of foreign spy agencies on Germany, Hitler and his entourage had a big surprise in store.

23. Most Germans—'British Propaganda in Germany', 21 Jan 1939, FO 371/23006 TNA. War record—Macassey to Halifax, 13 Apr 1939, FO 371/23007 TNA.

22

The Nazi–Soviet Pact

Throughout the spring and summer of 1939, both the British and French intelligence agencies received numerous reports about growing but covert links between Berlin and Moscow. But their reports did not win enough attention from their spymasters, who were in a position to allocate more time and resources exploring them, or their political leaders, who could have acted upon the information. Such action could conceivably have averted the non-aggression pact, struck up by Hitler and Stalin on 23 August.

In one sense, Hitler lost out from the deal, which caused consternation amongst bemused Germans who 'remember that, only the day before yesterday, Russia was still one of the arch-enemies: the harbour worker [in Hamburg] sums up the situation by saying "now we can say *Heil Moskau* again!"' Foreign observers noted 'fury over the Russian pact [and] everywhere people are saying that they would not dream of fighting for Moscow'. Ordinary Germans, in other words, were seeing red at the announcement. But the news also stunned London and Paris, and in spite of the intelligence warnings, the pact represented, in the words of DC Watt, 'one of the biggest disasters ever to overtake British foreign policy'. In a single stroke, the two dictators signed away the last effective barrier to a Nazi attack on Poland—the German fear of a war in both the east, against the Soviets, and against Britain and France in the west.[1]

But one individual who had not been surprised by the announcement of 23 August was Paul Stehlin. In Berlin some months before, in

1. Consternation—British consul, Hamburg to Whitehall, 23 Aug 1939, FO 371/23006 TNA. Foreign observers—'Disturbances in Germany', 30 Aug 1939, FO 371/23008 TNA; DC Watt, 'An Intelligence Surprise: The Failure of the Foreign Office to Anticipate the Nazi–Soviet Pact', *INS* (1989) 512.

early May, he had heard stories that he felt might have real substance, and enormous and alarming consequences for the Allies.

Stehlin's source was a Luftwaffe chief, General Karl Bodenschatz. The two men had struck up a close rapport over the preceding few years, not least because both had shared similar experiences as aviators in the First World War, when Bodenschatz had served under Göring's command in the elite Richthofen squadron. After the war, he had gone on to become Göring's personal adjutant, acting as a liaison officer between the *Reichsmarschall* and Hitler.

At the end of April, Bodenschatz had contacted Stehlin and told him, in the course of a 'long and logical talk', what he knew about Hitler's plans. Hitler was determined, he explained, not only to attack Poland but also to avoid fighting on two fronts. A pact with Stalin was therefore indispensable, and secret negotiations between Berlin and Moscow were already under way. 'Something', the German concluded, 'was about to happen in the east.' Stehlin was astonished by the mere suggestion of a pact between two regimes that seemed to be at each other's throats in so many different ways. But his visitor was adamant.[2]

The Frenchman realized that Bodenschatz, whom he trusted, might well be telling the truth: for during a speech to the Reichstag on 28 April, Hitler had not made any reference at all to Stalin's regime, which was usually an object of his vitriol. Silence spoke volumes and Stehlin had been surprised by the omission.[3]

After three years in the German capital, Stehlin had a good feel for a genuine story and immediately informed his ambassador, Robert Coulondre, who wrote a long despatch to Paris about the matter. Coulondre mentioned that there had already been secret contact in Berlin between Ribbentrop and Alexei Merekalov, the Soviet ambassador in Berlin, as well as between a number of Soviet military attachés and German officers.

In fact, some far-sighted intelligence analysts had long warned that relations between Hitler and Stalin could improve: as early as September 1933, a Deuxième Bureau report argued that 'the frosty relations between them can thaw or even melt altogether'. Nonetheless Bodenschatz's revelations, if true, made startling news. Without Soviet support, the Poles had no chance of fending off a German attack for more than a few days, long before the British and French were capable of organizing and fielding any relief force. Any such Berlin–Moscow alliance would make even the staunchest British or French supporter of Poland waver: there would simply be no point in trying to defend a country that, like Czechoslovakia in March 1939, would be overrun in a matter of days. Chamberlain would be forced to go back on his word, destroying his own credibility and that of his country.[4]

This was why both London and Paris were by this time setting their sights on Moscow, hoping to strike up a defensive alliance with the Soviets to deter German aggression. Despite his serious misgivings about a leader whom he did not trust and whose armed forces he did not hold in high regard, Chamberlain had relented and looked reluctantly towards Moscow, partly as a result of French pressure.

Coulondre shared his information with Henderson, who in turn relayed it straight back to London, although Bodenschatz had also made his own independent approaches to the Foreign Office, providing the same information. By this time, a number of other reports about growing German–Soviet collusion had also reached British Intelligence. The SIS station in Helsinki, for example, ran an agent, codenamed 'The Baron', with good contacts amongst Prussian aristocrats who, some weeks before Stehlin's report, had tipped him off about growing Soviet–German links. The Foreign Office, however, remained unconvinced, even when 'The Baron's' second report reached them in June, suspecting that they represented a deliberate campaign of disinformation aimed to disrupting talks between British, French, and Soviet officials.[5]

Then, towards the end of April, the SIS also received 'unconfirmed reports that secret Russo-German conversations of some sort' were about to start, while a 'Most Secret' Whitehall memorandum, dated 10 May, noted that 'German generals had had some communications with the Russians, as a result of which the former now seemed reconciled to the idea of a general war': such contact between the two dictators, if this report was to be believed, was not just about trade and commerce. Soon, rumours swirled: 'the possibility of a Soviet-German understanding is being much discussed', as one British source told Whitehall on 24 May. A trickle of other sources—including 'an

4. Report—'Plan de Renseignements 1933', 3 Feb 1933, 7NN 2530 SHD.
5. Coulondre—Henderson to London, 8 May 1939, FO 371/22972 TNA. Baron—Jeffery 322.

Englishman living and working in Rome [with] assured information from a most reliable source'—added to their suspicions.[6]

The SIS had also had another informer—General Walter Germanovich Krivitsky. A small, thin man with enormously bushy eyebrows, Krivitsky had spent several years in The Hague, using the name of 'Dr Martin Lessner' and posing as a rare book dealer from Austria. But his office, on Celebesstraat, really acted as the headquarters of Soviet military intelligence operation throughout the whole of Western Europe. In October 1937, however, perhaps fearful of falling victim to the purges in his homeland, he caused a worldwide sensation by announcing his defection and seeking political asylum in the West. After a brief stay in Paris, where he lived in constant fear of assassination by agents working for his vengeful former boss, Krivitsky then made a sudden departure for the United States.

Not long after his arrival, he wrote a series of articles in the American press about Stalin's domestic and foreign policies, working with another Soviet émigré, Don Levine, to write them. One of their pieces for the *Saturday Evening Post* had made the startling claim that Stalin had been seeking to strike up a secret deal with Hitler since 1934, but the claims were considered by British diplomats in Washington to be unreliable 'Russian day-dreaming' by a 'self-styled general' who was peddling 'twaddle' and 'nonsense'. Because the SIS knew so little about such an elusive man, Krivitsky was ultimately too much of an unknown quantity to be taken seriously.[7]

Over the next few weeks, further intelligence reports about contacts between Moscow and Berlin began to proliferate. In London, a visiting German economist, Helmut Wohltat, told the SIS about a Nazi plan to send a trade negotiator, Dr Karl Schnurre, to Moscow to conduct preliminary talks, while Moravec and his fellow exiles were closely networked with the well-informed former Czech war minister, General Jan Syrovy, whose own reports, although sometimes fanciful, confirmed the same picture. These versions of events corroborated information that was reaching Vansittart: on 17 May, he sent Halifax a detailed memorandum, marked 'Secret', based on information that was sent directly from the German general staff, alleging that 'Hitler has

6. Whitehall—Memos of 10, 11 May 1939, FO 1093/87 TNA. Rumours—Memo from the Munich Consulate, 24 May 1939, FO 371/23006 TNA. Other sources—British rep. to the Vatican, 6 May 1939, FO 371/22972 TNA.

7. Diplomats—FO 371/23697 TNA; Andrew 423.

been negotiating with Stalin through the Czech General Sirovy [*sic*]'. Vansittart urged Chamberlain and Halifax to strike a deal with Moscow before Hitler did, adding that 'there is no time to be lost in this Russian business'.[8]

The Deuxième Bureau also received around ten such reports on German–Russian talks while the Poles sent another military attaché to their embassy in Moscow solely to monitor the issue by keeping close tabs on the activities of German personnel in the Soviet capital. The Finnish and Estonian governments, which watched Soviet activity very closely, also picked up on the same rumours and judged that Stalin would prefer to deal with Hitler rather than strike an accord with the British and the French. And in Berlin, the Yugoslav attaché, Colonel Vladimir Vauhnik, claimed that the two countries had already struck a secret deal, which proved to be an accurate prophecy even if it was several weeks premature.[9]

By this time, British Intelligence had noted that there were 'an unusually large number of rumours' about a rapprochement circulating in foreign capitals. The problem was that not all of these rumours emanated from either known sources or reliable ones: Cadogan was highly mistrustful, for example, of Erich Kordt, the senior counsellor in Ribbentrop's office, who in mid-June travelled to London at great personal risk, telling Nazi officials that he was taking a holiday in Scotland. In fact, he delivered a stark warning to his contacts at the Foreign Office about a looming pact between Hitler and Stalin.[10]

The state of confusion, created by so many conflicting intelligence reports of undetermined and largely indeterminable veracity, became clear from a War Office report on 4 July. Noting 'an unusually large number of rumours', the document remarked upon the contradictory nature of the information which included 'one most secret report indicating that the Germans held the view that the elimination of Stalin was essential' and another 'from a reliable source on the Russian state [who] stated that Stalin was very bitter on account of German intrigues...and that no question of a rapprochement was possible'.

8. 17 May 1939, FO 371/22972 TNA.
9. Watt *How War Came* 296, 372.
10. Rumours—Andrew 424; on 1 June, Admiral Godfrey was informed that 'three of Ribbentrop's best assistants are in Moscow...to prevent the completion of an Anglo-Soviet agreement. Berlin is not by any means unhopeful that it may be possible to keep Russia neutral': FO 371/23006 TNA. Cadogan—Aster 274–5.

This meant that there was 'no real circumstantial evidence to show that any such rapprochement is in fact in progress of negotiation', although 'there is every possibility that Germany and Russia may reach a commercial agreement'.[11]

There was just one person who could have emphatically corroborated all these reports but who did not, unfortunately, go on to do so. In May, an anti-Nazi diplomat at the German embassy in Moscow had confided to 'Chip' Bohlen, an official based at the American embassy, about the growing rapport between the great dictators. Bohlen had immediately informed his bosses in Washington but did not tell his British or French counterparts, perhaps fearful that his supremely confidential information would catch the Soviet ear, compromising his source. And though Bohlen's information quickly reached the desk of the secretary of state, Cordell Hull, British and French diplomats in Washington were not informed until just before news of the German–Soviet pact broke, more than three months later: it was only on 15 August that the undersecretary of state, Sumner Welles, summoned the British ambassador and informed him that, according to 'a source which in the past had proved very reliable', a pact between the two countries was imminent.[12]

Without the confirmation they needed, British and French spies continued to work hard to get more information about what was really happening. In Moscow, Sir William Seeds kept a close eye on the German embassy, carefully observing and recording who was coming and going, and concluding that only a commercial deal was being discussed. But in the third week of August, French agents in Moscow noticed that Soviet workmen had suddenly started to work furiously hard on renovating the former Austrian embassy, which had stood vacant since *Anschluss*. They were right to take note, because the building was in fact being prepared for the arrival of Joachim von Ribbentrop, who visited the capital on 23 August to sign his deal with Stalin. The rumours and intelligence reports had been right all along.

The British and French, it emerged, had been 'misled, if not positively misdirected' by the reports of German–Soviet commercial negotiations, which had made them think that nothing more ambitious was afoot. The SIS had also picked up stories of German plans to subvert

---

11. 'Soviet–German Relations', FO 371/23686 TNA.
12. Diplomats—Herwath von Bittenfeld *Against Two Evils* Encore (1981) 154–60.

the Soviet government and assassinate Stalin, and of Stalin's supposed fury on hearing about this, but these were most likely to have been deliberately planted by German Intelligence in a bid to throw them off the trail. And in both London and Paris, many people had continued to assume that Nazism and Soviet communism were deadly enemies and that any sort of agreement between them, even a temporary one, was unthinkable.

But true or not, rumours of a Soviet–German pact still did not answer the big question that continued to loom so large in the summer of 1939: where would Hitler strike next? British Intelligence picked up more signs of German mobilization. These included the movement of reserve divisions and the confiscation by the army of civilian lorries; restrictions on the supply and distribution of petrol; and the inoculation of army officers against diseases such as cholera and typhoid. But against whom?[13]

Hitler's most likely motive for striking a deal with Moscow was of course to have a free hand to attack Poland, which shared such a long border with the Soviet Union, but he could equally have attacked the Balkans, which offered Romanian oil as well as control over the Mediterranean. In March 1939, this seemed a very likely move, as the SIS cited reports that 'all the German Tank Divisions and all the German motorized Divisions, i.e. all the specifically offensive troops, are concentrated in the East', prompting one senior diplomat to conclude that Germany might invade Romania together with Hungary and Bulgaria. Stalin could have potentially obstructed such a move, either by sending reinforcements across the Black Sea to Romania or else by launching a diversionary attack, further north, through the Ukraine. But some intelligence officers were also wondering if Hitler would launch his first strike in the west, either against Britain or, as the Bureau pondered in March 1939, against France. Again, a pact with Stalin left him free to do this, since the threat of Soviet intervention would deter the Poles from making their own diversionary attack against Germany.[14]

Wherever Hitler would strike, unmistakable signs of German war preparations emerged throughout the spring and summer months of 1939.

13. Signs—Henderson to Halifax, 8 Aug 1938, DBFP III series, Vol 4, 1939.
14. Reports—Minute by Mr Jebb, 21 Mar 1939, FO 371 22958 C3565/13/18 TNA. Officers—'Plan de Renseignements', 29 Mar 1939, 7NN 2530 SHD.

The Deuxième Bureau looked out for indications of renewed collusion between Hitler and Mussolini, introducing 'particularly close surveillance' of the transport network in Austria, which acted as the *zone de contact* between the two partners. By late spring, they had picked up clear indications of a rapprochement, heralding the 'Pact of Steel' that the two fascist leaders signed on 22 May. In June, French spies also discovered that German reservists were secretly being called up, while across the Reich, particularly in Berlin, food suddenly became scarcer and more expensive as the armed forces started to stockpile supplies. Such shortages, particularly of meat and vegetables, affected everyone, including Colonel Strong's housekeeper, who now had to cook whatever she could get hold of, and who found that she could no longer replace everyday household items, such as light bulbs, that had always previously been relatively plentiful. But still there was no clear, decisive indication of exactly when and where Hitler would attack.[15]

By this time, the British and French intelligence services still had too much 'intelligence information' on these matters. As Laurence Collier wrote from his desk at the Foreign Office:

We find ourselves, when attempting to assess the value of these secret reports, somewhat in the position of the Captain of the Forty Thieves when, having put a chalk mark on Ali Baba's door, he found that Morgiana had put similar marks on all the doors in the street and had no indication to show which mark was the true one.[16]

And Halifax told the cabinet in January 1939, 'the atmosphere was much like that which surrounded a child, in which everything was possible and nothing was impossible'.[17]

By this time, British officials had developed a system of intelligence evaluation that, on paper at least, shielded politicians from any erroneous information. 'Whenever a report conflicts with what one of our Missions has been saying', as Gladwyn Jebb wrote, 'a copy is either sent out to the head of that Mission or shown to him on the spot and his observations invited.' If it was judged to be plausible, the report was then forwarded to a 'co-ordinator' of intelligence within the SIS. This 'co-ordinator' was 'a man of remarkable intelligence and discretion

15. Indications—'Plan de Renseignements', 29 Mar 1939, 7NN 2530 SHD.
16. Laurence Collier, 26 Aug 1939, FO 371/23686 TNA.
17. 25 Jan 1939, CAB 23/97/2 TNA.

who has been doing the job for over fifteen years, reads all Foreign Office telegrams and despatches and is in constant contact' with the heads of the government. But in practice, in such difficult and challenging circumstances, such 'safeguards' counted for little. The Foreign Office and the SIS were often so distracted by false intelligence reports that they overlooked accurate and reliable information about such events as the occupation of Prague, which they failed to foresee until the last moment, and the Italian invasion of Albania in April 1939, which caught them entirely by surprise.[18]

A good many of these innumerable reports were not only unverifiable but also pointed in several different directions. On 30 June, Daladier told the British that he had heard 'from a first-rate source' that Hitler intended to 'settle Danzig' imminently, in the course of the next few days, and asked Whitehall to make a public stand against such a move. But in London, Cadogan was wary, suspecting Daladier of overreacting. While Cadogan fumed at the 'conflicting stories' that abounded in Europe, making it 'quite impossible to tell whether these were deliberately put about to confuse and alarm us or whether there was any truth in them', the British ambassador in Paris, Sir Eric Phipps, discovered that Daladier's source was in fact a German exile in Switzerland, who had been in contact with a Frenchman but whose value appears to have been unclear.[19]

Just days later, however, the SIS received a series of much more reassuring messages. 'We reported "faltering" in mid-July', as one SIS official later wrote, 'and MI5 information, mentioning "cold feet" in Berlin, tended to confirm this; it was a faltering which was apparently to be kept from the knowledge of all but a few at the top.' Hopes were raised even more when the German *gauleiter* of Danzig, Albert Forster, privately informed the UN representative that Hitler would henceforth be taking a more moderate and reasonable line over the city's future. This upbeat message was quietly relayed to the British, French, and American governments, and Halifax informed the cabinet on 26 July. Perhaps the Polish guarantee, and some other clear messages of support, were finally doing the trick that the long months of appeasement had failed to perform. War could be avoided after all.[20]

18. Jebb memo, 31 Mar 1939, FO 1093/86 TNA. Overlooked—Halifax, CAB 27/624 TNA; Cadogan *Diaries*, 21 Apr 1939.
19. Aster 208.   20. SIS—FO 371/22981 TNA; Aster 214.

Not everyone was sure. Kirkpatrick warned that, after breaking his word over Munich, Hitler had proved himself to be 'cunning and we must be on our guard'. Such measured voices were right to be cautious, especially when other sources of information suggested that Hitler was intending to move not eastwards, against Poland, but into the Balkans. In early July, a source informed Stehlin that the growing war scare over Poland was in fact a distraction from 'Germany's principal objective [which] remains the south-east'. A month later, the acting Romanian premier, Armand Călinescu, then informed the French that these reports had been corroborated by his own intelligence sources in Berlin, which included an anonymous industrialist linked to the former Nazi war minister, General Werner von Blomberg, and a German aristocrat by the name of the Prince zu Ward. At the same time, rumours abounded in London of a Nazi-inspired coup in Hungary that would reduce the country into a state of serfdom under German tutelage.[21]

These 'intelligence reports' may have been part of an ongoing and deliberate campaign of disinformation conducted by the enemies of the Nazis, as they tried to stir up more anti-German feeling in the Balkans. The Prince zu Ward, for example, was an exiled aristocrat who hated Hitler and Nazism so intensely that he had left his native Germany and settled in Romania, where he maintained close links with anti-Nazi circles inside the Reich as well as beyond. But much more of this false 'intelligence' was concocted by the Germans, as they once again tried to deceive their enemies. In Berlin, Paul Stehlin noticed how such disinformation could easily be lapped up by a gullible audience: 'I have an instinctive mistrust of diplomats who want to convey the impression of being well informed', as he wrote later, 'of rumours that are manipulated by private agendas, and of fake news spun out by Goebbels' press service.' In particular, he noted with amazement 'how a piece of information, from a trustworthy source and which has value, can be distorted by the time foreign embassies get hold of it and put it onto a secret telegram'.[22]

Deliberate German disinformation probably also explains how and why, at the end of March, British Intelligence received disturbing reports that the German navy had sent out to sea as many as fifteen submarines, far more than even the most pessimistic Whitehall analysts

21. Watt *How War Came* 301.   22. Stehlin 162.

even guessed it possessed. The SIS and the Royal Navy had no indication of these vessels' location but guessed that they were probably
mounting a continuous patrol in different areas, and expected them to
return to Kiel about every three months. The following month, the
sense of alarm in London grew even more sharply when Berlin openly
denounced the Anglo-German Naval Agreement.[23]

This 'submarine bogey', as it became known, had first surfaced during the Munich crisis, when British spies acquired information that a
number of U-boats had been deployed to the South Atlantic, where
the Royal Navy completely lacked any escorts and anti-submarine vessels, rendering British shipping extremely vulnerable to German
attacks. A few weeks later, the SIS then learned that the U-boats had
returned to Germany for refitting and refuelling, at just the same time
that the German Admiralty claimed to have matched the Royal Navy's
own submarine strength.

In fact, such reports of U-boat activity were completely false and
were deliberately concocted by the Abwehr and leaked to the Admiralty
and the SIS in a bid to sink British morale. The Royal Navy, Wesley
Wark has argued, was 'bamboozled by the wealth of supporting information which accompanied the story, a perfect piece of deception
work on the part of the Abwehr'. After the war, Admiral Godfrey
admitted that the 'intelligence' was the result of 'rumours [that] were
all based on single unchecked sources of unknown authenticity—very
intractable, and impossible to grade'. Some reports of German preparation were certainly accurate: the British embassy in Oslo, for example,
discovered that a Norwegian factory could not fulfil an order because
one of its suppliers was too busy building U-boat motors. But on the
outbreak of war, the British significantly overstated the size of the
German submarine fleet.[24]

23. Wark 'Baltic Myths'. Godfrey Vol 8 'Afterthoughts' 115–19.
24. Wark 'Baltic Myths' 76; Godfrey Vol 8, 119.

23

The Countdown to War

Chamberlain had now made a commitment to defend France but, in the months that preceded the outbreak of war, the two countries were constantly engaged in a diplomatic tug-of-war. The French had pulled one way, demanding British conscription, the opening of talks with Moscow, and a guarantee to Romania, and the British had given ground. Equally, the British had pulled the French closer towards London over the Polish guarantee, and tried, without success, to persuade Daladier to strike up negotiations with Mussolini. Both countries were committed, nonetheless, to spying on the Reich.

By this time, one of their best sources was a very familiar one. In a report written on 6 January, Christie had argued that 'Poland must be squeezed first' and that 'Colonel Beck must now make his final choice; either Poland must face a military squeeze by the Reich or put herself at the disposal of the Axis'. The main reason for Hitler's focus on Poland, Christie had argued, was that it held the key to further expansion eastwards. The Germans had no chance of launching a successful attack on the Soviet Union unless they had captured Poland first. If this assessment was correct, then of course Hitler, not for the first time, was playing an astonishingly cynical and duplicitous game, luring Stalin into a pact in the short term so that he would thereafter soon be free to attack his new ally. Two years later, this assessment did indeed prove accurate.[1]

Nearly three weeks later, Christie had filed another report, from an unspecified location in central Europe and also based on conversations with unspecified sources. Now he argued that there were clear signs of hubris in Berlin, where Hitler was seriously entertaining ideas that

1. Christie—quoted in Conwell-Evans 170.

bore no resemblance to reality. The *Führer*, claimed Christie, was planning not just to drive a wedge between Britain and France but also to promote the cause of fascism inside France in the same way that he had nurtured Henlein's fascist party in the Sudetenland. The new 'fascist state of France', in Hitler's imagination, would then join the Axis powers. Christie had also claimed, with unnerving accuracy, that 'Hitler would, in the last resort, even come to an agreement with Stalin. At all events a German–Russian trade treaty is to be concluded, and abuse of Russia has recently been much more subdued in the German press.'[2]

Other foreign observers looked for clues by detecting similarities and parallels with earlier crises. In the summer of 1939, for example, the Nazi press stepped up its attacks on Poland, making vitriolic accusations of atrocities against ethnic Germans living on Polish soil. In tone and content, such horror stories closely resembled the media attacks that Goebbels had unleashed against the Czechs the previous year. And in Berlin, Robert Coulondre commented on another parallel with the Sudeten crisis, noting how the Germans were now invoking, for the first time since the previous September, the same conception of 'honour'. 'Hitler's plan', he wrote on 15 August, 'continues to develop according to a well-known procedure.' Goebbels seemed to think that any supposed foreign insult to Germany's 'honour' would resonate with the wider public and win popular support. These reports coincided with indications of troop and arms movements as well as sudden shortages of petrol and other vital materials, all signs of an impending war.[3]

Vansittart's private network also provided other clues, for on 16 August Erich Kordt sent a message to his brother at the German embassy in London, claiming that Hitler had chosen war, in spite of Italian misgivings, and was preparing to launch an invasion of Poland at the end of the month. Vansittart immediately contacted Halifax and then Sir Alexander Cadogan to tell him the news. Despite his strong distrust of Kordt, who was known to have received top-secret information about British negotiations with Stalin from a traitor within the Foreign Office, Cadogan believed this particular report, which corroborated a number of other sources. In particular, the SIS

2. Conwell-Evans 171.

3. Coulondre—Watt *How War Came* 431. Indications—British consul, Hamburg to Whitehall, 9 Aug 1939, FO 371/23006 TNA.

had a very valuable informer inside the German railway network whose own information confirmed Kordt's version of events. By this time, the sense of impending doom was overwhelming: 'holiday-makers are leaving hurriedly, the British colony in Hamburg has dwindled [and] there is an appreciable thinning of traffic on the streets', as one diplomat wrote back to London.[4]

Meanwhile, from his office in Putney, which he shared with a handful of his fellow exiles, including Beneš, Moravec had been working hard to re-establish contact with the agents who had gone to ground after the Nazi occupation of their homeland. And in June, he received a letter, forwarded by his counterpart in Zurich, from someone claiming to be his 'nephew'. The note was short and simple: 'Dear Uncle, I think I am in love. I have met a girl.'[5]

But written on the same page, in secret ink, Moravec found something rather different:

I will be in The Hague shortly. Would like to meet you or your deputy. Place: Hotel des Indies: Time: June 15. Name: Lustig. Signed: Karl.

Moravec knew exactly who the real author was. Paul Thümmel. Agent A-54.

Within days, Thümmel had met one of Moravec's deputies in Holland, where he revealed details of Hitler's plans to attack Poland. Moravec immediately forwarded this dramatic news to both his British and French counterparts as well as to the Poles. The two countries that had been bitterly at loggerheads ever since their formation after the First World War, and even been on the verge of outright war during the Munich crisis, were now cooperating again. The international espionage network between Britain, France, Poland, and Czechoslovakia against Nazi Germany had come full circle.

Like Thümmel, Hans-Thilo Schmidt had by this time also shown a remarkable longevity for an individual who was operating in such a dangerous and hostile environment. In the summer of 1939, he continued to write several letters to Rivet, always using invisible ink, and on 27 May informed the Deuxième Bureau of a secret conference at which Hitler had stated his ambition to annex Poland as soon as the

4. British consul, Hamburg to Whitehall, 23 Aug 1939, FO 371/23006 TNA.
5. Moravec 181–2.

opportunity cropped up. Then, on 9 June, another letter arrived: Poland, Schmidt told Rivet, would be attacked at the end of August.

Information also came, or could have come, from visiting business-men who had a legitimate reason to visit Germany at this time. The risks they took as *honorables correspondants*, however, were enormous. In the summer of 1939, for example, a patriotic businessman called Mauritz Samson offered his services to the Bureau's Colonel Gauthier, who gave his new recruit precise instructions about the information that he needed. On 4 July, Samson then left Nancy to make his third trip to Germany, checking in at a hotel in Stuttgart for a two-week stay. For the first few days, Samson sent letters and postcards to his brother, who felt sure that everything was going well. But the corres-pondence suddenly stopped, and his distraught brother's increasingly frantic phone calls to the hotel, and desperate pleas to police chiefs in Paris, revealed nothing. Three weeks later, Samson appeared before a tribunal in Stuttgart, charged with espionage.[6]

In Berlin, meanwhile, the military attachés continued their work. But for Stehlin, watching matters unfold inside Germany became more difficult, even dangerous, in the course of the summer, as the Nazis placed him under constant surveillance, making little or no effort to disguise the fact. Two Gestapo agents tailed his car or followed him if he went anywhere by foot or on public transport. Wherever he went—to and from his home or office, or on an evening out—he found himself being shadowed. And when the phone sometimes rang but no one answered, he was sure that the Gestapo were checking up on his movements, perhaps because they hadn't sighted him for a while and wondered if he had given them the slip. Despite the growing sense of threat inside Germany, Stehlin tried to avoid them, sometimes swap-ping his own car with that of a friend who bore a slight resemblance to him, or else by using his own car for part of a journey before switching to public transport.[7]

Stehlin could still access his diplomatic plane, which he was allowed to use to follow pre-arranged flight paths over Germany. But in August, as the Germans began to concentrate massive numbers of troops along the border with Poland, he found that the Luftwaffe was starting to steer a much more confrontational course than before: on one occasion, for

6. Lettre du 24 Juillet 1939; Note pour M. Depas, 29 Aug 1939, 7NN 2335 SHD.
7. Stehlin 168–9.

example, several German planes approached him in a very aggressive and hostile manner as he approached a garrison and airfield. Stehlin was aware that, although he was a diplomat who had Göring's permission to fly over Germany, he could not stop the German domestic security chiefs from arranging an 'accident' if they wanted to do so. His days of flying over the Reich were soon over. Days later, he was told that his plane was unusable after being 'accidentally' damaged in its hangar when another pilot was taxiing past.

The British and French spy services had a number of other sources about developments within the Reich. Conwell-Evans, for example, was in close touch with a handful of disillusioned officials within the German Foreign Office who had sympathy with Hitler's expansionist aims but not with his reckless methods, which they regarded as entirely self-destructive. The intelligence services were also well aware of growing dissent within the German army. Although both the SIS and the Bureau judged Hitler to be an uncontrollable force, despite the efforts of some of his generals—notably Beck—to act as a restraint, their analysts also felt that there was a chance of a coup against him if the risk of a pan-European war loomed too large. To keep track of this dissent, the SIS had a contact who acted as an intermediary with dissidents inside the German army: this anonymous individual also played a quiet but important role at the end of August, when he accompanied a Swedish negotiator, Birger Dahlerus, from London back to Berlin bearing 'a platitudinous message' that expressed Britain's strong desire for peace. Göring, this contact told his SIS handlers in London, was looking favourably at the proposal.[8]

Meanwhile Paul Thümmel was providing Moravec with more information about Hitler's plans, meeting a Czech intelligence officer during another 'business trip' to The Hague, and providing him with details of Plan White against Poland. The Czechs were astounded by the amount of information he provided, which included the German army's precise order of battle, including the names and numbers of units and their commanders. The master spy also told his Czech contact that Hitler was bracing for an invasion in early September, and was going to make a staged attack on a German radio station, ostensibly by

8. Conwell-Evans 136–7. SIS—Robert J Young 'French Military Intelligence and Nazi Germany 1938–9' in Ernest May (ed.) *Knowing One's Enemies* Princeton (1984) 281. Contact—Watt *How War Came* 507. Cadogan—*Diaries* 27 Aug 1939.

'Polish commandos', as an excuse to launch his assault. The SS, he continued, was trying to acquire a hundred or so Polish uniforms in a bid to give such an 'attack' some cloak of plausibility. The information tailored perfectly with another report from Christie, who on 26 August provided Vansittart with the exact details of Germany's plans against Poland.

Before he left, Thümmel suggested a means of informing the Czech spies of any particularly urgent information he might have. In this scenario, he would send a telegram to a shop, 'De Favorit', in The Hague that acted as Moravec's cover address: since the shop sold gloves, handkerchiefs, and handbags, the telegram would simply state that 'merchandise would be arriving' on a specific day. That date would in fact state the day of the German army's planned mobilization for an attack against Poland. For added security, the date on the telegram would pre-date the pending attack by two days. Over the next few weeks, as the Germans postponed their attack, two such telegrams arrived, each with different dates.[9]

By this time, the Czechs had suddenly acquired another very valuable source of information. In June, the Czech consulate in Zurich, which was still organized and run by Captain Karel Sedlacek, began to transmit to London a series of top-quality military reports about developments inside the Reich. Sedlacek's source was a German refugee called Rudolf Roessler, 'a small thin man with a cadaverous face, half-hidden by glasses', who had fled to Zurich, where he was writing and publishing strongly anti-Nazi newspaper articles.

Roessler was very well connected inside Germany and had agreed to provide Sedlacek with information, on condition that his sources would remain anonymous. A steady flow of information now started to reach London, using codenames—'Werther' for the German army, 'Olga' for its air force, and 'Anna' for the navy—that were to become highly familiar during the wartime years. Much of this information was highly technical data but it also included forecasts and analysis that had great value. 'We passed on these reports to the British', as Moravec later wrote, 'producing almost daily changes in the huge War Office maps on which the deployments of the German forces were plotted.' Later, after the war, it emerged that amongst the informants were a group of ten German officers, five of whom ended the war as generals,

9. Moravec 185.

whose anti-Nazi sympathies prompted them to betray Germany's secrets in a desperate bid to prevent conflict.[10]

Finding new sources of information remained, however, a very hazardous affair, given the risks of falling for an *agent provocateur*. On 30 August, for example, an anonymous visitor came to meet the military attaché at the British embassy in Berlin. Claiming to be closely linked to the leading opponents of the Nazi regime, he stated that there was turmoil within its ruling circles, and that Hitler was secretly in a state of nervous collapse while several of his top generals had either already resigned their posts or else were on the verge of doing so. There was growing support for a coup against Hitler, he continued, but the instigators needed to know exactly how much support they would have from the British and French governments and what approach they would take, if Hitler was toppled, towards Danzig and Germany's security.

Whoever this informant really was, it is most likely that he was working for the German security services, who were probably fishing for information about Allied intentions or else trying to lead the attaché into a trap. The truth was that, in the summer of 1939, there was no risk of an army coup against Hitler amongst the ruling circles that surrounded him. The head of the German army, Field Marshal von Brauchitsch, was no longer sympathetic to the opponents of Hitler, largely because he had fallen under the influence of his second wife, a rabid pro-Nazi, whom he had married two years before. A more accurate picture was instead drawn by a second informant who also appeared at the British embassy on the same day, claiming that, despite a great deal of dissatisfaction with Hitler and his regime amongst most Germans, at every level of society, there was virtually no chance that the *Führer* would be toppled. This individual, unnamed in the diplomatic despatch that was sent to London, was most likely to have been Ewald von Kleist-Schmenzin, who had travelled to London the previous summer in an unsuccessful bid to win British support for a coup against Hitler.[11]

But in the long, hot summer weeks of 1939, there were other, quite factual, intelligence reports that drastically raised Allied hopes of averting war.

10. Moravec 186–7.   11. Watt *How War Came* 517.

In the middle and end of August, both the SIS and the Bureau received a flow of information suggesting that popular discontent inside Germany was growing rapidly. Czech spies informed them that 'bodies of German troops in Budovice [Budweiss] and Pilsen have mutinied...and that in each case a whole regiment was affected'. Days later, a 'reliable source' in Switzerland informed London that Austrian railway workers were undertaking a campaign of passive resistance, slowing down the movement of trains, while there were also 'disturbances of a serious nature in the Ruhr district and in the neighbourhood of Salzburg', which had prompted the Nazi authorities to 'recall a division from the eastern frontier to deal with it'. At the same time, the imposition of a new rationing system provoked 'major riots' in the Rhineland, near the Dutch frontier, and in Bavaria, prompting Henderson to comment that 'there is little doubt that considerable dissatisfaction exists among the masses and is growing in volume'. There were stories, too, of food shortages in Germany, 'more serious than is generally known and considerable dissatisfaction among German troops'.[12]

The following day, on 31 August, British Intelligence picked up an even more 'surprising development and a most hopeful sign'. This concerned 'a palace revolution' in Berlin that had allowed Göring, 'with the help of Generals and officials', to take charge. Observers at the Japanese embassy in Berlin also informed London that war was now less likely to break out 'because of the deterioration in German morale', prompting Ivone Kirkpatrick to conclude that 'we had the whip hand over Germany at all points'. Papal delegates in Berlin also concluded that 'the days of the Hitler regime are numbered', while Dutch officials told the British that 'there was widespread discontent [and] statues of Hitler had been overthrown in various places, and the Gestapo...feared to provoke outbreaks'.[13]

12. Discontent—Frank Roberts noted 'the French have had similar reports';'Disturbances in Germany', 30 Aug 1939, FO 371/23008 TNA. Czech spies—Home Office to Kirkpatrick, 18 Aug 1939, FO 371/23006 TNA. Trains—'From France', 29 Aug 1939 FO 371/23008 TNA. Disturbances—Secret Memo, 29 Aug 1939, FO 371/23008 TNA. Major riots—'From Germany', 30 Aug 1939, FO 371/23008 TNA. Bavaria— 'Disturbances in Germany', 30 Aug 1939, FO 371/23008 TNA. Stories—'Germany's Internal Situation', 30 Aug 1939, FO 371/23008 TNA.
13. Palace—Memo from Sir Orme Sargeant, 31 Aug 1939, FO 371/23008 TNA; Memo from Ivone Kirkpatrick, 30 Aug 1939, FO 371/23008 TNA. Papal and Dutch reports— Bland to Halifax, 31 Aug 1939, DBFP, Series III, Vol 7 No 626.

Such information arrived against a backdrop of other reports, received over the summer months, of discontent, strikes, and sabotage against Hitler's regime, notably in Austria and Czechoslovakia. Informers noted that large numbers of plain-clothed Gestapo officers had been posted throughout the big cities to keep a close watch on ordinary Germans who were 'becoming more and more dissatisfied with the conditions of everyday life, and explosions are expected'. And in Prague, anti-German feeling had moved 'from passivity to passive resistance', leading to 'sabotage, suppressed patriotic demonstrations', and 'anti-German propaganda in chain-letters, leaflets [and] lampoons', while there had also been 'successful and attempted bomb outrages'.[14]

On a more anecdotal level, a diplomat described what happened during the 'Theatre Week' that was held every year in Vienna. Seated in the audience, Dr Goebbels had been infuriated by the audience's rapturous applause for Austrian performers 'while the appearance of Germans was passed over in silence'. After the show, the enraged propaganda minister had ordered the organizers to stop all applause throughout future performances. A more serious incident arose two days later, when Hitler's arrival prompted an angry conductor to refuse to perform in front of a hand-picked audience comprising Nazi officials and, in his phrase, 'prostitutes from Berlin': politics was being played out to the sound of music. Many ordinary Austrians were also angered by the stories of extravagance that flowed at the end of week: at a dinner hosted by Goebbels, just twenty-eight guests polished off 'no less than 84 bottles of champagne . . . in addition to other wines' at a time of shortages and hardship in the streets outside.[15]

These reports, accurate though they may have been, reached Whitehall desks at a crucial hour, just as the cabinet was wrestling with the agonizingly difficult decision of how to deal with the threat of an imminent Nazi invasion of Poland. The prime minister and his chief advisers badly miscalculated, expecting Hitler to stand down and cancel his planned attack on the Poles: having already postponed it once before, there seemed every likelihood that he would do so again when,

14. Backdrop—'the Germans would need a considerable number of troops to make sure of their continued submission, for it is quite clear that the iron has entered their souls', Memo from Prague, 13 May 1939, FO 371/23008 TNA. Informers—'Germany and the International Situation', 10 July 1939, FO 371/23009 TNA. Prague—Memo from Katowice, 23 June 1939, FO 371/23009 TNA.
15. Vienna consul to Whitehall, 15 June 1939, FO 371/23009 TNA.

on 25 August, London made a 'decisive' commitment to defending Poland by signing an 'Agreement of Mutual Assistance'. When the cabinet met, at 11.30 on 30 August, to decide how to respond to a communication from Berlin, it was felt that Hitler was in an 'awful fix' and was 'a man...trying to extricate himself from a difficult situation'. The German leader, it seemed, was 'beaten' and dissension within Germany might prevent a war. This sense was reinforced, and to some extent created, by the intelligence reports that had reached them over the preceding hours.[16]

But the belief that Hitler would back down was catastrophically mistaken. From their supposed position of 'strength', Chamberlain and his cabinet now failed to seize their last remaining opportunity to avert war. They could have put far more pressure on Warsaw firstly not to mobilize its troops—which enraged a highly unstable German leader—and secondly, to open last-minute negotiations with Berlin to find a face-saving formula over the future of Danzig and the Corridor. Halifax claimed that 'His Majesty's Government could not press the Poles' to the negotiating table, and in the early hours of 1 September sent a telegram to Warsaw, one that was never acted on, 'politely asking' them to strike up last-second talks with Berlin. The British instead imposed conditions on Hitler, informing him that talks could not start under any threat of invasion and would have to be conducted on neutral soil. It soon became 'obvious that the Poles were obstructing the possibility of negotiation', as Sir Horace Wilson noted from 10 Downing Street on 31 August.[17]

This could have made a difference, if only by buying valuable time, because Hitler's military timetable for an attack on Poland allowed room for negotiations. Britain and France could have acted together to exert this pressure on Warsaw because Daladier's administration, and Bonnet in particular, had closer relations with Warsaw. Equally, they could have done so at the beginning of August, before the Polish lead-

16. Cowling 311–12, 342; Ismay said on 2 Sept that internal dissension might avert war— see R Wingate *Lord Ismay* Hutchinson (1970) 39.
17. Warsaw pressure—'News of Polish mobilization had obviously excited Hitler...[an] immediate visit of M. Beck' was now 'the sole chance of preventing war': Henderson to Halifax, 29 Aug 1939, DGFP III series, Vol 7 No 493. Wilson, Halifax—Aster 363, 365. Conditions—Cowling 310.

ers made their fateful decision to send an ultimatum to the Danzig Senate, provoking Hitler and precipitating the crisis that led to war.[18]

Steering the Poles along a more conciliatory course was no easy task. They felt that they were in a position to resist any German attack on their own, without any British or French support, and might well therefore have ignored any pressure from London or Paris. But any such refusal also gave Chamberlain an exit strategy that would have averted war while saving his political neck from his domestic critics: he and his cabinet could have refused to support Poland on the grounds that its leaders had failed to enter into the negotiations that Germany had offered. Coupled with the dramatic news of the Moscow–Berlin pact, which meant that nothing could now realistically be done to save Poland, this argument could have plausibly deflected the intense domestic pressure to 'stand up to Hitler'.[19]

Five months before, in the weeks and days that preceded his commitment to Poland, Chamberlain and his advisers had drawn the opposite conclusion about the reports of internal unrest inside Germany, suspecting that it would be more likely to prompt Hitler to go to war, in a bid to unite his increasingly fragmented country, than to lose his nerve. But now, in a change of heart, they believed what they wanted to believe by instead concluding that Hitler would back down and that Poland would be spared.

By doing so, they made another flawed assumption. Even if the reports of such low-level protests were accurate, there was no reason why the German authorities could not have quickly suppressed them. In such a tightly controlled and brutal police state as Nazi Germany, there was a huge difference between minor street protests on the one hand and a major rebellion on the other. Some of the intelligence reports did spell out this harsh reality: 'there is of course no question of any active or organized resistance', as the British consul wrote from Vienna in May, while his counterpart in Prague felt that resistance activities inside Czechoslovakia 'would not amount to much more than passive resistance'. And the previous November, General Ismay had cautioned that 'although there was much anti-Nazi sentiment...we

18. Difference—Aster 363. Warsaw relations—Henderson to Halifax, 29 Aug 1939, DGFP III series, Vol 7, No 493.
19. AJ Prazmowska *Britain, Poland and the Eastern Front 1939* Cambridge University Press (1987).

had no sure evidence of the existence of any cohesive opposition movement which could have shaken the regime [and] the bulk of the population would have followed the *Führer* into war'.[20]

These were also failings of the French intelligence service. Prior to Munich, it had typically emphasized the limits of effective protest. 'It is clear that a totalitarian state possesses considerable advantages in imposing its policies on the populace,' ran one such report in August 1937. 'This is especially true in a country like Germany, whose citizens are known for their willingness to accept rules and restrictions.' Other reports noticed that 'public expressions of dissatisfaction remained very rare...one must not imagine that Hitler's government is teetering merely because Germany is caught up in enormous economic difficulties'. And in 1938, the Bureau had emphasized that 'if faced with the prospect of war, there is no doubt the masses will obey with discipline but without enthusiasm'. But in the summer of 1939, Daladier, Gamelin, and the air and naval ministries also received daily briefings on the state of German popular opinion, falsely raising their hopes that Hitler might back down if France held firm. On 25 August, for example, Gauché forwarded a report to Daladier emphasizing 'the multiplicity of intelligence reports and the variety of sources, all of which indicate a breakdown in German morale'. Crucially, the senior French diplomat Alexis Léger used evidence of a 'general malaise' and the 'possibility of a moral and physical collapse on the part of Hitler' to reject an Italian initiative to open negotiations about Poland.[21]

This is not a criticism of those who wrote these intelligence reports, for they were not tasked with any such appraisal. Responsibility instead falls upon senior advisers, whose role was to assess the information from the ground, and upon the politicians who passed ultimate judgement.

In the very early hours of Friday 1 September, German tanks thundered across the Polish border and as the conflagration erupted, many of those involved remained faithful to their former selves.

In Berlin, at 10 o'clock that morning, Hitler told the Reichstag that he had spent 'more than 90 billion reichsmarks' building up his armed

20. Reports—British Consul, Prague to Whitehall, 13 May 1939, FO 371/23008 TNA. Ismay—'Most Secret Memo', 15 Nov 1938, CAB 104/43 TNA.
21. Reports—Jackson *France and the Nazi Menace* 219; Léger—Jackson *France and the Nazi Menace* 357.

forces, which were by this time 'the best equipped in the world'. This sum was a gross exaggeration, perhaps nearly double what he had really spent, that was intended to intimidate and threaten the outside world: he had started his political career as a street fighter, focused on violence and propaganda, and was now starting a world war in the same belligerent and boastful spirit.

In Warsaw, the Poles continued to underestimate the Nazi threat, insisting that many of the German 'tanks' were really just dummies, while in Paris the French went to the other extreme, continuing to seriously overestimate the German army's ability to resist a British–French counter-attack, and claiming that it could field as many as sixty divisions when the real number was in fact just eleven. The French spy service also argued, very questionably, that an economic blockade would be more effective against Germany than an armed attack.[22]

Meanwhile, there were sharp differences between London and Paris. In the French capital, Bonnet, 'putting forward every wriggle in favour of delay', scrambled to organize a ceasefire and to start negotiations that would keep France out of war. And while the French generals mobilized their armies and organized the evacuation of their women and children, Daladier insisted on a two-day delay before he presented Hitler with an ultimatum. In London, the hours ticked by, stretching the patience of even the most ardent Francophiles to breaking-point, as the cabinet wondered if the anti-war party in Paris, of which Bonnet was deemed 'the villain and rallying-point', was gaining the upper hand and if the French could not be trusted to join the looming fight, despite the high level of cross-Channel collusion between the two governments, their armies and departments. 'If France failed again and ratted on the Poles, as she had ratted on the Czechs', Churchill yelled down the phone at the French ambassador, then he would be 'utterly indifferent' to its fate. But at 9.30 on Saturday night, an exasperated and exhausted Chamberlain phoned Daladier to explain that, given the immense political pressure he was under at home, he would have to issue an ultimatum to Hitler early the following morning regardless.[23]

22. Porch *French Secret Service* 147; Adamthwaite *France and the Coming of the Second World War* 311.
23. Bonnet's delay—Bouverie 377. London, Bonnet as villain—FO 371/22982 TNA; Young *In Command of France* 242–3. Churchill—Bouverie 377.

The British ultimatum, put forward on Sunday morning, expired two hours later, at 11 o'clock London time, when Chamberlain addressed the nation to formally declare war against Germany. But only in the evening, hours after the prime minister's own statement, did Daladier also declare that 'we are at war because we have been forced to do so'.

Even at this desperate hour, the two old adversaries were marching together but still not quite in step.

Conclusion

On 10 March 1935, the Danish police raided several houses in Copenhagen and arrested a group of foreign visitors who had arrived there some weeks before and who were planning to slip across the porous border into Nazi Germany. The Danish police had been tipped off about their plans: the visitors were planning to assassinate Adolf Hitler, and were researching his movements to gauge a weak spot in his defences. The Danish authorities expelled all of them from the country except two, 36-year-old George Mink, from Philadelphia, and 43-year-old Nicholas Sherman, who was born in Yugoslavia but who, like Mink and four others in the group, had American citizenship. They were both detained and charged with passport offences, serving a brief prison sentence before also being thrown out of the country.

The Danish authorities had uncovered *une vaste affaire d'espionnage* but it was, and remains, unclear exactly who was implicated. They searched for clues to Soviet involvement but struggled to decipher some of the heavily coded notes that the assassins had written, prompting them to ask experts in the Deuxième Bureau for assistance. Perhaps they were just acting independently, supporting themselves out of their own pockets and entirely self-motivated.[1]

In the months and years that preceded the outbreak of the Second World War, other reports of assassination plots had come to the attention of British and French intelligence. Just weeks after Hitler came to

---

1. See in general, 'Affaire d'espionnage au Danemark', 28 May 1935, 7NN 3213 SHD. On motives, see the statement from the Danish Minister of Justice, 22 May 1935, quoted in 7NN 3213 SHD. Six of the detainees had US passports: Leon Josephson (aged 37); Adolph Rabinovitch (40); Georg Mink (36); and Nicholas Sherman (43, born in Yugoslavia); two were Austrian citizens—Hans Grunfeld; Karl Hammerman; David and Sybil Rosenthal had both Canadian and Soviet citizenship.

power, the Bureau reported that, according to 'a very good source', German communists had allegedly decided to kill the *Führer* in retaliation for the brutality he had shown towards them. Then, at the very end of December 1934, Communist Party representatives from Switzerland met secretly in Lausanne to discuss ways of instigating revolution in Germany. 'One of the principal aims' of the meeting, noted the Bureau, was to discuss the assassination of Hitler, and to do so without leaving any trace of who was responsible. And nearly a year later, in December 1935, the German border police shot dead five people, all belonging to the German Communist Party, as they made their way towards Berchtesgaden, less than 40 miles away, where they intended to kill Hitler at his mountain home. Needless to say, the incident caught the attention of French intelligence officers.[2]

Because their own homeland was under Nazi occupation from the spring of 1939, the Czechs went further. Some months prior to the outbreak of the Second World War, Moravec received a coded message, hidden inside a book that had been posted from occupied Czechoslovakia to his exiled headquarters in London, informing him that his counterparts had set up an organization, Obrana Naroda, the 'Defence of the Nation'. This was an underground army, led by a 'tall, lean figure [with] a sharply-pointed face' called General Josef Bílý, whose members were sworn to resist the German occupation with acts of sabotage and assassination. It also carried out a number of attacks outside Czechoslovakia, and one of its leaders, Colonel Josef Masin, allegedly had a hand in a failed attempt to kill Heinrich Himmler, planting a timebomb that exploded as his train passed near Anhalt station in Berlin. The assassination of Reinhard Heydrich in Prague in May 1942 was destined to become the army's most renowned feat, as well as its most controversial.[3]

In 1938, a 44-year-old Italian national called Giovanni Bertoni also had a remarkable story to tell, whatever substance it may or may not have held. He had been arrested in Belgium at the request of the Italian authorities, who had charged him with fraud and other minor crimes and issued an order for his extradition. But his return journey to Rome proved to be a long one because he suddenly developed ser-

2. Bureau report—'Communisme en Allemagne et Hitler', 1 Mar 1933, 7NN 3161 SHD. Principal aims—Renseignement, 10 Jan 1935, 7NN 2352 SHD. Incident—*Kurier*, Colmar, 18 Dec 1935; quoted in Renseignement, 19 Dec 1935, 7NN 2352 SHD.
3. Masin—Moravec 176–7.

ious health problems as his train made its way through France, prompting the Interior Ministry to refer him to hospital, under guard, for urgent treatment.

On his hospital bed, Bertoni made some startling claims. The Italian authorities, he stated, were concealing the real charges against him. His true crime was his involvement in an assassination plot against Hitler and Mussolini that was due to have taken place on 3 March 1938, during the *Führer's* visit to Rome. He and his accomplices, he continued, had planned to place a bomb underneath the train station at Rome. Another plan was to throw a grenade at their open car as the two leaders left the train station, just as it entered the street directly opposite the station, while their accomplices would unleash smoke bombs to panic the crowd and allow the assassins to escape. But the plot had been betrayed, forcing him to flee to Switzerland and thereafter to Belgium.[4]

The French authorities listened to the other details he gave. Bertoni claimed that the plot had had support from an Italian army officer, who was at that time living in Switzerland and who would be willing to give information to the French. A figure called 'Colonel Martelli' had used his expertise in explosives to make the bombs, while the plot was funded by a relative of the Austrian chancellor, Kurt Schuschnigg, and by figures within the Vatican, who had used an intermediary called Count Ruffo di Calabria to liaise with the executioners.

Bertoni's story seized interest at high levels in Paris. 'We must explore this lead urgently,' as a French intelligence officer argued. At the very least, their detainee was potentially a source of information on 'terrorism, its methods, and its agents' since he had 'offered to tell the French authorities all he [knew] about the organization of terrorism, and how they would carry out an attack on two heads of state'. But its veracity, all these decades later, remains unproven, and perhaps he was just making a mendacious and last-ditch effort to kill attempts to extradite him.[5]

Such episodes or, perhaps in the case of Bertoni, such stories, raise an important speculative question of what, with hindsight, foreign

---

4. Accomplices—'Giovanni Bertoli', Direction Générale de la Sûreté Nationale, 10 May 1939, 7NN 2519 SHD; Statement to the Inspector General of Police, Paris, 2 May 1939, 7NN 2519 SHD.
5. French officer—'Giovanni Bertoli', Direction Générale de la Sûreté Nationale, 29 Apr 1939, 7NN 2519 SHD. Detainee—'A/S Giovanni Bertoli', 5 May 1939, 7NN 2519 SHD.

intelligence services, as well as their political masters, could have done differently in the 1930s to deal with the fast-growing threat posed by Nazi Germany.

Much attention has been focused on the track record of these spy services at assessing the military prowess of Hitler's Germany, such as their successes at obtaining information from 'high-value assets' like Hans-Thilo Schmidt, and their failure to correctly assess the information they did receive, whether by overstating or underestimating German capabilities. Some historians have already argued persuasively that the British and French intelligence services were guilty of seriously misjudging the true armed strength of Hitler's Germany. In his landmark 1986 study *The Ultimate Enemy*, Wesley Wark showed how various intelligence bodies significantly underestimated the strength of the Luftwaffe and the Wehrmacht until 1936, before going on to considerably exaggerate its strength. The overestimation of German power, he continued, allowed Hitler to bluff and bully Britain and France into a state of submission at the Munich Conference in September 1938. Equally, the French spy services habitually inflated German power, perhaps because for France, more so than many other countries, Germany and its rearmament posed 'a question of national survival'.[6]

But more deserves to be said about the wider geopolitical picture, and of the different ways in which these spy services could conceivably have changed it: the role of an intelligence service is not just to collect and evaluate facts about foreign threats but also, more generally and loosely, to enhance the security of the country it represents, a very grey area that of course overlaps with the roles of both diplomats and politicians alike.

Chamberlain once lamented that the Jews 'obstinately' refused, or failed, to kill Hitler, and that such an act would have rendered his own life 'so much simpler'. But if such individuals as Mink, Sherman, and communist opponents of Hitler were able to conceive their own assassination plans and were prepared to take such drastic steps to implement them, could not and should not the British, French, Czech, and other spy services have been in a position to at least prepare for such a drastic course of action in the event of war? If military analysts in London and Paris were by this time gathering as much information as they could about the size, strength, and location of the Reich's war

6. Porch 'French Intelligence' 45.

machine, why could not their respective spy services have been at least
investigating the possibility of high-level assassination? They had
informers who were in a position to provide them with details about
Hitler's movements, allowing them to make assessments of his vulnerabilities and to assess the viability of using third parties—whose own
links with Western intelligence could have been plausibly denied—to
execute such plans.[7]

They were well aware of the degree to which Nazi Germany was
focused solely on the will of its leader, rendering the regime so vulnerable to a single, decapitating blow: Hitler, as a French intelligence
report noted in December 1938, 'had assumed an immense task for
himself...and there is no longer an ambassador, a military attaché or
even a German military command which carries much influence with
him'. And as Cadogan pointed out, shortly after the start of hostilities,
'get rid of Hitler...then you will win the War. Remove him, and there
will be such disunity in Germany that they *can't* win.' True, killing
Hitler risked making him a martyr—one reason why a wartime plot
to assassinate him was called off—but this hardly mattered if National
Socialism imploded. Any such failure on the part of the intelligence
services seems all the more inexcusable after the Munich agreement,
when the French government started to prepare for war, and certainly
after the occupation of Prague the following March.[8]

Such a plan would also have immensely benefited from collaboration between the spy services of Britain, France, and Czechoslovakia.
The French and the Czechs, for example, had close contact with
German exiles who were in a position to provide information about
Hitler's movements, while the growing number of Jewish refugees
from Germany provided a recruitment pool from which to find an
assassin whose loyalty and commitment would not have been in doubt.

It is possible, of course, that there were such contingency plans
whose details have never been released or discovered. But it seems
most unlikely, since no SIS or Deuxième Bureau officers of the time
have bequeathed any written or oral testimony that suggests that any

---

7. Chamberlain—Letter of 28 May 1939, *The Neville Chamberlain Diary Letters* Ashgate
(2005) Vol 4, 419.
8. French report—Memo from Didelet, 12 Dec 1938, 7NN 2602 SHD. Cadogan—
Diaries 7 Oct 1939, 221. Martyr—the wartime plot was Operation Foxley, a 1944 plan
to shoot Hitler at Berchtesgaden. See Roger Moorhouse *Killing Hitler* Viking (2007)
and HS 6/624 TNA.

such plan existed prior to the outbreak of war. Instead they made, in every likelihood, the convenient but false assumption that Hitler's domestic opponents inside the general staff would carry out regime change on their behalf.

Assassinating Hitler was the most effective way of dealing with an individual who, from the moment he became chancellor, was determined to wage aggressive war against foreign targets. Nazism, he insisted in 1936, was 'a doctrine of conflict', and there is overwhelming evidence of his long-standing determination to realize this doctrine. *Mein Kampf* and his *Second Book*—in which he described 'foreign policy [as] the art of safeguarding the momentary, necessary living space, in quantity and quality, for a people…and creat[ing] and secur[ing] vital prerequisites abroad'—expressed more than just dreams. As Alan Bullock has written, the German leader showed 'a consistency of aim with complete opportunism in method and tactics'. However, if war could not have been prevented or cut short—unless Hitler had been assassinated—then more time could have been bought, allowing the outside world more breathing space to prepare for onslaught.[9]

Foreign spying agencies could have done this by undertaking some other bold moves to favourably alter the geopolitical landscape before 1939. Such an overtly political role would not have fallen outside the scope of any foreign intelligence service because in the 1930s these services could, and frequently did, stray into such relatively political territory. This was particularly true in France, where all civil servants have traditionally taken a more political role to provide some continuity in a country that has frequently been rocked by serious instability, particularly in the mid-1930s. After German troops reoccupied the Rhineland on 7 March 1936, for example, the directors of the Deuxième Bureau argued in favour of closer alliances with Poland, Czechoslovakia, and Italy, adding that the Soviet Union did not figure in its 'system'. Even the SIS, which has traditionally been much less involved in policymaking than some of its European counterparts, took just such a role as the Czech crisis flared: in a 'most secret memo' of 18 September 1938, for example, Sinclair argued that the Czechs should accept the inevitable and surrender the Sudetenland.[10]

9. *Second Book* Ch 2; Alan Bullock, 'Hitler and the Origins of the Second World War', in Hans Gatzke (ed.) *European Diplomacy Between the Two Wars 1919–39* Quadrangle (1972) 224.
10. Directors—Buffotot JSS 550. Sinclair—'What Should We do?', 18 Sept 1938, FO 371/21659 TNA; Andrew 561.

In this more politically proactive role, both the SIS and the Bureau could arguably have done more to undermine the neutrality of the United States, which did not enter the Second World War until 1941. This did not necessarily mean that they, or anyone else, could have persuaded the American government to repeal the 1937 Neutrality Act but rather, more modestly, only to make such a drastic move appear more likely: even a heightened threat of American intervention in Europe might have swayed Hitler, forcing him to abort his plans to attack Poland in 1939. Foreign visitors to Germany noted the Nazi respect for, and fear of, America's military might, which had become so evident in the closing stages of the First World War: Hitler 'took no account of words, only deeds', as Schwerin told British officials in 1939. If the United States had had 5,000 planes at the time of Munich as well as the capacity to produce double that number, Roosevelt sighed, then 'Hitler would not have dared to take the stand he did'. In Washington, US officials 'gave the impression that the main German interest . . . was the hope of discouraging the development of closer ties between the United States on the one hand and England and France'. And in Berlin, in early March 1939, news that Roosevelt had declared his 'solidarity' for Britain and France was met with 'dismay', 'incredulity', and 'consternation'.[11]

But while the British government did undertake a covert campaign to influence American public opinion, this did not get properly under way until early 1941. Any such propaganda campaign would certainly have to have been conducted with immense care because many Americans were highly suspicious of any covert foreign efforts to lure the United States out of its state of isolation and, if exposed, such a campaign would have probably been counter-productive, provoking a reaction that lost, rather than won, popular sympathy. The British, in particular, could not afford to take such a risk. This was partly because of strong anti-British sentiment amongst America's Irish diaspora and its anti-colonial lobby groups, but also because of an unfortunate antecedent: prior to America's entry into the Great War, British Intelligence had invented a number of horror stories about 'the Huns', such as a fictitious German factory that had supposedly been devoted

11. Schwerin—Aster 236. Roosevelt—JM Blum, *From the Morgenthau Diaries* Houghton Mifflin (1959) Vol 2, 48–9. Washington—'Attitude of the German Government', 23 Jan 1939, FO 371/23004 TNA. Berlin—Phipps to Halifax, 3 Mar 1939, CAB 104/43 TNA.

to making soap out of the corpses of dead soldiers. This story was all froth and it was later exposed as a fake, rendering many people on both sides of the Atlantic highly sceptical about atrocity stories and equally mistrustful of those who concocted and disseminated them. '"Atrocities", as George Orwell later noted, 'had come to be looked on as synonymous with "lies".'[12]

But the SIS could have run a media campaign that emphasized British vulnerability to German aggression and its dependency on foreign assistance that was not forthcoming. Such a media campaign could have followed the German occupation of Austria, which also outraged American public opinion and even prompted Cordell Hull to condemn isolation as a 'fruitful source of insecurity'. And later on, it could have exploited Hitler's angry rhetoric towards the United States, where he accused Jewish influence of stirring up anti-German sentiment.[13]

On this count, a closer relationship between the British and French spy services could have proved productive. A French-led media campaign in the United States, subtly advocating a transatlantic alliance, had an obvious advantage: if discovered, such a campaign would have provoked antagonism not towards Great Britain but towards a country that the United States was never likely to have struck up an alliance with in any event. Such a campaign was eminently feasible because the Deuxième Bureau had a close link with the American ambassador in Paris, William C Bullitt: he passed a great many of its reports only to the president and not to a wider audience, which would have been alarmed by the pessimistic and inflated figures put forward by the French spies. Roosevelt also had close dealings with independent French officials, whom he was less mistrustful of than those of the Bureau.[14]

12. 1941—Henry Hemming *Agents of Influence* Hachette (2019). Campaign—see in general Nicholas Cull *Selling War: The British Propaganda Campaign Against American 'Neutrality' in World War II* OUP (1997) Ch 1. Sonia Orwell and Ian Angus (eds) *The Collected Essays, Journalism and Letters of George Orwell* Penguin (1979) Vol 3.
13. Speech to the Reichstag, 30 Jan 1939. On strained German–US relations, noted by the British embassy in December 1938, see in general FO 371/23004 TNA.
14. French campaign—a Gallup poll in 1937 found that 55% of US voters thought that Britain was the European country 'they liked best'. The runner-up was France, at 11%. Cull 7. Roosevelt—in Jan 1939, Roosevelt preferred not to deal directly with the French embassy 'since he did not want his message to pass through M. Bonnet', of whom he was 'suspicious'. Memo from the British embassy in Washington, 4 Jan 1939, FO 371/23004 TNA.

More could also have been done to challenge Soviet, and perhaps American, views of Imperial Japan. In July 1937, war had erupted between China and Japan, whose forces made dramatic advances into the Chinese mainland. But Emperor Hirohito's victories, quite apart from the atrocities his soldiers were responsible for, caused deep alarm in Moscow, which was now confronted by a powerful eastern power that threatened its grip on Mongolia. To a lesser extent, this advance also alarmed Washington, where many Americans, including President Roosevelt, had a strong emotional attachment to China, as well as a commercial interest. Stalin soon began to assist the Chinese nationalist resistance and fierce clashes frequently broke out between Soviet and Japanese troops, notably at Nomonhan, on the border of Outer Mongolia and Manchukuo, in August 1939.

The ties, real or imaginary, between Nazi Germany and Hirohito's Japan presented Western intelligence services with an opportunity not only to divide Hitler and Stalin but also to win stronger support from the United States. Germany and Japan had signed the Comintern Pact in November 1936, committing both countries to 'cooperation' against a perceived Soviet threat, but this had not been enough to deter Stalin from secretly negotiating with Hitler in the spring and summer of 1939. However, he would have been even more mistrustful of Hitler's motives if he had been alerted to intelligence, real or concocted, of Nazi contacts with Tokyo.

Equally, an Anglo-French propaganda campaign could have focused on the growing chorus of Japanese voices that, by 1939, were calling for an aggressive alliance with both Italy and Germany. Amongst those clamouring for such a move were the war minister, Seishirō Itagaki, the prime minister, Kiichirō Hiranuma, and the Japanese ambassadors in Rome and Berlin: in particular, General Hiroshi Oshima, who became the emperor's representative in the German capital in October 1938, had long been pressing Tokyo to strike up a formal military alliance with Germany and Italy. British Intelligence was aware of such moves from an 'absolutely certain source' and could conceivably have done more to exploit such information.[15]

This might not have been enough to drive Stalin into Anglo-French arms in the summer of 1939 for the simple reason that Chamberlain, whose suspicion and seething antipathy for the Soviet regime repre-

15. 25 Jan 1939, CAB 23/97/2 TNA.

sented the main obstacle to any alliance with Moscow, would still have resisted any such move. But it could well have sufficed to forestall the pact between Hitler and Stalin, who only decided at the last possible moment to side with Berlin and who was always intensely suspicious of German motives. 'Tell Stalin that if his government joined up with Hitler it was as certain as night followed day that as soon as Hitler had conquered France, he would turn on Russia and that it would be the Soviets' turn next,' as Roosevelt warned the Soviet ambassador to Washington in June 1939. It was just such fears that a propaganda campaign could have exploited, prompting Hitler to abort his plans to invade Poland.[16]

Both the SIS and the Deuxième Bureau could also have done more to drive a wedge between Nazi Germany and Mussolini's Italy. Had they and their respective governments accomplished such a diplomatic feat, then Hitler would, at the very least, have paused longer for thought before attacking Poland, or might even have been dissuaded by the *duce* from doing so: Hitler, after all, did rescind his attack order on 26 August when Mussolini said he would not join. But the *duce* refused to participate only at the last possible moment, as soon as he heard that the Nazis—once again without his prior knowledge or consultation— had struck a treaty with the Soviets. Mussolini's announcement shocked and infuriated Hitler, who worked hard to win back Rome's support, but the *Führer* was now determined not to change course. Mussolini had already proven that he was capable of influencing Hitler—it was, for example, at his instigation that the German leader had agreed to meet Chamberlain at Munich—and if he had protested and withdrawn his support earlier and declared his 'non-belligerency' or even his neutrality, then Hitler might conceivably have lost his nerve, changed track, and left Poland alone. In a worst-case scenario, if war had still broken out, then the British and French would have been able to divert desperately needed resources away from Italy and instead focus them on Germany.[17]

Such opportunities to prise apart the two fascist states arose after the murder of Dollfus in 1934, which prompted an enraged Mussolini to advance his army up as far as the Brenner Pass, a threatening gesture that suggested an imminent invasion. Then, in 1937, the British struck

16. Roosevelt—Joseph E Davies *Mission to Moscow* Simon & Schuster (1941) 450.
17. Italy did not participate in the invasion of Poland in 1939, but its alliance with Germany in 'the Pact of Steel' forced Britain and France to divert resources.

up a 'Gentleman's Agreement' with Rome that gave Mussolini more
room for manoeuvre in the Mediterranean. Blum's Popular Front
Ministry refused to participate, arguing that Italy and Germany were
already bound together, but better intelligence could have challenged
this false premise.

The most important opportunity emerged after the Nazi occupation of Prague in March 1939. 'Here was a chance, the last chance', as
the French ambassador in Rome, André François-Poncet, later wrote,
'to separate the *Duce* from his partner'. News of the occupation provoked fury and despair in Rome, where Mussolini and his foreign
minister, Count Ciano, raged against Hitler's duplicity as well as his
apparent contempt, since both had received only the barest of warnings and at the last possible moment. The following month, Mussolini
dropped his support for Hitler and soon began to talk openly of war
against Germany, while the French ambassador in Rome urged his
government to seize the opportunity to open up talks with Mussolini
and strike up an alliance.[18]

It was at this political juncture that the British and French intelligence services could have exploited and widened the rift between the
two capitals. The French were aware of 'struggles between Italy and
Germany for influence in Central Europe and the Balkans', as the
Bureau noted in January 1939, but there is no evidence that anything
was done to accentuate them. Equally, Sinclair argued that the 'Axis of
Steel' could be melted by 'playing up the pride' of the Italian leader,
but did not build on this initial suggestion with concrete proposals
about what to do next. An undercover propaganda campaign could
also have capitalized upon and fully exploited Mussolini's fears about
Hitler's interest and ambitions in the Balkans, which the *duce* regarded
as his own area of influence. Mussolini had by this time become aware,
for example, of German links with Croatian soldiers, who had formed
a legion based in Munich, and of broadcasts in Serbo-Croat from an
SS-controlled radio transmitter in Vienna. With the intervention of the
SIS and the Deuxième Bureau, he could at this vital hour have found
out, or seemed to find out, much more about Hitler's ambitions and
interest in the Balkans.[19]

18. François-Poncet 148.
19. Jan 1939—'Réunion des Chefs de Poste', Jan 1939, 7NN 2463 SHD. Sinclair—'What
    Should We Do?' FO 371/21659 TNA. Mussolini—Watt *How War Came* 203.

Close studies of Mussolini's mindset by the intelligence services would also have revealed psychological traits that the British and French governments could have exploited had they wanted, at this point, to strike up an alliance with Rome. Such studies would have revealed, for example, the *duce*'s respect for raw military might: while Hitler recognized and harped upon this vulnerability, most notably during Mussolini's visit to Berlin in September 1937, Baldwin and Chamberlain could equally have invited the Italian leader to visit Great Britain and allowed him to watch a naval review at Southampton or Plymouth that would have revealed the true might of the Royal Navy.

Neither service deserves the blame, however, for failing to foresee acts of Italian aggression that had highly adverse consequences. On 17 March 1936, for example, the Deuxième Bureau made a 'faultless' prediction of an Italian attack on Abyssinia but its warnings appear to have gone unheeded by a French administration whose threats, alongside those of the British, could have deterred Mussolini from acting. Instead, the invasion not only created a sharp rift between London and Paris but provoked a storm of international criticism and condemnation that drove Mussolini towards Hitler. It is possible, however, that more could have been done, by both the intelligence agencies and their respective governments, to predict Italy's invasion of Albania in April 1939 and issue warnings against it. Instead, this attack also created rifts between Britain, France, and Italy—Daladier still firmly refused to open negotiations with Rome, arguing that the Italians were just 'gangsters'—and this rendered an accord with Mussolini even more elusive.[20]

In addition, the two intelligence services could have fully exploited German fears of Soviet involvement in Czechoslovakia, even if the British and French governments had not wanted, or been able, to strike up any alliance with Moscow. Both the SIS and the Bureau were well aware of these German insecurities: in March 1935, for example, Whitehall officials noted that 'the Germans did fear the Russian air force and the possibility that they might find bases for operations

---

20. Criticism—Robert Young *French Military Intelligence and the Franco-Italian Alliance 1933–1939* CUP (2009) 148. Daladier—see in general CA Macdonald, 'Britain, France and the April Crisis of 1939', *European History Quarterly* (Apr 1972). Much of this mistrust stemmed from Galeazzo Ciano's anti-French speech in November 1938, when he demanded control over Djibouti, Tunisia, Corsica, and even Nice. This was followed by Italy's formal renunciation of the Franco-Italian alliance of 1935.

against Germany in Czechoslovakia...there were distinct Czech affinities with Russia and the Czechs might well be forced to lean on Russia as there was no other power which could save Czechoslovakia, especially as Poland is hostile'. German officials also spoke openly about their fears of a Soviet presence inside Czechoslovakia, which an 'anxious' Berlin also instructed German diplomats based in Moscow to find out more about.[21]

The SIS and the Bureau could have worked in conjunction with their Czech counterparts not just to challenge the negative assumptions about Soviet power that many officials in London and Paris harboured but also to exploit these Germans fears, particularly in September 1938, when Hitler might well have backed down over the Sudetenland if he had been confronted by a determined show of force. The Soviets sent a series of conflicting and contradictory signals about Stalin's willingness to honour their 1935 pact with Prague but a subtle and low-key propaganda campaign, with or without Stalin's knowledge or approval, could have lent such words extra weight, portraying a convincing if false and concocted picture of military preparations being undertaken for such an intervention. For example, Beneš, who told a British diplomat in March 1938 that 'he had been given...a promise of an absolute minimum of a thousand Russian planes for which aerodromes etc are prepared...and relies upon receiving equipment from Russia', could have deliberately leaked such comments to Berlin, and instructed Moravec to orchestrate a campaign based on bluff. Instead, this failure of intelligence forms part of a wider political and diplomatic failure to encourage and facilitate Czech–Soviet military cooperation.[22]

This is not to say that the two countries should necessarily have struck up an alliance with Moscow, a course of action that politicians and diplomats, rather than intelligence officials, considered and decided to reject until the summer of 1939 and which can be condemned only with the benefits of hindsight: in both London and Paris, some officials harboured a strong mistrust of Soviet intentions and commitment as

---

21. Mar 1935—'Note on a Meeting at the Foreign Office', 11 Mar 1935, WO 190/305 TNA. Officials—'Notes on a Conversation', 9 Jan, 8 June, and 6 July 1936, AIR 2/2797 TNA. Bittenfeld, 122.

22. Soviet preparations—the Soviets mobilized on 25 Sept 1938, by which time the British and French governments had already pressurized Prague to concede to German demands. Mar 1938—Adamthwaite *France and the Coming of the Second World War* 237.

well as a great deal of scepticism about Moscow's military capabilities, even if some other countries, notably the Czechs, did not share it.[23]

Finally, in the weeks that preceded the outbreak of war in September 1939, a comparable intelligence-led propaganda campaign might also have helped persuade Hitler, Ribbentrop, and their generals that Chamberlain's commitment to Poland was serious and whole-hearted. The British government was not willing to station its troops on Polish soil prior to the Nazi invasion, judging that this would have imperilled the western front and defence of the British homeland, but the SIS and the Deuxième Bureau could nonetheless have orchestrated a campaign to persuade Berlin that preparations were being made, and already in an advanced stage, for such a deployment.[24]

In all of these speculative scenarios, closer collaboration between the independent intelligence services of Britain, France, Czechoslovakia, and Poland could have exploited the specific vulnerabilities of the Third Reich and perhaps averted war. Pooling their resources, balancing each other's strengths and weaknesses, and led by the British, the four national spy agencies had opportunities, which they failed to take, to profoundly alter the path of twentieth-century history and save millions of lives by doing so.

23. Halifax argued that it was 'extremely doubtful whether Russia could be counted upon to make any great contribution, if indeed she could make any contribution at all'. Adamthwaite *France and the Coming of the Second World War* 231.
24. On 28 Aug, the Joint Planning Sub-Committee in London had decided to do 'little other than the execution of reconnaissance and the dropping of propaganda leaflets' to directly support the Polish front.

Index

For the benefit of digital users, indexed terms that span two pages (e.g., 52–53) may, on occasion, appear on only one of those pages.